Lecture Notes in Computer Science   8106

Commenced Publication in 1973
Founding and Former Series Editors:
Gerhard Goos, Juris Hartmanis, and Jan van Leeuwen

T0218379

Peter Achten   Pieter Koopman (Eds.)

The Beauty
of Functional Code

Essays Dedicated to Rinus Plasmeijer
on the Occasion of His 61st Birthday

 Springer

Volume Editors

Peter Achten
Pieter Koopman
Radboud University Nijmegen
Institute for Computing and Information Sciences (ICIS)
Heijendaalseweg 135, 6525 AJ Nijmegen, The Netherlands
E-mail: {p.achten, pieter}@cs.ru.nl

Cover illustration:
"Stad Nova" by Joop Plasmeijer, 2009

ISSN 0302-9743   e-ISSN 1611-3349
ISBN 978-3-642-40354-5   e-ISBN 978-3-642-40355-2
DOI 10.1007/978-3-642-40355-2
Springer Heidelberg New York Dordrecht London

Library of Congress Control Number: 2013945328

CR Subject Classification (1998): D.1.1, D.1, D.3, F.4, D.2

LNCS Sublibrary: SL 2 – Programming and Software Engineering

Typesetting: Camera-ready by author, data conversion by Scientific Publishing Services, Chennai, India

Printed on acid-free paper

Springer is part of Springer Science+Business Media (www.springer.com)

Rinus Plasmeijer

Preface

This Festschrift for Rinus Plasmeijer has been compiled to celebrate the combined occasion of Rinus's 61st birthday and the 25th Symposium on Implementation and Application of Functional Languages.

After the Plasmeijer family moved from Amsterdam to Hengelo in the eastern part of The Netherlands, Rinus was born on October 26 in 1952. Rinus completed secondary school at "De Grundel" in Hengelo without much effort. In 1971 he started studying Applied Mathematics at the Technical University Twente in Enschede. Although the university in Enschede is very close to Hengelo, he lived on campus instead of at home. These studies were also not a real challenge for Rinus and hence he obtained his Bachelor in 1975, which was quite prompt in those days. Rinus continued with a Master in Applied Mathematics within the Division of Computer Science. This was probably as close as you could get to an academic study in computer science in The Netherlands at that time.

After graduating as an engineer, Rinus attended the Catholic University in Nijmegen where he works to this very day, despite a change of the university name to Radboud University Nijmegen. Rinus started working in the Computer Graphics Department while Kees Koster was starting preparations for academic computer science education and the corresponding computer science department. Already in 1981 Rinus completed his PhD thesis entitled "Input tools – a language model for interaction and process communication." Although this title might suggest a close relationship with his current work on the iTask system and the associated generic input tools for browsers, the actual tools described in his thesis are quite different in many aspects. Nevertheless, both try to provide state-of-the-art abstractions to describe user interactions for programs. Back in 1981 the context was still an imperative paradigm.

At about the same time as Rinus finished his PhD, important changes occurred in computer science in The Netherlands. At ten different universities the academic study Computer Science was initiated. To handle the teaching associated with this study and to extend computer science research, additional staff was appointed. Raymond Boute became full professor in the field of operating systems and introduced functional programming very enthusiastically. In particular, a tape with the language SASL from David Turner stimulated the curiosity for "modern" functional programming languages. In November 1984, a cooperative research project was started at the universities of Amsterdam (hardware), Utrecht (theory), and Nijmegen (software), called the Dutch Parallel Reduction Machine Project, which was sponsored by the Dutch Ministry of Science and Education (Science Council). As the initial step for the first externally funded project on functional programming, Rinus made a tour throughout the UK together with Marko van Eekelen and Pieter Hartel in 1985 [18] in which they visited the most active research groups to bring them on par with the state of the art.

In those days achieving a reasonable performance was seen as one of the main challenges for functional programming research. Parallel reduction of functional programs was considered to be one of the most promising solutions. In 1987 this cooperation resulted in the first publication on the lazy functional programming language Clean [8]. The name Clean is a shorthand for Clean LEAN, and LEAN [4] stands for the Language of East Anglia and Nijmegen, which was the result of a long cooperation between the research groups at these universities. The main part of the Clean language implementation was done by Tom Brus and Maarten van Leer. In contrast to most functional programming languages, Clean is based on Term Graph Rewrite Systems rather than on λ-calculus [3, 26]. Henk Barendregt and his group and later Jan Willem Klop and his group helped to develop the required theoretical backing for the Clean implementation. Within the Clean group, Henk and Jan Willem were known as *mister λ-calculus* and *mister rewrite system*. As a result of this project, the future Spinoza prize winner Henk Barendregt moved from Utrecht University to the Radboud University in Nijmegen. Later, Jan Willem Klop was also appointed as professor at the Radboud University. To this day there is ongoing scientific cooperation between Henk, Jan Willem, and Rinus.

In addition to these international IFL meetings, an annual series of national, informal meetings focusing on the education of functional programming was started in 1993, called the Netherlands Functional Programming (NL-FP day). Rinus was one of the initiators and the first meeting was also in Nijmegen. Currently, this series of meetings is held on the first Friday of January. The 2013 meeting was again in Nijmegen. Over the years, the scope of the event has slowly broadened. It is no longer restricted to teaching functional programming, but includes nice topics in functional programming in general. As a result, there are also participants from software companies using functional programming languages. During the last few years, the NL-FP days have attracted an increasing number of participants as well as their first international guests.

During the late 1980s, many functional programming groups in Europe were working on creating efficient implementations of lazy functional programming languages. Over a dozen non-strict, purely functional programming languages existed. Most researchers were quite satisfied with Miranda [28] as a lazy functional language. However, the trade mark on this language made it impossible to implement it. In 1987, at the Functional Programming Languages and Computer Architecture Conference (FPCA [12]), in Portland, Oregon, these researchers decided to form a committee to define a common language [10]. In 1990 this committee presented Haskell 1.0. Originally, Rinus participated in this committee. He left the committee because he felt that too much effort was put into adding new experimental language constructs instead of defining a small, Miranda-like, language. The functional programming group in Nijmegen decided to stick to Clean.

In 1987, at the Parallel Architectures and Languages Europe conference (PARLE [21]) in Eindhoven, many functional programming research groups were present and discussed their common interests informally. They agreed that it would be good to have an informal meeting of a few days to discuss implementation issues in depth. This informal meeting became the first IFL, Implementation of Functional Languages Workshop, held in September 1989 in Nijmegen. Owing to its success it became an annual event. The first events were held in Nijmegen and were hosted by the functional programming research group of Rinus. Later, it started moving throughout Europe and the USA. Because of its informal character there are no proceedings of the first editions of IFL. During the years, IFL became bigger and the desire to record the results of the informal presentations grew. The 1996 edition of IFL was the first edition to publish formal proceedings of selected papers that are peer-reviewed to common conference standards.

Rinus was the main designer of Clean and has always been the leader of the associated research team. Right from the start, Clean was developed as an intermediate programming language with industrial strength. Speed of compilation and speed of the compiled code is of uttermost importance. Consequently, separate compilation is demanded in order to compile large programs quickly. In turn, this requires a proper module system and limits the possibilities for whole program optimizations. All optimizations over module boundaries must be done with the information available in the module interface definition. Another consequence is that Rinus always stressed the importance of a single version; all language extensions (e.g., the uniqueness type system [5, 7, 29], strictness annotations [17, 6], multi-parameter type classes, dynamics [22], generics [2] and so on) have to work smoothly together with the module system.

After the first exploratory implementations of Clean, all implementations used a compilation scheme via the abstract ABC-machine [19, 27, 15]. The first compiler from Clean to ABC-code was written in C for efficiency reasons. In 1994 it was decided that Clean no longer was an intermediate language for a compiler but should become a full-fledged lazy functional programming language [24]. After many language extensions, maintenance of the compiler written in C became an issue. A new compiler from Clean to ABC-code in Clean was written to cope with these problems. Later, even a front-end for Haskell 98 was added to this compiler [9]. For many years the language was Concurrent Clean [25] and had a parallel implementation on transputers [13] based on parallel graph rewriting [23]. Clean is extended with a fancy object-oriented GUI library [1], a proof system [16], a model-based test system [14], and an extension to run partly in the browser [11]. Clean has always been strongly typed, and types play an important role in its applications (e.g., [30, 20]).

In 1991, Prof. Zoltán Horváth from the Eötvös Loránd University in Budapest visited the group of Rinus on a TEMPUS grant. This was the start of an ongoing cooperation between these universities. Many of Prof. Horváth's colleques and students followed him and spent a successful research period in Nijmegen. The Central European Functional Programming summer schools (CEFP) are run in strong cooperation. These proceedings are also published in the LNCS series. Rinus is doctor and professor honoris causa of the Eötvös Loránd University.

For this Festschrift we invited all former PhD students of Rinus as well as researchers in the field of functional programming who are listed in joint publications with Rinus. We received only positive reactions to this initiative. We are very glad that many of these people, including those mentioned above, were able to find time to write a contribution to this Festschrift for Rinus. The contributions are scientific essays, and the theme of the book is *beautiful code*. We asked the authors to write about the influence the beauty of functional programming has had or still has on their work. The order of appearance in this Festschrift is inspired loosely by the timeline that is described above.

We are very happy that Springer recognizes the importance of the work of Rinus and was willing to publish this Festschrift as a volume in LNCS. Each submission was peer-reviewed to check the scientific correctness and received constructive feedback for improvements. We express our gratitude to the following persons who provided valuable support in the preparation of this Festschrift:

Wil van der Aalst	Alfred Hofmann	Betsy Pepels
Steffen van Bakel	Zoltán Horváth	Andrew Polonsky
Henk Barendregt	Jan Martin Jansen	Hajo Reijers
Erik Barendsen	Johan Jeuring	Reuben Rowe
Ingrid Berenbroek	Marco Kesseler	Pascal Serrarens
Tom Brus	Jan Willem Klop	Sjaak Smetsers
Atze Dijkstra	Tamás Kozsik	Doaitse Swierstra
László Domoszlai	Anna Kramer	Frits Vaandrager
Marko van Eekelen	Bas Lijnse	Edsko de Vries
Jörg Endrullis	Peter Lucas	Michael Westergaard
Herman Geuvers	José Pedro Magalhães	Nicolas Wu
John van Groningen	Steffen Michels	Viktória Zsók
Dimitri Hendriks	Maarten de Mol	Erik Zuurbier
Ralf Hinze	Marco T. Morazán	

Finally, we think that it is appropriate that this Festschrift is handed over to Rinus at the 25th edition of the IFL series returning to its roots at Nijmegen.

June 2013   Peter Achten
                                                             Pieter Koopman

References

1. Achten, P., van Groningen, J., Plasmeijer, R.: High level specification of I/O in functional languages. In: Launchbury, J., Sansom, P. (eds.) Proceedings of the 5th Glasgow Workshop on Functional Programming, GFP 1992, Ayr, UK. Workshops in Computing, pp. 1–17. Springer (1992)
2. Alimarine, A., Plasmijer, R.: A generic programming extension for Clean. In: Arts, T., Mohnen, M. (eds.) Proceedings of the 13th International Workshop on the Implementation of Functional Languages, IFL 2001, Stockholm, Sweden, pp. 257–278. Ericsson Computer Science Laboratory (2001)
3. Barendregt, H., van Eekelen, M., Glauert, J., Kennaway, J., Plasmeijer, M., Sleep, M.: Term graph rewriting. In: Bakker, Nijman, Treleaven (eds.) PARLE 1987. LNCS, vol. 259, pp. 141–158. Springer, Heidelberg (1987)
4. Barendregt, H., van Eekelen, M., Glauert, J., Kennaway, J., Plasmeijer, M., Sleep, M.: LEAN: An intermediate language based on graph rewriting. Parallel Computing 9, 163–177 (1988)
5. Barendsen, E., Smetsers, S.: Uniqueness typing for functional languages with graph rewriting semantics. In: Mathematical Structures in Computer Science, vol. 6, pp. 579–612 (1996)
6. Barendsen, E., Smetsers, S.: Strictness typing. In: Hammond, K., Davie, T., Hankin, C. (eds.) Proceedings of the 10th International Workshop on the Implementation of Functional Languages, IFL 1998, London, UK, pp. 101–116 (1998)
7. Barendsen, E., Smetsers, S.: Graph rewriting aspects of functional programming. In: Handbook of Graph Grammars and Computing by Graph Transformation, pp. 63–102. World Scientific (1999)
8. Brus, T., van Eekelen, M., van Leer, M., Plasmeijer, R.: Clean: a language for functional graph rewriting. In: Kahn, G. (ed.) Proceedings of the 3rd International Conference on Functional Programming Languages and Computer Architecture, FPCA 1987, Portland, OR, USA, pp. 364–384. Springer, London (1987)
9. van Groningen, J., van Noort, T., Achten, P., Koopman, P., Plasmeijer, R.: Exchanging sources between Clean and Haskell - A double-edged front end for the Clean compiler. In: Gibbons, J. (ed.) Proceedings of the Haskell Symposium, Haskell 2010, Baltimore, MD, USA, pp. 49–60. ACM Press (2010)
10. Hudak, P., Hughes, J., Peyton Jones, S., Wadler, P.: A history of Haskell: being lazy with class. In: Ryder, B., Hailpern, B. (eds.) Proceedings of the 3rd Conference on History of Programming Languages, HOPL III, San Diego, CA, USA, pp. 1–55. ACM Press (2007)
11. Jansen, J., Koopman, P., Plasmeijer, R.: Efficient interpretation by transforming data types and patterns to functions. In: Nilsson, H. (ed.) Revised Selected Papers of the 7th Symposium on Trends in Functional Programming, TFP 2006, Nottingham, UK, vol. 7, pp. 73–90 (2006) Intellect Books
12. Kahn, G. (ed.): FPCA 1987. LNCS, vol. 274. Springer, Heidelberg (1987)
13. Kesseler, M.: Concurrent CLEAN on transputers. In: Proc. of the Second Workshop of ESPRIT Parallel Computing Action (PCA). ISPRA, Italy (1990)
14. Koopman, P., Alimarine, A., Tretmans, J., Plasmeijer, R.: Gast: generic automated software testing. In: Peña, R., Arts, T. (eds.) IFL 2002. LNCS, vol. 2670, pp. 84–100. Springer, Heidelberg (2003)
15. Koopman, P., van Eekelen, M., Plasmeijer, R.: Operational machine specification in a functional programming language. Software: Practice & Experience 25(5), 463–499 (1995)

16. de Mol, M., van Eekelen, M., Plasmeijer, R.: Theorem proving for functional programmers. In: Arts, T., Mohnen, M. (eds.) IFL 2002. LNCS, vol. 2312, pp. 55–72. Springer, Heidelberg (2002)
17. Nöcker, E.: Strictness analysis using abstract reduction. In: Proceedings of the Conference on Functional Programming Languages and Computer Architecture, FPCA 1993, pp. 255–265. ACM, New York (1993)
18. van Eekelen, M., Hartel, P., Plasmeijer, M.: Report of a trip to the united kingdom, Sponsored by the Dutch Parallel Reduction Machine Project (January 1985)
19. van Groningen, J.: Implementing the abc-machine on m680x0 based architectures. Master's thesis, University of Nijmegen (1990)
20. van Noort, T., Achten, P., Plasmeijer, R.: A typical synergy. In: Morazán, M.T., Scholz, S.-B. (eds.) IFL 2009. LNCS, vol. 6041, pp. 179–197. Springer, Heidelberg (2010)
21. Odijk, E., Syre, J.-C., Rem, M. (eds.): PARLE 1989. LNCS, vol. 365. Springer, Heidelberg (1989)
22. Pil, M.: Dynamic types and type dependent functions. In: Hammond, K., Davie, T., Clack, C. (eds.) IFL 1998. LNCS, vol. 1595, pp. 169–185. Springer, Heidelberg (1999)
23. Plasmeijer, R., van Eekelen, M.: Functional programming and parallel graph rewriting. Addison-Wesley Publishing Company (1993) ISBN 0-201-41663-8
24. Plasmeijer, R., van Eekelen, M.: Concurrent Clean 1.0 - language manual, draft version. Technical report, Katholieke Universiteit Nijmegen (1994)
25. Serrarens, P.R., Plasmeijer, R.: Explicit message passing for concurrent clean. In: Hammond, K., Davie, T., Clack, C. (eds.) IFL 1998. LNCS, vol. 1595, pp. 229–245. Springer, Heidelberg (1999)
26. Sleep, R., Plasmeijer, R., van Eekelen, M. (eds.): Term graph rewriting: theory and practice. John Wiley and Sons Ltd., Chichester (1993)
27. Smetsers, S., Nöcker, van, E., Groningen, J.H., Plasmeijer, M.J.: Generating efficient code for lazy functional languages. In: Hughes, J. (ed.) FPCA 1991. LNCS, vol. 523, pp. 592–617. Springer, Heidelberg (1991)
28. Turner, D.A.: Miranda: a non-strict functional language with polymorphic types. In: Proc. of a Conference on Functional Programming Languages and Computer Architecture, pp. 1–16. Springer-Verlag New York, Inc., New York (1985)
29. de Vries, E., Plasmeijer, R., Abrahamson, D.M.: Uniqueness typing redefined. In: Horváth, Z., Zsók, V., Butterfield, A. (eds.) IFL 2006. LNCS, vol. 4449, pp. 181–198. Springer, Heidelberg (2007)
30. van Weelden, A., Plasmeijer, R.: Towards a strongly typed functional operating system. In: Peña, R., Arts, T. (eds.) IFL 2002. LNCS, vol. 2670, pp. 215–231. Springer, Heidelberg (2003)

Table of Contents

Beautiful Code, Beautiful Proof?

Maarten de Mol[1] and Marko van Eekelen[2,3]

[1] AiA Software B.V.
P.O. Box 38025, 6503 AA Nijmegen, The Netherlands
[2] Institute for Computing and Information Sciences
Radboud University Nijmegen
[3] School of Computer Science
Open University of the Netherlands
M.de.Mol@aiasoftware.com, M.vanEekelen@cs.ru.nl

Abstract. Functional programming languages are often praised for creating the capability of writing beautiful code. Furthermore, an often mentioned advantage is that it is easy to reason about properties of functional programs. Such reasoning can be either formal or informal. This might lead to the assumption that really beautiful code is also really easy to prove. One might even say that beautiful code can *only* be classified as really beautiful if the code also has a beautiful proof. This essay explores whether beautiful code written in a functional programming language also has a beautiful proof. Two small case studies discuss both the beauty of an informal mathematical proof and the beauty of a formal proof created in a dedicated theorem prover. General lessons are drawn from these studies and directions for future research directions are given.

This essay is written on the occasion of the celebration of the 61th *anniversary of Rinus Plasmeijer, coinciding with the 25*th *IFL conference, held in Nijmegen. Rinus was one of the supervisors of both the Ph.D. Thesis of Marko van Eekelen and the Thesis of Maarten de Mol. The authors of this essay co-authored many functional programming papers with him both on the design and application of the functional programming language Clean and on its dedicated theorem prover Sparkle.*

We are most grateful for his enthusiastic guidance and for the many hours of warm, creative and productive collaboration.

1 Introduction

The beauty of functional programming has been advocated by many authors. John Hughes [Hug89] focuses on the expressivity and the inherent compositionality of functional programming languages where Richard Bird and Phil Wadler [BW88] advocate both the ease of proving properties in functional programming languages and the beauty of the resulting proofs. Not every kind of program is as easy to express in a functional language. Some programming tasks are generally considered awkward [Pey01]. The code for this awkward squad may be less beautiful and it may be harder to proof things about them if possible at all. An example of such a class of hard-to-reason-about programs is the class of programs that involve input and output [BS01, DBE04, DB06].

P. Achten and P. Koopman (Eds.): Plasmeijer Festschrift, LNCS 8106, pp. 1–7, 2013.

Apart from such awkward program classes, functional programming languages are generally well-known both for the beauty of their code and for the beauty of reasoning about its code. It may seem reasonable to expect that these two often come together. Following Hughes, Bird and Wadler one might assume that really beautiful code is also really easy to prove. In fact, one even might say that code written in a functional programming language can only be classified as beautiful if the code also has a beautiful proof.

This essay sets out to perform a small case study studying the relation between the beauty of a code and the beauty of its proof. The lazy functional programming language *Clean* [vESP97, PE99, PE02] is used since it is the language we are most familiar with. It comes with the interactive proof assistant *Sparkle* [MEP02, KEM04, MEP08, Mol09]. *Sparkle* makes it possible to interactively define and prove theorems about *Clean* functions. It has special support for reasoning about strictness [vEdM05] to determine and analyze the definedness properties of the *EditorArrow* framework [AvdP13]. The features of *Sparkle* make it well suited for the case study in this essay. In two small examples we want to explore this expected relation between the beauty of the code and the beauty of its proof.

In Section 2 an example is taken from a standard text book of which the text book claims that the code and the proof are beautiful. The text book does the proof informally. The section explores whether the formal proof can also be considered to be beautiful.

Then, in Section 3 a classic beautiful code example, the *quicksort* algorithm, is taken for which we have not found a source that does the formal proof for a functional programming language. In [FH71] Michael Foley and Tony Hoare give both an informal proof and a formal proof of an *imperative* version of Quicksort. At the moment of publication a formal proof was not possible (*yet*), as was explicitly stated in the paper: *'general purpose theorem provers are not powerful enough to handle complex lemmas.'* Furthermore, there are some web pages referring to informal proofs or to prove parts in *Coq* but they have as goal the equivalence of an imperative program and a functional program. The goal of Section 3 is to formally prove the correctness of the functional program and to discuss the beauty of the formal proof for this classic example.

Finally, Section 4 describes lessons learnt from this small proof experiment and draws conclusions.

2   Classic Beautiful Code with a Beautiful Proof

Two often used functions from the standard library of *Clean* are 'map' and 'flatten'. Map is of course well-known, and applies an argument function to all elements of a list. Flatten turns a list of lists into a single list by means of repeated concatenation. These functions are defined in *Clean* as follows:

```
map :: (a -> b) ![a] -> [b]        flatten :: ![[a]] -> [a]
map f [x:xs]                       flatten [x:xs]
   = [f x: map f xs]                  = x ++ flatten xs
map f []                           flatten []
   = []                               = []
```

A nice property of map and flatten is that they do not interfere with each other, and can be interchanged freely. This can be expressed as follows:

$$\forall_{f,A}[\text{map } f \text{ (flatten } A) = \text{flatten (map (map } f) A)]$$

This property can be proved by induction. The base case is trivial, as for $A = \texttt{[]}$ both the left- and right-hand-side evaluate to $\texttt{[]}$. For $A = [x\!:\!X]$, the left-hand-side can be be rewritten into the right-hand-side as follows:

$$
\begin{array}{lll}
 & \text{map } f \text{ (flatten } [x\!:\!X]) & \text{(expand flatten)} \\
= & \text{map } f \text{ } (x \texttt{ ++ } (\text{flatten } X)) & \text{(map distributes over ++)} \\
= & (\text{map } f \text{ } x) \texttt{ ++ } (\text{map } f \text{ (flatten } f \text{ } X)) & \text{(IH)} \\
= & (\text{map } f \text{ } x) \texttt{ ++ } \text{flatten (map (map } f) X) & \text{(expand flatten, backwards)} \\
= & \text{flatten } [\text{map } f \text{ } x : \text{map (map } f) \text{ } X] & \text{(expand map, backwards)} \\
= & \text{flatten (map (map } f) \text{ } [x\!:\!X]) & \square
\end{array}
$$

This proof relies on induction and equational reasoning only[1]. These two techniques are considered to be the basic reasoning techniques for functional programs. The (small) proof is therefore both elegant and beautiful.

It is also straightforward to formalize the proof. In fact, *Sparkle*, can build the proof automatically with its built-in hint mechanism. The resulting proof, which is also part of the standard library of *Sparkle*, looks as follows:

```
Induction xs.
1. Introduce f.
   Reduce NF All (  ).
   Reflexive.
2. Introduce f.
   Reduce NF All (  ).
   Reflexive.
3. Introduce x xs IH f.
   Reduce NF All (  ).
   Rewrite -> All "map_++".
   Rewrite -> All IH.
   Reflexive.
```

Each line in this proof code corresponds to a single command, or proof step. The first step is the structural induction, and in *Sparkle* this leads to three cases, instead of two. The first case covers the possibility that $A = \bot$, which was omitted in the written proof. It is proved easily, however. The 'Reduce' steps correspond to program evaluation; 'Rewrite .. "map_++"' corresponds to the application of the map distribution lemma; and 'Rewrite ... IH' corresponds to the application of the induction hypothesis. The remaining 'Introduce' and 'Reflexive' steps are logic axioms that need to be specified explicitly. Consequently:

- (all the steps from) the paper proof can easily be found in the formal proof; and

---

[1] It relies on the auxiliary property that map distributes over ++ as well, but that property is proved by induction and equational reasoning itself.

– the overhead on top of that (which is unavoidable due to the transition to a formal level) is minimal

Therefore, the code, the paper proof, and the formal proof are **all** beautiful.

3   Classic Beautiful Code with an Ugly Proof

An elegant solution for sorting an arbitrary collection of elements is the famous *quicksort* algorithm. The idea of this algorithm is very straightforward: first pick a random element (the so called pivot); then divide the input into those that are smaller than the pivot, those that are equal to the pivot, and those that are greater than the pivot; then recursively sort the smaller and greater components; and finally concatenate the three parts back again.

The quicksort algorithm can be expressed into *Clean* as follows:

```
quickSort :: ![a] -> [a] | Ord a
quickSort [x:xs] =  quickSort [y \\ y <- xs      | y < x]
                 ++           [y \\ y <- [x:xs] | y == x]]
                 ++ quickSort [y \\ y <- xs      | y > x]
quickSort []     = []
```

This piece of code is a concise and readable representation of the algorithm, which makes it beautiful indeed. Note that for the sake of this paper, a less efficient version was chosen, which traverses the list three separate times. Instead, it is also possible to split the list into three components with one pass.

The correctness of a sorting algorithm entails two separate properties: the output list must be a permutation of the input list, and the elements of the output list must occur in increasing order. These auxiliary properties can be stated as follows:

$$perm\ A\ B \Leftrightarrow \forall_{a \in A}[a \in B \land perm\ (A \setminus a)\ (B \setminus a)]$$
$$sorted\ \langle a_1 \ldots a_n \rangle \Leftrightarrow \forall_{1 \leq i,j \leq n}[i < j \rightarrow a_i \leq a_j]$$

The correctness of quicksort as a whole can now be formulated as:

$$\forall_A[perm\ A\ (\texttt{quicksort}\ A)) \land sorted\ (\texttt{quicksort}\ A)]$$

Intuitively, it is clear that this correctness property holds. Firstly, quicksort does not remove elements from the input list, and each element is used exactly once. This is because $(< x)$, $(== x)$ and $(> x)$ are mutually exclusive, and in combination also total. Therefore, the permutation property holds. Secondly, by construction, the elements in each sublist of the algorithm are smaller than the elements of the subsequent sublists. This is preserved by the recursive calls (due to the permutation property). Also, each sublist is sorted on its own by induction. All things combined, the concatenated output list is sorted as a whole.

We have formalized this proof idea with *Sparkle*. This took a *Sparkle* expert about two working days, and the resulting formal proof is 2897 lines long, and consists of no less than 64 theorems. Section files for both proofs can be downloaded from `http://www.cs.ru.nl/~marko/BCBP`, and can be replayed with the latest versions of *Clean*[2] and *Sparkle*[3].

There are two theorems in the formal proof that roughly correspond to the presented proof idea, one for the permutation part and one for the sorted part. These two theorems combined occupy 265 lines of proof code, which is much larger that the original one paragraph proof idea. That is to be expected, however, because a formal proof cannot omit any details and consists of small steps only.

The remaining 58 theorems and 2632 lines of proof code do not correspond directly to any steps in the original proof idea, and are therefore pure overhead. An inspection of the formal proof brings up the following explanations for this overhead:

- The formal proof takes the possible *undefinedness* of data into account, while the informal proof does not. This manifests itself in two different ways. Firstly, properties require additional definedness conditions on their input parameters. Secondly, in order to satisfy these conditions, the definedness of the *output* of intermediate functions must be proved as well, resulting in additional *definedness theorems*.
  This factor explains 11 additional theorems, occupying 348 lines of proof code.
- The formal proof relies heavily on the interaction between basic operations (such as list concatenation, filtering, etc.) on properties that are relevant for sorting (such as one list being a permutation of another). These properties are intuitively straightforward, and have therefore been omitted in the proof idea. They have to be proved explicitly in the formal proof, however.
  This factor explains 43 additional theorems, occupying 1883 lines of proof code.
- The quicksort proof requires features that are poorly supported by *Sparkle*, such as *course of value induction* (only supported in an extension, see [LvE04]) and list comprehensions (which are translated automatically to incomprehensible local functions).
  This factor explains 4 additional theorems, occupying 253 lines of proof code.
- The remaining $2632 - (348 + 1883 + 253) = 148$ lines of proof code are due to the internal representation of proof files (i.e. empty lines between proofs, theorem headers, etc.).

Due to this overhead, the end result is a formal proof that is rather ugly. It is fair to ask oneself if this overhead is mainly caused by *Sparkle* itself, and could have been avoided by using another proof assistant. This especially goes for the second point above, which can be solved by having more library theorems available. However, there are currently no other proof systems for functional languages that have such a library. Also, using a non-dedicated proof assistant will result in additional overhead caused by semantic differences, which have to

---

[2] `http://www.cs.ru.nl/~clean`

[3] `http://www.cs.ru.nl/Sparkle`

be modelled explicitly. Therefore, as far as we know, in this particular case the performance of *Sparkle* cannot easily be improved by other proof systems.

4   Discussion and Conclusion

From both examples in the previous sections one can conclude that making a formal proof involves considerable overhead in comparison with an informal proof. This is quite common in the area of formal verification. The amount of overhead may a be good indication for the beauty of the proof. In Section 2 the overhead was minimal and the proof was considered beautiful. However, in Section 3 the overhead was quite considerable and the proof was considered ugly.

The question is whether this difference is accidental, due to the specific features of the dedicated theorem prover or due to other aspects such a the specific choice of example. The *quickSort* example is considered by many people as one of the nicest examples of beautiful code. Intuition tells us that it should be possible to create a beautiful proof for it but that the current status of the language dedicated theorem prover prevents that.

For a language dedicated theorem prover to support beautiful proofs it will have to have a large collection of proven theorems to start with. General theorem provers tend to have such large collections of theorems. They lack, however, the direct expression of theorems and proofs in the programming language itself. This indicates that one would want a kind of mix between a generic prover such as *Coq* [Tea98] or *PVS* [ORS92] and a language specific prover such as *Sparkle*. On one hand one needs the language specific extensions like there are in *Sparkle* for strictness and definedness [vEdM05] and for class properties [KEM04]. On the other hand one needs the libraries and tactics for general proof support from a generic theorem prover.

The lack of the combined power of a generic and a language specific theorem prover made the proof of *quickSort* not so beautiful. However, the proof is still doable, albeit with more effort. By adding more proven statements to the libraries of *Sparkle*, this situation can be improved upon in the future. Until then, we are afraid that we still have to conclude that beautiful code and beautiful proofs can go together but not in all cases where one might reasonably expect them to do so.

References

[AvdP13]   Achten, P., van Eekelen, M., de Mol, M., Plasmeijer, R.: EditorArrow: An Arrow-based Model for Editor-Based Programming. Journal of Functional Programming 23, 185–224 (2013)

[BS01]   Butterfield, A., Strong, G.: Proving Correctness of Programs with I/O - a paradigm comparison. In: Arts, T., Mohnen, M. (eds.) IFL 2002. LNCS, vol. 2312, pp. 72–88. Springer, Heidelberg (2002)

[BW88]   Bird, R.S., Wadler, P.: Introduction to Functional Programming. Prentice Hall (1988)

[DB06]   Dowse, M., Butterfield, A.: Modelling deterministic concurrent I/O. In: Reppy, J.H., Lawall, J.L. (eds.) ICFP, pp. 148–159. ACM (2006)

[DBE04]   Dowse, M., Butterfield, A., van Eekelen, M.: Reasoning About Determin-
          istic Concurrent Functional I/O. In: Grelck, C., Huch, F., Michaelson,
          G.J., Trinder, P. (eds.) IFL 2004. LNCS, vol. 3474, pp. 177–194. Springer,
          Heidelberg (2005)
[FH71]   Foley, M., Hoare, C.A.R.: Proof of a recursive program: Quicksort. Comput.
          J. 14(4), 391–395 (1971)
[Hug89]   Hughes, J.: Why Functional Programming Matters. Computer Jour-
          nal 32(2), 98–107 (1989)
[KEM04]   van Kesteren, R., van Eekelen, M., de Mol, M.: Proof support for general
          type classes. In: Loidl, H.-W. (ed.) Trends in Functional Programming 5:
          Selected papers from the 5th Int. Symposium on Trends in Functional
          Programming, TFP 2004, pp. 1–16. Intellect (2004)
[LvE04]   Lensink, L., van Eekelen, M.: Induction and co-induction in sparkle. Tech-
          nical Report NII–R0502, Radboud University Nijmegen (2004)
[MEP02]   de Mol, M., van Eekelen, M., Plasmeijer, R.: Theorem Proving for Func-
          tional Programmers. In: Arts, T., Mohnen, M. (eds.) IFL 2001. LNCS,
          vol. 2312, pp. 55–72. Springer, Heidelberg (2002)
[MEP08]   de Mol, M., van Eekelen, M., Plasmeijer, R.: Proving properties of lazy
          functional programs with Sparkle. In: Horváth, Z., Plasmeijer, R., Soós,
          A., Zsók, V. (eds.) CEFP 2007. LNCS, vol. 5161, pp. 41–86. Springer,
          Heidelberg (2008)
[Mol09]   de Mol, M.: Reasoning About Functional Programs - Sparkle: a proof as-
          sistant for Clean. PhD thesis, University of Nijmegen, The Netherlands
          (March 4, 2009) ISBN 978-90-9023885-2
[ORS92]   Owre, S., Rushby, J.M., Shankar, N.: PVS: A prototype verification system.
          In: Kapur, D. (ed.) CADE 1992. LNCS, vol. 607, pp. 748–752. Springer,
          Heidelberg (1992)
[PE99]   Plasmeijer, R., van Eekelen, M.: Keep it clean: a unique approach to func-
          tional programming. ACM Sigplan Notices 34(6), 23–31 (1999)
[PE02]   Plasmeijer, R., van Eekelen, M.: Clean language report version 2.1. Dept.
          of Software Technology, University of Nijmegen (2002)
[Pey01]   Peyton Jones, S.: Tackling the Awkward Squad: monadic input/output,
          concurrency, exceptions, and foreign-language calls in Haskell. In: Hoare,
          T., Broy, M., Steinbruggen, R. (eds.) Engineering Theories of Software
          Construction, pp. 47–96. IOS Press (2001) ISBN 1 58603 1724
[Tea98]   The Coq Development Team. The Coq Proof Assistant Reference Manual
          (version 7.0), Inria (1998),
          http://pauillac.inria.fr/coq/doc/main.html
[vEdM05] van Eekelen, M., de Mol, M.: Proof tool support for explicit strictness. In:
          Butterfield, A., Grelck, C., Huch, F. (eds.) IFL 2005. LNCS, vol. 4015,
          pp. 37–54. Springer, Heidelberg (2006)
[vESP97] van Eekelen, M., Smetsers, S., Plasmeijer, R.: Graph rewriting semantics
          for functional programming languages. In: van Dalen, D., Bezem, M. (eds.)
          CSL 1996. LNCS, vol. 1258, pp. 106–128. Springer, Heidelberg (1997)

Beauty and Code

Tom Brus

Modeling Value Group

"Beauty is more important in computing than anywhere else in technology because software is so complicated.
Beauty is the ultimate defence against complexity."
(David Gelernter) [1]

1 Introduction

Let me take you on an expedition in search of the beauty in code. Although not everybody links code and beauty, it has always been a natural link for me. Apparently I am not the only one, considering the hefty battles that show up regularly regarding syntax, coding practices, and how things should be written down. I have some strong feelings in this area myself and fought some battles in the past. But syntax and the appearance of code on screen or paper is not the only beauty axis that can be identified, there is more which I also hope to illustrate below.

I have always looked on coding (or code creation) as a creative process and 'creative' encapsulates a drive for beauty for me, at least in some direction. I always searched for satisfaction by creating something that I can look back on with a certain satisfaction, some intricate sensation of beauty. The more beauty, the more satisfaction. The coding process is more worthwhile, more satisfying when more beauty is created.

When you start thinking about beauty in code you realize that there are many aspects of code and code-creation that can be beautiful. For instance: the resulting program can have a nice GUI; the source code can look elegant; the program can have a pleasingly simple structure.

So, to identify beautiful code and distinguish it from the opposite (ugly code? mediocre code?) we need to identify what beautiful could mean for code. We need reasons to label code as beautiful or not. Only then we can find the real beauty.

But is a quest for beauty a good guidance for high quality code? To answer that question we should investigate what 'quality' exactly means for code and that is beyond this essay. For me personally, 'high quality' and 'beautiful code' go together like copy and paste. Whenever there seems to be only one you need to step back and rethink.

P. Achten and P. Koopman (Eds.): Plasmeijer Festschrift, LNCS 8106, pp. 8–17, 2013.

My plan in this essay is to first look at what beauty is. Then I look into what that specifically means for code. Finally I will look at different coding languages as well as programming paradigms and how they can be related to beauty.

In this essay I do not claim to be complete in any dimension nor do I intend to identify universal truths. It is not academic or scientific, and although some experience with programming helps to enjoy this essay, it is not technical either. I hope to shine a small light from a personal angle on what the art and beauty of programming is. I am convinced that it is an art and that it should remain an art [2]. In all humbleness I think I am old enough to look back and talk about the past. I even enjoy doing that, at least occasionally.

2   Some Historical Notes

When I started programming around 1976 (in 8080 assembler) I did not have any clear notion of beauty in mind. Getting the thing to do what I wanted it to do was my goal. I can remember, however, that I did rearrange code fragments only because it would look better or maybe feel better, even if there was no technical reason to do so. In hindsight I am tempted to conclude that I was already trying to create beauty, crude as it was. I also remember that code size really mattered and that cramping the same functionality into a smaller code size was a satisfying and rewarding process. You could also win points among peers for a yet smaller footprint. This had little to do with beauty I think, although some see beauty in small waists or small feet. Not me, so that must have just been a practical issue. Nowadays code size is not a real issue anymore and we tend to even spend more space to avoid riddles in maintenance or even for laziness. The quest for time on the other hand has not degraded that much. Machines have gotten ridiculously faster but we also seem to be more hungry for cycles. So squashing the last drop out of the available cycles is at times still a rewarding exercise.

Later I was charmed by the first Macintosh computer because of its elegance. Real fonts, a super intuitive mouse device, a wealth of GUI primitives and last but not least a fanless design. At that time I earned my first $5 in 1987 with 'm2beauty', a public domain code beautifier for Modula-2 (this was by the way also the only donation for this project). When researching for this essay I was surprisingly still able to find it on the internet. I guess we need to wait for the first retro-Mac-on-iPhone-emulator to be able to run it again (and find a Modula-2 programmer to use it, which might even prove to be more difficult).

When making the first Clean compiler, around 1988, based on graph reduction for a VAX, I can remember that performance was the big issue. This was mainly due to the fact that functional coding was regarded by the world as an academic exercise that was good for proving theorems but was not worthwhile for everyday programming. We, Rinus Plasmeijer and his team, tried to convince the world of the opposite and at that time we needed the performance to support our argument. I believe we gave Clean a good head start in that lane. The position of functional programming has changed since that time. Functional as well as declarative programming has become more mainstream. Still it has not reached the acceptance levels that C had at the time we designed Clean. It is actually amazing how much ground is still covered by C at the present time. I remember that in the 80's and 90's I was implicitly convinced that new programming languages and paradigms would follow each other like assembler was followed by C which was followed by Pascal/Modula. I see a far more scattered field now. Java has takes a big chunk (and rightfully so) but is still almost a par with C according to the TIOBE index for April 2013 [3]. The index for February 2013 mentions Clean in the number 51...100 popularity range of the TIOBE index, but has unfortunately dropped below 100 in the recent April issue. Functional languages in general only have a mere 3.1% popularity score in the TIOBE index of April 2013. I must add that the methods and accuracy of this index can rightly be questioned, but it is at least an indication.

Going back to beauty, one could state that there is not enough generally accepted beauty in functional languages to make them generally used. We can of course also be convinced that the intrinsic beauty is unrecognized by the wider audience. My personal opinion on this matter is that there is a lot more involved in getting a language accepted than just beauty. There is a complex collection of reasons why a language is picked up. Apart from all sorts of technical qualities, sheer luck is one of those factors, or in other words being the right language at the right time. Being fashionable is another (this hooks into beauty by the way).

3   What Is Beauty

What does beauty mean when we are not referring to code? What is beauty in our day to day life? There are aspects of *balance, harmony, feelings of well being, attraction, satisfaction.* In our western society there is, without doubt, a special relationship between beauty and humans, ourselves. This is generally interpreted as outer beauty. Generally, but not solely. There is also inner beauty, which is harder to get a grip on and needs time and experience to recognize.

I think you can identify those two beauty aspects in code as well. There is outer beauty, the arrangement of the lines, how pleasing it is to look at the code on screen or paper. There is also inner beauty: how well does the code describe and define the solution at hand. As with beauty in humans, the outer beauty aspects can be tweaked to a certain extent without changing the essence of the code. This is where code-beautifiers play a role, they are the beauty parlours for software engineers. Nothing much is changed, it just looks better. If we go a step further we can do some plastic surgery. I would like to compare that to refactorings of software: you are really changing your code, but the meaning of the code is not changed. You make semantic changes but they result in different but equivalent code. When we look at inner beauty it is harder to make make changes for the better. I would like to compare changes on that level to meditation for humans: you really have to sit down and think about algorithms and solutions and most of the time there are moments of insight where the essence of your code is changed. These kind of changes are harder, and as of yet impossible, to automate. They need human creativity and perseverance to be accomplished. As with meditation and other inner beauty changing processes they are hard to accomplish in code. First of all they are very hard to just do, but secondly they are hard to start because it involves rethinking your solution and possibly throwing away your initial one. Depending on the time you spent already it might seem a waste. The endeavour of rethinking everything from the ground might also seem a waste because you are (inherently) not sure if you are going to find a better solution. This is where our wonderful mind jumps in: we need to trust our instinct. If our instinct tells us that there should be a better (more beautiful) solution then it is worthwhile investigating. Finding it in the end is always uncertain and that is the beauty of the endeavour.

3.1   Outer Beauty

I have always been implicitly convinced that outer beauty is not the most important thing in life. On the other hand it is not completely unimportant either. I would like to introduce what I call 'modest beauty': the beauty that does not shout out: "I am beautiful". It is the beauty that needs to be discovered. You will have to find balance and the harmony in things and discover the true beauty that caused that feeling. I have been a lifelong fan of Apple products because of this. There have never been stickers on Mac's that shout out the GHz-s and other mega-multi-super qualifications. The thing is just there. You need to discover the beauty of it, feel the balance and use it with a smile.

This modest beauty concept equally applies to humans. I find little beauty in magazines with photoshopped people, they have beauty written all over them but I do not seem to find it. Real people have imperfections and if they have learned to live with those imperfections and convey balance and harmony there is a high chance they are beautiful in a modest way.

For objects as well as people this modest beauty does not come for free. It probably takes more effort to design a Mac laptop then an average windows laptop. Equivalently, getting in balance with your imperfections and be who you are is not a trivial exercise either. In my opinion modest beauty is real beauty.

Does this relate to code? Maybe it does, maybe not. The outer beauty aspects of code that I value are mainly based on making the meaning more easy to grasp. For instance: I like columnization. The visual appearance is more balanced, there is more harmony, maybe more beauty.

Take this arbitrary snippet for example:

```
private int cacheLength = ApnsConnection.DEFAULT_CACHE_LENGTH;
private boolean autoAdjustCacheLangth = true;
private ExecutorService executor = null;
private ReconnectPolicy reconnectPolicy = ReconnectPolicy.newObject();
private boolean isQueued = false;
private ApnsDelegate delegate = ApnsDelegate.EMPTY;
private Proxy proxy;
private boolean errorDetection = true;
```

I find more balance and harmony in this representation:

```
private int             cacheLength                = ApnsConnection.DEFAULT_LENGTH;
private boolean         autoAdjustCacheLangth = true;
private ExecutorService executor                   = null;
private ReconnectPolicy reconnectPolicy            = ReconnectPolicy.newObject();
private boolean         isQueued                   = false;
private ApnsDelegate    delegate                   = ApnsDelegate.EMPTY;
private Proxy           proxy                      = null;
private boolean         errorDetection             = true;
```

I also like to see uniformity in control structures and how they are written down (i.e. write all curly brackets and write them always at the same position). Another arbitrary snippet:

```
if (minutes) return minutes.minutes();
else if (hours) return hours.hours();
else return 0;
```

for which I would prefer this make-up:

```
if (minutes) {
    return minutes.minutes();
} else if (hours) {
    return hours.hours();
} else {
    return 0;
}
```

This example actually proves my earlier statement about beauty being personal, because the last example was taken from [4], where the author is talking about the beauty of braces being absent. The absence of braces is more 'zen' in his opinion while in my opinion it gives a more uniform structure. Two different views on beauty.

In general I think terseness can not clearly be related to beauty. In my opinion it is obvious that very verbose code or a programming language that requires it is not very beautiful, because the verbosity hides the essence of the solution. In contrast, a very terse program or language hides the essence in riddles. When I was first exposed to APL I was charmed by the beauty of the terse expressions that could express everything but the kitchen sink. Later on I realized that it was actually a way of hiding meaning for everybody but the experienced APL programmer. Take for instance this Sudoku solver in APL presented in [5]:

```
Sudoku←{
    box  ← {ω ⊦ ω/ω  ωριω*2}
    rcb  ← {(ιω), ¨box⊃ ω*0.5}
    cmap ← {⊂[ι 2] 1∈¨ ω°.=ω}
    CMAP ← cmap rcb ρω
    at   ← {ω+α×(ιρω)∈⊂ αα}
    avl  ← {(ι ⊃ ρω)˜ω× ⊃ α⌷CMAP}
    emt  ← {(,ω=0)/,ιρω}
    pvec ← {(α avl ω) (α at)¨ ⊂ ω}
    pvex ← {⊃,/α°pvec¨ω}
    svec ← {⊃pvex/(emt ω),⊂⊂ ω}
    svec ω
}
```

Very terse, very cryptic and hardly beautiful, at least for me. Beauty, again, turns out a matter of taste since the solution is literally presented as *"... the following more beautiful form..."* in the referenced document. You can watch a YouTube movie [6] if you like a detailed explanation of this solution.

All these outer beauty aspects give me a more balanced and uniform visual experience which in turn makes the program easier to interpret and understand. For me, this is the essence of beauty in programming: to help relaying the meaning of your program while still defining it in an executable (sometimes even provable) way.

It is not only important to relay the meaning of what you scribbled down to other people, but also to yourself. Many times I took code I had written years ago (voluntarily or not) and tried to make sense of it. Sometimes it was hard, more times it was harder.

I would like to add here that this last aspect of beauty in code (better understandable code is also more beautiful) does not necessarily coincide with our perception of beauty in the real world. A beautiful woman is not always the easiest to understand. A certain level of mystery can make a woman even more beautiful. I guess women and code are not completely comparable after all.

3.2 Decay over Time

As in everyday live, beauty seems to evaporate over time for code as well. The code you can still remember you were proud of ten years ago is not so beautiful anymore. For our human body this is mostly due to actual changes happening over time. Code does not change when you do not touch it so it must be a change in our mind that makes it less beautiful.

This is comparable to fashion: what was beautiful in the 70's does not get that qualification anymore, at least not from me. As with code, the material did not changed but we did.

There are, of course, timeless designs that keep their beauty over time. The designs of Frank Lloyd Wright are definitely in that category for me. Whether those designs are genuinely timeless or merely longer living, only time will tell.

The Sagrada Familia in Barcelona is a perfect example of beauty in a potentially timeless setting. Generations have been building it now and still it feels as one beautiful piece of art. We can only dream of IT projects of comparable magnitude to result in such splendor. (image: Gubin Yury / Shutterstock.com)

I always experience harmony, balance and serenity when looking at zen gardens. Will code ever look like this?

If you have kids of an older age you will probably recognize this: when your child was born you genuinely and objectively felt that it was by far the most beautiful child in the world. When seeing his or her baby photos after many years you might not be so sure anymore. I can see a parallel in code beauty here... When writing a program you really think it is cool and beautiful. On a higher level: when designing a programming language you also think it is the most beautiful language you have ever seen. After years of nurturing you find yourself with a product or language that is well equipped for life but also has its scars. When looking back at the first designs and implementations you might be a little furtively ashamed and at the same time touched by reminiscences.

What I aim for from the start is beauty, although it might be only raw beauty at first. Sometimes this raw beauty will shine later, sometimes it drowns. I must admit that at least some of my older code generates more sense of shame than arousal of beauty now. Nevertheless my goal is to write code (or design languages) that I can look back on with satisfaction, even after many years. This is the reason why I am hesitant to engulf myself in the latest hype, the fashion areas of our industry. At the same time I regard it as a challenge to pick out the hypes with long term potential. An intriguing and endless balancing game.

3.3   Inner Beauty

I discussed some aspects of inner beauty above already. When a program can be easily understood by reading, there is beauty. A program should not be written with the executing computer in mind but with the human reader in mind, he or she is your peer who needs to understand what you are concocting. Beauty is not something that a computer requires to execute a program. I can still remember one of my first professors at the university, Kees Koster, teach us to program top down in Algol 68. He advocated that subroutines or functions are also valuable if only used once. This was contradicting my feeling for machine efficiency but made sense in a peer to peer setting where you wanted to explain what is happening. We were stimulated to use spaces inside ridiculously long identifiers. This made you concentrate on describing the solution more than programming it. To get a feeling, consider this imaginary snippet (I do not remember the exact syntax of Algol 68):

```
PROC build a house according to the specifications of the designer
BEGIN
    remove any buildings from the land if they are present;
    build the house on cleared land;
END

PROC build the house on cleared land
BEGIN
    build a strong foundation;
    build the all walls for the whole house;
    put the roof on the house;
END

PROC make the foundation
BEGIN
    dig a hole for the foundation;
    pour concrete to make the foundation;
    pour concrete for the ground floor;
END

PROC build all the walls for the whole house
BEGIN
    WHILE the walls are not high enough for the average person in this area DO
        put another row of bricks on all the walls;
END
```

In hindsight it was a bit over the top for production environments but was definitely instructive in the educational setting. Without knowing it we were aiming for inner beauty: explainable program structures that were understandable and clearly identifiable.

Conveying meaning is the essence and beauty of code.

One of the essential spoilers of understandable and clear code is the inevitable time sequential specification in imperative languages. It is one of those little critters in programming we could happily do without. It always spoils things. There is always a sequence of events that you did not take into account. In catering for these rare sequences you add code and then more code, you add complexity and make it less understandable, less beautiful, often even ugly. An additional problem with sequential specifications in programming languages is that it is only essential at some points. At many points in your program it is not important and therefore an over specification. The main frustration comes from the fact that it can not be specified where sequential execution is essential and where it is not. It is then very hard, if not impossible, for humans as well as computers to separate the two. We need programming languages that do not require time sequential specifications to make truly beautiful code. We need to abstract away from time to encounter real beauty. This perhaps explains my preference for declarative and functional programming where sequentiality is not explicitly specified. When you free yourself from this over-specification there is more beauty.

So why then is functional and declarative programming used so little ($< 5\%$ currently and going down!). Well, it has taken Apple decades to become the biggest company on earth. Why was the beauty not picked up earlier? Maybe beauty is not the thing that drives the avarage human being, maybe it is because sheer beauty is not enough, maybe you need a killer-app for wide acceptance. I do not have the answers. What I know is that you need to follow your instincts and my instinct tells me to follow the trail of functional and declarative, because beauty can be found there. Maybe I will live long enough to see it widely accepted, it would make me happy and even more happy to play a modest role in that.

> *When I am working on a problem I never think about beauty.*
> *I think only how to solve the problem.*
> *But when I have finished, if the solution is not beautiful, I know it is wrong.*
> (Richard Buckminster Fuller) [7]

References

1. Gelernter, D.: Machine Beauty: Elegance And The Heart Of Technology. Basic Books (1998)
2. Knuth, D.: Computer programming as an art. Communications of the ACM 17, 667–673 (1974), ACM Turing Award Lecture

3. http://www.tiobe.com/index.php/content/paperinfo/tpci/index.html
4. http://tobyho.com/2009/02/01/programming-without-braces/
5. http://dfns.dyalog.com/n_sudoku.htm
6. http://www.youtube.com/watch?v=DmT80OseAGs
7. Buckminster Fuller, R.: US architect and engineer (1895 - 1983), quote taken from
   http://simple.wikiquote.org/wiki/Richard_Buckminster_Fuller

An Ontology of States

Andrew Polonsky[1] and Henk Barendregt[1,2]

[1] Institute for Computing and Information Sciences (iCIS),
Radboud University Nijmegen, The Netherlands
[2] Netherlands Institute for Advanced Study, Wassenaar

1 Introduction

The notion of state is ubiquitous in analysis of computational systems. State introduces intensional content into a dynamical process which cannot be directly observed from outside. Without a state, the process is defined purely by its input-output behaviour, and is thus expected to run itself out toward a final result, ie, compute some function. The injunction of internal data that has causal effect on the execution of a system can thus be said to be the step that extends the concept of a function to that of a process, which is no longer guaranteed to terminate.

On the hardware level, this step is observed as one ascends from combinational circuits to sequential circuits. The former concerns logical circuits that produce values that depend only on the given input. The latter refers to circuits that have 'memory': an internal state that depends on the previous history of execution in addition to the input data. The fundamental circuit element that allows for state behavior is the flip-flop, that can store one bit of data in a virtual feedback loop. (This circuit also exhibits another characteristic of systems with memory: the presence of some clock mechanism.) The significance of circuits with state is that they make it possible to construct a fully functional computer system — which requires registers, arithmetic processors, instruction sequencing, storage, etc.

On the software level, this distinction manifests itself as the difference between programs which execute some specific algorithm and then terminate (e.g. compilers, text analysers, theorem provers, database search) and those that interact with their environment while they are running (e.g. text editors, web servers, operating systems). In the latter family, the behavior of the program at a particular moment may be determined not only by the current user input, but by the previous history also, so that there is additional information needed to determine how the program will act at a given instant.

On the level of language design, the presence of intensional data is part of the great divide between the pure functional languages and imperative (also, object-oriented) languages. Because of *referential transparency*, the meaning of an expression in purely functional languages is defined independently of the context or history of execution. In contrast, languages in the latter family also allow destructive operations on data which makes it possible to have data structures whose internal content changes over time.

P. Achten and P. Koopman (Eds.): Plasmeijer Festschrift, LNCS 8106, pp. 18–26, 2013.

Functional languages are very convenient for writing programs of the first kind, where the input data must be transformed in some algorithmically complex way; indeed, the syntax of languages such as `Clean` very closely mirrors the actual mathematical definition of the function being computed. Thus functional programs are much easier to analyze and prove properties of than their imperative counterparts.

However, many real-world applications require programs of the second kind; for this, stateful programming becomes unavoidable (similarly to how purely combinational circuits become inadequate for building complex computational systems). Thus, much of the research in the field of functional programming has been devoted to finding the most clean way of incorporating intensional content into functional programs. The design of the `Clean` language is directly based on the fruits of this research, as is made evident in its very name. In addition to fundamental innovations in language design, this work also introduced ideas in programming language theory of independent mathematical interest, [3] and [4].

The practical possibilities offered by the `Clean`-style uniqueness typing solution to the state problem can be observed in the implementation of the iTasks system, [5] and [6].

In this paper, we offer a meta-level investigation of the notion of a state from the conceptual/logical points of view. We will show that there are several ways with which a state specifies the intensional content of a sytem.

2 Agents and Systems

An *agent* is a system that receives input from the environment and comes into action. Classes of agents are (in historical order)

1. Molecules and molecular machines.
2. Organims, from unicellular ones to homo sapiens.
3. Computer systems, from ad-hoc chips to super-computers.

The simplest way to describe an agent is recording its input-output (I/O) behaviour. This may be done in natural or testing circumstances. This leads to a behaviour function. Denoting the set of possible inputs by I and the set of possible actions by A, we see that such a purely behavioral system is nothing but a map

$$M : I \to A \tag{1}$$

which specifies which actions are to be taken for every input. One may rewrite this as

$$M(i) = a \in A \tag{1'}.$$

In most cases this behaviouristic approach is limited. Nevertheless some agents can be described in this way. Their actions uniquely result from the input, either in a deterministic way or in a non-deterministic way.

More interesting agents may react differently under the same circumstances. This is the reason that the notion of state is important, as the model (1) is inadequate.

3 What Is a State?

Observing an agent we may tentatively say that its behaviour depends on a state. The behaviour function now becomes

$$M : I \times S \rightarrow A. \tag{2}$$

One also may write

$$M(i, s) = a \in A. \tag{2'}$$

But do these states exist? To a biologist a state that fully determines together with the input the action may seem doubtful. Using some mathematical hubris one can nevertheless affirm that states do exist. An agent M_1 at moment t_1 can be said to be in the same state as a similar (having the same classes of I/O) agent M_2 at moment t_2 iff M_1 and M_2 react on an input $i \in I$ with the same action. In particular one has defined now when an agent M is at moment t_1 and t_2 in the same state by taking $M_1 = M_2 = M$. Now with the principle of abstraction, see [1], one can define 'state' from the relation 'to be in the same state':

DEFINITION. A *state* is an equivalence relation consisting of pairs (M, t) all being in the same state.

In this way a state is a higher-order concept: a specific I/O relation.

Like the notion of state of a gas in a closed vat (a vector in a $6 * 10^{23}$ space describing for all (10^{23}) gas molecules its 3 position and 3 momentum coordinates) the state of a biological organism or even of a digital device can never be fully known: the amount of data is over-astronomical. So one may wonder why to introduce states, being what seems to be an example of mathematical hubris. The reason to have states is that one may reason about them.

The ontology for state as determined by (2) is a (deterministic or non-deterministic) map. If $s : I \rightarrow A$, then one can interpret the action (2) as

$$M(i, s) = s(i) \in A. \tag{2''}$$

Although this ontology is satisfactory for the states used in (2), there is a need for a more complex notion of state.

4 Turing-Like Machines

It is well known that a classical Turing machine can be described as a triple $\langle \Sigma, Q, \delta \rangle$, where Σ is a set of symbols, with $b \in \Sigma$ is a special element ('blank'), Q is a set of 'states' with $q_0 \in Q$ a special state (start), and finally

$$\delta \colon \Sigma \times Q \rightharpoonup \Sigma \times Q \times \{L, R\},$$

is a partial map. A set of 'final states' is not needed as it can be simulated by states $q \in Q$ such that $\delta(q, -)$ is never defined. There is a two sided infinite linear tape consisting of cells of order type $\mathbb{Z}$ and a read-write head placed on one of the cells. If the machine is in state q and the head reads a symbol a and $\delta(a, q) = \langle a', q', L|R\rangle$ is defined, then

I   the machine jumps to state q' and symbol a is overwritten by a';
II the head moves over the tape to the left or right, depending
    on whether the last element of the output was an L or an R.

This description can be slightly generalized in such a way that the resulting 'Turing-like' machines describe 'agents' dealing with input/output (I/O) that include robots, animals and even humans in an abstract way. Now the machine is described as a 4-tuple $\langle I, Q, A, \delta\rangle$, where I is a set of inputs, Q is a set of states, A is a set of actions, and finally

$$\delta: I \times Q \rightharpoonup A \times Q$$

is a partial map. By taking $I = \sigma$ and $A = \{L, R\} \cup \{W(a) \mid a \in \Sigma\}$, with $W(a)$ having as meaning 'write the symbol a, the classical Turing machine can be seen as a Turing-like machine. But now I also can be seen as information presented from the outside world through sensors, or the inner world part of memory; and A can be seen as actions including movements of the robot, and focussing attention on a part of memory, relevant in the given environmental context.

If we now suppose that every step taken by the agent M depends also on some current state that is preserved between successive cycles of execution, then, letting S denote the set of these states, such a machine is specified by a map

$$M : I \times S \to A \times S \tag{3}$$

Thus M sends the pair (i, s) of an input and a state to a pair (a, s) consisting of the action to be taken as well as the new state the system is put into.

In this model, the state space S acts as a hidden parameter in the specification of the system.

Modelling living beings in this way, one can ask the question whether there does exists something like a state that determines action (and the next state). The extensional apporach is to say that an agent at different moments is in the same state whenever equal inputs deliver equal actions (and new states). So a state is seen as a map transforming input to action (and a possibly new state). This yields the recursive domain equation

$$S \cong (I \to (A \times S)) \tag{3'}$$

5 Solving the Recursive Domain Equation

We now solve the recursive domain equation

$$S \cong (I \to (A \times S)) \tag{4}$$

Since the variable S appears positively on the left side, the initial solution to this equation is an inductive type. Categorically, this universal solution turns out to be empty, because $\emptyset$ maps initially to every object and satisfies $(A \times \emptyset)^I \cong \emptyset^I \cong \emptyset$. (Unless I itself is empty, in which case the unique solution to (4) is the singleton set consisting of the empty map $\emptyset : \emptyset \to (A \times \{\emptyset\})$.)

It is therefore preferrable to assume that we begin with some initial set of states S_0, and take the closure by the functor $F(X) = (A \times X)^I$. (This solution is universal among all sets containing S_0.)

Explicitly, such a solution is found by infinitely iterating the functor F and taking the direct limit:

$$
\begin{aligned}
S_0 \quad &= S_0 \\
S_1 = F(S_0) &= (A \times S_0)^I = A^I \times S_0^I \\
S_2 = F(S_1) &= (A \times (A^I \times S_0^I))^I \\
&\cong A^I \times (A^I)^I \times (S_0^I)^I \\
&\cong A^{I+I^2} \times S_0^{I^2} \\
S_3 = F(S_2) &= (A \times (A^{I+I^2} \times S_0^{I^2}))^I \\
&\cong A^I \times (A^{I+I^2})^I \times (S_0^{I^2})^I \\
&\cong A^I \times A^{I^2+I^3} \times S_0^{I^3} \\
&\cong A^{I+I^2+I^3} \times S_0^{I^3} \\
S_4 = F(S_3) &\cong A^{I+I^2+I^3+I^4} \times S_0^{I^4} \\
&\quad\vdots \\
S_n \quad &= A^{I+\cdots+I^n} \times S_0^{I^n} \\
&\quad\vdots
\end{aligned}
$$

The limit of the above sequence is the type

$$
S := S_\omega = A^{I^+} \times S_0^{I^\omega}
$$

where

$$
X^+ := \sum_{n>1} X^n
$$

is the set of strings of *positive length* over a set X. It satisfies the equation

$$
X^+ \cong X + X \times X^+ \tag{5}
$$

On the other hand, X^ω is the set of all sequences (or *streams*) over X, which satisfies the equation

$$
X^\omega \cong X \times X^\omega \tag{6}
$$

Using (5) and (6), we trivially verify that

$$
\begin{aligned}
F(S) &= (A \times S)^I \\
&\cong A^I \times S^I \\
&= A^I \times (A^{I^+} \times S_0^{I^\omega})^I \\
&\cong A^I \times (A^{I^+})^I \times (S_0^{I^\omega})^I \\
&\cong A^I \times A^{I \times I^+} \times S_0^{I \times I^\omega} \\
&\cong A^{I + I \times I^+} \times S_0^{I \times I^\omega} \\
&\cong A^{I^+} \times S_0^{I^\omega} \\
&= S
\end{aligned}
$$

So that $F(S) \cong S$, as desired.

Notice that the inductive process that builds up S is correlated with the time axis of execution: the n'th approximant S_n contains precisely enough data to run the machine for n steps.

Another curiousity of this space of solutions is that it is a product of two function spaces. Indeed, $S = A^{I^+} \times S_0^{I^\omega}$ consists of pairs of maps (f, g), with $f : I^+ \to A$ and $g : I^\omega \to S_0$. We will now analyze the meaning of these constituent functions.

We note that the first factor, specifying a function $f : I^+ \to A$, serves to determine which action is taken by M after some finite sequence of inputs $i = (i_1, \ldots, i_n)$. This corresponds to the *extensional* part of the specification of M, as every value of this function can be observed by feeding M a required string of inputs. Note that it has no relation to the initial set S_0.

The second factor, on the other hand, declares a function $g : I^\omega \to S_0$. It is curious that no value of g can be known after finitely many inputs. Rather, g may be interpreted by stipulating that, given an *infinite* sequence $x = (x_n)$ of inputs (running the system 'to the end of time'), M ultimately comes to some 'state' $s_x \in S_0$, which ascribes it intrinsic identity that cannot be measured by any actions it takes. In other words, g is the *intensional* part of the specification of M.

By taking $S_0 := 1 = \{0\}$ to be a singleton, we find the space of purely extensional solutions, where the second component is projected away: $S_e = A^{I^+} \times 1^{I^\omega} \cong A^{I^+}$

If we furthermore stipulate any machine $M \in S$ takes some action $a \in A$ *before* the first input is given, then the space of solutions is

$$
S = A \times A^{I^+} \cong A^{1 + I^+} \cong A^{I^*}
$$

where I^* is the space of finite strings of non-negative length. This set S is nothing but the set of A-*labelled trees* over I.

In conclusion, every system specified by a map $m : I \times S \to A \times S$ consists of two components: an extensional (or *behavioral*) part, given by an A-labelled

I-branching tree, and an intensional part, that merely stipulates some 'hidden variable' determined only by the whole run of the system to infinity.

6 Solution via Scott Domains

The calculation of the recursive type $F(S) = S$ is somewhat better behaved if we work in the category of Scott domains, see [2]. This is effected by turning every set in question (I, A, S) into a flat cpo by adjoining a bottom element $\bot$ and declaring it to be below every other element.

In this setting, we may find S_0 as a subset of the limit S_ω via the embedding $s \mapsto (\bot_A, c_s)$ which sends $s \in S_0$ to the pair consisting of the bottom action and the constant function with value s. Here S_ω with this embedding is indeed universal among all algebras X for the functor F together with an embedding $S_0 \hookrightarrow X$.

Furthermore, since every cpo has a bottom element, the functor F itself has the universal solution in which S_0 is terminal cpo $\{\bot\}$. Note that this cpo doesn't grow during the iteration $\{\bot\}, \{\bot\}^I, \{\bot\}^{I^2}, \ldots$ So in the limit, the second factor appears as the 1-element cpo, giving the pure extensional solution, which is the initial algebra for the functor F in the category of cpos.

7 Continuous Time

As a final rumination, let us consider how the former analysis could be employed in a continuous setting. The first suggestion could be to take the sets I, S, A to be topological spaces, and consider a continuous map

$$\Phi = (u(i, s), a(i, s)) : I \times S \to S \times A$$

representing evolution of state and action with respect to input and previous state. Since we want the state $s \in S$ to evolve "continuously" with each application of Φ, it seems necessary that, whenever $\Phi(i, s) = (s', a')$, we must have $s = s'$. But then repeated iteration of Φ can never move the state!

The resolution of this dilemma is to consider $\Phi = (u, a)$ as a family of operators of smaller and smaller "clock ticks". The input, state, and action then become functions that depend on time.

Thus the question of realizability of a prescribed behavior using a stateful system takes the following form:

Given functions $i(t) : [0, 1] \to I$ and $b(t) : [0, 1] \to A$, when can we find a space S admitting functions $s : [0, 1] \to S$ and $a : I \times S \to A$ such that

1. $b(t) = a(i(t), s(t))$
2. $s(t + dt)$ depends on $i(t)$ and $s(t)$ in a "continuous way".

In order to expore a more precise formulation of the second condition, let us simplify the analysis by first considering the case where the input is held constant: $i(t) = i_0$. We want to think of the evolution of the state during this interval as a "continuous application" of some state function $v(s)$. This wish could be attained if we are provided a map $v_0 : S \to S$ together with an infinite collection of "compositional square roots": maps

$$v_n : S \to S, \qquad n \geq 0$$

such that

$$v_{n+1} \circ v_{n+1} = v_n$$

We then define v_t for every $t \in [0, 1]$ by prescribing its values on the dyadic rationals: for $t = \frac{t_1}{2} + \frac{t_2}{4} + \cdots + \frac{t_n}{2^n}$, put

$$v(s,t) = v_1^{t_1} \circ \cdots \circ v_n^{t_n}(s)$$

This would define a continuous map v from $S \times [0, 1]$ to S if we can provide, for each $s \in S$, that

$$\lim_{n \to \infty} v_n(s) \quad \text{exists}$$

and that the value of this limit varies continuously with s.

In fact, it must then follow that the limit above is actually equal to s, capturing the intuition that $v(s, t)$ represents infinitesimal evolution of $u(i, s)$.

Now, given $s_0 \in S$, we can define $s : [0, 1] \to S$ by

$$s(t) = \begin{cases} s_0 & t = 0 \\ v(s_0, t) & t > 0 \end{cases}$$

Thus, the right way to ask the question of what is the "next value" of Φ is to consider the infinitesimal change in the state after an infinitesimal tick of time. This naturally leads to the question of the derivative of s.

In fact, in order to accomodate the possibility of changing input, passing to the derivative cannot be avoided, because the small changes in the value of the input must be integrated into the changes of the state from the very beginning.

Now, suppose that the following expression is well-defined for each $s \in S$:

$$\dot{v}(s) = \lim_{n \to \infty} 2^n (v_n(s) - s)$$

Notice that $\frac{ds}{dt}(t) = \dot{s}(t) = \dot{v}(s(t))$. Considering $\dot{v}(t)$ as a known function and $s(t)$ an indeterminate one, this identity becomes a differential equation

$$s' = \dot{v}(s)$$

Having reduced the problem to this form, we can now accomodate non-constant input functions. Specifically, instead of having $s'(t)$ be defined by a function $\dot{v}$ that depends only on $s(t)$, we allow it to depend on $i(t)$ as well. That is, we write

$$s' = u(s, i)$$

for some given function u. (Notice that i may now contain information about time, as well as be equal to time.)

Together with a function $a(s, i)$ that computes the output, we now have precisely the data needed to specify a behavior of a stateful system subject to the boundary condition given by the input function $i(t)$, $t \in [0, 1]$. This can be seen as the infinitesimal limit of the specification of Φ.

REMARK. In order for the expression

$$\frac{1}{\epsilon} \cdot (s(t) - s(t + \epsilon))$$

to be meaningful, the space S must have linear structure on it. As it happens, the state spaces which usually appear in the dynamical systems of physics are in fact vector spaces. Thus, we see that the idea of having internal state realize a given continuous behavior naturally leads to the classical PDE view of dynamical systems.

8 Conclusion

We have seen that the notion of internal state arises naturally when one progresses from the concept of a function, which gives raw input–output relation, to that of a process, or a system, which evolves indefinitely as new input is provided.

In the discrete case, the extensional contribution of a state is captured by an infinite tree of its possible executions, which can be specified by a function from strings over inputs to actions. The length of the string provides how many clock ticks have elapsed since the execution has started.

In the continuous case, we are lead to the notion of dynamical systems as solutions of differential operators. As in the previous case, the crucial role is played by an intermediate structure, within which the intensional data of computation resides.

References

1. Tarski, A.: Introduction to logic and to the methodology of deductive sciences. Oxford university press (1941)
2. Gunter, C.A., Scott, D.S.: Semantic Domains. Handbook of Theoretical Computer Science, Volume B: Formal Models and Sematics (B), pp. 633–674 (1990)
3. Plasmeijer, R., van Eekelen, M.: Functional programming and parallel graph rewriting. Addison-wesley (1993)
4. Achten, P., Plasmeijer, R.: The Ins and Outs of Clean I/O. JFP 5(01), 81–110 (1995)
5. Lijnse, B.: TOP to the Rescue. PhD thesis (2013)
6. Plasmeijer, R., Lijnse, B., Michels, S., Achten, P., Koopman, P.: Task-Oriented Programming in a Pure Functional Language. In: Proceedings of the International Conference on Principles and Practice of Declarative Programming, PPDP 2012, Leuven, Belgium, pp. 195–206 (2012)

Functional Type Assignment for Featherweight Java
To Rinus Plasmeijer, in Honour of His 61st Birthday

Steffen J. van Bakel and Reuben N.S. Rowe

Department of Computing, Imperial College London, 180 Queen's Gate, London SW7 2BZ, UK
s.vanbakel@imperial.ac.uk, r.rowe@doc.ic.ac.uk

Abstract. We consider functional type assignment for the class-based object-oriented calculus Featherweight Java. We start with an *intersection type assignment systems* for this calculus for which types are preserved under conversion. We then define a variant for which type assignment is decidable, and define a notion of unification as well as a principal typeing algorithm.

We show the expressivity of both our calculus and our type system by defining an encoding of Combinatory Logic into our calculus and showing that this encoding preserves typeability. We thus demonstrate that the great capabilities of functional types can be applied to the context of class-based object orientated programming.

Introduction

In this paper we will study a notion of functional type assignment for Featherweight Java (FJ) [15]. We will show its elegance and expressiveness, and advocate its use in type assignment systems for fully fledged Java; of course it would need to be extended in order to fully deal with all the features of that language, but through the system we present here we show that that should be feasible, giving a better notion of types.

Type assignment has more than shown its worth in the context of functional programming, like ML, Clean [11,17], and Haskell. Not only are types essential for efficient code generation, they provide an excellent means of (an abstract level of) error checking: it is in most programmers' experience that once the type checker has approved of a functional program, said program will be almost error free.[1] But, more importantly, the approach to types in functional programming is that of *type assignment*: programmers have the freedom to not specify types for any part of their code. A type inference algorithm embedded in the compiler guarantees a partial correctness result: the type found for a program is also the type for the result of running the program, a property most commonly known as *subject reduction* or *type soundness*, although that latter term has different meaning as well.

In the context of imperative programming, which contains the Object-Oriented approach (OO) as well, the reality is very different. There it is more common to demand that *all* types are written within the code; then type checking is almost trivial, and mainly concerns checking if special features like inheritance are well typed. The difference between the *functional* approach and the *imperative* one then boils down to the

---

[1] Almost, yes, not completely; we can but dream of static error checking systems that only approve of error free code, and catch all errors.

P. Achten and P. Koopman (Eds.): Plasmeijer Festschrift, LNCS 8106, pp. 27–46, 2013.

difference between *untyped* and *typed* calculi. Often, in the untyped approach, if a term has a type, it has infinitely many, a feature that is exploited when introducing *polymorphism* into a programming language's type system. In the typed approach, each term has (normally) only *one* type. This implies that it is difficult, if not impossible, to express polymorphism in imperative languages.

With that in mind, we set out to investigate if the functional approach is feasible for imperative languages as well. The results presented in this paper are part of the results of that investigation, but in the more concrete setting of functional type assignment for object orientation. In order to be able to concentrate on the essential difficulties, we focus on Featherweight Java [15], a restriction of Java which can be regarded as the minimal core fragment of Java, defined by removing all but the most essential features of the full language; Featherweight Java bears a similar relation to Java as the λ-calculus (LC) [12,9] does to languages such as ML and and Haskell.

But rather than defining a notion of type assignment that is implementable, we thought it necessary to first verify that the kernel of our approach *made sense, i.e.* accords to some particular kind of abstract semantics.[2] Normally, just *operational semantics* is used: then the only check is that subject reduction is satisfied. This is certainly the minimal requirement for type assignment systems (although variants are proposed that do not even satisfy this), but normally much more can be achieved.

Rather, in [19] we proposed an approach that has strong links with *denotational semantics*, in that it gives a full equational semantics for FJ-programs. The best-known way to achieve that is through setting up a notion of types inspired by Coppo and Dezani's *intersection type discipline* (ITD) [13,10,2] and this was the path we followed in [19]. ITD, first defined for LC, is a system that is closed under β-equality and gives rise to a filter model and semantics; it is defined as an extension of Curry's basic type system for LC by allowing term-variables to have many, potentially non-unifiable, types. This generalisation leads to a very expressive system: for example, strong normalisation of terms can be characterised by assignable types.

Inspired by this expressive power, investigations have taken place of the suitability of intersection type assignment for other computational models: for example, van Bakel and Fernández have studied intersection types in the context of Term Rewriting Systems (TRS) [7,8] and van Bakel studied them in the context of sequent calculi [3,5]. In an attempt to bring intersection types to the context of OO, van Bakel and de'Liguoro presented a system for the ς-calculus [6]; the main characteristic of that system is that it sees assignable types as an *execution* or *applicability predicate*, rather than as a functional characterisation as is the view in the context of LC and, as a result, recursive calls are typed individually, with different types. This is also the case in our system.

The system we presented there is essentially based on the strict system of [1]; the decidable system we present here, a system with simple record types, is likewise essentially based on Curry types. Our system with intersection types has been shown to give a semantics in [19] of which we will state the main results here; that paper also defined

---

[2] Too often *ad-hoc* changes to type systems are proposed that only solve a specific problem; the proposer typically gives an example of an untypeable term that in all reasonability should be typeable, and gives a change to the type system in order to make that example typeable.

a notion of *approximation*, inspired by a similar notion defined for the λ-calculus [20], and showed an approximation result.[3]

Our types are *functional*, contain *field* and *method* information, and characterise how a typeable object can interact with a context in which it is placed. The notion of type assignment we developed can be seen as a notion of 'flow analysis' in that assignable types express how expressions can be approached; as such, the types express run-time behaviour of expressions. Our type system was shown to be closed for *conversion*, *i.e.* closed for both *subject reduction* and *subject expansion*, which implies that types give a complete characterisation of the execution behaviour of programs; as a consequence, type assignment in the full system is undecidable.

That FJ is Turing complete seems to be a well accepted fact; we illustrate the expressive power of our calculus by embedding Combinatory Logic (CL) [14] – and thereby also LC – into it, thus establishing that our calculus is Turing complete as well. To show that our type system provides more than a semantical tool and can be used in practice as well, in this paper we will define a variant of our system by restricting to a notion of Curry type assignment; the variant consists of dealing with recursion differently. We show a principal type property and a type preservation result for this system.

The Curry system we propose here is a first, and certainly not the most expressive, illustrative, or desirable system imaginable. We allow intersection types only in the form of records; for FJ this is natural, since a class should be seen as a combination of all its capabilities. As a special property, our principal typeing algorithm calculates (normally) records as types for classes, and the return type of a method can be a record as well. And thirdly, the way the system types recursive classes could be improved by using recursive types.

1 Featherweight Java without Casts

In this section, we will define the variant of Featherweight Java we consider in this paper. As in other class-based object-oriented languages, it defines *classes*, which represent abstractions that encapsulate both data (stored in *fields*) and the operations to be performed on that data (encoded as *methods*). Sharing of behaviour is accomplished through the *inheritance* of fields and methods from parent classes. Computation is mediated by *instances* of these classes (called *objects*), which interact with one another by *calling* (also called *invoking*) methods on each other and accessing each other's (or their own) fields. We have removed cast expressions since, as the authors of [15] themselves point out, the presence of *downcasts* is unsound[4], so cannot be modelled semantically; for this reason we call our calculus FJ$^{\not\subset}$. We also leave constructors as implicit.

Notation. We use $\underline{n}$ (where n is a natural number) to represent the set $\{1,\dots,n\}$. A sequence s of n elements $a_1,\dots,a_n$ is denoted by $\vec{a}_n$; the subscript can be omitted

---

[3] Although the latter firmly rooted our system semantically, it plays no role when implementing, so we will skip its details here. Suffice that say that, because the language of FJ is first order, we had to define *derivation reduction* and show it strongly normalisable in order to prove the approximation result and the normalisation results that follow as a consequence.

[4] In the sense that typeable expressions can get stuck at runtime by reducing to an expression containing *stupid* casts.

when the exact number of elements in the sequence is not relevant. We write $a \in \vec{a}_n$ whenever there exists some $i \in \underline{n}$ such that $a = a_i$. The empty sequence is denoted by ϵ, and concatenation on sequences by $s_1 \cdot s_2$.

We use familiar meta-variables in our formulation to range over class names (C and D), field names (f), method names (m) and variables (x).[5] We distinguish the class name Object (which denotes the root of the class inheritance hierarchy in all programs) and the self variable this, used to refer to the receiver object in method bodies.

Definition 1 (FJ$^\mathcal{l}$ Syntax). An FJ$^\mathcal{l}$ program P consist of a *class table* $\mathcal{CT}$, comprising the *class declarations*, and an *expression* e to be run (corresponding to the body of the main method in a real Java program). Programs are defined by the grammar:

$$
\begin{aligned}
e &::= x \mid \mathtt{this} \mid \mathtt{new}\ C(\vec{e}) \mid e.f \mid e.m(\vec{e}) \\
fd &::= C\ f; \\
md &::= D\,m(C_1\ x_1,\ \ldots,\ C_n\ x_n)\ \{\mathtt{return}\ e;\} \\
cd &::= \mathtt{class}\ C\ \mathtt{extends}\ C'\ \{\ \overline{fd}\ \overline{md}\} \qquad (C \neq \mathtt{Object}) \\
\mathcal{CT} &::= \overrightarrow{cd} \\
P &::= (\mathcal{CT}; e)
\end{aligned}
$$

The remaining concepts that we will define below are dependent (or, more precisely, parametric) on a given class table. For example, the reduction relation we will define uses the class table to look up fields and method bodies in order to direct reduction and our type assignment system will do likewise. Thus, there is a reduction relation and type assignment system *for each program*. However, since the class table is a fixed entity (*i.e.* it is not changed during reduction, or during type assignment), as usual it will be left as an implicit parameter in the definitions that follow.

As we have just mentioned, the sequence of (class) declarations that comprises the class table induces a family of lookup *functions*. In order to ensure that these functions are well defined, we only consider programs which conform to some sensible well-formedness criteria: that there are no cycles in the inheritance hierarchy, that each class is declared only once, that fields and methods in any given branch of the inheritance hierarchy are uniquely named, and that method definitions correspond to closed functions. An exception is made to allow *method override*, i.e. the redeclaration of methods, providing that only the *body* of the method differs from the previous declaration.

We define the following functions to look up elements of class definitions.

Definition 2 (Lookup Functions). The following lookup functions are defined to extract the names of fields and bodies of methods belonging to (and inherited by) a class.

1. The following retrieve the name of a class, method, or field from its definition:

$$
\begin{aligned}
\mathcal{CN}\,(\mathtt{class}\ C\ \mathtt{extends}\ D\{\overline{fd}\ \overline{md}\}) &= C \\
\mathcal{MN}\,(C\,m(\vec{x}).e;) &= m \\
\mathcal{FN}\,(C\ f;) &= f
\end{aligned}
$$

2. By abuse of notation, we will treat the *class table*, $\mathcal{CT}$, as a partial map from class names to class definitions:

---

[5] We use roman teletype font for concrete FJ$^\mathcal{l}$-code, and italicised teletype font for meta-code.

$$\mathcal{CT}(c) \;=\; cd \qquad (\mathcal{CN}(cd) = c,\; cd \in \mathcal{CT})$$

3. The list of fields belonging to a class c (including those it inherits) is given by:

$$\mathcal{F}(\texttt{Object}) \;=\; \epsilon$$
$$\mathcal{F}(c) \;=\; \mathcal{F}(c') \cdot \vec{f}_n \quad (\mathcal{CT}(c) = \texttt{class } c \texttt{ extends } c' \;\{\overrightarrow{fd}_n \; \overrightarrow{md}\},$$
$$\mathcal{FN}(fd_i) = f_i \quad (i \in \underline{n}))$$

4. The list of methods belonging to a class c is given by:

$$\mathcal{M}(\texttt{Object}) \;=\; \epsilon$$
$$\mathcal{M}(c) \;=\; \mathcal{M}(c') \cdot \vec{m}_n \quad (\mathcal{CT}(c) = \texttt{class } c \texttt{ extends } c' \;\{\overrightarrow{fd}_n \; \overrightarrow{md}\},$$
$$\mathcal{MN}(md_i) = m_i \quad (i \in \underline{n}))$$

(notice that method names can appear more than once in $\mathcal{M}(c)$).

5. The function $\mathcal{M}b$, given a class name c and method name m, returns a tuple $(\vec{x}, e)$, consisting of a sequence of the method's formal parameters and its body:

$$\mathcal{M}b(c,m) \;=\; (\vec{x}_n, e) \qquad (\mathcal{CT}(c) = \texttt{class } c \texttt{ extends } c' \;\{\overrightarrow{fd} \; \overrightarrow{md}\}$$
$$\&\; c_0 \, m\,(c_1\,x_1, \ldots, c_n\,x_n)\; \{\texttt{return } e;\} \in \overrightarrow{md})$$
$$\mathcal{M}b(c,m) \;=\; \mathcal{M}b(c',m) \quad (\mathcal{CT}(c) = \texttt{class } c \texttt{ extends } c' \;\{\overrightarrow{fd} \; \overrightarrow{md}\}$$
$$\&\; m \text{ not in } \overrightarrow{md})$$

6. The function $fv\,(e)$ returns the set of variables used in e.

Substitution of expressions for variables is the basic mechanism for reduction in our calculus: when a method is invoked on an object (the *receiver*) the invocation is replaced by the body of the method that is called, and each of the variables is replaced by a corresponding argument, and this is replaced by the receiver.

Definition 3 (Reduction).   1. A *term substitution*

$$\mathsf{S} \;=\; \langle\, \texttt{this} \mapsto e', x_1 \mapsto e_1, \ldots, x_n \mapsto e_n \,\rangle$$

is defined in the standard way as a total function on expressions that systematically replaces all occurrences of the variables x_i and this by their corresponding expression. We write e^{S} for $\mathsf{S}(e)$.

2. The single-step reduction $\rightarrow$ is defined by:

$$\texttt{new } c\,(\vec{e}_n . f_i) \;\rightarrow\; e_i \qquad (\mathcal{F}(c) = \vec{f}_n, i \in \underline{n})$$
$$\texttt{new } c\,(\vec{e})\,.m\,(\overrightarrow{e'}_n) \;\rightarrow\; e^{\mathsf{S}} \qquad (\mathcal{M}b(c,m) = (\vec{x}_n, e),\; \text{where } \mathsf{S} =$$
$$\langle\, \texttt{this} \mapsto \texttt{new } c\,(\vec{e}),\; x_1 \mapsto e'_1,\; \ldots,\; x_n \mapsto e'_n \,\rangle)$$

We call the left-hand term the *redex* (*red*ucible *ex*pression) and the right hand the *contractum*. As usual, we define $\rightarrow^*$ as the pre-congruence generated by $\rightarrow$.

The nominal system as presented in [15], adapted to our version of Featherweight Java, is defined as follows.

$$(\text{NEW}) : \frac{\Gamma \vdash e_i : C_i \quad (\forall i \in \underline{n})}{\Gamma \vdash \text{new } C(\vec{e}) : C} \; (\mathcal{F}(C) = \vec{f} \;\&\; \mathcal{FT}(C,f_i) = D_i \;\&\; C_i <: D_i \quad (\forall i \in \underline{n}))$$

$$(\text{INVK}) : \frac{\Gamma \vdash e : E \qquad \Gamma \vdash e_i : C_i \quad (\forall i \in \underline{n})}{\Gamma \vdash e.m(\vec{e}) : C} \; (\mathcal{MT}(E,m) = \vec{D} \rightarrow C \;\&\; C_i <: D_i \; (\forall i \in \underline{n}))$$

$$(\text{VAR}) : \frac{}{\Gamma, x{:}C \vdash x : C} \quad (\text{FLD}) : \frac{\Gamma \vdash e : D}{\Gamma \vdash e.f : C} \; (\mathcal{FT}(D,f) = C) \quad (\text{U-CAST}) : \frac{\Gamma \vdash e : D}{\Gamma \vdash (C)e : C} \; (D <: C)$$

$$(\text{D-CAST}) : \frac{\Gamma \vdash e : D}{\Gamma \vdash (C)e : C} \; (C <: D, C \neq D) \qquad (\text{S-CAST}) : \frac{\Gamma \vdash e : D}{\Gamma \vdash (C)e : C} \; (C \not<: D, D \not<: C)$$

Fig. 1. Type assignment rules for the nominal system for FJ$^{\not\zeta}$

Definition 4 (Member type lookup). The *field table* $\mathcal{FT}$ and *method table* $\mathcal{MT}$ are functions which return type information about the elements of a given class in an execution. These functions allow us to retrieve the types of any given field f or method m declared in a particular class C: $\mathcal{FT}(C,f) =$

$$\begin{cases} D & (\mathcal{CT}(C) = \text{class } C \text{ extends } C' \; \{\overline{fd}\,\overline{md}\}, D\,f \in \overline{fd}) \\ \mathcal{FT}(C',f) & (\mathcal{CT}(C) = \text{class } C \text{ extends } C' \; \{\overline{fd}\,\overline{md}\}, f \text{ not in } \overline{fd}) \end{cases}$$

$\mathcal{MT}$ is defined similarly: $\mathcal{MT}(C,m) =$

$$\begin{cases} \vec{C}_n \rightarrow D & (\mathcal{CT}(C) = \text{class } C \text{ extends } C' \; \{\overline{fd}\,\overline{md}\}, \\ & \hspace{4cm} D\,m(\overline{C}\,\vec{x}) \; \{e\} \in \overline{md}) \\ \mathcal{MT}(C',m) & (\mathcal{CT}(C) = \text{class } C \text{ extends } C' \; \{\overline{fd}\,\overline{md}\}, m \text{ not in } \overline{md}) \end{cases}$$

Notice both are not defined on Object.

Nominal type assignment in FJ$^{\not\zeta}$ is a relatively easy affair, and more or less guided by the class hierarchy.

Definition 5 (Nominal type assignment for FJ$^{\not\zeta}$ [15]). 1. The sub-typing relation on class types is generated by the extends construct, and is defined as the smallest pre-order satisfying: if class C extends D $\{\overline{fd}\ \overline{md}\} \in \mathcal{CT}$, then $C <: D$.[6]

2. *Statements* are pairs of expression and type, written as $e : C$; *contexts* Γ are defined as sets of statements of the shape $x{:}C$, where all variables are distinct, and possibly containing a statement for this.

3. Expression type assignment for the nominal system for FJ is defined through the rules given in Figure 1, where (VAR) is applicable to this as well.

4. A declaration of method m is well typed in C when the type returned by $\mathcal{MT}(m,C)$ determines a type assignment for the method body.[7]

$$(\text{METH}) : \frac{\vec{x}{:}\vec{C}, \text{this}{:}C \vdash e_b : D}{E \; m(\overline{C}\,\vec{x}) \; \{ \text{ return } e_b; \; \} \text{ OK IN } C} \; (\mathcal{MT}(m,D) = \vec{C} \rightarrow E, D <: E, \text{class } C \text{ extends } D \; \{\cdots\})$$

5. Classes are well typed when all their methods are and a program is well typed when all the classes are and the expression is typeable.

---

[6] Notice that this relation depends on the class-table, so the symbol <: should be indexed by $\mathcal{CT}$; as mentioned above, we leave this implicit.

[7] Notice that, by the well-formedness criterion, e_b has no other variables than $\vec{x}$, so all variables are bound in a method declaration, thus avoiding dynamic linking issues.

$$\left(\text{CLASS}\right): \frac{md_i \text{ OK IN } C \quad (\forall i \in \underline{n})}{\texttt{class } C \texttt{ extends } D\{\overrightarrow{fd}; \ \overrightarrow{md_n}\} \text{ OK}} \qquad \left(\text{PROG}\right): \frac{\overrightarrow{cd} \text{ OK} \quad \Gamma \vdash e : C}{(\overrightarrow{cd}; e) \text{ OK}}$$

Notice that in the nominal system, classes are typed (or rather type-*checked*) once, and the types declared for their fields and methods are static, unique, and used at invocation.

As mentioned above, we have decided to not consider casts in our work; using a cast is comparable to a promise by the programmer that the casted expression will at run time evaluate to an object having the specified class (or a subclass thereof), and so (for soundness) requires doing a run-time check of the shape

$$(\texttt{C}) \texttt{ new D}(\dots) \ \rightarrow \ \texttt{new D}(\dots) \qquad \left(\texttt{D} <: \texttt{C}\right)$$

Once this check has been carried out the cast disappears. Of course, for full programming convenience, and to be able to obtain the correct behaviour in overloaded methods, casts are essential.

2 Semantic Type Assignment

In [19], we defined a type system for FJ^ℓ that is loosely based on the strict intersection type assignment system for the λ-calculus [1,2] (see [4] for a survey) and is influenced by the predicate system for the ς-calculus [6]; we showed that it satisfies both *subject reduction* and *subject expansion*. Our types can be seen as describing the capabilities of an expression (or rather, the object to which that expression evaluates) in terms of (1) *the operations that may be performed on it* (i.e. *accessing a field or invoking a method*), and (2) *the* outcome *of performing those operations,* where dependencies between the inputs and outputs of methods are tracked using (type) variables. In this way, our types express detailed properties about the contexts in which expressions can safely be used. More intuitively, they capture a certain notion of *observational equivalence*: two expressions with the same set of assignable types will be observationally indistinguishable. Our types thus constitute *semantic predicates*.

Definition 6 (Semantic Types [19]). The set of *intersection types* (or *types* for short), ranged over by ϕ, ψ, and its subset of *strict* types, ranged over by σ, τ are defined by the following grammar (where φ ranges over a denumerable set of *type variables*, C ranges over the set of class names, and ω is a type constant, the universal type and the top element of the type hierarchy):

$$\phi, \psi ::= \omega \mid \sigma \mid \phi \cap \psi$$
$$\sigma ::= \varphi \mid C \mid \langle f : \sigma \rangle \mid \langle m : (\phi_1, \dots, \phi_n) \rightarrow \sigma \rangle \quad (n \geq 0)$$

Notice that our types do not depend on the types that would be assigned in the nominal system; in fact, we could have presented our results for an *untyped* variant of FJ, where all class annotations on parameters and return types are omitted. We have decided not to do so for reasons of compatibility with other work, and to avoid leaving the (incorrect) impression that our results would somehow then depend on the fact that expressions carry no type information.

The key feature of types is that they may group information about many operations together into *intersections* from which any specific one can be selected for an expression

$$(\text{NEWM}) : \frac{\text{this}{:}\psi, x_1{:}\phi_1, \ldots, x_n{:}\phi_n \vdash e_b : \sigma \quad \Pi \vdash \text{new } C(\vec{e}) : \psi}{\Pi \vdash \text{new } C(\vec{e}) : \langle m{:}(\vec{\phi}_n){\to}\sigma\rangle}$$
$$(\mathcal{M}b(C,m) = (\vec{x}_n, e_b),\ n \geq 0)$$

$$(\text{NEWF}) : \frac{\Pi \vdash e_1 : \phi_1 \quad \cdots \quad \Pi \vdash e_n : \phi_n}{\Pi \vdash \text{new } C(\vec{e}_n) : \langle f_i{:}\sigma\rangle} \ (\mathcal{F}(C) = \vec{f}_n,\ i \in \underline{n},\ \sigma = \phi_i,\ n \geq 1)$$

$$(\text{OBJ}) : \frac{\Pi \vdash e_1 : \phi_1 \quad \cdots \quad \Pi \vdash e_n : \phi_n}{\Pi \vdash \text{new } C(\vec{e}_n) : C} \ (\mathcal{F}(C) = \vec{f}_n,\ n \geq 0) \qquad (\omega) : \frac{}{\Pi \vdash e : \omega}$$

$$(\text{INVK}) : \frac{\Pi \vdash e : \langle m{:}(\vec{\phi}_n){\to}\sigma\rangle \quad \Pi \vdash e_1 : \phi_1 \ \ldots \ \Pi \vdash e_n : \phi_n}{\Pi \vdash e.m(\vec{e}_n) : \sigma} \qquad (\text{FLD}) : \frac{\Pi \vdash e : \langle f{:}\sigma\rangle}{\Pi \vdash e.f : \sigma}$$

$$(\text{JOIN}) : \frac{\Pi \vdash e : \sigma_1 \ \ldots \ \Pi \vdash e : \sigma_n}{\Pi \vdash e : \sigma_1 \cap \ldots \cap \sigma_n} \ (n \geq 2) \qquad (\text{VAR}) : \frac{}{\Pi, x{:}\phi \vdash x : \sigma} \ (\phi \trianglelefteq \sigma)$$

Fig. 2. Type assignment rules for the semantical system for FJ$^{\not c}$

as demanded by the context in which it appears. In particular, an intersection may combine two or more different (even non-unifiable) analyses of the *same* field or method. Types are therefore not *records*: records can be characterised as intersection types of the shape $\langle \ell_1{:}\sigma_1, \cdots, \ell_n{:}\sigma_n\rangle$ where all σ_i are intersection-free, and all labels ℓ_i are distinct; in other words, records are intersection types, but not vice-versa (see Definition 12).

We include a type constant for each class, which we can use to type objects which therefore always have a type, like for the case when an object does not contain any fields or methods (as is the case for `Object`) or, more generally, because no fields or methods can be safely invoked. The type constant ω is a *top* (maximal) type, assignable to all expressions and serves typically to type subterms that do not contribute to the normal form of an expression. The following *subtype* relation facilitates the selection of individual behaviours from an intersection.

Definition 7 (Subtype Relation). The subtype relation $\trianglelefteq$ is induced by the fact that an intersection type is smaller than each of its components, and is defined is the smallest preorder satisfying:

$$\phi \trianglelefteq \omega \qquad \phi \cap \psi \trianglelefteq \phi \qquad \phi \cap \psi \trianglelefteq \psi \qquad \phi \trianglelefteq \psi\ \&\ \phi \trianglelefteq \psi' \Rightarrow \phi \trianglelefteq \psi \cap \psi'$$

We write $\sim$ for the equivalence relation generated by $\trianglelefteq$, extended by

$$\sigma \sim \sigma' \Rightarrow \langle f{:}\sigma\rangle \sim \langle f{:}\sigma'\rangle$$
$$\forall i \in \underline{n}\,[\,\phi_i' \sim \phi_i'\,]\ \&\ \sigma \sim \sigma' \Rightarrow \langle m{:}(\phi_1, \ldots, \phi_n){\to}\sigma\rangle \sim \langle m{:}(\phi_1', \ldots, \phi_n'){\to}\sigma'\rangle$$

We consider types modulo $\sim$; in particular, all types in an intersection are different and ω does not appear in an intersection. It is easy to show that $\cap$ is associative and commutative with respect to $\sim$, so we will abuse notation slightly and write $\sigma_1 \cap \ldots \cap \sigma_n$ (where $n \geq 2$) to denote a general intersection, where all σ_i are distinct and the order is unimportant. In a further abuse of notation, $\phi_1 \cap \ldots \cap \phi_n$ will denote the type ϕ_1 when $n = 1$, and ω when $n = 0$.

Definition 8 (Type Contexts [19]). 1. A *type statement* is of the form $e : \phi$, with e as *subject*.

2. A context Π is a set of type statements with (distinct) variables as subjects; $\Pi, x{:}\phi$ stands for the context $\Pi \cup \{x{:}\phi\}$ (so then either x does not appear in Π or $x{:}\phi \in \Pi$) and $x{:}\phi$ for $\varnothing, x{:}\phi$.

3. We extend $\unlhd$ to contexts: $\Pi' \unlhd \Pi \Leftrightarrow \forall x{:}\phi \in \Pi \exists \phi' \unlhd \phi x{:}\phi' \in \Pi'$.
4. If $\overrightarrow{\Pi}_n$ is a sequence of contexts, then $\cap \overrightarrow{\Pi}_n$ is the context defined as follows: $x{:}\phi_1 \cap \ldots \cap \phi_m \in \cap \overrightarrow{\Pi}_n$, if and only if $\{x{:}\phi_1, \ldots, x{:}\phi_m\}$ is the non-empty set of all statements in the union of the contexts that have x as subject.

We will now define our notion of type assignment.

Definition 9 (Semantic Type Assignment [19]). Semantical type assignment for $\text{FJ}^{\not{c}}$ is defined by the natural deduction system of Figure 2.

Notice that new objects like new $\text{C}(\cdots)$ can be dealt with by both the rules (OBJ) and (NEWM); then the context Π can be any. Moreover, we do not need any of the information of the nominal type system here, other than that provided by the rule (OBJ).

We should perhaps emphasise that, as remarked above, we *explicitly do not type classes*; instead, the rules (NEWF) and (NEWM) create a field or method type for an object, essentially stating that this field or method is available, and what its current type is. So method bodies are checked *every time* we need that an object has a specific method type, and the various types for a particular method used throughout a program need not be the same, as is the case for the nominal system (see Definition 5). So, in our system, we would have, in principle, an infinite type for each class, which we cannot establish when typing the class separately; rather, we let the context of each new $\text{D}()$ decide which type is needed, so the type for an occurrence of new $\text{D}()$ is 'constructed' by need, and not from an analysis of the class.

The rules of our type assignment system are fairly straightforward generalisations of the rules of the strict intersection type assignment system for LC to OO, whilst making the step from a higher order to a first order language: for example, (FLD) and (INVK) are analogous to $(\to E)$; (NEWF) and (NEWM) are a form of $(\to I)$; and (OBJ) can be seen as a universal (ω)-like rule for *objects* only.

The only non-standard rule from the point of view of similar work for TRS and traditional nominal OO-type systems is (NEWM), which derives a type for an object that presents an analysis of a method that is available in that object. Note that the analysis involves typing the method body and the assumptions (*i.e.* requirements) on the formal parameters are encoded in the derived type (to be checked on invocation). However, a method body may also make requirements on the *receiver*, through the use of the variable this. In our system we check that these hold *at the same time* as typing the method body (so-called *early self typing*; with *late self typing*, as used in [6], we would check the type of the receiver at the point of method invocation). This checking of requirements on the object itself is where the expressive power of our system resides. If a method calls itself recursively, this recursive call must be checked, but – crucially – carries a *different* type if a valid derivation is to be found. Thus only recursive calls which terminate at a certain point (*i.e.* which can then be assigned ω or C, and thus ignored) will be typeable in the system.

As is standard for intersection type assignment systems, our system is set up to satisfy both subject reduction *and* subject expansion.

Theorem 10 (Subject reduction and expansion [19]). Let $e \to e'$; then $\Pi \vdash e : \phi$ if and only if $\Pi \vdash e' : \phi$.

Notice that, as usual, computational equality between expressions in FJ^{ℓ} is undecidable; as a consequence, through Theorem 10 we obtain that type assignment in our system is undecidable as well.

We have also shown (variants of) the characterisation of normalisation properties:

Theorem 11 ([19]).   1. If e is a head-normal form then there exists a strict type σ and type context Π such that $\Pi \vdash e : \sigma$; moreover, if e is not of the form $\text{new } C(\vec{e}_n)$ then for any arbitrary strict type σ there is a context such that $\Pi \vdash e : \sigma$.
2. $\Pi \vdash e : \sigma$ if and only if e has a head-normal form.
3. If $\mathcal{D} :: \Pi \vdash e : \sigma$ with $\mathcal{D}$ and Π ω-free then e has a normal form.

3   Curry Type Assignment

The nominal type system for Java is so far the accepted standard, but many researchers are looking for more expressive type systems that deal with intricate details of object oriented programming and in particular with side effects. It will be clear that through the system we presented above, we propose a different path, an alternative to the nominal approach. We illustrate the strength of our approach in this section by presenting a basic (decidable) functional system, that allows for us to show a preservation result with respect to a notion of Curry type assignment for CL. This basic system is based on a true restriction of our semantical type system; the restriction consists of removing the type constant ω as well as intersection types from the type language, but not completely: we will still allow for types to be combined as by rule (JOIN) above, but only if the labels involved are different: the intersection types we allow, thereby, correspond to *records*. The additional change we made was to type classes (and the class table and programs) explicitly, and in that use a different approach when dealing with recursive classes.

It is worthwhile to point out that, above, the fact that we allow more than just record types is crucial for the results: without allowing arbitrary intersections (and ω) we could not show that type assignment is closed under conversion. The undecidability of type inference in our type assignment system follows as a consequence of the conversion result shown in the previous section. Thus, to be of *practical* use for program analysis we must restrict the type assignment system in a decidable fashion.

The notion of the type assignment system we present here is based on Curry's type system for CL (or simply-typed LC), and is inspired by Milner's system for ML [16]. As such, it is not a true restriction of the system we defined above, and therefore different from the Curry system we presented in [19]. However, we can show that our encoding of CL into FJ^{ℓ} (Section 3) preserves typeability; this is mainly because CL is a notion of computation defined without recursion. The basic approach of our restriction is to only assume a *single* behaviour for each element of a program - that is, we remove intersections. So, for example, when deriving a type for a method each argument and each field of the receiver may only have one type. While this may seem overly restrictive, we show that our system is expressive enough to type those programs that correspond to computable functions, λ-terms typeable in Curry's system of simple types.

We demonstrate the decidability of this restricted form of type assignment by first showing that the system has a *principal typings* property, and then arguing that there is a terminating algorithm which computes these typings. A principal typings property for a type system states that for each typeable term there is a typing (an context-type pair) which is *most general*, in the sense that all other typings assignable to that term can be generated from it. Typeability is decidable, then, if there is a (terminating) algorithm which computes whether a principal typing exists for any given term. In the latter half of this section, we discuss the implementation of such an algorithm for our restricted type assignment system, which we will now define.

Definition 12 (Curry types for FJ$^\ell$).   1. *Curry (object) types* for FJ are defined by:

$$\sigma, \tau ::= \phi \mid \langle f_1:\sigma, \ \ldots, \ f_n:\tau, \ m_1:(\vec{\alpha}){\to}\beta, \ \ldots, \ m_k:(\vec{\gamma}){\to}\delta \rangle \quad (n+k \geq 1)$$

2. We will call a type of the shape $\langle f:\sigma \rangle$ a *field* type, one of the shape $\langle m:(\vec{\alpha}){\to}\beta \rangle$ a *method* type, and $\langle \cdots \rangle$ with 2 or more components a *record* type and let ρ range over those. We write ℓ for arbitrary labels and, by abuse of notation, will also use $\langle \ell:\sigma \rangle$ to represent $\langle m:\sigma \rangle$, even though in $\langle m:(\vec{\alpha}){\to}\beta \rangle$, the structure $(\vec{\alpha}){\to}\beta$ is *not* a type. We write $\langle \ell:\sigma \rangle \in \rho$ (or $\ell \in \rho$) when $\ell:\sigma$ occurs in ρ, and assume that all labels are unique in records.
3. We call two types ρ and ρ' *compatible* when: if $\langle \ell:\sigma \rangle \in \rho$ and $\langle \ell:\sigma' \rangle \in \rho'$, then either: σ and σ' are compatible types, or $\sigma = \sigma'$.
4. We define the operator $\sqcup$ (*join*) on types by: $\rho_1 \sqcup \rho_2$ is the type composed out of the union of two compatible types, defined as: $\langle \ell:\sigma \rangle \in \rho_1 \sqcup \rho_2$ if and only if either:
   - $\langle \ell:\sigma \rangle \in \rho_1$ and $\ell \notin \rho_2$; or
   - $\langle \ell:\sigma \rangle \in \rho_2$ and $\ell \notin \rho_1$; or
   - $\sigma = \sigma_1 \sqcup \sigma_2$, with $\langle \ell:\sigma_1 \rangle \in \rho_1$, $\langle \ell:\sigma_2 \rangle \in \rho_2$ and σ_1 and σ_2 are compatible; or
   - $\sigma = \sigma_1$, with $\langle \ell:\sigma_1 \rangle \in \rho_1$ and $\langle \ell:\sigma_2 \rangle \in \rho_2$ and $\sigma_1 = \sigma_2$.
5. When we write a record type as $\langle \ell:\sigma \rangle \sqcup \rho$, then $\ell \notin \rho$.

Notice that compatible records can have different labels, even distinct. Moreover, even when we allow for the notation $\langle m:\sigma \rangle$ for a method type, then σ is never a record type: we can only derive those for variables, fields, and objects; see Definition 18. As an example of compatible types, consider $\langle f_1:\langle f_2:\sigma, f_3:\tau \rangle \rangle$ and $\langle f_1:\langle f_3:\tau, f_4:\rho \rangle \rangle$; on the other hand, $\langle f_1:\langle f_2:\sigma, f_3:\tau \rangle \rangle$ and $\langle f_1:\langle f_3:\mu, f_4:\rho \rangle \rangle$ with $\tau \neq \mu$ are not compatible.

Definition 13 (Curry contexts and environments).   1. A *Curry context* is a mapping from term variables (including this) to Curry types.
2. We call two contexts Γ_1 and Γ_2 compatible whenever: if $x:\sigma \in \Gamma_1$ and $x:\tau \in \Gamma_2$, then σ and τ are compatible record types.
3. The operation of $\sqcup$ can be extended to compatible contexts as follows:

$$
\begin{aligned}
Join \ \Gamma, x:\sigma \ \Gamma', x:\tau &= (Join \ \Gamma \ \Gamma'), x:\sigma \sqcup \tau \\
Join \ \Gamma, x:\sigma \quad \Gamma' &= (Join \ \Gamma \ \Gamma'), x:\sigma \qquad (x \notin \Gamma') \\
Join \quad \varnothing \quad\quad \Gamma' &= \Gamma'
\end{aligned}
$$

4. An environment $\mathcal{E}$ is a mapping from class names to types (normally records).

Notice that compatible contexts can have different variables, even distinct; but even if a variable appears in both, the labels in its types can be different as well.

The operation of substitution, which replaces type variables with types (and type variables with simple types), allows one type (or record) to be generated from another.

$$(\text{NEW}_r): \quad \frac{\emptyset; \mathcal{E}, C{:}\rho \vdash e_i : \sigma_i \quad (i \in \underline{n})}{\Gamma; \mathcal{E}, C{:}\rho \vdash \text{new } C(\vec{e}) : \rho} \; (\langle\overrightarrow{f{:}\sigma_i}\rangle \in \rho) \qquad\qquad (\text{VAR}): \quad \frac{}{\Gamma, x{:}\sigma; \mathcal{E} \vdash x : \sigma}$$

$$(\text{NEW}_c): \quad \frac{\emptyset; \mathcal{E}, C{:}\rho \vdash e_i : \sigma_i \quad (i \in \underline{n})}{\Gamma; \mathcal{E}, C{:}\rho \vdash \text{new } C(\vec{e}) : S\rho} \; (\langle\overrightarrow{f{:}\sigma_i}\rangle \in S\rho) \qquad (\text{PROJ}): \quad \frac{\Gamma; \mathcal{E} \vdash e : \rho}{\Gamma; \mathcal{E} \vdash e : \langle\ell{:}\sigma\rangle} \; (\langle\ell{:}\sigma\rangle \in \rho)$$

$$(\text{INVK}): \quad \frac{\Gamma; \mathcal{E} \vdash e : \langle m{:}(\vec{\sigma}_n){\to}\sigma\rangle \quad \Gamma; \mathcal{E} \vdash e_i : \sigma_i \; (i \in \underline{n})}{\Gamma; \mathcal{E} \vdash e.m(\vec{e_i}) : \sigma} \qquad (\text{FLD}): \quad \frac{\Gamma; \mathcal{E} \vdash e : \langle f{:}\sigma\rangle}{\Gamma; \mathcal{E} \vdash e.f : \sigma}$$

$$(\text{CT}): \quad \frac{\begin{array}{ll} \text{this}{:}\rho, \overrightarrow{x{:}\sigma}_{n_1}; \mathcal{E}, C{:}\rho \vdash e_1 : \tau_1 & (\mathcal{M}b(C,m_1) = (\vec{x}_{n_1}, e_1)) \quad \cdots \\ \quad\quad \text{this}{:}\rho, \overrightarrow{x{:}\sigma}_{n_m}; \mathcal{E}, C{:}\rho \vdash e_m : \tau_m & (\mathcal{M}b(C,m_m) = (\vec{x}_{n_m}, e_m)) \quad \mathcal{E}, C{:}\rho \vdash CT : \diamond \end{array}}{\begin{array}{c} \mathcal{E}, C{:}\rho \vdash \text{class } C \text{ extends } C' \; \{\vec{f}\vec{d} \; \vec{m}\vec{d}\}; CT : \diamond \\ (\rho = \langle\vec{f}{:}\vec{\phi}_n, m_1{:}(\vec{\sigma}_{n_1}){\to}\tau_1, \ldots, m_m{:}(\vec{\sigma}_{n_m}){\to}\tau_m\rangle, \mathcal{F}(C) = \vec{f}_n, \mathcal{M}(C) = \vec{m}_m) \end{array}}$$

$$(\varepsilon): \quad \frac{}{\Pi \vdash \varepsilon : \diamond} \qquad\qquad\qquad\qquad\qquad (\text{PROG}): \quad \frac{\mathcal{E} \vdash CT : \diamond \quad \Gamma; \mathcal{E} \vdash e : \sigma}{\Gamma; \mathcal{E} \vdash (CT, e) : \sigma}$$

Fig. 3. Type assignment rules for the Curry type system for FJ^{ℓ}

Definition 14 (Substitution). 1. The type *substitution* $\langle \varphi \mapsto \sigma \rangle$, which is a function from types to types, is defined as follows:

$$
\begin{array}{lll}
(\varphi \mapsto \sigma)\,\varphi & = & \sigma \\
(\varphi \mapsto \sigma)\,\varphi' & = & \varphi' \quad \varphi \neq \varphi' \\
(\varphi \mapsto \sigma)\,\langle f{:}\sigma'\rangle & = & \langle f{:}(\varphi \mapsto \sigma)\,\sigma'\rangle \\
(\varphi \mapsto \sigma)\,\langle m{:}\vec{\sigma}_n {\to} \sigma'\rangle & = & \langle m{:}((\varphi \mapsto \sigma)\,\sigma_1, \ldots, (\varphi \mapsto \sigma)\,\sigma_n){\to}(\varphi \mapsto \sigma)\,\sigma'\rangle
\end{array}
$$

The extension to records $(\varphi \mapsto \sigma)\,\rho$ is defined as can be expected.

2. If S_1 and S_2 are substitutions, then so is $S_2 \circ S_1$ where $(S_2 \circ S_1)\,\sigma = S_2\,(S_1\,\sigma))$; we write $\vec{S}_n$ for $S_n \circ \cdots \circ S_1$.
3. $S\Gamma = \{x{:}S\sigma \mid x{:}\sigma \in \Gamma\}$.
4. *Id* denotes the *identity* substitution.
5. For two types σ_1 and σ_2, if there exists a substitution S such that $S\sigma_1 = \sigma_2$ then we say that σ_2 is an *instance* of σ_1.
6. We say that a type variable is *fresh* if it does not occur in any type we are considering at that moment; we also say that a *fresh instance of* σ is the type created out of σ by substitution each type variable in σ by a fresh one.

Simple type assignment is defined through:

Definition 15 (Curry type assignment for FJ^{ℓ}). *Curry type assignment* for FJ^{ℓ}-expressions is defined through the rules in Figure 3.

Notice that judgements depend not only on contexts, but also on environments; the first six rules type expressions, whereas the others deal with the class table and the program.

Rule (CT) comes in place of the rules deriving OK for the nominal system. It checks the occurrence of $C{:}\rho$ in the environment for class C. By using $\text{this}{:}\rho$ when typeing the methods, it insists that the types derived for the methods and fields in a class are the same as used for the receivers; also rule (NEW_r) is used for occurrences of new $C(\vec{e})$ inside the definition of C which insists that the same record type is used for the 'recursive' instances of C as well. This corresponds to the usual way of dealing with recursion as in ML's rule $(\texttt{fix})$ (note that OO languages have *two* types of recursion) and corresponds to the nominal rule (CLASS) above.

Notice that ρ is not unique; the rule accepts any type that fits. Below, in the algorithm $\mathcal{PT}$, we will calculate the smallest; then when we use a type for C, as in rule (NEW_c) which is used for occurrences of new $C(\vec{e})$ *outside* the definition of C, this type will be a substitution instance of the one calculated. Thereby, this introduces a notion of *polymorphism* into our system; each instance of class C will be typed differently, but any of its types can be generated from $\mathcal{E}(C)$ by (projection and) substitution.

Also, (NEW_r) and (NEW_c), in combination with rule (PROJ), come in place of the rules (NEWF) and (NEWM) of the semantical system. We could have removed the separation of the two NEW rules and only used rule (NEW_c); this would give a 'Mycroft'-like way of dealing with recursion, which is only semi-decidable, rather than a 'Milner'-like way as we do now; it could be used for a *type-check* system, however.

Note also that rules (ε) and $(\mathcal{CT})$ checks the typeability of a class table, and rule (PROG) specifies how to type a FJ$^\ell$ program.

We can show that type substitution is sound for expressions.

Theorem 16. For all substitutions S, if $\Gamma; \mathcal{E} \vdash e : \sigma$ then $S(\Gamma; \mathcal{E}) \vdash e : S\sigma$.

We will now show that simple type assignment has a *principal typings* property. At the heart of type inference lies the problem of *unification* - finding a common instance of two types; since we deal with records, we will also need to join those, after we have made them compatible through unification.

Definition 17 (Type Unification). The operation of unification is defined on types, and extended to contexts as follows:

1. The function *Unify*, which takes two simple types and returns a substitution, is defined by cases through:

$$
\begin{array}{llll}
\textit{Unify} & \varphi & \varphi' & = (\varphi \mapsto \varphi') \\
\textit{Unify} & \varphi & \sigma & = (\varphi \mapsto \sigma) \quad (\varphi \text{ not in } \sigma) \\
\textit{Unify} & \sigma & \varphi & = (\varphi \mapsto \sigma) \quad (\varphi \text{ not in } \sigma) \\
\textit{Unify} & \langle f{:}\sigma \rangle & \langle f{:}\alpha \rangle & = \textit{Unify } \sigma \; \alpha \\
\textit{Unify} & \langle m{:}(\vec{\sigma}_n) \rightarrow \tau \rangle & \langle m{:}(\vec{\alpha}_n) \rightarrow \beta \rangle & = \vec{S}_n
\end{array}
$$
$$
\begin{array}{ll}
\text{where} & S_1 = \textit{Unify } \tau \; \beta \\
& S_{i+1} = \textit{Unify } (\vec{S}_i \, \sigma_i) \, (\vec{S}_i \, \alpha_i) \;\; (i \in \underline{n-1})
\end{array}
$$

These are the cases where unification is defined, *i,e,* where either a substitution is created, or unification fails (when φ occurs in σ in the second and third case). This implies that no action is taken when unifying two method types that have different method names; rather, those are joined in a record.

2. On records, unification is defined through:

$$
\textit{Unify } \langle \ell{:}\sigma \rangle \sqcup \rho \; \langle \ell{:}\tau \rangle \sqcup \rho' = S_2 \circ S_1
$$
$$
\begin{array}{ll}
\text{where} & S_1 = \textit{Unify } \sigma \; \tau \\
& S_2 = \textit{Unify } (S_1 \, \rho) \, (S_1 \, \rho')
\end{array}
$$
$$
\textit{Unify } \langle \ell{:}\sigma \rangle \sqcup \rho \quad \rho' = \textit{Unify } \rho \; \rho' \quad (\ell \notin \rho')
$$

3. Unification can be extended to contexts as follows:

$$
\begin{aligned}
\text{Unify } \Gamma, x{:}\sigma \ \Gamma', x{:}\tau \ &= \ S' \circ S \\
\text{where} \quad S \ &= \ \text{Unify } \sigma \ \tau \\
S' \ &= \ \text{Unify } (S\Gamma) \ (S\Gamma') \\
\text{Unify } \Gamma, x{:}\sigma \quad \Gamma' \ &= \ \text{Unify } \Gamma \ \Gamma' \quad (x \notin \Gamma') \\
\text{Unify } \quad \varnothing \quad \Gamma' \ &= \ Id
\end{aligned}
$$

4. By abuse of notation, we will allow also the unification of any number of types or contexts '*at one fell swoop*', by defining

$$
\begin{aligned}
\text{Unify } \sigma_1 \ \sigma_2 \ \ldots \ \sigma_n \ &= \ \text{Unify } (S\sigma_2) \ (S\sigma_3) \ \ldots \ (S\sigma_n) \circ S \\
\text{where } S \ &= \ \text{Unify } \sigma_1 \ \sigma_2
\end{aligned}
$$

Notice that unification on records (as specified in the last two cases of the first part) recurses on the number of types in the record, ending up with the unification of simple types, which is dealt with in the first five cases.

It is easy to show that unification creates compatible contexts, which it is designed to do; it is, however, not fully satisfactory for use in our principal typing algorithm, since it does not always adequately checks that the 'offered type' of the argument is not less specific that the 'demanded type' of the parameter of a method invocation in terms of labels that occur. For example, as can be seen in the algorithm, for the expression `e.m(e')`, it can be that we infer that the principal type of e is $\langle m{:}\langle f{:}\sigma, f'{:}\sigma'\rangle{\rightarrow}\rho\rangle$, and the principal type of e' is $\langle f{:}\tau\rangle$. Assuming σ and τ are unifiable,

$$
\text{Unify } \langle m{:}\langle f{:}\sigma, f'{:}\sigma'\rangle{\rightarrow}\rho\rangle \ \langle m{:}(\langle f{:}\tau\rangle){\rightarrow}\varphi\rangle
$$

would succeed; however, there is no guarantee that e' has type $\langle f'{:}\tau'\rangle$ as well.

We could have amended the unification algorithm, but that would have made it a great deal more intricate. Rather, in the principal typing algorithm, we add an additional test that checks if the offered type matches the demanded type, by checking that the labels in the demanded type all occur in the offered type. This implies, of course, that type assignment can fail not just because unification fails.

Using the concepts of substitution and unification, we can now define what principal typings are for our system. Since our types express information about fields and methods, and since objects may have many different fields and methods (each with their own unique behaviours), our principal types must actually be *records*. This makes defining the principal typings somewhat complicated, as can be seen below.

Also, we in fact calculate the principal typing for a *program*, by traversing the class table, building up the environment that contains the types for the classes, and type the final expression in that environment.

Definition 18 (Principal Typing).   1. A *typing* is a pair $\langle \Gamma ; \sigma \rangle$ of a context (including `this`) and a type.

2. The function $\mathcal{PT}$ (*principal typing*), from expressions and environments to typings and environments, is defined inductively as follows:

$$PT(x; \mathcal{E}) \quad = \langle x{:}\varphi; \varphi \rangle; \mathcal{E} \qquad\qquad (\varphi \; fresh)$$

$$PT(\texttt{this}; \mathcal{E}) \; = \langle \texttt{this}{:}\varphi; \varphi \rangle; \mathcal{E} \qquad\qquad (\varphi \; fresh)$$

$$PT(\texttt{e.f}; \mathcal{E}) \quad = S \langle \Gamma; \varphi \rangle; S\,\mathcal{E}'$$

$$\text{where} \quad PT(e; \mathcal{E}) \; = \langle \Gamma; \rho \rangle; \mathcal{E}'$$
$$S \qquad\qquad = \textit{Unify} \langle \texttt{f}{:}\varphi \rangle \, \rho \quad (\varphi \; fresh)$$

$$PT(\texttt{e.m}(\vec{\texttt{e}}_n); \mathcal{E}_0) = \vec{S}_2 \langle \Gamma \sqcup \Gamma_1 \sqcup \cdots \sqcup \Gamma_n; \varphi \rangle; \vec{S}_2 \, \mathcal{E}_{n+1}$$

$$\text{where} \quad PT(e; \mathcal{E}_0) \; = \langle \Gamma; \rho \rangle; \mathcal{E}_1$$
$$PT(e_i; \mathcal{E}_i) \; = \langle \Gamma_i; \gamma_i \rangle; \mathcal{E}_{i+1} \qquad (i \in \underline{n})$$
$$S_1 \qquad\qquad = \textit{Unify} \langle \texttt{m}{:}(\vec{\gamma}_n){\to}\varphi \rangle \, \rho \quad (\varphi \; fresh,$$
$$\text{all labels in } \sigma_i \text{ in } \langle \texttt{m}{:}(\vec{\sigma}_n){\to}\tau \rangle \in \rho \text{ appear in } \gamma_i)$$
$$S_2 \qquad\qquad = \textit{Unify} \, (S_1\Gamma) \, (S_1\Gamma_1) \cdots (S_1\Gamma_n)$$

$$PT(\texttt{new } C(\vec{\texttt{e}}_n); \mathcal{E}_1) = S' {\circ} \vec{S}_n \langle \Gamma_1 \sqcup \cdots \sqcup \Gamma_n; \rho \rangle; S' {\circ} \vec{S}_n \mathcal{E}_{n+1}$$

$$\text{where} \quad \rho \; = \begin{cases} \mathcal{E}_1\, C & (\textit{definition of } C \textit{ depends on this}) \\ \textit{fresh instance of } \mathcal{E}_1\, C & (\textit{otherwise}) \end{cases}$$
$$PT(e_i; \mathcal{E}_i) = \langle \Gamma_i; \sigma_i \rangle; \mathcal{E}_{i+1} \qquad (i \in \underline{n})$$
$$S_i \; = \; \textit{Unify} \, (\vec{S}_{i-1}\langle \texttt{f}_i{:}\sigma_i \rangle) \, (\vec{S}_{i-1}\rho) \quad (i \in \underline{n}, \; S_0 = Id,$$
$$\text{all labels } \vec{\texttt{f}}_n \text{ appear in } \rho)$$
$$S' \; = \; \textit{Unify} \, (\vec{S}_n\Gamma) \, (\vec{S}_n\Gamma_1) \cdots (\vec{S}_n\Gamma_n)$$

3. We use PT also for the function that calculates the principal type for a each class definition in the class table, and builds the environment:

$$PT(\varepsilon : e; \mathcal{E}) \; = \; PT(e; \mathcal{E})$$
$$PT(\texttt{class } C \texttt{ extends } C' \; \{\overline{\texttt{fd}}_n \; \overline{\texttt{md}}_m\}, CT : e; \mathcal{E}) = PT(CT : e; S\,\mathcal{E}_{m+1})$$
$$\text{where} \quad PT(e_{b_j}; \mathcal{E}_j) = \langle \overline{x_i{:}\sigma_i}, \texttt{this}{:}\alpha_j; \tau_j \rangle; \mathcal{E}_{j+1} \quad ^{(*)}$$
$$\mathcal{Mb}(C, m_j) = (\vec{x}_i, e_{b_j}) \in \overline{md}$$
$$\mathcal{E}_1 \; = \; \mathcal{E}, C{:}\varphi \qquad\qquad (\varphi \; fresh)$$
$$S \; = \; \textit{Unify} \, \overline{\alpha_j} \, (\mathcal{E}_{m+1}C) \, \langle \overline{\texttt{f}{:}\varphi}, \overline{\texttt{m}{:}(\vec{\sigma}){\to}\tau} \rangle$$
$$(\mathcal{F}(C) = \vec{\texttt{f}}, \; \vec{\varphi}_n \; fresh)$$

$^{(*)}$ σ_i or α_j are fresh variables whenever $x_i \notin fv(e_{b_j})$ or $\texttt{this}$ does not occur in e_{b_j}; of course the assumption is here that all free variables in a method body are mentioned in the parameters list: methods have no free variables. Notice that if $\texttt{new } C(\vec{\texttt{e}}_n)$ occurs in e_{b_j}, then the type stored in the environment is taken itself, rather than instantiated, so might be affected by the unifications that are calculated.

Notice that, in the case for $PT(\texttt{new } C(\vec{\texttt{e}}_n); \mathcal{E})$, we have to take a fresh instance of the type calculated for C. We have stored the principal type for C into the environment in $PT(CT; \mathcal{E})$ and need to access it when creating a new object; however, we have to work from a *copy*: otherwise, we would change $\mathcal{E}C$ during the unification process, making it change before a new access. Thereby, this operation introduces a notion of *polymorphism* into our system; each instance of class C will be typed differently, but any of its types can be generated from $\mathcal{E} \, C$ by (projection and) substitution; the substitutions will be calculated by $\mathcal{PT}$, as demanded by the context in which the object appears, and depending on exactly what expressions it gets initialised with.

We can show the expected properties for $\mathcal{PT}$:

Theorem 19 (Soundness of $\mathcal{PT}$). If $\mathcal{PT}(e; \mathcal{E}) = \langle \Gamma; \sigma \rangle; \mathcal{E}'$, then $\Gamma; \mathcal{E}' \vdash_{\overline{C}} e : \sigma$.

Theorem 20 (Completeness of $\mathcal{PT}$). If $\Gamma; \mathcal{E} \vdash_{\overline{C}} e : \sigma$ (where e is not part of a class definition), then there exists a typing $\langle \Gamma'; \sigma' \rangle; \mathcal{E}$ such that $\mathcal{PT}(e; \mathcal{E}) = \langle \Gamma'; \sigma' \rangle; \mathcal{E}$ and a substitution S such that $S\Gamma' \subseteq \Gamma$, and $\sigma = S\sigma'$.

As an example of a program we can type, consider the following which constitutes perhaps the simplest example of a term without head-normal form in OO:

```
class C extends Object {
    C m() { return this.m(); }
}
```

This program has a method m which simply calls itself recursively, and new C().m() *loops*:

$$\text{new C().m()} \rightarrow \text{this.m()} \left[\text{new C()/this} \right] = \text{new C().m()}$$

so, in particular, new C().m() has no normal form, not even a head-normal form; this correspond to the ML-program $(\text{fix } x.x)$. Running $\mathcal{PT}$ returns $C:\langle m:()\rightarrow\varphi\rangle$ and therefore running $\mathcal{PT}(\text{new C().m()}; \mathcal{E})$ gives $(\emptyset; \varphi)$ which is also the typing for $(\text{fix } x.x)$. Notice that, since new C().m() has no head-normal form, it is not typeable in our intersection system, so we cannot show '$\Gamma \vdash_{\overline{C}} e : \sigma \Rightarrow \Gamma \vdash e : \sigma$'; the same observation can be made with respect to type assignment for the λ-calculus and ML.

4   OOCL

We will now relate this notion of type assignment to one from the world of functional programming, by defining an encoding of Combinatory Logic [14] (CL) into FJ^{ℓ}, and showing that assignable types are preserved by this encoding.

Definition 21. Combinatory Logic consists of the function symbols $\mathbf{S}, \mathbf{K}$ where terms are defined over the grammar

$$t ::= x \mid \mathbf{S} \mid \mathbf{K} \mid t_1\, t_2$$

and the reduction is defined via the rewrite rules:

$$\begin{aligned}\mathbf{K}\, x\, y &\rightarrow x \\ \mathbf{S}\, x\, y\, z &\rightarrow x\, z\, (y\, z)\end{aligned}$$

CL can be seen as a higher-order TRS.

Our encoding of CL in FJ^{ℓ} is based on a Curryfied first-order version of the system above (see [7] for details), where the rules for $\mathbf{S}$ and $\mathbf{K}$ are expanded so that each new rewrite rule has a *single* operand, allowing for the partial application of function

```
class Combinator extends Object {
    Combinator app(Combinator x) { return this; }
}
class K extends Combinator {
    Combinator app(Combinator x) { return new K_1(x); }
}
class K_1 extends K {
    Combinator x;
    Combinator app(Combinator y) { return this.x; }
}
class S extends Combinator {
    Combinator app(Combinator x) { return new S_1(x); }
}
class S_1 extends S {
    Combinator x;
    Combinator app(Combinator y) { return new S_2(this.x, y); }
}
class S_2 extends S_1 {
    Combinator y;
    Combinator app(Combinator z) { return this.x.app(z).app(this.y.app(z)); }
}
```

Fig. 4. The class table for Object-Oriented Combinatory Logic (OOCL) programs

symbols. We model application, the basic engine of reduction in TRS, via the invocation of a method named app. The reduction rules of Curryfied CL each apply to (or are 'triggered' by) different 'versions' of the **S** and **K** combinators; in our encoding these rules are implemented by the bodies of five different versions of the app method which are each attached to different classes representing the different versions of the **S** and **K** combinators. In order to make our encoding a valid (typeable) program in full Java, we have defined a Combinator class containing an app method from which all the others inherit, essentially acting as an *interface* to which all encoded versions of **S** and **K** must adhere.

Definition 22 ([19]). The encoding of Combinatory Logic (CL) into the FJ$^{\not{c}}$ program OOCL (Object-Oriented Combinatory Logic) is defined using the execution context given in Figure 4 and the function $\llbracket \cdot \rrbracket$ which translates terms of CL into FJ$^{\not{c}}$ expressions, and is defined as follows:

$$\begin{aligned}
\llbracket x \rrbracket &= x \\
\llbracket t_1\ t_2 \rrbracket &= \llbracket t_1 \rrbracket.\mathtt{app}(\llbracket t_2 \rrbracket) \\
\llbracket \mathbf{K} \rrbracket &= \mathtt{new\ K()} \\
\llbracket \mathbf{S} \rrbracket &= \mathtt{new\ S()}
\end{aligned}$$

We can show that the reduction behaviour of OOCL mirrors that of CL.

Theorem 23 ([19]). If t_1, t_2 are terms of CL and $t_1 \rightarrow^* t_2$, then $\llbracket t_1 \rrbracket \rightarrow^* \llbracket t_2 \rrbracket$ in OOCL.

Through this encoding - and the results we have shown above - we can achieve a type-based characterisation of all (terminating) computable functions in OO. Since CL is a Turing-complete model of computation, as a side effect we show that FJ^{ℓ} is Turing-complete. Although we are sure this does not come as a surprise, it is a nice formal property for our calculus to have, and comes easily as a consequence of our encoding.

In addition, our type system can perform the same 'functional' analysis as ITD does for LC and CL. This is illustrated by a *type preservation* result. We present Curry's type system for CL and then show we can give equivalent types to OOCL programs.

Definition 24 (Curry Type Assignment for CL [19]).   1. The set of *simple types* (also known as Curry types) is defined by the grammar: $A, B ::= \varphi \mid A {\to} B$.
2. A *basis* Γ is a mapping from variables to Curry types, written as a set of statements of the form $x{:}A$ in which each of the variables x is distinct.
3. Simple type assignment to CL-terms is defined by the following system:

$$(Ax): \frac{}{\Gamma \vdash_{\mathrm{CL}} x : A} \,(x{:}A \in \Gamma) \quad (\to E): \frac{\Gamma \vdash_{\mathrm{CL}} t_1 : A{\to}B \quad \Gamma \vdash_{\mathrm{CL}} t_2 : A}{\Gamma \vdash_{\mathrm{CL}} t_1 t_2 : B}$$

$$(\mathbf{K}): \frac{}{\Gamma \vdash_{\mathrm{CL}} \mathbf{K} : A{\to}B{\to}A} \quad (\mathbf{S}): \frac{}{\Gamma \vdash_{\mathrm{CL}} \mathbf{S} : (A{\to}B{\to}C){\to}(A{\to}B){\to}A{\to}C}$$

The elegance of our approach is that we can now link types assigned to combinators to types assignable to object-oriented programs. To show this type preservation result, we need to define what the equivalent of Curry's types are in terms of our FJ^{ℓ} types. To this end, we define the following translation of Curry types.

Definition 25 (Type Translation [19]).   The function $\lVert \cdot \rVert$, which transforms Curry types[8], is defined as follows:

$$\begin{aligned} \lVert \phi \rVert &= \phi \\ \lVert A{\to}B \rVert &= \langle \mathtt{app} {:} (\lVert A \rVert) {\to} \lVert B \rVert \rangle \end{aligned}$$

It is extended to contexts as follows: $\lVert \Gamma \rVert = \{x{:}\lVert A \rVert \mid x{:}A \in \Gamma\}$.

We can now show the type preservation results.

Theorem 26 (Preservation of Types (cf. [19])).   1. If $\Gamma \vdash_{\mathrm{CL}} t : A$ then $\lVert \Gamma \rVert \vdash \lVert t \rVert : \lVert A \rVert$
2. Let $\mathcal{E}_{\mathrm{CL}}$ be defined as: $\mathcal{E}_{\mathrm{CL}} \, \mathbf{S} = \lVert (A{\to}B{\to}C){\to}(A{\to}B){\to}A{\to}C \rVert$
$\mathcal{E}_{\mathrm{CL}} \, \mathbf{K} = \lVert A{\to}B{\to}A \rVert$
If $\Gamma \vdash_{\mathrm{CL}} t : A$ then $\lVert \Gamma \rVert; \mathcal{E}_{\mathrm{CL}} \vdash_{\mathrm{C}} \lVert t \rVert : \lVert A \rVert$.

Furthermore, since Curry's well-known translation of the simply typed LC into CL preserves typeability (see [8]), we can also construct a type-preserving encoding of LC into FJ^{ℓ}; it is straightforward to extend this preservation result to full-blown strict intersection types. We stress that this result really demonstrates the validity of our approach.

To conclude this section, we give some example derivations of OOCL programs in our semantic system that illustrate our results; we could, of course, type these expression in our Curry system as well.

---

[8] Note we have *overloaded* the notation $\lVert \cdot \rVert$, which we also use for the translation of CL terms to FJ^{ℓ} expressions.

$$\dfrac{\overline{\text{this:}\langle x{:}\varphi_1\rangle, y{:}\varphi_2 \vdash \text{this} : \langle x{:}\varphi_1\rangle} \;(\text{VAR})}{\dfrac{\text{this:}\langle x{:}\varphi_1\rangle, y{:}\varphi_2 \vdash \text{this.x} : \varphi_1}{\text{this:K, x:}\varphi_1 \vdash \text{new } K_1(x) : \langle \text{app:}(\varphi_2) \to \varphi_1 \rangle}\;(\text{FLD})}$$

$$\dfrac{\overline{\text{this:K, x:}\varphi_1 \vdash x : \varphi_1}\;(\text{VAR})}{\dfrac{\text{this:K, x:}\varphi_1 \vdash \text{new } K_1(x) : \langle x{:}\varphi_1\rangle}{}\;(\text{NEWF})}\;(\text{NEWM})$$

$$\dfrac{\vdots \qquad \dfrac{\overline{x{:}\varphi_1, y{:}\varphi_2 \vdash \text{new } K() : K}\;(\text{VAR})}{x{:}\varphi_1, y{:}\varphi_2 \vdash \text{new } K() : \langle \text{app:}(\varphi_1) \to \langle \text{app:}(\varphi_2) \to \varphi_1 \rangle \rangle}\;(\text{NEWM})}{\dfrac{x{:}\varphi_1, y{:}\varphi_2 \vdash \text{new } K().\text{app}(x) : \langle \text{app:}(\varphi_2) \to \varphi_1 \rangle \qquad \vdots}{x{:}\varphi_1, y{:}\varphi_2 \vdash \text{new } K().\text{app}(x).\text{app}(y) : \varphi_1}\;(\text{INVK})}\;(\text{INVK})$$

with on the right:
$$\dfrac{\overline{x{:}\varphi_1, y{:}\varphi_2 \vdash x : \varphi_1}\;(\text{VAR})}{} \qquad \dfrac{\vdots \quad \overline{x{:}\varphi_1, y{:}\varphi_2 \vdash y : \varphi_2}\;(\text{VAR})}{}$$

$$\dfrac{\overline{\text{this:}\langle x{:}\varphi\rangle, y{:}\omega \vdash \text{this} : \langle x{:}\varphi\rangle}\;(\text{VAR})}{\dfrac{\text{this:}\langle x{:}\varphi\rangle, y{:}\omega \vdash \text{this.x} : \varphi}{\text{this:K, x:}\varphi \vdash \text{new } K_1(x) : \langle \text{app:}(\omega) \to \varphi \rangle}\;(\text{FLD})}$$

$$\dfrac{\overline{\text{this:K, x:}\varphi \vdash x : \varphi}\;(\text{VAR})}{\dfrac{\text{this:K, x:}\varphi \vdash \text{new } K_1(x) : \langle x{:}\varphi\rangle}{}\;(\text{NEWF})}\;(\text{NEWM})$$

$$\dfrac{\vdots \qquad \dfrac{\overline{x{:}\varphi \vdash \text{new } K() : K}\;(\text{OBJ})}{x{:}\varphi \vdash \text{new } K() : \langle \text{app:}(\varphi) \to \langle \text{app:}(\omega) \to \varphi \rangle \rangle}\;(\text{NEWM})}{\dfrac{x{:}\varphi \vdash \text{new } K().\text{app}(x) : \langle \text{app:}(\omega) \to \varphi \rangle \qquad \overline{x{:}\varphi \vdash x : \varphi}\;(\text{VAR})}{x{:}\varphi \vdash \text{new } K().\text{app}(x).\text{app}(\|\,\delta\delta\,\|) : \varphi}\;(\text{INVK})}\;(\text{INVK})$$

with on the right:
$$\dfrac{\overline{x{:}\varphi \vdash \|\,\delta\delta\,\| : \omega}\;(\omega)}{} \qquad \vdots \quad (\text{INVK})$$

$$\dfrac{\dfrac{\overline{\text{this:}K_1, x{:}\omega \vdash x : \omega}\;(\omega)}{\text{this:K, x:}\omega \vdash \text{new } K_1(x) : K_1}\;(\text{OBJ})}{\dfrac{\varnothing \vdash \text{new } K() : \langle \text{app:}(\omega) \to K_1 \rangle}{}\;(\text{NEWM})} \qquad \dfrac{\overline{\varnothing \vdash \text{new } K() : K}\;(\text{OBJ})}{}$$

$$\dfrac{}{\varnothing \vdash \text{new } K().\text{app}(\|\,\delta\delta\,\|) : K_1}\;(\text{INVK})$$

with:
$$\dfrac{\overline{\varnothing \vdash \|\,\delta\delta\,\| : \omega}\;(\omega)}{}$$

where δ is the CL-term **S** (**S K K**) (**S K K**) – *i.e.* $\delta\delta$ has no head-normal form.

Fig. 5. Derivations for Example 27

Example 27. Figure 5 shows, respectively, (1) *a derivation typing a strongly normalising expression of* OOCL*; (2) an ω-safe derivation of a normalising (but not strongly normalising) expression of* OOCL*; and (3) a non-ω-safe derivation deriving a nontrivial type for a head-normalising (but not normalising)* OOCL *expression.*

Conclusions and Future Work

We have considered a type-based semantics defined using an intersection type approach for FJ. Our approach constitutes a subtle shift in the philosophy of static analysis for class-based OO: in the traditional (nominal) approach, the programmer specifies the class types that each input to the program (field values and method arguments) should have, on the understanding that the type *checking* system will guarantee that the inputs do indeed have these types.

In the approach suggested by our type system, the programmer is afforded expressive freedom. Thanks the polymorphic character of our types and to type *inference*, which presents the programmer with an 'if-then' input-output analysis of class constructors and method calls, if a programmer wishes to create instances of some particular class (perhaps from a third party) and call its methods in order to utilise some given functionality, then it is then up to them to ensure that they pass appropriate inputs (either field values or method arguments) that guarantee the behaviour they require.

We will reintroduce more features of full Java back into our calculus, to see if our system can accommodate them whilst maintaining the strong theoretical properties that we have shown for the core calculus. For example, similar to $\lambda\mu$ [18], it seems natural to extend our simply typed system to analyse the exception handling features of Java.

References

1. van Bakel, S.: Complete restrictions of the Intersection Type Discipline. Theoretical Computer Science 102(1), 135–163 (1992)
2. van Bakel, S.: Intersection Type Assignment Systems. Theoretical Computer Science 151(2), 385–435 (1995)
3. van Bakel, S.: Completeness and Partial Soundness Results for Intersection & Union Typing for $\overline{\lambda}\mu\tilde{\mu}$. Annals of Pure and Applied Logic 161, 1400–1430 (2010)
4. van Bakel, S.: Strict intersection types for the Lambda Calculus. ACM Computing Surveys 43, 20:1–20:49 (2011)
5. van Bakel, S.: Completeness and Soundness results for $\mathcal{X}$ with Intersection and Union Types. Fundamenta Informaticae 121, 1–41 (2012)
6. van Bakel, S., de Liguoro, U.: Logical equivalence for subtyping object and recursive types. Theory of Computing Systems 42(3), 306–348 (2008)
7. van Bakel, S., Fernández, M.: Normalisation Results for Typeable Rewrite Systems. Information and Computation 2(133), 73–116 (1997)
8. van Bakel, S., Fernández, M.: Normalisation, Approximation, and Semantics for Combinator Systems. Theoretical Computer Science 290, 975–1019 (2003)
9. Barendregt, H.: The Lambda Calculus: its Syntax and Semantics, revised edition. North-Holland, Amsterdam (1984)
10. Barendregt, H., Coppo, M., Dezani-Ciancaglini, M.: A filter lambda model and the completeness of type assignment. Journal of Symbolic Logic 48(4), 931–940 (1983)
11. Brus, T., van Eekelen, M.C.J.D., van Leer, M.O., Plasmeijer, M.J.: Clean - A Language for Functional Graph Rewriting. In: Kahn, G. (ed.) FPCA 1987. LNCS, vol. 274, pp. 364–368. Springer, Heidelberg (1987)
12. Church, A.: A Note on the Entscheidungsproblem. Journal of Symbolic Logic 1(1), 40–41 (1936)
13. Coppo, M., Dezani-Ciancaglini, M.: An Extension of the Basic Functionality Theory for the λ-Calculus. Notre Dame Journal of Formal Logic 21(4), 685–693 (1980)
14. Curry, H.B.: Grundlagen der Kombinatorischen Logik. American Journal of Mathematics 52, 509–536, 789–834 (1930)
15. Igarashi, A., Pierce, B.C., Wadler, P.: Featherweight Java: a minimal core calculus for Java and GJ. ACM Trans. Program. Lang. Syst. 23(3), 396–450 (2001)
16. Milner, R.: A Theory of Type Polymorphism in Programming. Journal of Computer and System Sciences 17, 348–375 (1978)
17. Nöcker, E.G.J.M.H., Smetsers, J.E.W., van Eekelen, M.C.J.D., Plasmeijer, M.J.: Concurrent Clean. In: Aarts, E.H.L., van Leeuwen, J., Rem, M. (eds.) PARLE 1991. LNCS, vol. 506, pp. 202–219. Springer, Heidelberg (1991)
18. Parigot, M.: An algorithmic interpretation of classical natural deduction. In: Voronkov, A. (ed.) LPAR 1992. LNCS, vol. 624, pp. 190–201. Springer, Heidelberg (1992)
19. Rowe, R.N.S., van Bakel, S.J.: Approximation Semantics and Expressive Predicate Assignment for Object-Oriented Programming. In: Ong, L. (ed.) TLCA 2011. LNCS, vol. 6690, pp. 229–244. Springer, Heidelberg (2011)
20. Wadsworth, C.P.: The relation between computational and denotational properties for Scott's D_∞-models of the lambda-calculus. SIAM Journal on Computing 5, 488–521 (1976)

Verifying Functional Formalizations – A Type-Theoretical Case Study in PVS

Sjaak Smetsers and Erik Barendsen

Institute for Computing and Information Sciences,
Radboud University Nijmegen,
Toernooiveld 1, 6525 ED Nijmegen, The Netherlands
{S.Smetsers,E.Barendsen}@cs.ru.nl

Dedicated to Rinus Plasmeijer on the occasion of his 61th birthday

Abstract. In this case study we investigate the use of PVS for developing type theoretical concepts and verifying the correctness of a typing algorithm. PVS turns out to be very useful for the efficient development of a sound basic theory about polymorphic typing. The PVS formalization is also intended as the first step towards a functional training vehicle for the education of compiler construction.

Keywords: functional programming, compiler construction, typing, automated theorem proving.

1   Introduction

This paper reports on a case study in computer aided verification of theories about syntactic objects.

Syntactic theories such as *type theories* play an important role in the (static) analysis of computer programs and construction of reliable implementations of programming languages. The usability and reliability of syntactic techniques can potentially be improved by using automated proof assistants, thus bridging the gap between theory and implementations.

For example, subtle syntactical matters such as the treatment of variables and bindings are usually not addressed in theoretical expositions. However, these matters are crucial when implementing a typing algorithm as a compiler module. Syntactical details are a source of errors which can entirely be avoided using a more detailed design and verification.

In this paper we propose to use of a proof assistant (PVS, [17]), not only to develop new language theoretic concepts, but also to provide a framework for the experimentation with existing implementations of programming languages. In particular, we advocate the use of theorem provers for constructing compilers, for instance to provide the foundation for a course on compiler construction. To implement the various phases that occur during the compilation process, a compiler typically involves high level data structures and complex algorithms. In functional languages one can express these data structures and operations in a very concise and comprehendible manner.

P. Achten and P. Koopman (Eds.): Plasmeijer Festschrift, LNCS 8106, pp. 47–59, 2013.
© Springer-Verlag Berlin Heidelberg 2013

The specification language of the theorem prover PVS is based on classical typed higher-order logic, allowing quantification over propositions and predicates. Functions in PVS are first-class citizens, providing the same expressive power as in any (other) functional programming language. An important feature of PVS's type system is its capability to define *dependent types*: types depending on values. Dependent types enable a profound and accurate description of a function's domain and codomain.

Our paper can be seen as the first step towards a framework for a compiler construction course, permitting students to experiment with concepts and algorithms which prevail during the compilation process. The presence of a proof assistent enables students not only to examine and execute program fragments, but also to formally prove the correctness of methods applied. There is no doubt that such a form of experimentation will significantly increase the student's comprehension and knowledge of the complex compilation process.

In this paper we present the machine verification of a typing algorithm. We prove the soundness and completeness of a specific refinement of the well-known Milner-Wand typing algorithm. This result is new, and cannot be forthrightly derived from existing results. The novelty of our approach constitutes the treatment of the various variable classes, necessary for reasoning about systems with quantified types. Due to the specific nature of the type theoretic challenge, our formalization needs to deal with three classes of variables instead of the usual two (free and bound by universal quantification). We avoid problems with α-conversion by application of a labeling mechanism. Our method is flexible enough to be applied to similar systems with mixed free and bound variables such as rank-2 polymorphism and existential types [13].

2   Type Theory

Typing is a powerful tool for static analysis of programs. Especially in the area of functional programming, numerous typing systems are used to capture properties varying from simple consistency of function applications to complex reference requirements, see e.g. [3], [4].

This paper is about type systems with *weak polymorphism*. We focus on the type reconstruction problem for these systems. It is well-known that typability of full polymorphism (*System-F* or $\lambda 2$ in typed lambda calculus) is undecidable, but there are many systems with some restricted ('weak') form of polymorphism, such as let-polymorphism and rank-2 polymorphism.

In this section we will introduce some basic type-theoretic notions.

First-Order Typing.   Let us consider combinatory expressions built up from variables (from a given set V) and constants (C) using application and definition-abstraction:

$$E ::= V \mid C \mid E\,E \mid \text{let } V = E \text{ in } E.$$

Types are constructed from type variables ($\mathbb{V}$) with a function type constructor:

$$\mathbb{T} ::= \mathbb{V} \mid \mathbb{T} {\to} \mathbb{T}.$$

A type substitution is a function $* : \mathbb{V} \to \mathbb{T}$. The result of applying $*$ to σ is denoted by σ^*. In the sequel, we let $e, e_1, \ldots$ range over E, $\sigma, \tau, \ldots$ over $\mathbb{T}$.

Typing statements are of the form $\Gamma \vdash e : \tau$, where Γ is a set of declarations of the form $x{:}\sigma$. We suppose that the constants have some fixed type given by a type environment $\text{env} : C \to \mathbb{T}$. The typing rules are straightforward:

$$\Gamma, x{:}\sigma \vdash x : \sigma \qquad\qquad \Gamma \vdash c : \text{env}(c)$$

$$\frac{\Gamma \vdash e_1 : \sigma{\to}\tau \quad \Gamma \vdash e_2 : \sigma}{\Gamma \vdash e_1\, e_2 : \tau} \qquad \frac{\Gamma \vdash e_1 : \sigma \quad \Gamma, x{:}\sigma \vdash e_2 : \tau}{\Gamma \vdash \mathsf{let}\ x = e_1\ \mathsf{in}\ e_2 : \tau}$$

The computation of a type for an expression is called *type inference*. There are several implementations of typing algorithms for functional languages. Most of these are based on Milner's algorithm, commonly denoted by $\mathcal{W}$ [12]. The approach by Wand ([21]) differs from Milner's approach in that type reconstruction is split into two phases. During the first phase, expressions are traversed and typing constraints (following from the rules for the respective syntactic constructions) are collected as type equations. Type variables are used to denote the unknowns in these equations. Solving the constraints (via unification) takes place during the second phase. In $\mathcal{W}$ the identified constraints are solved immediately. See also [2].

The *principal typing algorithm* decides for each e whether it is typable; in the positive case it computes a *principal pair* Γ, σ such that

$$\Gamma \vdash e : \sigma$$

and moreover each other typing can be obtained from Γ, σ by substitution:

$$\Gamma' \vdash M : \sigma' \;\Rightarrow\; \Gamma' \supseteq \Gamma^*,\ \sigma' = \sigma^* \text{ for some } *.$$

The first property is called *soundness*, the second expresses *completeness* of the algorithm.

A variant of the principal typing algorithm computes a *principal type* σ given Γ and e. The substitution in the soundness property then only affects σ. We will focus on this variant in our formalization.

Weak Polymorphism.   We will describe a system which allows types with universal quantification of variables at the outermost level, such as $\forall \alpha. \alpha{\to}\alpha$. The resulting set of *type schemes* is denoted by $\mathbb{T}^\forall$:

$$\mathbb{T}^\forall ::= \mathbb{T} \mid \forall \mathbb{V}.\mathbb{T}^\forall.$$

$S, T, \ldots$ range over $\mathbb{T}^\forall$. Type schemes are assigned to expression variables (by Γ), and to constants (by the type environment $\text{env} : C \to \mathbb{T}^\forall$). These schemes can be *instantiated* by substituting types for the quantified variables. To this end, the first order system is extended with rules such as

$$\frac{\Gamma \vdash e : \forall \alpha.S}{\Gamma \vdash e : S[\alpha := \tau]} \qquad \frac{\Gamma \vdash e : S}{\Gamma \vdash e : \forall \alpha.S} \quad (\alpha \text{ not free in } \Gamma)$$

For this system one can prove principal typing results like for the first-order case. To allow for an inductive generation of type constraints one can transform the system into a 'syntax directed' one, in which each rule corresponds to exactly one syntactic construction. We will not go into the details.

3   Formalizing Expressions and Types

In this section we will prepare for the representation of types and show how to formalize the basic notions in PVS [17]. In our formalization we will consider a variant of the weakly polymorphic system introduced in the previous section. In our case study we wish to focus on the (sometimes subtle and error-prone) administration and manipulation of *types* and the various rôles of type variables. We therefore restrict the *expression* syntax to the simplest interesting example: the applicational fragment, so without let expressions. This is not a serious restriction, since [20] shows that let-polymorphism can be translated into a purely combinatoric system via substitutions.

Types with Markings

In the typing algorithm for weak polymorphism one has to distinguish two substitution-like operations on types. *Instantiation* should affect the (quantified) scheme variables, but not the other (free) variables. The *solving substitutions* should be restricted restricted to auxiliary type variables (denoting the unknowns in equations). For a transparent formalization we introduce the notion of *marked type variables* and two replacement operations on marked types. We will use this for a 'secure' formalization of the changing rôles of the variables in the subsequent steps of the algorithm.

The collection $\mathbb{T}$ of *marked first-order types* is built up from type variables that can appear either plain or marked (denoted by underlining):

$$\mathbb{T} ::= \mathbb{V} \mid \underline{\mathbb{V}} \mid \mathbb{T} \rightarrow \mathbb{T}.$$

Let $\sigma \in \mathbb{T}$ and let $* : \mathbb{V} \rightarrow \mathbb{T}$ be a substitution. The *instantiation effect* of $*$ on σ, denoted by $[\sigma]^*$, is defined inductively by

$$[\alpha]^* = \underline{\alpha},$$
$$[\underline{\alpha}]^* = *(\alpha),$$
$$[\sigma \rightarrow \tau]^* = [\sigma]^* \rightarrow [\tau]^*.$$

Observe that the free (i.e. unmarked) scheme variables of σ are marked in $[\sigma]^*$. The *substitution effect* of $*$ on σ, denoted by $(\sigma)^*$, is defined by

$$(\alpha)^* = *(\alpha),$$
$$(\underline{\alpha})^* = \underline{\alpha},$$
$$(\sigma \rightarrow \tau)^* = (\sigma)^* \rightarrow (\tau)^*.$$

Typing in the weakly polymorphic system can be expressed using marked first-order types: quantified variables can be represented as marked variables. The instantiation mechanism becomes

$$\frac{\Gamma \vdash e : \sigma}{\Gamma \vdash e : [\sigma]^*}$$

or $\Gamma, x{:}\sigma \vdash x : [\sigma]^*$ and $\Gamma \vdash c : [\text{env}(c)]^*$ in the syntax directed variant.

Representing Syntax in PVS

We formalize the syntax in our proof tool. While explaining the formalization we will give a brief introduction to PVS.

PVS offers an interactive environment for the development and analysis of formal specifications. The system consists of a specification language and a theorem prover. The specification language of PVS is based on classical, typed higher-order logic. It resembles common functional programming languages, like Haskell, LISP or ML. PVS supports inductive definitions.

We use the following representation of expressions.

```
EXPR[V:TYPE, C:TYPE] : DATATYPE
BEGIN
     e_var    (v_id: V)              : e_var?
     e_const  (c_id: C)              : e_const?
     e_appl   (e_fun, e_arg: EXPR)   : e_appl?
END EXPR
```

The basic syntactical categories V and C appear as the *parameters* V and C of the inductive data type EXPR. The data type itself has three *constructors*, e_var, e_const and e_appl for representing values in EXPR. In addition, three *recognizers* e_var?, e_const? and e_appl? are defined (PVS allows question marks as constituents of identifiers), which can be used as predicates to test whether or not an EXPR object starts with the respective constructor. It will be more convenient, however, to define operations on inductive datatypes by pattern matching.

For each data type, PVS generates a collection of so-called *theories*. One of those theories contains the basic declarations and axioms formalizing the data type, including an induction scheme for proofs. Moreover, instantiations of some generic operations such as map (for lifting functions) and the recursor reduce are generated.

For example, the function fvs (giving the *free variables* of an expression) can be defined using the recursor by specifying the results for each case of the inductive data type (variable, constant, application):

```
fvs: [EXPR → PRED[V]] = reduce(singleton,λ(c:C):∅,∪)
```

When applied to an expression e, this function will return the subset of V (in PVS denoted as PRED[V]) consisting of the variables occurring in e. We have used the predefined set operations singleton and ∪.

More involved inductive definitions can be given using a general pattern matching scheme (CASES). In particular, the function **reduce** itself is defined internally as follows. Note that the recursor (on EXPR) can be used to construct operations from EXPR to any result type **ran** ('range').

```
reduce (vf:[V → ran],cf:[C → ran],af:[[ran, ran] → ran]): [EXPR → ran]
   = λ (e: EXPR): LET red:[EXPR → ran] = reduce(vf,cf,af)
                 IN CASES e OF
                       e_var(v):    vf(v),
                       e_const(c):  cf(c),
                       e_appl(f,a): af(red(f), red(a))
                 ENDCASES
```

We will use the concept of marked types both for type schemes in environments (Γ and env) and for special variables in type assignments ($e : \sigma$). For convenience, however, we will use different names for these two occurrences of the collection of marked types: we represent them as two separate data types. This is shown in the following declarations.

```
SCHEME[V  : TYPE]: DATATYPE        MTYPE[V:TYPE]: DATATYPE
BEGIN                              BEGIN
    s_bv  (bv:V): s_bv?                t_mv  (t_var:V): t_mv?
    s_fv  (fv:V): s_fv?                t_fv  (t_var:V): t_fv?
    s_arr (arg, res:SCHEME): s_arr?    t_arr (t_arg, t_res:MTYPE): t_arr?
END SCHEME                         END MTYPE
```

```
discard(x:V) :PRED[V] = ∅

fvs:[SCHEME → PRED[V]] = reduce(discard,singleton,∪)
bvs:[SCHEME → PRED[V]] = reduce(singleton,discard,∪)

fvs:[MTYPE → PRED[V]]  = reduce(discard,singleton,∪)
mvs:[MTYPE → PRED[V]]  = reduce(singleton,discard,∪)
```

Contrary to our approach, in [14] and [15] expressions are typed with *monomorphic* types (i.e. types with only one kind of type variables). A consequence is that type variables occurring free in the type scheme can, after instantiation, be altered during type reconstruction. The advantage of using two kinds of variables is that they remain distinguishable, even after unification. We will explain this in more detail in section 5.

The instantiation and substitution operations (denoted earlier by $[\cdot]^*$ and $(\cdot)^*$) can be defined easily using the recursors for SCHEME and MTYPE.

```
SUBST : TYPE = [V → MTYPE];

inst(s:SUBST)  : [SCHEME → MTYPE] = reduce(s,t_mv,t_arr)
subst(s:SUBST): [MTYPE → MTYPE]   = reduce(t_mv,s,t_arr)
```

Observe that **inst** changes free scheme variables into marked type variables, implying that they cannot be further instantiated via substitution. In [20], an operation is introduced which converts a type back into a scheme. Usually this is called *generalization*. The result depends on the context in which the operation is performed, in particular on the type variables appearing in the used base. Generalization corresponds to the $\forall$-introduction rule in the weakly polymorphic type system. In PVS:

```
gen(p:pred[V]): [V → SCHEME]
    = λ(v:V): IF p(v) THEN s_fv(v) ELSE s_bv(v) ENDIF

generalize(p:pred[V]): [MTYPE → SCHEME]
    = reduce(gen(p), s_bv, s_arr)
```

Typically, the function `generalize` will be parameterized with the free variables of the present basis. Generalization (below indicated as $\mathcal{G}$) plays a crucial role in the proof of the following property concerning substitutions.

$$\Gamma \vdash e_1[x := e_2] : \sigma \;\Rightarrow\; \Gamma \vdash e_2 : \tau, \quad \Gamma, x{:}\mathcal{G}(\Gamma, \tau) \vdash e_1 : \sigma \text{ for some } \tau.$$

This property is used by [20] to justify the way let-polymorphism is translated into our combinatoric system.

For convenience, we prefer to use the infix operation ****** instead of `subst`. Moreover, the operator $\leq$ is used to express 'is an instance of'. We have two different versions, one for schemes and one for types.

For the definition of infix operations, PVS requires a specific syntax that does not allow parameter types to be included in the argument list.

```
s             : VAR SUBST
t, t1, t2  : VAR MTYPE
ts            : VAR SCHEME

**(t,s): MTYPE = subst(s)(t)
≤(t1, t2) : bool = ∃ (s) : t2 = t1 ** s;
≤(ts, t)  : bool = ∃ (s) : t = inst(s)(ts);
```

4   Formalizing the Typing System

To specify the type inference rules, we make use of PVS's facility to define *inductive predicates*. The type system is specified as a separate PVS theory `typingEXPR`. This theory has the environment `env` assigning types to constants as parameter.

```
typingEXPR [V, X, C:TYPE,
              (IMPORTING SCHEME[V]) env: [C → SCHEME[V]]]: THEORY
BEGIN
    BASE : TYPE     = [X → SCHEME]
    b  : VAR BASE
    st : VAR [EXPR,MTYPE]

    |-(b,st) : INDUCTIVE bool =
        CASES st'1 OF
```

```
         e_var(w)      : b(w)   ≤  st‘2,
         e_const(c)    : env(c) ≤  st‘2,
         e_appl(f, a)  : ∃ (t:MTYPE): (b |- (f,t_arr(t,st‘2)))
                                    ∧ (b |- (a, t))
     ENDCASES
END typingEXPR
```

Above, the variable st is declared as a pair consisting of an expression and its type. The notation st‘n is used to select the nth component of st.

An important property for our final theorem stating that type derivation is closed under substitution, is the following:

```
typable_subst : LEMMA
    ∀(e:EXPR, t:MTYPE, b:BASE, s:Substitution):
        (b |- (e,t)) ⇒ (b |- (e, t ** s))
```

The proof by induction on the structure of e is straightforward.

5 Formalizing the Algorithm

Until now, we only considered the monomorphic subset of MTYPE. In the present section, the role of the free variables will become apparent: they serve as unknows in type equations. These type equations are represented as a list of pairs. Solving these equations is usually done via *unification*: the process of finding a substitution that is a *unifier* for all equations appearing in the list.

In PVS equations and solutions can be defined as follows:

```
EQS : TYPE   = list[[MTYPE, MTYPE]]
solves(s): pred[EQS]  = every(λ(t1, t2: MTYPE): t1 ** s = t2 ** s)
```

The predefined combinator every checks if all elements of a list satisfy a given predicate. In this case we verify whether the given substitution s is a unifier for each pair of types.

It is well-known that unification is decidable. However, correctness of type inference does not depend on a particular implementation of unification, but merely on some general properties. As is, we do not give a unification algorithm but specify its properties via *axioms*. A machine verified proof of these properties (also by using PVS) for the Robinson unification [18] is given in [8]. The second axiom (mgu_complete) is based on the usual ordering on substitutions:

```
s, s1, s2: VAR SUBST
≤(s1, s2) : bool = ∃ s : s2 = (s o s1)
mgu: [EQS → lift[SUBST]]

mgu_sound : AXIOM
    ∀(eqs:EQS): mgu(eqs) = up(s) ⇒ solves(s)(eqs)
mgu_complete : AXIOM
    ∀(eqs:EQS): solves(s)(eqs) ⇒ up?(mgu(eqs)) ∧ down(mgu(eqs)) ≤ s
```

The predefined lift datatype adds a bottom element to a given base type, in this case SUBST. This is useful for defining partial functions, particularly to indicate the cases that unification fails.

The next step is to associate a set of type equations with each expression e, in such a way that typability of e can be expressed in terms solvability of those equations.

The generation of these equations is recursively defined on the structure of e. This algorithm needs to generate new free type variables. In hand written proofs this issue is often disposed of in a single remark stating that at certain points *fresh* variables are introduced. This merely means that these variables do not clash with variables used elsewhere. Obviously this solution will not work in a machine verified proof, which forces us to formalize such a notion of *freshness*. The easiest way to do this is by using natural numbers as type variables and by explicitly maintaining a counter indicating the next free variable number. The counter is incremented each time a fresh variable is required. This counter (below named heap) is returned as an additional component of the result of generate. Similar to [14], in our definition of generate we use two auxiliary functions called fresh and next_bv. The first function is used to create a fresh instance of a type scheme, i.e. a type in which bound scheme variables are substituted by fresh free variables. The second function computes the offset with which our heap must be increased such that uniqueness of fresh variables remains guaranteed.

```
fresh(heap:nat): [SCHEME → MTYPE] = inst(λ(n:nat):t_fv(n+heap))
next_bv: [SCHEME → nat] = reduce (λ(n:nat):n+1,λ(n:nat):0,maximum)
equa(t1,t2:MTYPE): EQS = cons((t1,t2),null)

generate(b:BASE)(e:EXPR,t:MTYPE)(h:nat): RECURSIVE [nat, EQS] =
  CASES e OF
    e_var(v):   (next_bv(b(v))+h,  equa(t,fresh(h)(b(v)))),
    e_const(c): (next_bv(en(c))+h, equa(t,fresh(h)(en(c)))),
    e_appl(f, a): LET (fh,feqs) = generate(b)(f,t_arr(t_fv(h),t))(h+1),
                      (ah,aeqs) = generate(b)(a,t_fv(h))(fh)
                  IN (ah, append(feqs,aeqs))
  ENDCASES
MEASURE e BY ≪
```

The MEASURE specification is a standard part in the definition of recursive functions such as generate. In PVS all functions are total. The measure is used to show that the function terminates. This is done by generating a proof obligation (a so-called Type Correctness Condition, *TCC*) indicating that the measure strictly decreases at each recursive call. In this case we can use the standard subtree-ordering on elements inductive data types ≪. This ordering is part of the standard theory generated with each inductive data type.

As can be deduced from the PVS code, generate uses free type variables as placeholders which are filled in later via unification. The advantage of separating these free variables from marked variables is that the substitution resulting from unification is restricted to placeholders only. This appears to crucial when formulating and proving the principal types property.

6   The Correctness Proof

In this section we show that type assignment has the *principal type property*. The proof is divided into three steps. The first two steps concern correctness of our procedure, i.e. *soundness* and *completeness*. In the third step our main theorem is proven using both correctness and the properties of the unification algorithm.

Soundness

The soundness property can be formulated as follows:

```
generate_sound: PROPOSITION
    ∀(b:BASE,e:EXPR,t:MTYPE,n:nat,s:SUBST):
        solves(s)(generate(b)(e,t)(n)'2) ⇒ (b  |- (e,t ** s))
```

This proposition is proven by induction on the structure of e. In contrast to [14], we do not have any side-conditions with respect to the free variables occurring in b. The proof itself is actually not difficult and relatively short (approximately 50 proof steps). This size is slightly misleading because it depends on many intermediate results which were proved separately. The main lemma occurring in the proof (relating the instance of a scheme ts to a substitution on a fresh copy ts) is:

```
fresh_inst : LEMMA
    ∀(n:nat,ts:SCHEME,s:SUBST):
        inst(λ(m:nat):s(n+m))(ts) = fresh(n)(ts) ** s
```

This lemma can be proven in just 15 steps, using structural induction on ts.

Completeness

The formulation as well as the proof of the completeness property is more subtle.

```
generate_complete: PROPOSITION
    ∀(m:nat,n:(below?(m)),b:BASE,e:EXPR,t:(betweenT?(n,m)),s1:(bsubst?(n,m))):
        (b |- (e, t ** s1)) ⇒
            LET (nheap,eqs) = generate(b)(e,t)(m)
            IN ∃(s2:(bsubst?(n,nheap))): solves(s2)(eqs)
                    ∧ restrict(s2)(between?(n,m))= s1
```

To complete the proof we had to make some specific assumptions on the free type variables occurring in the input type t and the substitution s1. These assumptions are formulated using *dependent types*: types depending on values. E.g. the predicate betweenT?(n,m) states that any variable v occurring in t lies between n and m. For substitutions the predicate bsubst?(n,m) does something similar: both domain and range of a substitution should be bounded by n and m. The function restrict restricts s2 to elements of the specified set, in this case between?(n,m). The complexity of the proof is significantly greater than the soundness proof: it requires some 1500 proof steps, not to mention the numerous sublemmas that are involved. Similar to the proof in [14], the e_appl-case is not only lengthy but also quite difficult.

Principal Types

We finally arrive at one of the main goals of our exercise: the principal type property. A necessary technicality is that we show that the principal type itself is *clean*, meaning that there is no overlap between free and marked variables. The latter is important because the generalization (as defined in section 3) of a 'unhygienic' type may lead to undesired name clashes.

```
Clean? : PRED[MTYPE] = { t : MTYPE | disjoint?(fvs(t),mvs(t)) }
```

```
principal_types: THEOREM
    ∀(b:BASE, e:EXPR): ∀(t1, t2:MTYPE):
       (b |- (e,t1)) ∧ (b |- (e,t2)) ⇒
          ∃(t:(Clean?)): (b |- (e,t)) ∧ t ≤ t1 ∧ t ≤ t2
```

Roughly, the proof proceeds as follows. Create a fresh variable, say v, and two singleton substitutions assigning t1 and t2 respectively to v. Use `generate_complete` twice with `t_fv(v)` as t and the above singleton substitutions as s1. This results in two new substitutions, both solving the set of generated equations. By `mgu_complete` we obtain the most general solution for these equations. Then the combination of `mgu_sound` and `generate_sound` gives us a type t for e. Transforming this type into a clean variant and showing that this variant is smaller than or equal to both t1 and t2. This is just a matter of simple case distinctions.

7   Discussion

The use of the proof tool for conceptual development turned out to be very beneficial. Inaccuracies stemming from implicit assumptions in theoretical expositions were quickly discovered and repaired. The formalization of the correctness proof did not lead to any alterations in the basic theory: stability was achieved after checking some basic properties.

The formalization of the correctness proof[1] took about 2000 steps, comparable to formalizations of similar syntactic theories. Our proofs could be optimized further by adding more lemmas, replacing repeating patterns.

The present research is part of a larger project using PVS for both the verification of existing software [7] and the development of new software [8]. For instance, the correctness of a scheduling protocol for a smart-card personalization machine has been proven in [10]. This protocol was used as a case study to test the power of model checkers. Due to their nature, model checkers were only capable of verifying correctness for a machine with a limited amount of personalization units. Using PVS it is shown that the correctness holds for any number of units.

Comparable with e.g. [11], [9], our work should be considered as a contribution to a broader goal leading to fully formalized (both functional and imperative)

---

[1] All the proofs presented in this paper can be downloaded from
http://www.cs.ru.nl/S.Smetsers/files/principal.zip

languages and fully verified compilers. Most theorem proving in this area has been done in Coq or LF. We prefer the more flexible proof style of PVS.

One of the POPLMARK challenges is the treatment of variable binding. Several solutions to this challenge have been reported, e.g., [5]. Most of these are based on de Bruijn indices. Though [1] argues that this representation introduces too much overhead in formal proofs, and therefore should be avoided, this is not confirmed by any of the presented solutions. Moreover, our own experience also points in this direction: we have proved *subject reduction* in PVS using the same representation. It would be interesting to compare our approach with that of [19] in more detail.

We have used the formalization of the principal type property to prove type preservation for a program transformation using PVS [20]. It turned out to be easy to connect our formalization to existing work on the particular transformation. It is crucial that our result allows the typing basis to be fixed in a proof. A result about principal *pairs* would not be usable. The combination of these results shows that in a core functional language like Mini-ML [6] principal types can be computed effectively.

A variant of the principal type property has been proved in Isabelle [16], see [15] and [14]. Our result is slightly more general. The main difference, however, is our treatment of bases as parameters in the formal proof.

8 Conclusion

We have successfully formalized the syntax of expressions and types, as well as a typing system with weak polymorphism. Our formalization includes a variable administration to deal with mixed rôles of variables in systems with quantifiers (such as polymorphic and existential type systems). The representation allows for reasoning about these technical matters at a conveniently high level.

We have used PVS for two goals: consistent development of syntactical concepts (such as typing) and verification of an algorithm.

References

1. Aydemir, B.E., Bohannon, A., Fairbairn, M., Nathan Foster, J., Pierce, B.C., Sewell, P., Vytiniotis, D., Washburn, G., Weirich, S., Zdancewic, S.: Mechanized metatheory for the masses: The POPLMARK challenge. In: Hurd, J., Melham, T.F. (eds.) TPHOLs 2005. LNCS, vol. 3603, pp. 50–65. Springer, Heidelberg (2005)
2. Barendregt, H.P.: Lambda calculi with types. In: Abramsky, S., M. Gabbai, D.M., Maibaum, T.S.E. (eds.) Handbook of Logic in Computer Science, vol. 2, pp. 117–309. Oxford Univ. Press (1992)
3. Barendsen, E., Smetsers, J.E.W.: Uniqueness typing for functional languages with graph rewriting semantics. MSCS 6, 579–612 (1996)
4. Barendsen, E., Smetsers, J.E.W.: Graph rewriting aspects of functional programming. In: Ehrig, H., Engels, G., Kreowski, H.-J., Rozenberg, G. (eds.) Handbook of Graph Grammars and Computing by Graph Transformation, vol. 2, pp. 63–102. World Scientific Publishing (1999)

5. Berghofer, S.: A solution to the poplmark challenge in Isabelle/Hol. Technical report, Department of Computer Science, Technical University of Munich, Germany (2006)

6. Clément, D., Despeyroux, T., Kahn, G., Despeyroux, J.: A simple applicative language: mini-ml. In: LFP 1986: Proceedings of the 1986 ACM Conference on LISP and Functional Programming, pp. 13–27. ACM, New York (1986)

7. Hohmuth, M., Tews, H.: The semantics of C++ data types: Towards verifying low-level system components. In: Basin, D., Wolff, B. (eds.) TPHOLs 2003, pp. 127–144. Technical Report No. 187. Institut für Informatik Universität Freiburg (2003)

8. Jacobs, B., Smetsers, S., Schreur, R.W.: Code-carrying theories. Form. Asp. Comput. 19(2), 191–203 (2007)

9. Lee, D.K., Crary, K., Harper, R.: Towards a mechanized metatheory of standard ml. In: Hofmann, M., Felleisen, M. (eds.) POPL, pp. 173–184. ACM (2007)

10. Lensink, L., Smetsers, S., van Eekelen, M.: Machine checked formal proof of a scheduling protocol for smartcard personalization. In: Leue, S., Merino, P. (eds.) FMICS 2007. LNCS, vol. 4916, pp. 115–132. Springer, Heidelberg (2008)

11. Leroy, X.: A formally verified compiler back-end. J. Autom. Reason. 43(4), 363–446 (2009)

12. Milner, R.: A theory of type polymorphism in programming. J. Comput. Syst. Sci. 17(3), 348–375 (1978)

13. Mitchell, J.C.: Foundations for Programming Languages. MIT Press (1996)

14. Naraschewski, W., Nipkow, T.: Type inference verified: Algorithm $\mathcal{W}$ in Isabelle/HOL. Journal of Automated Reasoning 23, 299–318 (1999)

15. Nazareth, D., Nipkow, T.: Formal verification of algorithm $\mathcal{W}$: The monomorphic case. In: von Wright, J., Harrison, J., Grundy, J. (eds.) TPHOLs 1996. LNCS, vol. 1125, pp. 331–346. Springer, Heidelberg (1996)

16. Nipkow, T., Paulson, L.C., Wenzel, M.T.: Isabelle/HOL. LNCS, vol. 2283. Springer, Heidelberg (2002)

17. Owre, S., Shankar, N., Rushby, J.M., Stringer-Calvert, D.W.J.: PVS language reference (version 2.4). Technical report, Computer Science Laboratory, SRI International, Menlo Park, CA (November 2001)

18. Robinson, J.A.: A machine-oriented logic based on the resolution principle. Journal of the ACM 12, 23–41 (1965)

19. Urban, C., Tasson, C.: Nominal techniques in isabelle/HOL. In: Nieuwenhuis, R. (ed.) CADE 2005. LNCS (LNAI), vol. 3632, pp. 38–53. Springer, Heidelberg (2005)

20. van Weelden, A.: Putting Types to Good Use. PhD thesis, Radboud University Nijmegen (2007)

21. Wand, M.: A simple algorithm and proof for type inference. Fundamenta Infomaticae X, 115–122 (1987)

Functional Semantics

Pieter Koopman

Institute for Computing and Information Sciences (iCIS),
Radboud University Nijmegen, The Netherlands
pieter@cs.ru.nl

Abstract. In ordinary interpreters and executable specifications of operational semantics the interpreted language is represented by an algebraic data type and the operations are functions having this data type as argument. In this essay we reverse the roles of functions and data structures. Here the language constructs are represented by state transforming functions belonging to some class. There are instances of this class for the operations on the specified language. Typical examples of operations are reduction, pretty printing, and transformations. The state is a data structure indicating the desired operation. The advantage of this approach is that it is easy to add language constructs and operations independently of each other.

1 Introduction

It is known for a long time that there is a close resemblance between semantic descriptions and their implementation in functional programming languages. My Ph.D. thesis [8] gives a description of bracket abstraction and the translation of Clean to ABC-code [10] in Miranda [26]. Nielson and Nielson [15] give a nice overview of different kinds of semantics and the connection with their implementations in functional programming. Many other papers use one programming language to express the semantics of other languages, e.g. [12,21]. In [9] we reviewed this technique and applied it to the semantics of more complex systems like the iTask system [17]. Common to all these approaches is that the language described is represented as an algebraic data type. The semantics of the described language are functions taking the algebraic data type as an argument. We can add other functions like pretty printers for the described language or a function to determine the free variables. In a semantic framework operations like pretty printing and transformations assign just an other meaning to a language.

To specify the semantics of iTask constructs in a typed way [19] Rinus proposed to use functions instead of data structures to specify the meaning of iTask primitives. This appears to work remarkably well since we can use function types of the host language (here Clean) to describe type dependencies in the described language (here the domain specific language iTask).

The idea to represent elements of the defined language by functions in the defining language has been used before by Reynolds [21] and Carette et al. [2]. Function types are in most programming languages more expressive than algebraic data types. The advantage of this approach is that we can add constructs

P. Achten and P. Koopman (Eds.): Plasmeijer Festschrift, LNCS 8106, pp. 60–78, 2013.

to the language by just adding a new function. The drawback is that the semantic function takes a single type of event as argument and produces a tuple containing all results. This makes it harder to add new operations. Each new operation must be coded as a new constructor in the algebraic data type representing the events. In our iTask example there are constructors to model an input event (reduction), print the current iTask structure etcetera. The result must be embedded in the resulting tuple type.

Ideally we can add new operations as easily as in the algebraic data type approach, and add language elements as simple as in the function based architecture. A class based approach can in principle cope with these wishes. Different instances of the classes match the different operations. We can use functions with the same names to implement the needed manipulations of the language constructs. By defining new classes as extension of former classes we can extend our language. In this essay we study how well a class based approach works for the translation of λ-calculus [1] to SKI-combinators [22,25].

Since we can extend the language and its manipulations independently we have a real choice in the order of presenting these topics. Presenting them along the language extension axis works as well as introducing the topics as a sequence of new manipulations. In this essay we have chosen to use the manipulations as the main structure of sections. Within each section we show how the various language constructs are handled. Since this is an essay in the festschrift for Rinus Plasmeijer we use Clean [20] as the host language to redefine the translation of λ-calculus to SKI-combinators from [8].

2   The Expression Problem

Our desire to extend the language described and its manipulations independently is in fact just another instance of the *expression problem*. This expression problem is the ongoing quest for ways to extend data types and operations on them independently without the need to change existing code. Phil Wadler [27] phrased the expression problem as:

> *The goal is to define a data type by cases, where one can add new cases to the data type and new functions over the data type, without recompiling existing code, and while retaining static type safety.*

In the standard way to define data types and functions on these data types in a functional language like Clean it is straightforward to define new functions on a data type. Consider for example the well-known Peano numbers:

```
:: Num = Zr | Sc Num
```

A show function for these numbers can be defined in the default fashion as:

```
:: Show :== [String]
```

```
show  :: Num → Show
show  Zr    = ["Zero"]
show  (Sc n) = ["Succ": show n]
```

In the same style we can define any number of operations we need.

The drawback of this approach is that all of these functions need to be updated and recompiled when we extend the data type, for instance with the construct Pred Num for predecessors.

2.1   Representing Data Types

Our solution is based on classes and interchanging the role of data and functions on this data. Basically the functions take a state S as input and produce a result of type R. In order to model the different manipulations we use a class of functions with the same name instead of normal function. This allows us to use the same name for a language constructs and define tailor-made meanings for it; one meaning for each manipulation of the data structure. A class of functions of type s → r and making instances for various s and r is the most general solution for this programming task. The drawback of the general approach is that the compiler is often unable to solve the overloading by determining the types to be used as input and result. To prevent problems with solving overloading we use the same type as input and result. This implies that an expression is a function of type t → t in some class. We introduce the name Expr t for those functions:

```
:: Expr t    :== t → t
```

The 'type' for Peano numbers in this representation is defined as:

```
class nat t
where
    zr ::                Expr t
    sc :: (Expr t) → Expr t
```

To increase the correspondence with ordinary data type definitions we can use the uppercase identifiers Nat, Sc and Zr instead of the lowercase variants used here. We used the lowercase variants to emphasize that these are no ordinary types and data constructors.

2.2   Representing Functions

The show function from above is rephrased for the new representation as:

```
instance nat Show
where zr    = Cons "zero"
      sc n = Cons "succ" o n

Cons :: t [t] → [t]
Cons a x = [a: x]
```

The conversion to integers is defined very similarly:

```
instance nat Int
where zr   = const 0
      sc n = (+) 1 o n
```

We can apply these definitions in a function like:

```
three :: Expr t | nat t
three = sc (sc (sc zr))
```

The argument supplied to this data type determines its interpretation.

```
Start = (three ["."], three int)
```

```
int :: Int
int = undef
```

The definition of int is only used to determine the type of three in the second part of the tuple. Since the value is never used we can safely use undef as actual value. The show of three demonstrates that it is very well possible to use the input state. Evaluation of this Start rule yields (["succ","succ","succ","zero","."],3).

2.3   Extending the Data Type

We can extend the 'type' nat to whole numbers, z, by adding a predecessor construct named pr. We introduce a class z to extend the expressions in nat.

```
class z t | nat t where pr :: (Expr t) → Expr t
```

As expected the predecessor is very similar to the successor, sc. The class restriction nat t indicates that this 'type' is an extension of the natural numbers. We can apply the 'constructor' pr only to expressions of type nat and z.

The 'functions' show and Int introduced above can be extended by appropriate instances of z for the data types Show and Int respectively.

```
instance z Show where pr n = cons "pred" o n
instance z Int   where pr n = flip (−) 1 o n
```

2.4   Binary Operations

The classes nat and z illustrate how we can define extendable types. The instances of these classes define functions manipulating a single instance of such a type. To demonstrate how multiple arguments of such a type can be handled we define addition of our Peano numbers. For binary operators like addition there are several possibilities. An instance of the overloaded operator + for the integer interpretation of expressions is:

```
instance + (Expr Int) where (+) x y = λs . x s + y s
```

Evaluating Start = 10 * (three + three) int yields 60.

For a more general addition we define the class plus to add objects of type Expr t and instances of this class to add integers and strings.

```
class plus t where plus :: (Expr t) (Expr t) → Expr t
instance plus Int where   plus x y = λs . x s + y s
instance plus Show where plus x y = λs . x [" + ":y s]
```

With these definitions we can add our nat numbers for integers and strings:

```
Start = (six int, six [","])
where six :: Expr t | plus, nat t
      six = plus three three
```

This expression yields 6 succ succ succ zero + succ succ succ zero, when we show only the basic values. It is obvious that plus applies the initial state to both of its arguments and applies the appropriate 'plus' operation to the resulting values. It is also possible to compose the result of the addition before we apply it to the initial state with the help of a data type Sum:

```
:: Sum t = Sum (Expr t)
```

```
instance nat (Sum t) | nat t
where zr = id
      sc n = λ(Sum f). n (Sum (sc f))
instance z (Sum t) | z t where pr n = λ(Sum f). n (Sum (pr f))
```

```
fromSum :: (Sum t) → Expr t
fromSum (Sum f) = f
```

The resulting expression is very similar to the standard Church representation of Peano numbers in λ-calculus [1]. In order to use this new addition in the previous Start rule we just have to replace the definition of six by:

```
six :: Expr t | plus, nat t
six = fromSum (three (Sum three))
```

A limitation of our approach is that it can only 'match' the othermost constructor. Well known optimisations of the form sc (pr n) = n and pr (sc n) = n cannot be defined directly in this formalism. A traditional algebraic data type and the associated conversions are needed for such optimisations:

```
:: Peano = Zr | Sc Peano | Pr Peano
```

```
instance nat Peano
where zr = const Zr
      sc n = λp . case n p of
                   Pr m = m
                   p    = Sc p
instance z Peano
where pr n = λp . case n p of
                   Sc m = m
                   p    = Pr p
```

```
fromPeano :: Peano → Expr t | z t
fromPeano Zr = zr
```

```
fromPeano (Sc n) = sc (fromPeano n)
fromPeano (Pr n) = pr (fromPeano n)
```

A variant of the Start rule given above is used to demonstrate the use of these optimisation rules.

```
Start = (twoOpt int, twoOpt [""])
where twoOpt :: Expr t | z t
      twoOpt = fromPeano (two Zr)
      two    :: Expr t | z t
      two    = fromSum (one (Sum one))
      one    :: Expr t | z t
      one    = sc (sc (pr zr))
```

The value two yields the value c (sc (pr (c (sc (pr zr)))))) while twoOpt yields the class sc (sc zr). The applications of twoOpt demonstrate that this value is a class that can still be applied to different states to obtain different behaviour. The reduction result is (2,["succ","succ","zero","."]).

The price to be paid for the advantage of nested pattern matches is that we cannot extend our type for Peano numbers no longer step by step.

2.5   Related Work

Much work has been done to solve the expression problem. We discuss the closest related approaches in some detail. Lämmel and Ostermann [11] have used type classes in a more standard way to tackle the expression problem. Essential steps in their approach are: **1** each constructor is placed in a separate data type, **2** each operation is modelled by a class. In Clean terms the data type for natural numbers becomes:

```
:: Zr = Zr
:: Sc x = Sc x
```

The conversion to integers and pretty printing can be defined as:

```
class int x :: x → Int
instance int Zr where int Zr = 0
instance int (Sc x) | int x where int (Sc x) = int x + 1

class show x :: x → [String]
instance show Zr where show Zr = ["Zr"]
instance show (Sc x) | show x where show (Sc x) = ["Sc": show x]
```

We can extend this to the whole numbers and associated operations by defining:

```
:: Pr x = Pr x
instance show (Pr x) | show x where show (Pr x) = ["Pr": show x]
instance int  (Pr x) | int x  where int  (Pr x) = int x − 1
```

A simple application computes the value of an expression and shows its structure:

```
Start = (int one, show one)
where one = Sc (Pr (Sc Zr))
```

This program yields (1,["Sc","Pr","Sc","Zr"]). This approach enables the required type safe possibilities to extend data types and their manipulations independently. A limitation of this approach is that there is very limited control over the use of the type constructs. For instance the type system does not help us to make pure natural numbers (containing only Zr and Sc) in a context where the definition of Pr is available. In fact, any 'constructor' can be added to such a natural number if the required operations are defined as a class instance. It is also hard to define optimisation rules of the form opt (Pr (Sc x)) = x and apply them to all constructors in an instance of a data type like Sc (Pr (Sc Zr)).

In [23] Swierstra rephrases a GADT based approach from current day functional programming folklore. The basic idea is to embed all actual data types in a uniform representation. All manipulations unpack this representation to access the real arguments. Upon finishing their job the function stores the result again in the generic representation. The required packing and unpacking complicates programming.

The open data types and open functions proposed by Löh and Hinze are a language extension to solve the expression problem [13].

3   Expressions for an Executable Semantics

In this section we apply our attempt to solve the expression problem to define an extendable executable semantics of simple expressions. We use the same type t → t to represent expressions and assign the name Expr t to this type. As basic expressions, Exp, in the described language we have constants, cons, function application, app, and functions, fun.

```
class Exp t
where cons  :: x                      → Expr t | toString, TC x
      app   :: (Expr t) (Expr t) → Expr t
      fun   :: Fun       String  → Expr t
```

Any type x can be used with a cons provided that instances of the classes toString and TC (for dynamics) are defined for the type x. The reasons for those type constraints will be explained below. Although the types in an application, app, are parameterised, there is no type constraint an the function and its argument guarantying that the arguments fits the function. A function, fun, takes an expression transformer function, Fun, as argument that can only be used during reduction. Since we want to model only primitive functions the only thing we can do with them is apply them to arguments during evaluation of the expression. This implies that we cannot do anything else with these functions, hence we add a string as name for the primitive function for printing purposes.

Since we do not want to restrict ourselves to the values manipulated within these expressions we pack them into dynamics whenever needed and unpack them again when the real value is needed [16,18].

```
:: Fun   :== (Expr Eval) → Expr Eval
:: Eval  =   Eval Val | Fun Fun String
:: Val   :== Dynamic
```

We discuss evaluation of expressions in detail in Section 6. First we present some extensions of these expressions.

3.1 Variables and λ-Abstraction

In order to extend these expressions to a full λ-calculus we need abstraction of the form λv . expr and variables. We represent those expressions by the functions abst and var respectively. Together these functions form the class Lambda. The class restriction Exp t indicates that it is an extension of the expressions in the class Exp. Every instance of Lambda should also have an instance of Exp, the basic cases for expressions.

```
class Lambda t  |  Exp t
where
    abst        :: Var (Expr t)  →  Expr t
    var         :: Var            →  Expr t

:: Var          :== String
```

The type synonym Var indicates that we use strings as names for variables.

3.2 Local Recursive Definitions

The final extension of expressions in this essay are potentially recursive, local definitions. The **let** expressions are indicated by the function Let. Do not let the uppercase identifier used as name for this function fool you, this is really a function. We only use an identifier starting with an uppercase symbol since the obvious names **let** and **where** are predefined keywords in Clean.

```
class Let t  |  Lambda t
where
    Let        :: Var (Expr t) (Expr t)  →  Expr t
```

Note that this is an extension of expressions in the class Lambda rather than another independent extension of Exp. This is not a limitation of the semantic constructions, but appears to be convenient during reduction of Let expressions.

It is of course possible to add more expression constructs in the same fashion. However, the given constructs are sufficient for the purpose of this paper.

4 Pretty Printing

As first manipulation, or meaning, of these expressions we implement pretty printing. A pretty print is just a list of strings. When this list of strings is a pretty printed version of the expression when is shown on a console or written to a file. We define a data structure Show to be used as state in this class for the expressions. The instance for free variables below shows why we define an instance for the tailor made type Show instead of a plain list of strings, [String].

This example shows that the role of data structures and functions is reversed in this function based description of semantics.

The simple expressions are printed by the class instance for Show of the functions in the class Exp. The instance for cons uses the class restriction toString in the class definition to ensure that there is toString function for this constant. Apart from both class restrictions there are no other limitations on constants. By design any type of values can be used here. We insert parentheses to disambiguate nested occurrences of app in the pretty printed version.

```
:: Show = Show [String]
```

```
instance Exp Show
where cons x  = show (toString x)
      app f a = show "(" o f O a o show ")"
      fun f s = show s
```

This uses the auxiliary function Show to add elements to the list of strings. The infix operator O behaves very similar to the infix function composition, it only adds a space between the shown elements.

```
show :: t Show → Show | toString t
show s (Show l) = Show [toString s: l]
```

```
(O) infixr 9 :: (Expr Show) (Expr Show) → Expr Show
(O) f g = f o show " " o g
```

Pretty printing the expression app (fun (oneBasic ((+) 1)) "inc") (cons 60) yields (inc 60). The used primitive function oneBasic is defined in Section 6.1.

4.1 Pretty Printing λ-Expressions

Variables are pretty printed by adding their name in the list of strings. An abstraction is pretty printed similar to λ-expressions in a functional programming style, using a backslash to represent the λ. The variable and the body are separated with a dot. Parentheses disambiguate any nested expressions.

```
instance Lambda Show
where var  v   = show v
      abst v b = show "(\\" o show v o show "." o b o show ")"
```

This prints the expression abst "x" (app (var "x") (cons 60)) as (\x.(x 60)). Note that this example mixes pretty printing of Lambda and Exp.

It is straightforward to extend the state Show with information to indicate whether parentheses are really necessary in a particular situation.

4.2 Pretty Printing Local Definitions

In exactly the same manner we can pretty print Let-expressions:

```
instance Let Show
where Let v body expr
        = show "let" O show v o show " = " o body o show " in\n" o expr
```

5   Free Variables

In this section we show how to compute the free variables of an expression. We define a type Free to be used as state in the class instance to be defined for this operation.

Since a variable of type Var is just a string indicating its name, it is obvious that we cannot use a single state of type [String] for pretty printing and for determining free variables. Clean needs different type of states to distinguish those different operations.

Constants and primitive functions do not contain free variables, hence they yield the identity functions id for this state. For an application we search both subexpressions for free variables by a function composition.

```
:: Free = Free [Var]
```

```
instance Exp Free
where cons x  = id
      app f a = f o a
      fun f s = id
```

5.1   Free Variables in λ-Expressions

Determining the free variables in λ-expressions is more interesting. For a variable expression we inject the name of the current variable name in the list of variable names in the state. For an abstraction we determine the free variables in the argument expression, remove the given variable from these variables and finally yield a new state with free variables that is the union of the old variables in the state and the free variables in this abstraction.

```
instance Lambda Free
where var  v  = λ(Free vars) . Free (inject v vars)
      abst v b = λ(Free vars) . let (Free local) = b (Free [])
                                in  Free (union vars (remove v local))
```

These definitions use the functions inject, union and remove to mimic set operations in lists. These functions have the obvious implementation.

```
inject ::  a  [a] → [a] | < a
union  ::  [a] [a] → [a] | < a
remove ::  a  [a] → [a] | < a
```

The class restriction < a ensures an ordering to allow a somewhat efficient implementation.

5.2   Free Variables in Local Definitions

In very much the same way we determine free variables in Let-expressions. We determine the free variables in the body of the local definition and the expression. For the result we take their union and remove the name of the local definition.

Finally we yield the union of the variables of this definition and the definitions that were already present in the state.

```
instance Let Free
where  Let v body expr
         = λ(Free vars) .
             let  (Free fb) = body (Free [ ])
                  (Free fe) = expr (Free [ ])
             in   Free (union vars (remove v (union fb fe)))
```

6   Evaluation of Expressions

For the evaluation of expressions we define a state containing the result of reduction. Since we do not know the type of the result, nor want to put any restriction on the type of the result we store it as a dynamic in the state. Hence, a constant expression cons just transforms the given value to a dynamic. This explains the presence of the class restriction TC given in the definition of a constant. This class restriction ensures that it is possible to transform the given value to a dynamic. To enable tracing we do not only store a function in a dynamic as result of evaluation, but we pair this function with its name in a tuple stored in the dynamic.

The instance of expression, Exp for evaluation, Eval (from Section 3), just does this. In the definition for application, app, we first evaluate the left sub-expression. If this yields a function we apply it to the right sub-expression of the app as function argument. This implements lazy evaluation, the function argument is not evaluated before the function is applied.

```
instance Exp Eval
where  cons x  = λe . Eval (dynamic x)
       app f a = λe . case f e of
                         Fun f s = f a e
                         eval = abort ("Cannot apply " + toString eval)
       fun f s     = λr . Fun f s
```

These definitions show that the state is only used to hold results. The type of expressions, Expr, forces us to pass a state to expressions in order to evaluate them, but no information from the state passed top-down to an expression is used.

At the expense of an additional constructor Fun Fun String in the type Eval we can prevent the packing and unpacking of functions into and from dynamics. This give a speedup of about a factor 30 in the evaluation of expressions. To specify the semantics this speed is not relevant and we prefer a single constructor data type as state in the evaluation.

6.1   Primitive Functions

Before we continue with the evaluation of other expressions we define some primitive functions. Note that we can store any function of the appropriate type in a fun expression. Hence the number of primitive functions is in no way limited by the given representation of expressions.

The instance of app for Eval shows that our expressions really use Currying, they take their arguments one by one [3,1] Each primitive function takes an expression as argument. It yields either a new function or a constant.

The function oneBasic is parameterised by the function of type a→b to be applied. It gets an expression as argument, evaluates this expression (by applying it to the given toBasic). Next the given function is applied to the basic value and the result is stored in an expression evaluation state with return.

```
oneBasic :: (a→b) (Expr Eval) → Expr Eval | TC a & TC b
oneBasic f x = return o f o toBasic x

toBasic :: (Expr Eval) Eval → a | TC a
toBasic expr eval
    = case expr eval of
        (Eval (x::a^)) = x
        eval = abort ("Value expected instead of " + toString eval)

return :: x → Eval | TC x
return x = Eval (dynamic x)
```

As a typical example the increment function for our expressions can be defined as fun (oneBasic inc) "inc". The expression that can compute the increment of sixty is defined as app (fun (oneBasic inc) "inc") (cons 60).

In a similar way we can define functions with more arguments. It appears to be convenient to have also functions with a more specific type, like the function twoInts that requires two integer expressions as argument. This solves the overloading when we use overloaded functions, like +, −, *, < and ==.

```
twoInts :: (Int Int → b) String → Expr t | TC b & Exp t
twoInts f s = fun (λx e . Fun (oneBasic (f (toBasic x e)))) (s + " x")) s
```

This function solves the overloading in an application like the function plus that defines addition for our expressions and eq that compares two integers.

```
plus :: (Expr t) | Exp t
plus = twoInts (+) "plus"

eq :: (Expr t) | Exp t
eq = twoInts (==) "eq"
```

By defining an appropriate instance for the infix operation +, we can even define an infix addition for our expressions:

```
instance + (Expr t) | Exp t where (+) x y = app (app plus x) y
```

A simple application of these applications is:

```
Start = (cons 18 + cons 42) (Eval undef)
```

Executing this yields a dynamic containing the integer 60. We can pretty print the expression cons 18 + cons 42 by replacing the state Eval undef by the state Show []. The results in ((plus 18) 42).

Conditionals. In pretty much the same way we can add the conditional as just another function to our expressions. The conditional collects three arguments. As soon as all arguments are available the first argument is evaluated to a Boolean. Depending on the Boolean value either the then-part (second argument), or the else-part (third argument) is evaluated.

```
IF :: (Expr t) | Exp t
IF = fun If "IF"
where If :: (Expr Eval) → (Expr Eval)
      If c = fun then "then"
      where then :: (Expr Eval) → (Expr Eval)
            then t = fun else "else"
            where else :: (Expr Eval) → (Expr Eval)
                  else e = λeval. if (toBasic c eval) (t eval) (e eval)
```

For clarity we have named and typed every function used to process the next element in this conditional. Often we will use λ-expressions since they produce more compact code.

Note that all these primitive functions can be added to our expressions locally. The class definitions representing our expressions are untouched. We only define some functions that can be used as primitive functions by supplying them as argument to the fun case of our expressions.

6.2   Evaluating λ-Expressions and Expressions with Local Definitions

Instead of defining evaluation for λ-expressions by implementing a β-reduction rule we use a combinator based implementation of these expressions. The reason for this choice is that in general we cannot prevent name conflicts. These name conflicts can of course be solved by an appropriate renaming, an α-conversion, but these problems are elegantly avoided by combinator reduction. That is why we leave the evaluation of Lambda-expressions and Let-expressions undefined:

```
instance Lambda Eval
where
    var  v   = undef
    abst v b = undef

instance Let Eval
where
    Let v b e = undef
```

7   Bracket Abstraction

In order to reduce Lambda-expressions and Let-expressions we translate them to combinators. Combinators are here just some primitive functions. We only use four of those combinators: S, K, I, and Y. Minimalists can reduce the number of combinators and people aiming for efficiency can introduce more combinators.

7.1   Combinators

As mathematical functions the combinators are defined as [22,25,1,8]:

$$I \ x = x$$
$$K \ x \ y = x$$
$$S \ f \ g \ x = (f \ x) \ (g \ x)$$
$$Y \ f = f \ (Y \ f)$$

The definition of those combinators as primitive functions in our framework is:

```
I :: (Expr t) | Exp t
I = fun (λx.x) "I"

K :: (Expr t) | Exp t
K = fun (λx.fun (λy.x) "K x") "K"

S :: (Expr t) | Exp t
S = fun (λf. fun (λg. fun (λx.app (app f x) (app g x)) "S f g") "S f") "S"

Y :: (Expr t) | Exp t
Y = fun (λf.app f (app Y f)) "Y"
```

7.2   Bracket Abstraction

The translation of λ-expressions to combinator expressions is known as bracket abstraction. In a simple approach we can define this bracket abstraction as a phase in the evaluation of expressions. Bracket abstraction becomes a function of type Expr Eval.

Here we use a slightly more sophisticated approach. Instead of an expression that can only be evaluated, we use a version of the algorithm that produces the expressions encoded as classes. This implies for instance that we will be able to pretty print the produced combinator expressions as well as to evaluate them. Since the Clean system assumes that in every application of some class member in a single Clean function the same class instance will be used, we have to apply a trick to circumvent the restrictions this assumption imposes on our expressions. The simplest solution to this problem is to pack the class members in a dynamic and unpack them by need.

The state for bracket abstractions, BracAbs, has three different values. Scan just traverses an expression looking for possibilities to apply abstraction. With the state Abs v the algorithm is abstracting variable v. The state SKI d is used to yield the dynamic d.

```
:: BracAbs = Scan | Abs Var | SKI Dynamic
```

Bracket abstraction for basic expressions is defined as:

```
instance Exp BracAbs
where
    cons c  = λba . case ba of
                  Scan  = lambda2bracAbs (cons c)
                  Abs v = lambda2bracAbs (app K (cons c))
    app f x = λba . appSKI (f ba) (x ba) ba
    where
        appSKI :: BracAbs BracAbs BracAbs → BracAbs
        appSKI (SKI (f :: ∀t: (Expr t) | Lambda t))
               (SKI (x :: ∀t: (Expr t) | Lambda t)) ba
          = case ba of
              Scan  = lambda2bracAbs (app f x)
              Abs _ = lambda2bracAbs (app (app S f) x)
    fun f s = λba . case ba of
                  Scan  = lambda2bracAbs (fun f s)
                  Abs v = lambda2bracAbs (app K (fun f s))
```

This uses the following function to pack an expression as a class in a dynamic.

```
lambda2dynamic :: (∀a: (Expr a) | Lambda a) → Dynamic
lambda2dynamic f = dynamic f :: ∀a: (Expr a) | Lambda a

lambda2bracAbs :: (∀a: (Expr a) | Lambda a) → BracAbs
lambda2bracAbs f = SKI (lambda2dynamic f)
```

7.3   Bracket Abstraction for λ-Expressions

Bracket abstraction for λ-expressions is the real reason why we perform this transformation. When we are abstracting a variable x and encounter the same variable as expression we yield the combinator I, and if we encounter a different variable y we construct the expression $K\ y$.

When we encounter an abstraction in scanning mode we abstract the variable for the given body: body (Abs v). When we are already abstracting a variable we first abstract the locally defined variable v and next the variable we were abstracting. As optimisation we throw away the actual argument with a K-combinator when both variables are identical.

```
instance Lambda BracAbs
where
    var v = λba . case ba of
                Scan = lambda2bracAbs (var v)
                Abs w | v == w
                    = lambda2bracAbs I
                    = lambda2bracAbs (app K (var v))
    abst v body
      = λba . case ba of
          Scan = body (Abs v)
          Abs w
              | v == w // some optimising code
```

```
= lambda2bracAbs (app K (bracAbs2lambda (body (Abs v))))
= bracAbs2lambda (body (Abs v)) (Abs w)
```

7.4   Bracket Abstraction for Local Definitions

Instead of doing something smart for the transformation of local definitions, we simply transform a local definition to a λ-expression. We insert a Y combinator to handle recursion in the local definition.

instance Let BracAbs
where
```
    Let v body expr = app (abst v expr) (app Y (abst v body))
```

8   Some Applications

In order to demonstrate that these transformations of expressions work as intended we show some examples. Our first example introduces two local definitions with the same variable. The definition of fac is the common recursive definition of the factorial function.

```
e1 :: (Expr t) | Let t
e1 = Let "half"
         (abst "n" (var "n" / cons 2))
         (Let "fac"
           (abst "n"
              (app (app (app IF (app (app eq (var "n")) (cons 0)))
                        (cons 1))
                   (var "n" * app (var "fac") (var "n" - cons 1))
              )
           )
         (app (var "half") (app (var "fac") (cons 5)))))
```

This definition is pretty printed as:

```
let half = (\n.((divide n) 2)) in
let fac = (\n.(((IF ((eq n) 0)) 1) ((times n) (fac ((minus n) 1)))))) in
(half (fac 5))
```

By applying this expression to the state Scan we execute the bracket abstraction algorithm. By applying the obtained combinator expression to the state Eval undef we can reduce it. This produces the desired result 60.

Our second example is a well know higher order expression with four applications of the function twice; the expression twice twice twice twice (plus 1) 0.

```
e2 :: (Expr t) | Let t
e2
 = Let "twice"
     (abst "f" (abst "x" (app (var "f") (app (var "f") (var "x")))))
     (app (app (app (app (app (var "twice") (var "twice")) (var "twice"))
         ( var "twice")) (app plus (cons 1))) (cons 0))
```

Pretty printing this expression yields:

```
let twice = (λf.(λx.(f (f x)))) in
(((((twice twice) twice) twice) (plus 1)) 0)
```

In the same way we can translate this to a combinator expression. The result of pretty printing the obtained combinator expression is:

```
(((S ((S ((S ((S ((S ((S I) I)) I)) I)) I)) ((S (K plus)) (K 1)))) (K 0)) (Y ((S
((S (K S)) ((S ((S (K S)) ((S (K K)) (K S))))) ((S ((S (K S)) ((S (K K))
(K K)))) (K I))))) ((S ((S (K S)) ((S ((S (K S)) ((S (K K)) (K S))))) ((S
((S (K S)) ((S (K K)) (K K)))) (K I))))) ((S (K K)) (K I))))))
```

Evaluating the combinator expression yields the desired result 65536.

9   Discussion

This essay shows how to formulate the semantics of expressions by functions. These functions are bundled in classes. We can extended the language by defining new classes as extension of existing classes. The operations on these expressions become instances of the classes.

Compared to traditional formulation of semantics we have swapped the role of functions and data types. Traditionally the language described and manipulated is represented by an algebraic data structure and the manipulations are functions taking this data structure as argument. Here the language constructs are functions and there are data structures indicating the desired manipulation. The advantage of this approach is that it is easy to add language constructs and operations independently of each other. In fact we introduced yet another attempt to solve the expression problem: the ongoing quest for type save ways to extend data types and operations on them independently without the need to change existing code. Although our approach work well for the examples shown there are some limitations. First, we cannot use nested pattern matching without the needed to introduce a standard algebraic data type and all the associated limitations. In addition we inherit all the limitations associated with type classes.

Much work has been done on GADTs to improve the type correctness of interpreters and semantic descriptions, e.g. [14,4,7]. GADTs provides a type safe way to construct expressions in the described languages. We will investigate how these approaches can be mixed.

An alternative approach to specify semantics of extensible languages can be based on extensible algebraic data types, as available in Clean and other languages [28,24]. The described language is represented by such an extensible data type and hence can be extended. The limitation of such an approach is that the manipulation functions usually cannot be extended is a similar way. Compared to the work of Lämmel [11] we can indicate the desired structure in the described expressions. Compared to the approach described by Swierstra [23] our expressions does not require repeated packing and unpacking.

In the future we want to polish this approach to describe the semantics. It is worthwhile to try to get rid of as many dynamics as possible. The introduction of user defined data structures is a desirable extension of the described language. These data structures can be transformed functions as outlined in [6,5].

Acknowledgement. First and for all many thanks to Rinus Plasmeijer. He has always encouraged writing clear functions to describe the semantics of other languages in a functional language like Clean. He also proposed the idea to use functions instead of data structures to describe language constructs in [19].

John van Groningen made an excellent compiler for Clean enabling these kind of experiments. He also advised on the dynamics wizarding used in this essay. Many thanks to Peter Achten for many productive discussions about this paper as well as any other topic we discussed as room mates. Finally, I acknowledge the useful feedback of an anonymous referee.

References

1. Barendregt, H.: The lambda calculus, its syntax and semantics, revised edition. Studies in Logic, vol. 103. North-Holland (1984)
2. Carette, J., Kiselyov, O., Shan, C.-C.: Finally tagless, partially evaluated: Tagless staged interpreters for simpler typed languages. J. Funct. Program. 19(5), 509–543 (2009)
3. Curry, H., Feys, R.: Combinatory logic. Studies in Logic and the Foundations of Mathematics Series, vol. 2. North-Holland Publishing Company (1972)
4. Hinze, R.: Fun with phantom types. In: Gibbons, J., de Moor, O. (eds.) The Fun of Programming, pp. 245–262. Palgrave Macmillan (2003)
5. Jansen, J.: Functional Web Applications – Implementation and Use of Client Side Interpreters. PhD thesis, Radboud University Nijmegen, 8 (July 2010) ISBN 978-90-9025436-4
6. Jansen, J., Koopman, P., Plasmeijer, R.: Efficient interpretation by transforming data types and patterns to functions. In: Nilsson, H. (ed.) Proceedings of the 7th Symposium on Trends in Functional Programming, TFP 2006, Nottingham, UK, April 19-21, pp. 157–172 (2006) ISBN 978-1-84150-188-8
7. Johann, P., Ghani, N.: Foundations for structured programming with gadts. SIGPLAN Not. 43(1), 297–308 (2008)
8. Koopman, P.: Functional Programs as Executable Specifications. PhD thesis, University of Nijmegen (1990)
9. Koopman, P., Plasmeijer, R., Achten, P.: An Effective Methodology for Defining Consistent Semantics of Complex Systems. In: Horváth, Z., Plasmeijer, R., Zsók, V. (eds.) CEFP 2009. LNCS, vol. 6299, pp. 224–267. Springer, Heidelberg (2010)
10. Koopman, P.W.M., van Eekelen, M.C.J.D., Plasmeijer, M.J.: Operational machine specification in a functional programming language. Softw., Pract. Exper. 25(5), 463–499 (1995)
11. Lämmel, R., Ostermann, K.: Software extension and integration with type classes. In: Proceedings of the 5th International Conference on Generative Programming and Component Engineering, GPCE 2006, pp. 161–170. ACM, New York (2006)
12. Landin, P.J.: The next 700 programming languages. Commun. ACM 9(3), 157–166 (1966)
13. Löh, A., Hinze, R.: Open data types and open functions. In: Proceedings of the 8th ACM SIGPLAN International Conference on Principles and Practice of Declarative Programming, PPDP 2006, pp. 133–144. ACM, New York (2006)

14. Middelkoop, A., Dijkstra, A., Swierstra, D.: A leaner specification for GADTs. In: Achten, P., Koopman, P., Morazán, M. (eds.) Trends in Functional Programming, vol. 9, pp. 65–80. Intellect (2009) ISBN 978-1-84150-277-9
15. Nielson, H., Nielson, F.: Semantics with applications: a formal introduction. John Wiley & Sons, Inc. (1992)
16. Pil, M.: Dynamic types and type dependent functions. In: Hammond, K., Davie, T., Clack, C. (eds.) IFL 1998. LNCS, vol. 1595, pp. 169–185. Springer, Heidelberg (1999)
17. Plasmeijer, R., Achten, P., Koopman, P.: iTasks: executable specifications of interactive work flow systems for the web. In: Hinze, R., Ramsey, N. (eds.) Proceedings of the International Conference on Functional Programming, ICFP 2007, Freiburg, Germany, pp. 141–152. ACM Press (2007)
18. Plasmeijer, R., Achten, P., Koopman, P.: Generic Functions Dynamically Applied. In: Porkoláb, Z., Pataki, N. (eds.) Proceedings of Workshop on Generative Technologies, WGT 2010, Paphos, Cyprus, March 27, pp. 1–2 (2010)
19. Plasmeijer, R., Lijnse, B., Michels, S., Achten, P., Koopman, P.: Task-Oriented Programming in a Pure Functional Language. In: Proceedings of the 2012 ACM SIGPLAN International Conference on Principles and Practice of Declarative Programming, PPDP 2012, Leuven, Belgium, pp. 195–206. ACM (September 2012)
20. Plasmeijer, R., van Eekelen, M.: Clean language report (version 2.1) (2002), http://clean.cs.ru.nl
21. Reynolds, J.: Defunctional interpreters for higher-order programming languages. Higher-Order and Symbolic Computation 11(4), 363–397 (1998)
22. Schönfinkel, M.: über die bausteine der mathematischen logik. Mathematische Annalen 92, 305–316 (1924)
23. Swierstra, W.: Data types à la carte. J. Funct. Program. 18(4), 423–436 (2008)
24. Syme, D., Neverov, G., Margetson, J.: Extensible pattern matching via a lightweight language extension. In: Proceedings of the 12th ACM SIGPLAN International Conference on Functional Programming, ICFP 2007, pp. 29–40. ACM, New York (2007)
25. Turner, D.A.: A new implementation technique for applicative languages. Software: Practice and Experience 9(1), 31–49 (1979)
26. Turner, D.A.: Miranda: a non-strict functional language with polymorphic types. In: Jouannaud, J.-P. (ed.) FPCA 1985. LNCS, vol. 201, pp. 1–16. Springer, Heidelberg (1985)
27. Wadler, P.: The expression problem. Message to Java-genericity Electronic Mailing List (November 1998)
28. Zenger, M., Odersky, M.: Extensible algebraic datatypes with defaults. SIGPLAN Not. 36(10), 241–252 (2001)

Why Functional Programming Matters to Me

Peter Achten

Institute for Computing and Information Sciences
Radboud University Nijmegen, P.O. Box 9010, 6500 GL Nijmegen, The Netherlands
p.achten@cs.ru.nl

Abstract. Functional programming advocates a style of programming in which the programmer seeks to find a sufficiently small, yet powerful, set of abstractions that capture an entire class of problems, and use these abstractions to solve a concrete problem. I illustrate this by means of a case study in which I implement the game *Trax*™. In this turn-based game two players attempt to create either a closed loop of a line of their own color, or make the line connect opposite ends of a tile set of some pre-scribed minimal dimensions. *Trax*™ is an attractive case because it has interesting computational problems, for which I use classical functional techniques, but also because it is a distributed multi-user application, for which I use the more recently developed *iTask* formalism.

1 Introduction

During my computer science studies at the University of Nijmegen my first exposure to functional programming was in 1987 – 1988 in a series of courses taught by Rinus Plasmeijer and Marko van Eekelen. Two appealing aspects of these courses were that we were asked to develop programs in David Turner's programming language *Miranda*[1] [1,2] and we were taught how functional programs can be compiled to efficient code using the intermediate language *Clean* (version 0.6 at that time). I learned to appreciate the beauty of functional programming (languages) and the semantic beauty of *term graph rewriting* [3,4] of which *Clean* was and still is an implementation.

In this essay I explain why ever since my first exposure to it, functional programming matters to me. As a starting point, I refer to John Hughes' seminal 1984 paper [5] in which he argues that functional programming matters because it offers *glue* with which to structure programs in an improved modular and reusable way, through the use of *higher order functions* and *lazy evaluation*. He sets the stage for how to go about solving a problem: *"It is also the goal for which functional programmers must strive - smaller and simpler and more general modules, glued together with the new glues we shall describe."* ([5], pg.4).

When solving a computational problem, higher order functions improve the level of abstraction of a solution because instead of solving one particular problem a solution for an entire class of problems is developed. Lazy evaluation is a

---

[1] *Miranda* is a trademark of Research Software Ltd.

P. Achten and P. Koopman (Eds.): Plasmeijer Festschrift, LNCS 8106, pp. 79–96, 2013.

consequence of the fundamental *referential transparency* property of pure functional programming languages. No matter in what order a computing device goes about determining the final result of my program, it is guaranteed to be uniquely defined if it exists. Hence, during problem solving I can concentrate on whether my program *has* a solution and worry much less *how* this solution is going to be computed. Developing a functional program feels a lot like playing a game in which I know that the programming language and compiler stick to the same rules as myself.

I demonstrate the style of functional programming by showing how to implement the game *Trax*™, which was brought to my attention by Rinus a couple of years ago. It is a 2-person turn-based tile game in which the players attempt to create either a closed loop of a line of their color (white or red) or make the line connect the far ends of the board that must have some minimal dimensions. Fig. 1 gives two examples of these winning states.

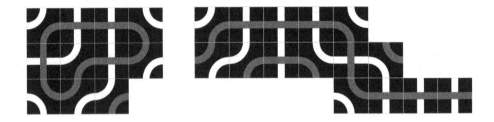

Fig. 1. Winning states for red: a closed loop (left) or a winning line (right)

Although *Trax*™ is a small and elegant game, it contains a number of sufficiently challenging problems, such as determining what tiles a player is allowed to place at which locations, determining if a configuration of tiles contains closed loops or winning lines, and how to prescribe and control the player actions. The specification of any game consists of two major parts: one part that introduces its *concepts and operations* – *what* the game is about – and one part that specifies what the *valid actions* are for each player – *how* to play the game –. The first part, described in Sect. 2, uses classical functional programming language features such as the above mentioned *higher order functions* and *lazy evaluation*, but also *algebraic and record data types* to model the domain of discourse accurately, *generic functions* [6,7] to avoid boiler plate specifications, and *list comprehensions* to deal elegantly with collections, finite maps, streams, and operations on them. The second part, described in Sect. 3, uses the *iTask* formalism [8,9]. Following John Hughes' adage, the peculiarities of *Trax*™ are abstracted from first, after which it is easier to actually implement the game. It turns out that this abstraction has striking similarities with the Racket big-bang approach [10,11]. I discuss this in more detail in Sect. 4. Finally, in Sect. 5, I hope to have explained to you why functional programming matters to me.

2   What Trax Is About

This part of the *Trax*™ specification deals with the elements of the game. I proceed bottom-up and start with basic elements (Sect. 2.1), show how to match two tiles (Sect. 2.2), create only correct tile configurations (Sect. 2.3), define the concept of mandatory moves (Sect. 2.4), and finally compute the sets of closed loops and winning lines (Sect. 2.5).

2.1   Tiles, Lines, Coordinates

In this section all basic elements are defined that are needed in the *Trax*™ specification. This amounts to modeling the entities as well as operations on these entities by means of data types and access functions.

A *Trax*™ tile has two sides, each displaying a white line and a red line. On the one side the lines cross each other, and on the other side they evade each other. These sides are placed in six different configurations (Fig. 2). A tile configuration

vertical   horizontal   northwest   northeast   southeast   southwest

Fig. 2. The six possible tile configurations

is modeled by defining which edges are connected by the red line:

```
:: Tile = { end1 :: !Edge, end2 :: !Edge }
:: Edge = North | East | South | West
```

The names `vertical`, `horizontal`, and so on are each of type `Tile` and identify the tiles as depicted in Fig. 2. For instance:

```
vertical = { end1 = North, end2 = South }
```

When modeling entities with data types it is a good habit to think right away which basic operations (such as comparison, arithmetic, printing, parsing) are sensible because this unlocks useful general purpose functions (such as sorting, searching, printing, storage via (de)serialization). These functions exist as higher-order polymorphic functions and overloaded functions. The basic operation is typically an argument of these general purpose functions (explicit in case of higher-order functions and implicit in case of overloaded functions). Many basic operations can be expressed by *induction on the structure of types* for which purpose generic functions can be deployed. The concise declarations:

```
derive gEq      Edge
derive gLexOrd  Edge
```

make structural equality and lexical ordering available for Edge values.

In this case study it is useful to be able to enumerate all elements of a finite (and small) domain. This is a typical example of a custom generic function:

```
generic gFDomain a :: [a]
gFDomain{|Bool|}         = [False,True]
gFDomain{|Char|}         = map toChar [0 .. 255]
gFDomain{|UNIT|}         = [UNIT]
gFDomain{|PAIR|}   dx dy = [PAIR x y \\ x <- dx, y <- dy]
gFDomain{|EITHER|} dx dy = map LEFT dx ++ map RIGHT dy
gFDomain{|CONS|}   dx    = map CONS   dx
gFDomain{|FIELD|}  dx    = map FIELD  dx
gFDomain{|OBJECT|} dx    = map OBJECT dx
```

A detailed explanation of this function is out of the scope of this essay. In a nutshell, the last six lines define the induction on the structure of types, and the first two lines define the meaning for the basic types Bool and Char. Enumeration of all Edge values can be derived from this recipe:

```
derive gFDomain Edge
```

For Tile values the generic scheme generates too many values, so the generic scheme must be overruled:

```
gFDomain{|Tile|} = map fromTuple [(West,East),(North,South),(North,West)
                                 ,(North,East),(South,East),(South,West)
                                 ]
```

Other sensible basic operations on Tile and Edge values are comparison (== and <), printing (toString), and taking the opposite value (~). Their definitions are straightforward:

```
instance == Tile
where    == {end1=a1,end2=a2} {end1=b1,end2=b2}
                    = (a1,a2) == (b1,b2) || (a2,a1) == (b1,b2)
instance toString Tile
where    toString tile = lookup1 tile [(horizontal,"horizontal")
                                      ,(vertical,  "vertical" )
                                      ,(northwest, "northwest" )
                                      ,(northeast, "northeast" )
                                      ,(southeast, "southeast" )
                                      ,(southwest, "southwest" )
                                      ]
instance ~ Tile
where    ~ tile        = lookup1 tile [(horizontal, vertical   )
                                      ,(vertical,   horizontal )
                                      ,(northwest,  southeast  )
                                      ,(northeast,  southwest  )
                                      ,(southwest,  northeast  )
                                      ,(southeast,  northwest  )
                                      ]
gEq      {|Tile|} t1 t2 = t1 == t2
```

```
instance ==     Edge where == e1 e2 =  e1 === e2
instance <      Edge where <  e1 e2 = (e1 =?= e2) === LT
instance ~      Edge where ~  e     = case e of
                                       North = South
                                       South = North
                                       West  = East
                                       East  = West
```

On many occasions, it is necessary to find a value v in a list of key-value pairs (k, v) using a key k. The lookup and lookup1 search functions capture this pattern (they are similar to the Haskell Prelude lookup function):

```
lookup          :: !k ![(k,v)] -> [v] | Eq k
lookup  key table = [v \\ (k,v) <- table | k == key]


lookup1         :: !k ![(k,v)] -> v | Eq k
lookup1 key table = hd (lookup key table)
```

The *line color* entity is defined in the same spirit as *edges*:

```
:: LineColor = RedLine | WhiteLine
derive   gFDomain LineColor
derive   gEq      LineColor
instance ==      LineColor where == c1 c2     = c1 === c2
instance ~       LineColor where ~ RedLine    = WhiteLine
                                 ~ WhiteLine  = RedLine
```

A configuration of tiles such as those depicted in Fig. 1 is called a *trax*. A simple way to model a trax is by listing the tiles and their coordinates:

```
:: Trax       = { tiles :: ![(Coordinate,Tile)] }
:: Coordinate = { col :: !Int, row :: !Int }


derive   gEq      Coordinate
derive   gLexOrd  Coordinate
derive   gPrint   Coordinate
instance ==      Coordinate where == c1 c2   = c1 === c2
instance <       Coordinate where <  c1 c2   = (c1 =?= c2) === LT
instance toString Coordinate where toString c = printToString c
instance zero     Coordinate where zero       = {col=zero, row=zero}
instance zero     Trax        where zero       = { tiles = [] }
instance ==      Trax         where == t1 t2  = sortBy fst_smaller t1.tiles
                                                ==
                                               sortBy fst_smaller t2.tiles
gEq{|Trax|} t1 t2                              = t1 == t2


col {col}                 = col
row {row}                 = row
fst_smaller (a,_) (b,_) = a < b
```

For navigation, we introduce functions to compute next coordinates:

```
north c  = {c & row = c.row-1}
south c  = {c & row = c.row+1}
west  c  = {c & col = c.col-1}
east  c  = {c & col = c.col+1}

go North = north
go South = south
go West  = west
go East  = east
```

Finally, of a Trax we need to know its current number of tiles (nr_of_tiles), the minimum and maximum values of the coordinates (bounds), the number of columns and rows that a trax occupies (dimension), and which tile, if any, can be found at a coordinate (tile_at). We wind up this section with their definitions:

```
nr_of_tiles :: !Trax -> Int
nr_of_tiles trax       = length trax.tiles

bounds :: !Trax -> (!(!Int,!Int), !(!Int,!Int))
bounds trax
| nr_of_tiles trax > 0 = ((minList cols,maxList cols), (minList rows,maxList rows))
| otherwise            = abort "bounds␣applied␣to␣empty␣set␣of␣tiles.\n"
where coords           = map fst trax.tiles
      cols             = map col coords
      rows             = map row coords

dimension :: !Trax -> (!Int,!Int)
dimension trax
| nr_of_tiles trax > 0 = (maxx - minx + 1, maxy - miny + 1)
| otherwise            = abort "dimension␣applied␣to␣empty␣set␣of␣tiles.\n"
where ((minx,maxx),(miny,maxy)) = bounds trax

tile_at :: !Trax !Coordinate -> Maybe Tile
tile_at trax c         = case lookup c trax.tiles of
                           [tile : _] = Just tile
                           none_found = Nothing
```

2.2   Matching of Tiles

A new tile can only be added to the current trax at a specific location if the colors of the lines at its edges *match* with those of the currently present neighbouring tiles. For this purpose, I need to know the line colors of an empty location and the line colors of a tile. If some edge at a coordinate is not next to a tile, there is no color (Nothing), otherwise the color is associated with the edge (Just color).

```
:: LineColors :== [(Edge,Maybe LineColor)]
```

The core function to determine line colors of empty locations and tiles is tile-colors which inspects a tile and returns all edge-color pairs. The derived function color_at_tile tells what color the tile has at some edge.

```
tilecolors :: !Tile -> LineColors
tilecolors tile = [(North,Just n),(East,Just e),(South,Just s),(West,Just w)]
where (n,e,s,w) = lookup1 tile [(horizontal,(WhiteLine,RedLine,WhiteLine,RedLine))
                               ,(vertical,  (RedLine,WhiteLine,RedLine,WhiteLine))
                               ,(northwest, (RedLine,WhiteLine,WhiteLine,RedLine))
                               ,(northeast, (RedLine,RedLine,WhiteLine,WhiteLine))
                               ,(southwest, (WhiteLine,WhiteLine,RedLine,RedLine))
                               ,(southeast, (WhiteLine,RedLine,RedLine,WhiteLine))
                               ]

color_at_tile :: !Edge !Tile -> LineColor
color_at_tile edge tile = fromJust (lookup1 edge (tilecolors tile))
```

The line colors of an empty location are assembled by looking at the line color of the opposite edge of a neighbour tile at each of its edges. In this definition, gFDomain{|*|} enumerates all Edge values, and gMap{|*->*|} is the functor that applies its first function argument to Just a value if there is one.

```
linecolors :: !Trax !Coordinate -> LineColors
linecolors trax c
    = [ (edge,gMap{|*->*|} (color_at_tile (~edge)) (tile_at trax (go edge c)))
      \\ edge <- gFDomain{|*|}
      ]
```

Two such line colors match if at each edge they either have the same color or if either one has no color:

```
linecolors_match :: !LineColors !LineColors -> Bool
linecolors_match a b       = and [match c1 c2 \\ (_,c1) <- sortBy fst_smaller a
                                               & (_,c2) <- sortBy fst_smaller b
                                 ]
where
    match (Just c1) (Just c2) = c1 == c2
    match _          _        = True
```

With the matching function, the collection of tiles that match particular line colors can be determined:

```
possible_tiles :: !LineColors -> [Tile]
possible_tiles colors
    = [tile \\ tile <- gFDomain{|*|} | linecolors_match colors (tilecolors tile)]
```

2.3   Correct Configurations by Construction

In a trax a new tile must be placed at one of the free edges. The collection of free coordinates is the union of all free neighbours of all tiles.

```
free_coordinates :: !Trax -> [Coordinate]
free_coordinates trax  = removeDupSortedList
                            (sort (flatten (map (free_neighbours trax)
                                                (map fst trax.tiles))))
```

```
free_neighbours :: !Trax !Coordinate -> [Coordinate]
free_neighbours trax c = [ c' \\ c' <- neighbours c | isNothing (tile_at trax c') ]

neighbours :: !Coordinate -> [Coordinate]
neighbours c           = map (flip go c) gFDomain{|*|}
```

Using the matching function and knowing valid free locations, it is now possible to safely add a tile to a trax:

```
add_tile :: !Coordinate !Tile !Trax -> Trax
add_tile c tile trax
| nr_of_tiles trax == 0 || isMember c (free_coordinates trax)
                            &&
                    linecolors_match (linecolors trax c) (tilecolors tile)
        = {trax & tiles = [(c,tile) : trax.tiles]}
| otherwise = trax
```

Starting with the zero instance of Trax and using only add_tile it is guaranteed that the trax is always in a valid configuration.

2.4   Mandatory Moves

After a player has added a tile to a trax all free locations that have no freedom as to what tile can be placed must be filled with their only tile candidate. These are the *mandatory moves*. It is sufficient to examine only the free neighbours of the placed tile. Those at which red or white occurs more than once belong to the collection of *mandatory tiles*.

```
mandatory_tiles :: !Trax !Coordinate -> [Coordinate]
mandatory_tiles trax c
    = case tile_at trax c of
        Nothing = []
        _       = [free \\ free <- free_neighbours trax c
                        | hasDup (filter isJust (map snd (linecolors trax free)))
                  ]
```

The mandatory moves need to be performed until there are no more mandatory tiles. Each move adds one tile to a trax. Hence, the structure of this algorithm is similar to the classic *fold* functions, except that each move may append extra list elements to be folded. Let's introduce *queued fold* functions that have an extra first function that determines which elements are to be appended:

```
qfoldl :: (a -> b -> [b]) (a -> b -> a) a ![b] -> a
qfoldl _ _ a []     = a
qfoldl f g a [b:bs] = let a' = g a b in qfoldl f g a' (bs ++ f a' b)

qfoldr :: (a -> b -> [b]) (b -> a -> a) a ![b] -> a
qfoldr _ _ a []     = a
qfoldr f g a [b:bs] = let a' = g b a in qfoldr f g a' (bs ++ f a' b)
```

The computation `mandatory_tiles` determines which free locations need to be filled, and is the first argument of the queued fold function. The function `move` updates the trax by adding the only possible tile at a given location.

```
mandatory_moves :: !Trax !Coordinate -> Trax
mandatory_moves trax c
| isNothing (tile_at trax c)
          = abort ("mandatory_moves:␣no␣tile␣at␣" <+++ c <+++ "\n")
| otherwise = qfoldl mandatory_tiles move trax (mandatory_tiles trax c)
where move trax filler
          = add_tile filler (hd (possible_tiles (linecolors trax filler))) trax
```

2.5   Closed Loops and Winning Lines

As illustrated in Fig. 1, a game of *Trax*™ ends as soon as a player constructs a *closed loop* or a *winning line*. In either case, it is necessary to extract a line of some given color from a trax. This results in a core function, `track`:

```
:: Line :== [Coordinate]

track :: !Trax !LineColor !Edge !Coordinate -> Line
track trax color edge c
    = case tile_at trax c of
        Nothing        = []
        Just tile      = let edge' = other_edge (perspective color tile) edge
                         in [c : track trax color (~edge') (go edge' c)]

perspective :: !LineColor !Tile -> Tile
perspective colour tile = if (colour == RedLine) tile (~tile)

other_edge :: !Tile !Edge -> Edge
other_edge tile edge    = if (edge == tile.end1) tile.end2 tile.end1
```

As explained at the start of Sect. 2.1, tiles are defined from the point of view of the red line. The function **perspective** gives the proper representation of a tile from the given perspective. The line is constructed by 'following' tiles at some edge and determining at which next edge to proceed. A line either terminates at an empty location or it does not terminate, in which case it is a closed loop. In the latter case, the **track** algorithm computes an infinitely long line, but thanks to lazy evaluation this is not a problem. Despite their infinite nature, closed loops can be detected and made finite:

```
is_loop :: !Line -> Bool
is_loop [c:cs]  = isMember c cs
is_loop empty   = False

cut_loop :: !Line -> Line
cut_loop [c:cs] = [c : takeWhile ((<>) c) cs]
```

Let's first find all closed loops in a trax and do this separately for the two colors:

```
loops :: !Trax -> [(LineColor,Line)]
loops trax = [(RedLine,  loop) \\ loop <- color_loops trax trax.tiles RedLine]
               ++
             [(WhiteLine,loop) \\ loop <- color_loops trax trax.tiles WhiteLine]
```

The basic idea is to inspect each tile in a trax, use **track** to follow it, and collect the found line if it is a loop. Before proceeding with another tile, the tiles from the line can be removed from the trax because they cannot be part of another line of the same color:

```
color_loops :: !Trax ![(Coordinate,Tile)] !LineColor -> [Line]
color_loops trax [(c,tile):tiles] color
| is_loop line       = [line : loops]
| otherwise          = loops
where line           = track trax color (start_edge tile color) c
      tiles'         = removeMembersBy (\(c,t) c' -> c == c') tiles (cut_loop line)
      loops          = color_loops trax tiles' color
color_loops _ [] _   = []


start_edge :: !Tile !LineColor -> Edge
start_edge tile color = choose (lookup1 tile [(horizontal,(West, North))
                                             ,(vertical,  (North,West ))
                                             ,(northwest, (North,South))
                                             ,(northeast, (North,South))
                                             ,(southeast, (South,North))
                                             ,(southwest, (South,North))
                                             ])
where choose         = if (color == RedLine) fst snd
```

Determining all winning lines in a trax is a matter of finding lines that connect either the far west with the far east or the far north with the far south. Obviously, an empty trax cannot contain a winning line:

```
winning_lines :: !Trax -> [(LineColor,Line)]
winning_lines trax
| nr_of_tiles trax == 0 = []
| otherwise             = winning_lines_at trax West ++ winning_lines_at trax North
```

The set of winning lines can be specified with a single list comprehension:

```
winning_lines_at :: !Trax !Edge -> [(LineColor,Line)]
winning_lines_at trax edge
| max - min + 1 < minimum_winning_line_length = []
| otherwise
  = [ (color,line)
    \\ (c,tile)   <- trax.tiles              | min == coord c
    , color       <- [color_at_tile edge tile]
    , line        <- [track trax color edge c] | not (is_loop line)
    , end         <- [last line]             | max == coord end
    , Just tile   <- [tile_at trax end]      | color_at_tile (~edge) tile == color
    ]
where ((minx,maxx),(miny,maxy)) = bounds trax
```

```
(min,max,coord)         = lookup1 edge [ (West, (minx,maxx,col))
                                       , (East, (maxx,minx,col))
                                       , (North,(miny,maxy,row))
                                       , (South,(maxy,miny,row))
                                       ]
```

If the trax is not big enough, then a winning line is not found. The first tile of a winning line must start at the given edge of the trax. Following its track must not result in a closed loop. Moreover, its last tile must be at the far other end of the trax, and also its line color must be at the opposite edge.

3 How to Play Trax

This part of the specification of *Trax*™ is concerned with coordinating and visualizing the actions of the two players. The *iTask* formalism is used to model this behavior. This is done in three stages: first, the concept of *turns* is formalized (Sect. 3.1); second, the peculiarities of *Trax*™ are abstracted away to create a general specification of n-player turn-based games (Sect. 3.2); third, the abstraction is used to implement a two player *Trax*™ game (Sect. 3.3).

3.1 Turns

A Turn is specified as follows:

```
:: Turn = { bound :: !Int, current :: !Int }
derive class iTask Turn
instance ==    Turn where == t1 t2   = t1 === t2
instance toInt Turn where toInt turn = turn.current

new bound | bound > 0     = {bound = bound, current = 0}
next turn=:{current,bound} = {turn & current = (current + 1)         rem bound}
prev turn=:{current,bound} = {turn & current = (current - 1 + bound) rem bound}
match nr turn              = nr == turn.current
```

Thus, in a game with a bounded number of players, each player is identified with a unique number. The functions **next** and **prev** identify the next and previous player, and with the function **match** a player can check whether her number matches with the current turn.

3.2 n-Person Turn-Based Games

To abstract away from the details of a specific n-person turn-based game, a collection of characteristics functions that operate on a state st is introduced:

```
:: Game st = { game   :: String
             , state  :: [User]    -> st
             , over   :: (Turn,st) -> Bool
             , winner :: (Turn,st) -> Task Turn
```

```
, move   :: (Turn,st) -> Task st
, board  :: (Turn,st) -> [HtmlTag]
}
```

The `game` field identifies the game. The `state` function makes the players known to the game state. The zero-based index position i in this list of users matches with a players turn in the game, so `match` i t is `True` only if it is player i's turn. When the game is `over`, the `winner` task declares which player has won. The `move` task prescribes a single move by the current player. Finally, the state is rendered by means of the `board` function.

Given these characteristic functions, it is possible to define the general structure of n-person turn-based games:

```
play_for_N :: !Int !(Game st) -> Task Turn | iTask st
play_for_N n game
   =            get_players n
      >>= \all -> withShared (new n,game.Game.state all)
         (\sharedGameSt -> anyTask [ user @: play_for_1 game nr sharedGameSt
                                   \\ user <- all & nr <- [0..]
                                   ])
```

A game is a task that returns a winner defined by the turn. First, n players are selected, using the `get_players` task that is described below. During the game, players can see the current state of the game at all times. Only one of them can actually change the state of the game. Hence, their task descriptions *share* the state, which is captured with the `withShared` task combinator. The player actions are controlled with the `play_for_1` task. The `anyTask` combinator evaluates all tasks in the list until one terminates.

The `get_players` task describes the selection of the participants, which is modeled as a multiple choice of all currently registered `users`:

```
get_players :: !Int -> Task [User]
get_players n
   = enterSharedMultipleChoice ("Select " <+++ max 0 n <+++ " players") [] users
      >>* [ WhenValid (\selection -> length selection == max 0 n) return
          , Always    ActionCancel (throw "Selection of players cancelled.")
          ]
```

Whenever the correct number of players are chosen, the list can be returned by the current user. It is also always possible to simply terminate this task, in which case the entire game terminates.

Each player basically does two things: gaze at the rendered game and make a move during their turn:

```
play_for_1 :: !(Game st) !Int !(Shared (Turn,st)) -> Task Turn | iTask st
play_for_1 game my_turn sharedGameSt
           = gaze ||- play
where gaze = viewSharedInformation ("Play with " <+++ my_turn)
                  [ ViewWith game.board ] sharedGameSt
      play = watch sharedGameSt
             >>* [ WhenValid game.over game.winner
```

```
             , WhenValid (\(turn,_)  -> match my_turn turn)
                         (\(turn,st) ->           game.move (turn,st)
                                       >>= \st -> set (next turn,st) sharedGameSt
                                       >>| play
                         )
             ]
```

Gazing at the game is realized with the viewSharedInformation task which uses the rendering function to display the current value of the shared game state. Not only the player gazes at the game, the task also monitors the current value of the shared game state, using the watch task function which merely echoes the current value of the shared game state. Whenever it is detected that the game is over, the winner is declared and the game terminates. At a player's turn, she performs the move task, the next player is chosen, and the game state is updated.

3.3   The Specialization of Trax

With the generalized framework for n-person turn-based games available, the specification of *Trax*™ amounts to deciding upon a suitable game state and characteristic functions. The game state needs to know the current trax and the persons who are playing the game.

```
:: TraxSt = { trax  :: !Trax, names :: ![User] }
derive class iTask TraxSt

initial_state :: ![User] -> TraxSt
initial_state users = { trax = zero, names = users }

play_trax :: Task Turn
play_trax              = play_for_N 2 { game   = "Trax"
                                      , state  = initial_state
                                      , over   = game_over
                                      , winner = declare_winner
                                      , move   = make_a_move
                                      , board  = show_board
                                      }
```

The game is over as soon as a closed loop or winning line exists:

```
game_over :: !(Turn,TraxSt) -> Bool
game_over (_,traxSt)
   = not (isEmpty (loops traxSt.trax ++ winning_lines traxSt.trax))
```

If the previous player managed to create a closed loop or winning line, then that player has won the game, otherwise the current player has won:

```
declare_winner :: !(Turn,TraxSt) -> Task Turn
declare_winner (turn,traxSt=:{trax,names})
   = viewInformation "The winner is:" [ViewWith (toString o (player names))] winner
where winners     = loops trax ++ winning_lines trax
      last_player = prev turn
```

```
winner      = if (isMember (toLineColor last_player) (map fst winners))
                 last_player turn
```

```
toLineColor turn = if (match 0 turn) RedLine WhiteLine
player [a,b] turn = if (match 0 turn) a b
```

Performing a move in the game amounts to letting the player choose a free coordinate, and then select a matching tile. This tile is added to the current trax, and the mandatory moves are performed.

```
make_a_move :: !(Turn,TraxSt) -> Task TraxSt
make_a_move (turn,traxSt=:{trax})
    =               chooseCoordinate trax
     >>= \new  -> chooseTile   new trax
     >>= \tile -> return {traxSt & trax = mandatory_moves
                                   (add_tile new tile trax) new}
```

At the start of the game, only the zero coordinate is free. In any other case, the player can select one of the available free coordinates:

```
chooseCoordinate :: !Trax -> Task Coordinate
chooseCoordinate trax
| nr_of_tiles trax == 0 = return zero
| otherwise            = enterChoice "Choose coordinate:"
                           [ChooseWith ChooseFromComboBox toString]
                           (free_coordinates trax)
```

At the start of the game, any tile can be selected. If the free coordinate is known, the player must select a tile that matches the line colors at that specific location.

```
chooseTile :: !Coordinate !Trax -> Task Tile
chooseTile c trax
    = enterChoice "Choose tile:"
        [ChooseWith ChooseFromRadioButtons (TileTag (16,16))]
        (if (nr_of_tiles trax == 0) gFDomain{|*|}
                      (possible_tiles (linecolors trax c))
        )
```

All that is left to do is to define a rendering of the trax. To this end, it is useful to specify a few helper definitions to create this *html*-based rendering:

```
TileTag :: !(!Int,!Int) !Tile -> HtmlTag
TileTag (w,h) tile = ImgTag [ SrcAttr    ("/" <+++ toString tile <+++ ".png")
                            , WidthAttr  (toString w)
                            , HeightAttr (toString h)
                            ]
tr               = TrTag []
td               = TdTag []
h3   x           = H3Tag [] [text x]
text x           = TdTag [AlignAttr "center"] [Text (toString x)]
```

In the *iTask* architecture, a task can place additional resources in a folder named *Static*. For each of the possible tiles, it contains a *.png* file (in fact, the ones of

Fig. 2). The `TileTag` function generates an image tag that displays this file with suitable dimensions. With these helper definitions, the trax is rendered as a *html* table. A cell displays either a tile, or the coordinate of a free location, or nothing at all. In addition, the name of the current player is displayed.

```
show_board :: !(Turn,TraxSt) -> [HtmlTag]
show_board (turn,traxSt=:{trax,names})
| nr_of_tiles trax == 0 = [h3 ("Select␣any␣tile,␣" <+++ current_player)]
| otherwise             = [h3 current_player, board]
where board             = TableTag [BorderAttr "0"]
                              [ tr [ cell {col=minx + x - 1,row=miny + y - 1}
                                     \\ x <- [0 .. nrcol + 1]
                                     ]
                                \\ y <- [0 .. nrrow + 1]
                                ]
      cell c                = case tile_at trax c of
                                  Nothing  = if (isMember c free) (text c) (text "")
                                  Just tile = td [TileTag (42,42) tile]
      current_player      = player names turn
      free                = free_coordinates trax
      (nrcol,nrrow)       = dimension         trax
      ((minx,maxx),(miny,maxy)) = bounds       trax
```

4   Related Work

The *n*-person turn-based game abstraction that is described in Sect. 3.2 bears a striking similarity with the `big-bang` abstraction that is provided in the *Racket world approach* [10]. This approach is designed to lower the threshold for beginning programmers to create interactive applications [12,11]. The key element of this abstraction is the `big-bang` expression:

(**big-bang** *state-expr clause*⁺)

in which *state-expr* represents the initial state value that is shared in the world program (similar to the `st` type parameter of the `Game st` record) and *clause* is a tagged list that specifies the attributes and event handlers of the world program:

```
clause  =  (on-tick     tick-expr)
        |  (on-tick     tick-expr rate-expr)
        |  (on-tick     tick-expr rate-expr limit-expr)
        |  (on-key      key-expr)
        |  (on-pad      pad-expr)
        |  (on-release  release-expr)
        |  (on-mouse    mouse-expr)
        |  (to-draw     draw-expr)
        |  (to-draw     draw-expr width-expr height-expr)
        |  (stop-when   stop-expr)
        |  (stop-when   stop-expr last-scene-expr)
        |  (check-with  world?-expr)
```

```
|  (record?     r-expr)
|  (state       boolean-expr)
|  (on-receive rec-expr)
|  (register    IP-expr)
|  (name        name-expr)
```

The event handlers are only concerned with the logical state of the world program and can be expressed as pure functions. For instance, the *tick-expr* of the on-tick clause is a pure function that computes a new state from the current one. The clause list must contain at least one to-draw member: *draw-expr* is a function that computes an image from the current state. Each time a new state is computed, this function is evaluated to create a new rendering of the game. In the n-person turn-based Game st abstraction, this corresponds with the board function, except that the latter generates a *html* rendering. The *stop-expr* of the stop-when clause has a similar role as the over predicate of the game abstraction and the *name-expr* of the name clause corresponds with the game member.

Racket world programs can be part of a distributed application using the *universe* abstraction. In a nutshell, a world program registers itself on a *server* identified by *IP-expr*. Event handlers either compute only a new state, as described above, or a pair of a new state *and* a message of some type. In the latter case, the message is sent to the server. A world program can receive messages from the server via the on-receive *rec-expr* function. The final component to be defined is the *server* which keeps track of registered world programs and the messages that are sent. It can serve as a broadcasting unit, or inspect messages to decide to what other worlds these should be sent.

The *Racket* universe approach to create distributed applications differs from the *iTask* approach. The main difference is that in *iTask* task distribution is accomplished from within the task specification and that communication occurs via observing each other's task value and shared data. In the *Racket* universe, world applications are more or less independent applications that use explicit message passing and receiving for communication.

5   Why Functional Programming Matters to Me

The case study in sections 2 and 3 shows that the glue that was identified by John Hughes is put to good use: higher order functions and lazy evaluation are used throughout the specification. This is also the case for other functional language features: list comprehensions deal with sets, lists, and streams in a uniform manner, the type class system unlocks useful functions for dedicated model data types, and generic functions capture type-dependent functionality in a single definition. However, having these language features available in a functional language only partially answers the question why functional programming matters to me. The other part of the answer concerns their impact on the way they help me to *solve problems*. Regardless of the programming paradigm, when solving a programming problem, I need to answer questions about that problem. I illustrate this in terms of the case study. The first kind of question is always about the entities of the problem domain:

1. What are the entities in a game of *Trax*™?

The answer is a collection of data types and their basic operations (most of them were defined in Sect. 2.1). Except for the choice to use streams to represent closed loops (Sect. 2.5), the data types in the case study are likely to result in similar representations in other programming languages and paradigms.

The second kind of question investigates the relation between these entities:

2. Which are the line colors of a (possibly empty) location in a trax?
3. When do two sets of line colors match?
4. Which tiles can be placed correctly at a free locations in a trax?
5. What trax results from performing the mandatory moves in a trax?
6. Which closed loops and winning lines does a trax contain?

The key observation is that these questions want to discover the relation between the entities and a well-defined result: this is exactly what functions and functional programming are about. *Functions are computable answers.* (Sections 2.2 – 2.5.)

The third kind of question investigates the relation with the end-users:

7. What is the order in which players take turns?
8. What is a player allowed to do?
9. When is a game of *Trax*™ over and who is the winner?

They investigate the concerted action between computable functions and user actions: this is exactly what tasks and *iTask* is about. Therefore, by specifying the corresponding tasks, you make the entities and functions tangible for users in the form of an executable application (Sect. 3).

Functional programming matters to me because it is a way of thinking and speaking that helps me to give the right answers to the right questions when solving computational problems.

Acknowledgements. I thank Pieter Koopman and Bas Lijnse for their advice during this case study. The reviewer's constructive comments have helped to greatly improve this essay. Finally, I thank Rinus for sharing his passion for functional programming, teaching, research, music, comic books, and elegant games.

References

1. Turner, D.A.: Miranda: A non-strict functional language with polymorphic types. In: Jouannaud, J.-P. (ed.) FPCA 1985. LNCS, vol. 201, pp. 1–16. Springer, Heidelberg (1985)
2. Turner, D.: An overview of Miranda. SIGPLAN Notices 21(12), 158–166 (1986)
3. Barendregt, H., van Eekelen, M., Glauert, J., Kennaway, J., Plasmeijer, M., Sleep, M.: Term graph rewriting. In: de Bakker, J.W., Nijman, A.J., Treleaven, P.C. (eds.) PARLE 1987. LNCS, vol. 259, pp. 141–158. Springer, Heidelberg (1987)

4. Barendregt, H., van Eekelen, M., Glauert, J., Kennaway, J., Plasmeijer, M., Sleep, M.: Towards an intermediate language based on graph rewriting. In: de Bakker, J.W., Nijman, A.J., Treleaven, P.C. (eds.) PARLE 1987. LNCS, vol. 259, pp. 159–175. Springer, Heidelberg (1987)
5. Hughes, J.: Why functional programming matters. Computer Journal 32(2), 98–107 (1989)
6. Hinze, R.: A new approach to generic functional programming. In: Reps, T. (ed.) Proceedings of the 27th International Symposium on Principles of Programming Languages, POPL 2000, Boston, MA, USA, pp. 119–132. ACM Press (2000)
7. Alimarine, A.: Generic Functional Programming - Conceptual Design, Implementation and Applications. PhD thesis, Radboud University Nijmegen (2005) ISBN 3-540-67658-9
8. Plasmeijer, R., Achten, P., Koopman, P.: iTasks: executable specifications of interactive work flow systems for the web. In: Hinze, R., Ramsey, N. (eds.) Proceedings of the International Conference on Functional Programming, ICFP 2007, Freiburg, Germany, pp. 141–152. ACM Press (2007)
9. Plasmeijer, R., Lijnse, B., Michels, S., Achten, P., Koopman, P.: Task-Oriented Programming in a Pure Functional Language. In: Proceedings of the 2012 ACM SIGPLAN International Conference on Principles and Practice of Declarative Programming, PPDP 2012, Leuven, Belgium, pp. 195–206. ACM (September 2012)
10. Felleisen, M., Findler, R., Flatt, M., Krishnamurthi, S.: How to Design Programs, 2nd edn. MIT Press (2012), http://www.ccs.neu.edu/home/matthias/HtDP2e/
11. Morazán, M.T.: Functional Video Games in the CS1 Classroom. In: Page, R., Horváth, Z., Zsók, V. (eds.) TFP 2010. LNCS, vol. 6546, pp. 166–183. Springer, Heidelberg (2011)
12. Felleisen, M., Findler, R., Flatt, M., Krishnamurthi, S.: A Functional I/O System * or, Fun for Freshman Kids. In: Proceedings International Conference on Functional Programming, ICFP 2009, Edinburgh, Scotland, UK. ACM Press (2009)

Clocks for Functional Programs[*]

Jörg Endrullis[1], Dimitri Hendriks[1],
Jan Willem Klop[1,2], and Andrew Polonsky[1,3]

[1] VU University Amsterdam, Department of Computer Science
[2] Centrum Wiskunde & Informatica (CWI)
[3] Radboud Universiteit Nijmegen
{j.endrullis,r.d.a.hendriks,j.w.klop,a.polonsky}@vu.nl

Dedicated to Rinus Plasmeijer for his 61st birthday:
to a clean functional programmer, in friendship and admiration.

1 Introduction

Of the current authors the oldest one remembers with fondness numerous meetings with Rinus from the ancient times of the European Basic Research Actions and from personal tutorials in Nijmegen about λ-terms, term graphs and processes on the one hand, and the practice of functional programming in the Clean environment on the other hand.

The youngest author as well remembers with gratitude the AFP 2008 summer school on functional programming that Rinus had helped organize. Taking place in the idyllic Center Parcs, in Boxmeer, this gratifying experience from his PhD years has left behind a number of wonderful memories.

Now that the clock for Rinus himself has arrived at 61 years, we like to offer him the present elaboration of an inherent clock mechanism in functional programs. A clock mechanism that is not only interesting from the perspective of curiosity, but that serves two very concrete goals.

The first goal is to *distinguish* between different functional programs, different in the sense that they are not convertible to each other by some canonical conversion rules, such as β-reduction and the ensuing convertibility. The usual procedure to establish such a discrimination is using the infinite unfolding, known as the Böhm Tree; if their respective Böhm Trees are different, then the programs are also inconvertible in the finite sense. But what if their Böhm Trees are identical? Then the classical Böhm Tree discrimination argument is not applicable. But here our clock method steps in: by means of an annotated version of Böhm Trees we often can observe a difference in the tempo in which the Böhm Trees are generated, and if this tempo is sufficiently different (in a sense to be made precise), the original λ-terms (or functional programs) are inconvertible in the finite sense.

[*] The research has been partially funded by the Netherlands Organization for Scientific Research (NWO) under grant numbers 612.000.934, 639.021.020, and 612.001.002.

P. Achten and P. Koopman (Eds.): Plasmeijer Festschrift, LNCS 8106, pp. 97–126, 2013.

So the discrimination can often be done on the basis of a difference in clock velocity, but note that we do not mean the clock velocity in the actual computer implementation, but a clock on a much higher level, on the level of the λ-terms that ultimately encode the program.

The second concrete goal is to use the inherent clock phenomenon described below for *optimization* of programs, or rather to measure the extent of such an optimization. To give a quick example: the two simplest fixed point combinators are the one of Church, Y_0, and the one of Turing, Y_1. While they perform similarly, in the sense that $Y_0 x$ and $Y_1 x$ both reduce to the infinite iteration of x written as x^ω, the first one delivers its output, the fixed point, in a faster tempo than the second one.

In fact we will not go all the way back to good old λ-calculus to describe the functional programs. First, we will adopt the *simply typed* version, because this conforms much more to actual functional programming practice than pure, untyped λ-terms would.

The second adaptation is that we consider the *extension* with the well-known μ-operator for recursion. This is equivalent with using a fixed point combinator, but it is more direct, and it again conforms more to actual functional programming practice as it can be considered to be tantamount to the letrec operator.

In previous work [EHK10, EHKP12] we have worked out this inherent clock feature in pure λ-terms. As the ticks of the clock, *head reduction steps* were used, that lead one from one node in the Böhm Tree being developed to a successor node. It is a simple observation that contracting internal redexes in a term can only diminish the number of head redexes needed to reach the next node. In other words, reducing a term can only speed-up its internal clock.

In subsequent work [EHKP13], we have internalized this 'external' counting of the head steps, in favour of a τ-operator, like the silent step in process theory. In the present work we do the same, but now with an additional ι-step to count applications of the μ-rules. In fact, we work with *weak head reduction*.

We include some examples suggesting the use of the clock method for simply typed $\lambda\mu$-terms, and thereby for functional programs.

As a historical note, we mention that [NI89] already proposed to use the number of root steps used in evaluating a term in a term rewriting system as a measure of efficiency in comparing terms.

2   A Glossary of Requisites

We will start with a glossary of preliminary notions. For general reference to λ-calculus we refer to [Bar84], for typed versions of λ-calculus to [BDS13, HS08]. For a general reference to term rewriting systems we refer to [BN98, Ter03]. For an introduction to functional programming, see [Hut07, dMJB$^+$]. Rather than repeat in detail much of what these general references offer, we present several of the prerequisites for understanding this paper in the form of a somewhat informal glossary. Some basic familiarity with λ-calculus and term rewriting systems is assumed.

Lambda Calculus. The kernel of all calculi figuring in this paper (except for the $\lambda\mu$-calculus introduced later) will be the $\lambda\beta$-calculus with as single reduction rule the β-reduction rule $(\lambda x.M)N \to_\beta M[x := N]$. Here $x \in \mathcal{X}$, the set of variables. This rule may be applied in a context, a λ-term $C[]$ with a hole, resulting in one-step β-reduction $C[\lambda x.M] \to_\beta C[M[x := M]]$. The transitive-reflexive closure of $\to_\beta$ is written as $\twoheadrightarrow_\beta$ and the equivalence relation generated by $\to_\beta$, also called β-convertibility, is $=_\beta$. The $\lambda\beta$-calculus has $Ter(\lambda)$ as set of terms. It has the Church–Rosser or confluence property (CR) stating that for $M =_\beta N$ there is a common reduct L such that $M \twoheadrightarrow_\beta L \twoheadleftarrow_\beta N$. A normal form is a term N that does not admit $\to_\beta$-steps. The property SN, strong normalization, stating that there are no infinite reduction sequences $M_0 \to_\beta M_1 \to_\beta \ldots$ does not hold in $\lambda\beta$, and neither does WN, weak normalization, stating that every $M \in Ter(\lambda\beta)$ has (reduces to) a normal form. Both $\neg$SN and $\neg$WN are witnessed by the 'unsolvable' term $\Omega \equiv \omega\omega$ with $\omega \equiv (\lambda x.xx)$ which has a β-loop to itself: $\Omega \to_\beta \Omega$. Here '$\equiv$' denotes syntactic identity, to be distinguished from $=_\beta$.

Fixed Point Combinators. An fpc, fixed point combinator, is a term $Y \in Ter(\lambda\beta)$ such that $Yx =_\beta x(Yx)$. The two simplest fpc's are Curry's fpc $Y_0 \equiv \lambda f.\omega_f\omega_f$ where $\omega_f \equiv \lambda x.f(xx)$, and Turing's fpc $Y_1 \equiv \theta\theta$ where $\theta \equiv \lambda ab.b(aab)$. Using the term $\delta \equiv \lambda ab.b(ab)$, called the Owl in [Smu85], we have $Y_0\delta =_\beta Y_1$.

An fpc Y is called reducing if not only $Yx =_\beta x(Yx)$, but even $Yx \twoheadrightarrow_\beta x(Yx)$. So Y_1 is reducing, but Y_0 is not. If Y is a reducing fpc, also $Y\delta$ is one.

Of interest are also weak fpcs, or wfpcs. These are terms $Z \in Ter(\lambda\beta)$ such that $Zx = x(Z'x)$ where Z' is again a wfpc. (This is a coinductive definition.) So any fpc is a wfpc but not conversely. An example of such a 'proper' wfpc is $A(BAB)$ where $B = \lambda xyz.x(yz)$ and $A \equiv B\omega$ given by Statman, see [EHK12].

Unsolvable Terms. are terms that cannot be evaluated to positive information, to a hnf. The ur-example is Ω as above. A $\lambda\beta$-term is unsolvable if it has no hnf, which is the case if it admits an infinite reduction containing infinitely many head reduction steps, i.e., where a head redex R is contracted (reduced); such a redex R occurs in a term $\lambda\boldsymbol{x}.R\boldsymbol{N}$ where $\boldsymbol{x}$ is a vector of variables, and $\boldsymbol{N}$ a vector of terms.

Böhm Trees. are the infinite expansions of λ-terms, analogous to expansions in number theory such as $\pi = 3.1415926535\ldots$ For Böhm Trees (BTs) there are two kinds of building blocks; positive information carriers which have the form of a head normal form (hnf) $\lambda\boldsymbol{x}.y\square\ldots\square$, where $\boldsymbol{x}, y \in \mathcal{X}$, the set of variables, and $\square\ldots\square$ are empty places; and negative information carriers (no information) of the form $\bot$ or Ω. Definition 13 gives a more precise description suitable for the present setting.

Next to the Böhm Tree semantics there is a slightly more refined semantics, based on Lévy–Longo Trees (LLTs), and a third and finest semantics based on Berarducci Trees (BeTs). See [EHK12].

Term Rewriting Systems. This name is most often reserved for first-order rewrite systems, where by definition there is no binding of variables as in the β-reduction rule above, or the μ-reduction rule $\mu x.t \to_\mu t[x := \mu x.t]$. Sometimes the name is used in a generic sense to include all term rewrite systems, first-order but also higher-order; but not e.g. term graph rewrite systems where terms have been generalized to term graphs.

Some Notations. As said, $\twoheadrightarrow$ or $\to^*$ denotes the transitive-reflexive closure of a rewrite relation $\to$; $\twoheadrightarrow$ always denotes infinitary reduction (of arbitrary ordinal length). For the substitution operation we use the notation $s[x := t]$ to indicate that in term s all free occurrences of x are replaced by the term t.

Types. We will be very short about types and refer to the before mentioned standard reference works. Only this: we mostly use (as in [HS08]) the Church style of writing the simple types, as superscripts A of subterms s, so as s^A, rather than the judgments $s : A$. Only occasionally we will have to mention a typing as a judgment.

Infinitary Rewriting. A development in term rewriting and λ-calculus which has been elaborated in a relatively late stage, is that of infinitary rewriting, which emerges naturally, and gives a domain where infinite Böhm Trees are at home. The fpc $\mathsf{Y}_1 \equiv \theta\theta$ where $\theta \equiv \lambda ab.b(aab)$ already gives the idea:

$$\mathsf{Y}_1 x \to^2 x(\mathsf{Y}_1 x) \to^2 x(x(\mathsf{Y}_1 x)) \to^2 x^3(\mathsf{Y}_1 x) \twoheadrightarrow x^n(\mathsf{Y}_1 x) \twoheadrightarrow \ldots$$

The natural extension here is to go on and continue rewriting to a limit $x^\omega \equiv x(x(x(...)))$, so that we have $\mathsf{Y}_1 x \twoheadrightarrow x^\omega$. Here $\twoheadrightarrow$ stands for an infinite reduction, in this case of length ω; we therefore also write $\mathsf{Y}_1 x \to^\omega x^\omega$. In general we may have reductions $s \to^\alpha t$ for every countable ordinal α. Infinitary rewriting requires a limit notion, which is that of ordinary Cauchy convergence with respect to the usual metric distance d. That is to say, $\mathrm{d}(s, t) = 2^{-n}$ if n is the first level where the formation term trees of s and t differ. There is however one extra requirement that is put on top of Cauchy convergence: when approaching a limit ordinal such as ω, $\omega \cdot 2$, ω^2, ϵ_0, ..., the 'action' has to go down all the way, more precisely, the depth of the contracted redexes has to tend to ∞. Note that this is indeed the case in the example $\mathsf{Y}_1 x \twoheadrightarrow x^\omega$ above. But note also that we do not have $\Omega \to^\omega \Omega$, as here the action stays confined at the top, the root. (A trivial subtlety: we do have $\Omega \twoheadrightarrow \Omega$, because we have $\twoheadrightarrow \supseteq \to \twoheadrightarrow \supseteq \equiv$: infinitary rewriting comprises finitary rewriting which in turn comprises identity.)

Let us mention that in recent work [EHH$^+$13] a coinductive definition of infinitary rewriting $\twoheadrightarrow$ is given that is 'coordinate-free', i.e., avoids all mention of ordinals and depth of redex contractions, which has the virtue of making the notion of infinitary rewriting much more amenable to an automated treatment and a formalization in theorem provers.

Main Syntactic Properties. For finite rewriting as in $\lambda\beta$-calculus, $\lambda\beta\mu$-calculus or their simply typed versions, but also in first-order term rewriting systems (without bound variables) we have some important syntactic properties of the rewrite or reduction relation. These are:

CR the confluence property, $\twoheadleftarrow \cdot \twoheadrightarrow \subseteq \twoheadrightarrow \cdot \twoheadleftarrow$;

PML Parallel Moves Lemma $\leftarrow \cdot \twoheadrightarrow \subseteq \twoheadrightarrow \cdot \twoheadleftarrow$;

WN weak normalization: every term has (reduces to) a normal form;

SN strong normalization: every reduction ends in a normal form when prolonged long enough; otherwise said, there are no infinite reductions;

UN every term has at most one normal form.

The infinitary counterparts of these properties are:

CR^∞ the infinitary confluence property, $\twoheadleftarrow\!\!\!\!\twoheadleftarrow \cdot \twoheadrightarrow\!\!\!\!\twoheadrightarrow \subseteq \twoheadrightarrow\!\!\!\!\twoheadrightarrow \cdot \twoheadleftarrow\!\!\!\!\twoheadleftarrow$;

PML^∞ the infinitary Parallel Moves Lemma, $\leftarrow \cdot \twoheadrightarrow\!\!\!\!\twoheadrightarrow \subseteq \twoheadrightarrow\!\!\!\!\twoheadrightarrow \cdot \twoheadleftarrow\!\!\!\!\twoheadleftarrow$;

WN^∞ every term has a (possibly infinite) normal form;

SN^∞ every reduction sequence, when prolonged long enough, even infinitarily, will strongly converge to a (possibly infinite) normal form; in other words, there are no diverging reductions;

UN^∞ every term has at most one (possibly infinite) normal form. Here 'has' means 'reduces to' ($\twoheadrightarrow$).

Miscellaneous. Next to first-order rewrite systems (so without bound variables), and higher-order rewrite systems such as the calculi featuring in this paper which all involve bound variables (by λ or μ), we have a general notion of higher-order rewrite system, that unifies the afore-mentioned rewrite systems. These are the Combinatory Reduction Systems (CRSs), see [Ter03]. All rewrite systems in this paper belong to this general family. An important notion in such systems is 'orthogonality', meaning that the reduction rules do not overlap harmfully; there are no critical pairs (and moreover the rules must be left-linear, no duplicated variables in lefthand-sides of the rules). For such orthogonal CRSs (once called OCRSs in this paper), we have the confluence property CR, and hence also the property UN, unique normal forms. The family of orthogonal CRSs also includes by definition subcalculi, where (e.g.) a typing restriction is adopted. For such subcalculi the CR property also holds.

3   A Cube of Calculi

The $\lambda\beta$-calculus can be considered to be the mother of all term rewriting systems—it is the origin corner of our cube of calculi in Figure 1. But it is not

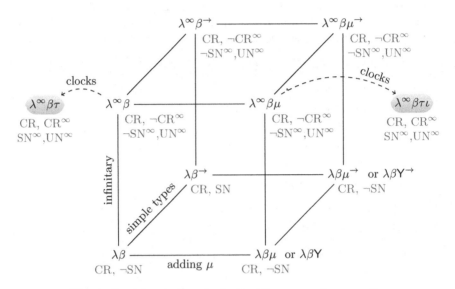

Fig. 1. Partial ordering of calculi with some main properties

the 'main calculus' of this paper, which is the simply typed λ-calculus with the β-rule and extended with the variable binding operator μ and the corresponding reduction rule. We use the notation $\lambda\beta\mu^{\rightarrow}$ for this λ-calculus. Writing $Ter(\lambda)$ for the set of λ-terms we first extend the terms to $Ter(\lambda\mu)$, and next restrict the terms to the typable ones, $Ter(\lambda\mu^{\rightarrow})$, according to the definition below. Let us note that, for simplicity, in this paper we do not consider the η-reduction rule (except for a brief appearance in Section 7.3).

The interest of the $\lambda\beta\mu^{\rightarrow}$-calculus is that it has a clear relevance for actual functional programming, both by the discipline of simple typing, and by the inclusion of the μ-operator which provides an abstraction over particular implementations of the fixed point combinators, so that a term which is defined by recursive equations can be analyzed without reference to the particular fixed point combinator used to construct the solutions.

The $\lambda\beta\mu^{\rightarrow}$-calculus will be our platform for an extension with a clock mechanism (by τ and ι ticks of a clock) that will enable us to discriminate between many fixed point combinators and the recursive solutions they facilitate. Thus we can discriminate terms with general "periodic" behavior. For example, passing to the $\lambda\beta\mu^{\rightarrow}$-calculus will allow us to discriminate functional programs defined by `letrec` expressions that have the same extensional behavior but cannot be converted from one to another by a finite sequence of syntactic rewrite steps.

As hinted at in the introduction, while the output of such programs could well be the same, their computation may often be distinguished by considering the time it takes to produce a value from one recursive step to the next one.

First, let us present the formal definition. The cube of calculi in Figure 1 displays the finitary and infinitary calculi that we define and study.

The following system is obtained by extending the simply typed lambda calculus ($\lambda\beta^{\rightarrow}$) with a term constructor $\mu x^A.t$ together with corresponding typing and reduction rules.

Types:

$$\mathbb{T} ::= \alpha \mid \mathbb{T} \rightarrow \mathbb{T}$$

Terms:

$$t ::= x \mid t\,t \mid \lambda x^{\mathbb{T}}.t \mid \mu x^{\mathbb{T}}.t$$

Typing:

$$\frac{(x^A) \in \Gamma}{\Gamma \vdash x^A} \qquad \frac{\Gamma \vdash s^{A \rightarrow B} \quad \Gamma \vdash t^A}{\Gamma \vdash (st)^B} \qquad \frac{\Gamma, x^A \vdash t^B}{\Gamma \vdash (\lambda x^A.t)^{A \rightarrow B}} \qquad \frac{\Gamma, x^A \vdash t^A}{\Gamma \vdash (\mu x^A.t)^A}$$

Reduction:

$$\beta : \quad (\lambda x^A.s)t \rightarrow s[x := t]$$
$$\mu : \quad \mu x^A.t \rightarrow t[x := \mu x^A.t]$$

Having made a formal acquaintance with the main calculus $\lambda\beta\mu^{\rightarrow}$ of our paper, in the cube of Figure 1 located at the corner 110, let us look at the whole cube. In the origin 000 we find the $\lambda\beta$-calculus. From there new calculi are obtained in three directions:

(i) by adding μ and its reduction rule (x-direction);
(ii) by adopting the simple type discipline (y-direction);
(iii) and by making the calculus infinitary by a coinductive reading of all the definitions (z-direction).

Furthermore there are some related calculi outside of this cube. The result is a family of a dozen related λ-calculi as in Table 1.

Remark 1. (i) One could also consider the *untyped* $\lambda\beta\mu$-calculus as the main calculus of our exposition, but we prefer the typed version because it admits natural intuitive interpretation in terms of Scott domains [Plo77], and rules out pathological terms such as $\mu x.xx$, which has Böhm Tree

$$@(@(@..)(@..))(@..)$$

Its term tree is depicted in Figure 2.

Table 1. Family of λ-calculi

position	notation	name
000	$\lambda\beta$	$\lambda\beta$-calculus
001	$\lambda^\infty\beta$	infinitary $\lambda\beta$-calculus
010	$\lambda\beta^\rightarrow$	simply typed $\lambda\beta$-calculus
011	$\lambda^\infty\beta^\rightarrow$	infinitary simply typed $\lambda\beta$-calculus
100	$\lambda\beta\mu$	$\lambda\beta\mu$-calculus
101	$\lambda^\infty\beta\mu$	infinitary $\lambda\beta\mu$-calculus
110	$\lambda\beta\mu^\rightarrow$	simply typed $\lambda\beta\mu$-calculus
111	$\lambda^\infty\beta\mu^\rightarrow$	infinitary simply typed $\lambda\beta\mu$-calculus
	$\lambda\beta Y$	$\lambda\beta Y$-calculus
	$\lambda\beta Y^\rightarrow$	simply typed $\lambda\beta Y$-calculus
	$\lambda^\infty\beta\tau^{(\rightarrow)}$	(simply typed) clocked $\lambda\beta$-calculus
	$\lambda^\infty\beta\mu\tau\iota^{(\rightarrow)}$	(simply typed) clocked $\lambda\beta\mu$-calculus
	$\lambda\mu$	$\lambda\mu$-calculus

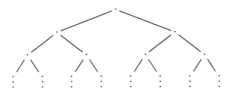

Fig. 2. Term tree of the Böhm Tree of $\mu x.xx$

(ii) The simply typed $\lambda\beta\mu^\rightarrow$-calculus is very interesting, as it harmoniously combines some seemingly opposite features. On the one hand, the presence of the simple type discipline seems to forbid infinite reductions, as it does in the sub-calculus $\lambda\beta^\rightarrow$, the simply typed $\lambda\beta$-calculus. However, then we also loose fixed point combinators (fpc's), as these all have by definition an infinite reduction. Now this loss is cured by reinstating fpc's by virtue of the μ-operator and the corresponding reduction rule. This simultaneous restriction and extension is still harmonious, in that it has the confluence property (CR). This is so because $\lambda\beta\mu^\rightarrow$ is a sub-calculus of an orthogonal CRS, namely the $\lambda\beta\mu$-calculus.

(iii) It is a rewarding exercise to check where the usual SN-proofs for simply typed lambda-calculus fail in the presence of the μ-operator. For the proof using multisets of degrees of redexes, the reason is that created redexes do not have a degree which is less complicated. What is the reason for failure of the other main type of SN proof via computability?

(iv) Another interesting aspect of this restricted-extended calculus, and some of its related calculi, is that its meta-theory hovers on the brink of decidability.

The related calculus $\lambda\beta Y$ has undecidable convertibility, but decidable unsolvability and normalizability [Sta02]. Presumably the same holds for the present calculus.

4   Variations of the Main Calculus

In this section we will describe some variations of the main calculus $\lambda\beta\mu^{\rightarrow}$, three finite calculi, and one infinitary extension. The three finite versions are well-known in practice; the infinite extension is less well-known, but provides a firm foundation for functional programming.

4.1   The $\lambda\beta Y$ Variant

Instead of the μ-constructor, we could instead assume the existence of a family of terms
$$Y_A^{(A\rightarrow A)\rightarrow A}$$
together with the reduction rule

$$Y:\qquad Y_A f \rightarrow f(Y_A f)$$

This system, when extended with a native type of natural numbers, is a Turing-complete programming language for functionals of higher types. It was introduced in 1966 by Platek [Pla84] in order to define higher-order computability in an "index-free" manner. Plotkin [Plo77] extensively studies the semantics of this calculus, culminating in the *full abstraction problem* for PCF. Bezem discusses $\lambda\beta Y$ in [BDS13, Ch. 5].

Without the type of natural numbers, Irina Bercovici [Ber85] shows that having a head normal form is decidable. Similarly, normalization and compactness (Böhm Tree finiteness) are decidable. Despite these results, Statman [Sta02] shows that the full word problem (convertibility with respect to the reduction rules β and Y) remains undecidable.

However, restricting to the lowest type level, and admitting only Y's of type $(0 \rightarrow 0) \rightarrow 0$, the word problem is solvable. Statman employs in the short proof of this fact an auxiliary reduction which is just our μ-reduction:

$$Y(\lambda x.s) \rightarrow s[x := Y(\lambda x.s)]$$

Our main calculus $\lambda\beta\mu^{\rightarrow}$ has an interesting sub-calculus, namely the one consisting of the fragment of only μ-binders, variables and applications. In our current notation it can be called $\lambda\mu$. So there is no β-reduction, only μ-reduction. Now one can ask whether this calculus has a solvable word problem, or in other words, whether its convertibility relation is decidable. Indeed this is the case. There are two sources for a proof of this fact: first, it is a corollary of Statman's result [Sta02] mentioned above, and second, it was also proved for the untyped setting in [EGKvO11].

For the rest of the paper, we will stick with the μ-constructor formulation of the fixed point lambda calculus, which is our main calculus $\lambda\beta\mu^{\rightarrow}$.

4.2   The `letrec` Variant

Another system of equal expressive power is that obtained by postulating the existence of solutions to arbitrary systems of equations of the form

$$x_1 = t_1[\boldsymbol{x}]$$
$$\vdots$$
$$x_n = t_n[\boldsymbol{x}]$$

That is, instead of formally adding a unary fixed point constructor, the language provides the ability to solve multiple fixed point equations *simultaneously*.

This idea is implemented by the `letrec` construction commonly found in functional programming languages such as `Clean` [dMJB+]. Its syntax is given as follows:

$$t ::= x \mid t\,t \mid \lambda x^A.t \mid \texttt{let } x_1{:=}t, \ldots, x_n{:=}t \texttt{ in } t$$

For convenience, we will write $(\texttt{let } \boldsymbol{x} := \boldsymbol{t} \texttt{ in } u)$ in place of

$$\texttt{let } x_1{:=}t_1, \ldots, x_n{:=}t_n \texttt{ in } u$$

Similarly, in the typing rule below, we will write $\boldsymbol{x}^{\boldsymbol{A}}$ in place of

$$x_1^{A_1}, \ldots, x_n^{A_n}$$

The typing rule is

$$\frac{\Gamma, \boldsymbol{x}^{\boldsymbol{A}} \vdash t_1^{A_1} \quad \cdots \quad \Gamma, \boldsymbol{x}^{\boldsymbol{A}} \vdash t_n^{A_n} \quad \Gamma, \boldsymbol{x}^{\boldsymbol{A}} \vdash u^B}{\Gamma \vdash (\texttt{let } \boldsymbol{x} := \boldsymbol{t} \texttt{ in } u)^B}$$

The computation of $(\texttt{let } \boldsymbol{x} := \boldsymbol{t} \texttt{ in } u)$ returns u in which occurrences of x_i get replaced by t_i, possibly creating new occurrences, which can subsequently be replaced again, and so on. As a rewrite rule, this can be formalized as

$$\texttt{let } \boldsymbol{x} := \boldsymbol{t} \texttt{ in } u \quad \to \quad u[x_i := (\texttt{let } \boldsymbol{x} := \boldsymbol{t} \texttt{ in } t_i)]_{i=1..n}$$

For our purposes, this rule is much less convenient to work with than that of the μ-constructor, hence we will stick with the original formulation. The two systems are mutually interpretable, although there are some subtleties related to the possibility of "horizontal sharing" (as it was called in [AK95]) in the `letrec` system which we will not investigate here. In any case, the `letrec` syntax is precisely what we find in `Clean`-like functional languages.

4.3   Simultaneous Fixed Point Solutions via the μ-Operator

Clearly, every $\lambda\mu$-term can be captured within the previous syntax: the expression $\mu x^A.t$ is represented by the single-variable expression $\texttt{let } x := t \texttt{ in } x$.

Going the other way, we can represent any term M defined by a simultaneous recursion system $(\texttt{let } \boldsymbol{x} := \boldsymbol{t}(\boldsymbol{x}) \texttt{ in } u)$ by a cascade of μ-expressions.

We show this by an example. Suppose we are a given a `letrec` expression

$$M = \text{let } x_1 = t_1(x_1, x_2, x_3)$$
$$x_2 = t_2(x_1, x_2, x_3)$$
$$x_3 = t_3(x_1, x_2, x_3)$$
$$\text{in}$$
$$u(x_1, x_2, x_3)$$

Define the terms

$$f_3(x_1, x_2) = \mu x_3.t_3(x_1, x_2, x_3)$$
$$f_2(x_1) = \mu x_2.t_2(x_1, x_2, f_3(x_1, x_2))$$
$$f_1 = \mu x_1.t_1(x_1, f_2(x_1), f_3(x_1, f_2(x_1)))$$

Finally, put

$$M^\mu = u(f_1, f_2(f_1), f_3(f_1, f_2(f_1)))$$

and it can be easily seen that M^μ the same extensional behavior as M (i.e., M^μ is bisimilar to M).

Convention 2. Using the previous technique of solving simultaneous recursive systems using the μ-operator, we will sometimes write

$$\mu \boldsymbol{x}^{\boldsymbol{A}}.\boldsymbol{t}(x_1, \ldots, x_n)$$

for the corresponding μ-term solving the system given in the matrix. Here we take as given that $t_i(x_1^{A_1}, \ldots, x_n^{A_n})$ has type A_i.

Example 3. Here are some examples of $\lambda\mu^\rightarrow$-terms.

(i) The simplest meaningful example is the definition of a fixed point combinator by way of the μ-notation. Put

$$Y = \lambda f^{A \to A}.\mu y^A.fy$$

Then $Yf =_{\beta\mu} f(Yf)$. We have the head reduction

$$Yf \to \mu y.fy \to f(\mu y.fy) \to f(f(\mu y.fy)) \to \cdots \to f^n(\mu y.fy) \to \cdots$$

(Here and throughout, we spare annotation of the types of bound variables when they are unambiguously determined by the immediate context.)

(ii) Applying the above term to the identity yields the canonical unsolvable $\lambda\mu$-term for any type A:

$$\perp_A = \mu x^A.x$$

which has the head reduction

$$\perp \to \perp \to \cdots$$

See [EGKvO11] for a characterization of all unsolvables arising in the $\lambda\mu$-calculus, e.g., $\mu xyz.x$ and $\mu xyz.y$ are examples.

4.4   Infinitary Calculi

It is interesting to extend $\lambda\beta\mu^{\rightarrow}$ to include infinitary rewriting. We call the resulting infinitary simply typed calculus: $\lambda^{\infty}\beta\mu^{\rightarrow}$. Not only the calculus itself, but also its definition method is an interesting application of the recently developed method to define infinitary rewriting, both the terms and the reductions, using coinduction and coalgebraic techniques [CC96, EP13, EHH+13]. In the present case the new elements are the μ-construct and the simple types. Both can be lifted to the infinite setting by a straightforward coinductive reading of the defining clauses. Intuitively, the benefit is that in this way the somewhat coinductive flavour of the typing rule for μ-terms is elucidated. It follows straightforward by a consideration of the infinite normal form of the μ-term, and its obvious simple typing. Figure 3 contains an example.

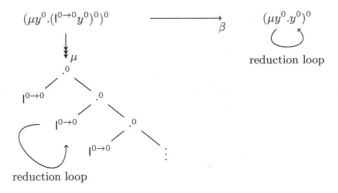

Fig. 3. Failure of infinitary confluence (CR^{∞}) in the main calculus $\lambda^{\infty}\beta\mu^{\rightarrow}$

How about the fundamental theorems for $\lambda^{\infty}\beta\mu^{\rightarrow}$? We have the failure of PML^{∞}, the infinitary parallel moves lemma, as the following counterexample witnesses:

$$\mu y.\,|y \twoheadrightarrow_{\mu} |^{\omega} \qquad\text{and also}\qquad \mu y.\,|y \rightarrow_{\beta} \mu y.\,y$$

Both reducts can only reduce to themselves, in one step. Hence $\neg PML^{\infty}$, and therefore also $\neg CR^{\infty}$. (See Figure 3.)

Note that the looping terms in Figure 3 are unsolvable. This observation suggest to restore infinitary confluence (CR^{∞}) by quotienting out the unsolvable terms, see [EHK12]. In spite of the failure of CR^{∞}, UN^{∞} holds, by an appeal on a theorem of Ketema and Simonsen [KS09], stating UN^{∞} for all infinitary OCRSs; here we have a substructure of such an iOCRS, which by its closure properties admits the same proof of UN^{∞}.

Remark 4. Pure μ-terms $\mu x_1, \ldots, x_n.x_i$ are unsolvable. The μ-reductions between theses terms constitute an interesting reduction graph, see [EGKvO11]. In particular, the terms $\mu x_1, \ldots, x_n.x_1$ are looping terms. All these μ-unsolvables reduce to $\mu x.x$.

Question 5. Looping terms (admitting a one-step reduction cycle) are interesting as they constitute the difference between the canonical notion of convergence in infinitary rewriting, namely strong convergence (see Glossary), and mere Cauchy convergence:

(i) For the finite $\lambda\beta$-calculus the looping terms are easily classified: they are of the form $C[\Omega]$ for some context $C[]$. For the infinitary λ-calculus $\lambda^\infty\beta$ the full characterization of looping terms was given by Endrullis and Polonsky in [EP13]. Two questions arise at this point:
   (a) What are the looping terms in the main calculus $\lambda^\infty\beta\mu^\rightarrow$?
   (b) And without typing, so in $\lambda^\infty\beta\mu$?
(ii) For $\lambda\beta\mu$ the question is easy, using the remark above and item (i).

5   Adding Clocks

In this section we prove the main results, the clock theorems, of this paper. We introduce clocked Böhm Trees [EHK10, EHKP12, EHKP13] for the $\lambda\beta\mu$-calculus. For this purpose, we extend the $\lambda\beta\mu^\rightarrow$-calculus with unary constructors τ and ι that are witnesses of β-steps and μ-steps, respectively. The resulting calculus is orthogonal and infinitary normalizing. The unique infinitary normal forms are Böhm Trees enriched with τ and ι providing information on the speed at which the tree was formed (the number of steps needed to head normalize the corresponding subterm).

Definition 6. The set $Ter^\infty(\lambda\mu\tau\iota)$ of (finite and infinite) terms of the clocked $\lambda\mu$-calculus is coinductively defined[1] by the following grammar

$$M ::=^{co} x \mid MM \mid \lambda x.M \mid \mu x.M \mid \tau(M) \mid \iota(M) \qquad (x \in \mathcal{X})$$

The set of contexts is inductively defined by

$$C ::= \Box \mid \lambda x.C \mid CM \mid MC \mid \tau(C) \qquad (x \in \mathcal{X}, M \in Ter^\infty(\lambda\mu\tau\iota))$$

Definition 7. The rewrite rules of the clocked $\lambda\mu$-calculus are:

$$\beta : \quad (\lambda x.t)s \rightarrow \tau(t[x := s]) \qquad\qquad \tau : \quad \tau(x)y \rightarrow \tau(xy)$$
$$\mu : \quad \mu x.t \rightarrow \iota(t[x := \mu x.t]) \qquad\qquad \iota : \quad \iota(x)y \rightarrow \iota(xy)$$

The rewrite relation $\rightarrow_{\because}$ is defined as the closure under contexts of these rules.

---

[1] This means that $Ter^\infty(\lambda\mu\tau\iota)$ is defined as the greatest fixed point of the underlying set functor.

The shift rules for τ and ι (on the right) are adopted for a better correspondence between the unclocked and the clocked version of the calculus. Without the shift rules, we could not lift reduction from the unclocked to the clocked calculus since the τ or ι may be in the way of a β-redex. For example, the unclocked reduction $\mathsf{II}x \to_\beta \mathsf{I}x \to x$ yields in the clocked calculus $\mathsf{II}x \to_\beta \tau(\mathsf{I})x \to_\tau \tau(\mathsf{I}x) \to_\beta \tau(\tau(x))$ where the shift step is needed to reveal the β-redex.

In this section we can do without the simple type discipline but it would be easy to adopt it. In that case we assume the trivial typing rules for τ and ι, that is to say: a τ-term has the type of its argument, and likewise for ι.

We write $\to$ for the usual (non-clocked) $\lambda\beta\mu$-rewrite relation. We write $\tau^n(t)$ for the term $\tau(\tau(\cdots\tau(t)))$ with n τ's, and likewise for $\iota^n(t)$.

Example 8. Consider $\mu x.x$. We have the reduction

$$\mu x.x \to_{\mathcal{C}} \iota(\mu x.x) \to_{\mathcal{C}} \iota(\iota(\mu x.x)) \to_{\mathcal{C}} \cdots \twoheadrightarrow_{\mathcal{C}} \iota^\omega$$

An infinite stack of τ's and ι's in the normal form indicates that the corresponding position in the term could not be evaluated to a weak head normal form. In the Böhm Tree such unsolvable subterms are replaced by $\bot$ or Ω.

The motivation for choosing different witnesses for β- and μ-steps is to extract more information from the reduction to the normal form. By distinguishing between τ's and ι's, we can extract information about the working of unsolvables. For example, let $\omega \equiv \lambda x.xx$, then we have:

$$\omega\omega \to_{\mathcal{C}} \tau(\omega\omega) \to_{\mathcal{C}} \tau(\tau(\omega\omega)) \to_{\mathcal{C}} \cdots \twoheadrightarrow_{\mathcal{C}} \tau^\omega$$

Note that τ^ω is a different form of undefined than ι^ω. We can also have infinite towers of alternating τ's and ι's as illustrated by the reduction:

$$\mu x.\mathsf{I}x \to_{\mathcal{C}} \mu x.\tau(x) \to_{\mathcal{C}} \iota(\tau(\mu x.\tau(x))) \to_{\mathcal{C}} \iota(\tau(\iota(\tau(\mu x.\tau(x))))) \to_{\mathcal{C}} \cdots \twoheadrightarrow_{\mathcal{C}} (\iota\tau)^\omega$$

This example has lead to failure of CR^∞ in the $\lambda\beta\mu^\to$-calculus as shown in Figure 3. In the clocked setting, the infinitary confluence is restored as shown in Figure 4. For the elementary diagrams involved we refer to Figure 5.

Example 9. Let us have a look at the fixed point combinators of Curry and Turing. In the $\lambda\beta\mu^\to$-calculus these fpc's can be rendered as follows.

(i) Curry's fpc Y_0 corresponds to $\lambda f.\mu x.fx$; *par abus de langage* we also use Y_0 for the latter term. Then we have

$$\mathsf{Y}_0 f \equiv (\lambda f.\mu x.fx)f$$
$$\to_{\mathcal{C}} \tau(\mu x.fx)$$
$$\to_{\mathcal{C}} \tau(\iota(f\mu x.fx))$$
$$\to_{\mathcal{C}} \tau(\iota(f(\iota(f\mu x.fx))))$$
$$\to_{\mathcal{C}} \cdots \twoheadrightarrow_{\mathcal{C}} \tau((\iota f)^\omega) \quad (= \tau(\iota(f(\iota(f\ldots)))))$$

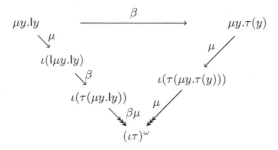

Fig. 4. Restoring of infinitary confluence with clocks (compare with Figure 3)

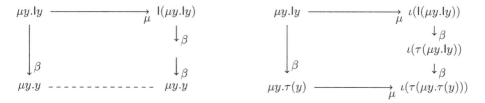

Fig. 5. Elementary diagrams: unclocked (left) and clocked (right)

(ii) Turing's fpc Y_1 corresponds to $\mu x.\lambda f.f(xf)$. Again we also use Y_1 to denote this μ-term. Then we have

$$
\begin{aligned}
Y_1 f &\equiv (\mu x.\lambda f.f(xf))f \\
&\to_{\ast} (\iota(\lambda f.f(Y_1 f)))f \\
&\to_{\ast} \iota((\lambda f.f(Y_1 f))f) \\
&\to_{\ast} \iota(\tau(f(Y_1 f))) \\
&\to_{\ast} \cdots \twoheadrightarrow_{\ast} (\iota\tau f)^\omega \quad (= \iota(\tau(f(\iota(\tau(f\ldots))))))
\end{aligned}
$$

The term Y_0 is more efficient than Y_1 in the sense that between the f's in the infinitary normal forms of Y_0 and Y_1, we have ι in contrast with $\iota\tau$, respectively.

Remark 10. The clocked $\lambda\mu$-calculus can be extended to *atomic clocks*, as they are called in [EHK10, EHKP13], as follows:

$$
\begin{aligned}
\beta &: (\lambda x.t)s \to \tau_\varepsilon(t[x:=s]) & \tau &: \tau_p(x)y \to \tau_{Lp}(xy) \\
\mu &: \mu x.t \to \iota_\varepsilon(t[x:=\mu x.t]) & \iota &: \iota_p(x)y \to \iota_{Lp}(xy)
\end{aligned}
$$

Positions are defined as words over the alphabet $\{\lambda, L, R\}$ in the obvious way; the letter L stands for 'left'; ε denotes the empty word. Then the symbols τ_p and μ_p witness not only the type of the rewrite step but also its (relative) position p. In order to keep the presentation simple, we stick to the non-atomic clocks.

Lemma 11. *The rewrite relation $\to_{\ast}$ has the properties* UN^∞, SN^∞ *and* CR^∞.

Proof. Observe that any contraction of a root redex will introduce a τ or ι at the root, hence every term admits at most one root step. We get SN^∞ by the non-existence of root-active terms [KdV05]. Finally, UN^∞ follows from orthogonality of the rules, see [KS09] and CR^∞ immediately follows from UN^∞ and SN^∞.

For terms M, we use $nf_{\lambda\mu}(M)$ to denote the unique infinitary normal forms of M with respect to $\rightarrow_{\lambda\mu}$. We note that $nf_{\lambda\mu}(M)$ corresponds to the Lévy–Longo Tree [EHK12] of M enriched with symbols τ and ι that provide information about the speed in which this tree has been developed.

Definition 12. We define τ, ι*-removal* $\rightarrow_{acc} \subseteq Ter^\infty(\lambda\mu\tau\iota)^2$ as the closure under contexts of the rules

$$\tau(M) \rightarrow M \qquad\qquad \iota(M) \rightarrow M$$

and use $=_{acc}$ to denote the equivalence closure of $\rightarrow_{acc}$ (the subscript "acc" abbreviates "acceleration"). For $M, N \in Ter^\infty(\lambda\mu)$, we define

(i) $M \succeq_{\lambda\mu} N$, M *is globally improved by* N iff $nf_{\lambda\mu}(M) \twoheadrightarrow_{acc} nf_{\lambda\mu}(N)$;
(ii) $M =_{\lambda\mu\exists} N$, M *eventually matches* N iff $nf_{\lambda\mu}(M) =_{acc} nf_{\lambda\mu}(N)$.

So global improving means that we may drop everywhere in the normal form of M occurrences of τ and ι, even in infinitely many places; while eventual matching means that we may drop these symbols in finitely many places only, so that there is almost everywhere a precise match.

Definition 13. A *head context* is a context of the form $D[\square N_1 \ldots N_m]$ where D is built from $\lambda x.\square$, $\tau(\square)$ and $\iota(\square)$. A *head reduction step* $\rightarrow_h$ is a step in a head context (the position of the step is the position of the hole).

A *head normal form (hnf)* is a λ-term of the form $C[y]$ where C is a head context and $y \in \mathcal{X}$. A *weak head normal form (whnf)* is an hnf or an abstraction, that is, a whnf is a term of the form $xM_1 \ldots M_m$ or $\lambda x.M$. A term *has a (weak) hnf* if it reduces to one.

The following proposition states that clocks are accelerated under reduction:

Proposition 14. *If* $M \twoheadrightarrow N$, *then* N *improves* M *globally, i.e.,* $nf_{\lambda\mu}(M) \twoheadrightarrow_{acc}$ $nf_{\lambda\mu}(N)$.

Proof. We reduce terms to their unique infinite normal form in a top-down fashion. A position in a term t is *(weakly) stable* if it is not (strictly) contained in a subterm $t' \equiv t''N_1 \ldots N_m$ of t for which t'' is a redex. Observe that stable symbols (i.e., symbols at stable positions) cannot be touched by any reduction. A *top-redex* in a term t is a redex occurrence ρ whose position is weakly stable. Note that top-redexes stay top when other redexes are contracted. Fair contraction of top-redexes guarantees to reach the infinitary normal form in $\leq \omega$ steps.

By induction on the length of the reduction $M \twoheadrightarrow N$ it suffices to consider a single rewrite step $M \rightarrow N$. The step $\rightarrow$ can be modeled by a step $\rightarrow_{\lambda\mu}$ with the only difference that the step $\to_{\text{※}}$ creates an additional symbol $\xi \in \{\tau, \iota\}$. Thus $M \to_{\text{※}} N'$ with $N' \to_{\text{acc}} N$ by dropping the symbol ξ. We trace the residuals of ξ over reductions with respect to $\to_{\text{※}}$. For this purpose we employ the standard notion of tracing [Ter03, BKdV00] except for the rules

$$\tau : \quad \tau(x)y \to \tau(xy) \qquad\qquad \iota : \quad \iota(x)y \to \iota(xy)$$

where we consider the τ and ι displayed in the right-hand sides to be residuals of the τ and ι displayed in the left-hand sides, respectively.

Consider a rewrite sequence $N' \equiv N'_1 \to_{\text{※}} N'_2 \to_{\text{※}} N'_3 \to_{\text{※}} \ldots$ of length $\leq \omega$ to infinitary normal form $\text{nf}(N')$ contracting only top-redexes. By uniqueness of normal forms (Lemma 11) we have $\text{nf}(N') \equiv \text{nf}(M)$. For $n = 1, 2, \ldots$, we define N_i as the result of dropping all residuals of ξ from N'_i (that is, contracting all residuals of ξ with $\twoheadrightarrow_{\text{acc}}$). The results N_i of the dropping are well-defined since the residuals of ξ are finitely nested (every step $\to_{\text{※}}$ can at most double the nesting depth). We then have a rewrite sequence $N \equiv N_1 \to_{\text{※}} N_2 \to_{\text{※}} \ldots$ with limit $\text{nf}(N)$. We have $\text{nf}(N') \twoheadrightarrow_{\text{acc}} \text{nf}(N)$ as the limit of the reductions $N'_i \twoheadrightarrow_{\text{acc}} N_i$ for $i \to \infty$.

This immediately yields the following discrimination method:

Theorem 15 (First Discrimination Criterion). *If N cannot be improved globally by any reduct of M, then $M \neq_{\beta\mu} N$.*

Proof. If $M =_{\beta\mu} N$ then by confluence these terms have a common reduct. By Proposition 14 this common reduct globally improves M.

We now define a class of 'simple' terms for which the clock is invariant under reduction (changes only in finitely many positions). The idea is that in reductions of simple terms there are no duplications of redexes. In fact, we only need to require this for the top-down reduction to Lévy–Longo Tree normal form. The following definition makes this precise:

Definition 16. [Simple terms] A redex $(\lambda x.M)N$ is called:

(i) *linear* if x has at most one occurrence in M;
(ii) *call-by-value* if N is a normal form; and
(iii) *simple* if it is linear or call-by-value.

A redex $\mu x.M$ is called *simple* if M is in normal form.

The set of *simple terms* is coinductively defined as follows (that is, the largest set such that the following conditions holds): A term M is *simple* if

(a) M is not in whnf, $M \to_h M'$ contracting a simple redex and M' is simple,
(b) $M \equiv \lambda x.M'$ with M' a simple term, or
(c) $M \equiv yM_1 \ldots M_m$ with $M_1, \ldots, M_m$ simple terms.

In contrast to previous work [EHKP13] this definition of 'simple' also considers reduction steps inside of unsolvables. While previously every unsolvable had the infinite normal form τ^ω, the clocked $\lambda\mu$-calculus allows to extract information from unsolvables as they are mapped to infinite towers consisting of τ's and ι's, see Example 8.

Example 17. Let us consider two unsolvables:

(i) The term $\Omega \equiv \omega\omega$ reduces in one step to Ω without duplicating a redex (the term ω does not contain a redex). Thus the terms $\Omega \equiv \omega\omega$ is simple.

(ii) The term $\mu x.\mathsf{l}x$ is not simple, but can be simplified, that is, reduced to a simple term. The term itself is not simple since the reduction step $\mu x.\mathsf{l}x \to \mathsf{l}\mu x.\mathsf{l}x$ duplicates the redex l. However, a reduction step $\mu x.\mathsf{l}x \to \mu x.x$ yields a simple term $\mu x.x$. Note that for discriminating terms M, N it is always sufficient to convertible terms $M' = M$ and $N' = N$.

Proposition 18. *Let N be a reduct of a simple term M. Then N eventually matches M (i.e., $\mathrm{nf}_{\text{\tiny⚙}}(M) =_\tau \mathrm{nf}_{\text{\tiny⚙}}(N)$).*

The following is a reformulation of [EHK10, Corollary 32] for Lévy–Longo Trees:

Corollary 19 (Second Discrimination Criterion). *If simple terms M, N do not eventually match ($\mathrm{nf}_{\text{\tiny⚙}}(M) \neq_{\mathrm{acc}} \mathrm{nf}_{\text{\tiny⚙}}(N)$), then they are not β-convertible: $M \neq_\beta N$.*

Proof. The proof proceeds the same as the proof of Theorem 15 with the additional observation that due to M, N being simple, the symbol ξ cannot be duplicated (stems from a redex). □

Example 20. We discriminate the unsolvables in Example 8. The term Ω is simple, and $\mu x.\mathsf{l}x =_\beta \mu x.x$ with $\mu x.x$ simple; see Example 17. We have $\mathrm{nf}_{\text{\tiny⚙}}(\Omega) = \tau^\omega$ and $\mathrm{nf}_{\text{\tiny⚙}}(\mu x.x) = \iota^\omega$. Hence by the second discrimination criterion (Corollary 19), the terms Ω and $\mu x.x$ are not $=_{\beta\mu}$-convertible.

Note that every term without weak head normal form in the $\lambda\beta\mu$-calculus gives rise to a clocked normal form which in fact is an infinite stream of τ's and ι's. For simple terms without whnf the discrimination criterion thus amounts to eventually matching of their corresponding streams. The initial segments are not relevant, it is the behavior at infinity that counts.

In Section 7 we give more example applications of this discrimination method.

6 A Functional Programming Application

We discuss a potential application of clocks for the performance optimization of functional programs. The transformations we mention here are well-known in functional programming and form a part of compile-time optimizations. Our point is merely that the clocked $\lambda\beta\mu$-calculus gives rise to a measure for comparing the performance of programs, thereby illustrating why a certain variant is preferable.

We have the following distributivity law

$$\mu f^{A \to B}.\lambda x^A.t(x, fx) = \lambda x^A.\mu y^B.t(x, y) \tag{1}$$

First of all, notice that computation of the Böhm Tree of the term on the left side of (1) does indeed contract an additional redex every time a recursive node is reached (corresponding to occurrences of fx). It follows by the discrimination theorem that these two terms are not convertible via finitary reduction steps. At the same time, the term on the right is to be preferred in any practical implementation of a recursive function of type $A \to B$. It may thus be of some interest that such patterns are actually quite common in programming practice.

Example 21. Consider the standard map function (we use **Clean** notation):

```
map f [] = []
map f [a:as] = [f a : map f as]
```

In this code, the argument f must be passed on during each recursive call, yielding an additional β-reduction step at every turn. This additional time step can be recovered by reimplementing **map** as follows:

```
map f as = map' as where
    map' [] = []
    map' [a:as] = [f a : map' as]
```

There is a close correspondence with the fixed point combinators of Curry and Turing, see Example 9. The first implementation of **map** corresponds to Turing's fpc Y_1 which passes the argument f from recursive call to recursive call, while the second implementation of **map** corresponds to Curry's fpc Y_0 which abstracts over f outside of the recursion. As shown in Example 9, Y_0 has a faster clock than Y_1.

We note that, fixing all recursive definitions in a program by abstracting their constant arguments over the recursion (as above) might not in itself eliminate all threats to efficiency. Functional programs are often built up from various combinators. Yet when one such combinator is applied to another, new "hidden redexes" may appear.

For example, the above map function could be invoked in order to "whiteout" a list by some constant c:

```
fill lst = map (\x = c) lst
```

At every invocation, this turns into the equivalent code

```
fill [] = []
fill [a:as] = [(\x = c) a : fill as]
```

(In the notation of the λ-calculus, we could write **fill** = **map'**$[f := \lambda x.c]$.)

We note that this code is suboptimal: it has a redex $(\lambda x.c)a$ which appears in every recursive call, but which gives the same value. In this case the program is convertible to its best version:

```
fill [] = []
fill [a:as] = [c : fill as]
```

But the example illustrates how the functional clock can become slow because there is an extraneous redex that is created at every iteration.

(The clock is also slower when the redex in question occurs inside the function supplied to map. However, this situation is well-studied: it is precisely the argument in favor of strict evaluation of those function arguments that come to the head position in the body of the function.)

All these optimizations are related to the concept of *inlining* from compiler theory. In a sense, inlining is an operation that lifts redexes out from run-time into compile-time, where they can be contracted before program execution begins. This optimization comes with obvious associated space costs. Yet when time is of priority, it is generally a good idea to inline as much as possible.

Our current framework provides a possibility to detect inlining opportunities based on static syntactic inspection of code. It does not appear that all modern compilers of functional languages take advantage of this possibility in full generality. We wonder whether the Clean compiler can make use of such information!

7   Sequences of Fixed Point Combinators

Fixed point combinators are very suitable to test discrimination methods, because there are so many of them, and because they all have the same Böhm Tree $\lambda f.f^\omega$. When they are constructed in different ways, they can be inconvertible, in the case of this paper with its main calculus $\lambda\beta\mu^\rightarrow$, using the β- and μ-reduction rules. In this section we consider the most 'canonical' sequence of fpc's, that we call the Böhm sequence, and next a less well-known sequence, that we call the Scott sequence, due to the history and background of its construction (see [EHK10, EHKP12]). As a third topic in this section we analyze the question whether in the calculus $\lambda\beta\mu^\rightarrow$ there are more singleton fpc-generators like $\square\delta$, using Barendregt's inhabitation machines to help us enumerate certain simple types.

7.1   The Böhm Sequence

Just as in the case of untyped λ-calculus we can conjure up an infinite sequence of fpc's $Y_0, Y_1, \ldots$ where $Y_0 \equiv \lambda f.\mu y.fy$ and $Y_{n+1} \equiv Y_n\delta$ with $\delta \equiv \lambda ab.b(ab)$. It is easily checked that all Y_n are fpc's. What is much harder to check is that they are mutually different with respect to $=_{\beta\mu}$:

$$Y_n =_{\beta\mu} Y_m \iff n = m$$

We have $Y_{n+1} = Y_1\delta^{\sim n}$ and the infinite clocked normal form of $Y_1\delta^{\sim n}$ can be computed as follows:

$$
\begin{aligned}
Y_1\delta^{\sim n} \equiv (\mu x.\lambda f.f(xf))\delta^{\sim n} \to_\mu \cdot \to_\iota^* \ & \iota(\,(\lambda f.f(Y_1 f))\delta^{\sim n}\,) \\
\to_\beta \cdot \to_\tau^* \ & \iota\tau(\,\delta(Y_1\delta)\delta^{\sim(n-1)}\,) \\
\to^* \ & \iota\tau^{1+2(n-1)}(\,\delta(Y_1\delta^{\sim n})\,)
\end{aligned}
$$

$$\to^* \iota\tau^{2n}(\ \lambda f.f(\mathsf{Y}_1\delta^{\sim n}f)\ )$$
$$\to^* \iota\tau^{2n}(\ \lambda f.f(f(\iota\tau^{2n+1}(\ \mathsf{Y}_1\delta^{\sim n}f\ )))\ )$$
$$\twoheadrightarrow \iota\tau^{2n}(\lambda f.f(\iota\tau^{2n+1}(f(\iota\tau^{2n+1}(\ldots)))))$$
$$\equiv \iota\tau^{2n}\ \lambda f.f(\iota\tau^{2n+1}f)^\omega$$

Thus $\mathrm{nf}_{\text{...}}(\mathsf{Y}_1\delta^{\sim n}) \equiv \iota\tau^{2n}\ \lambda f.f(\iota\tau^{2n+1}f)^\omega$. Note that in the computation of the clocked normal form of $\mathsf{Y}_1\delta^{\sim n}$ we really need the shift-rules for τ and ι in order to let these constants not impede the necessary reductions. Here we used the notation M^ω for $M(M(M(\ldots)))$, so e.g. $(\iota\tau f)^\omega \equiv \iota\tau f\iota\tau f\iota\tau f\ldots$ with all brackets associating to the right.

Note further that we have carried out the reduction in a top-down fashion, and none of the steps has duplicated a redex. Thus the terms $\mathsf{Y}_1\delta^{\sim n}$ are simple. By the second discrimination criterion (Corollary 19), we can discriminate these fixed point combinators pairwise with respect to $=_{\beta\mu}$ since their clocked normal forms do not eventually match.

7.2   The Scott Sequence

As shown in [EHK10, EHKP12], there is another way to generate new fpc's as follows: if Y is a reducing fpc, then $Y(\mathsf{SS})\mathsf{I}$ is an fpc. Indeed we calculate

$$Y(\mathsf{SS})\mathsf{I}x \to_\beta \mathsf{SS}(Y(\mathsf{SS}))\mathsf{I}x \twoheadrightarrow_\beta \mathsf{SI}(Y(\mathsf{SS})\mathsf{I})x \twoheadrightarrow_\beta x(Y(\mathsf{SS})\mathsf{I}x)$$

In fact we have for every $n \geq 0$: Y is a reducing fpc $\implies Y(\mathsf{SS})\mathsf{S}^{\sim n}\mathsf{I}$ is a reducing fpc. Here we use the notation $AB^{\sim n}$ defined by $AB^{\sim 0} = A$ and $AB^{\sim n+1} = ABB^{\sim n}$.

In this way we can generate many new fpc's. The question however is how to show that they are indeed new, i.e., that for different sequences of 'fpc-building blocks' $\pi_1, \ldots, \pi_k$ and $\pi_1', \ldots, \pi_k'$ where each π_i and π_j' is $[]\delta$ or $[](\mathsf{SS})\mathsf{S}^{\sim n}\mathsf{I}$ for some $n \geq 0$, we have $M_1 \equiv Y_0\pi_1, \ldots, \pi_k \neq_{\beta\mu} Y_0\pi_1', \ldots, \pi_k' \equiv M_2$.

To perform the discrimination argument we can proceed in analogy with the treatment above for $[]\delta$ with two stipulations. First, we have to simplify the terms by reducing the subterms SS to their normal forms $\lambda abc.bc(abc)$. Second, we need the refined atomic clocks defined in Remark 10. Otherwise we could not distinguish the effect of swapping two blocks in the sequence $\pi_1, \ldots, \pi_k$.

7.3   Other Fpc-Generators

As we have seen above, the term $\delta \equiv \lambda ab.b(ab)$ has the peculiar property that it generates new fpc's when postfixed to an already available fpc: Y is an fpc $\implies Y\delta$ is an fpc. We shall now consider the following problem:

> Give the set of λ-terms G such that, for an fpc Y, YG is again an fpc.

For general G this problem becomes intractable due to the usual pathologies of the type-free λ-calculus. However, it is interesting to solve this problem for the simply-typed setting. That is, we shall work in $\lambda\beta\mu^{\rightarrow}$. In fact, with $\lambda\beta\eta\mu^{\rightarrow}$ as it is natural in this subsection to include the η-rule

$$\eta: \quad \lambda x.Mx \rightarrow M \qquad \text{if } x \text{ not free in } M$$

and long $\beta\eta$-normal forms (this is the only part of the paper where the η-rule is used).

In this context, we solve the above problem using the technique of Barendregt's Inhabitation Machines [BDS13].

Suppose G is such that YG is a fixed point combinator in $\lambda\beta\mu^{\rightarrow}$, for Y fpc. Since YG must have type $(\alpha \rightarrow \alpha) \rightarrow \alpha$ for any α, while Y has type $(A \rightarrow A) \rightarrow A$, for some A, we must have that $A = (\alpha \rightarrow \alpha) \rightarrow \alpha$.

For $\sigma \in \mathbb{T}$, write σ^o for the type $(\sigma \rightarrow \sigma) \rightarrow \sigma$. With this notation, the above becomes

$$YG : \alpha^o$$

$$Y : (\alpha^o \rightarrow \alpha^o) \rightarrow \alpha^o \quad (= \alpha^{oo})$$

whence we see that G must have type $\alpha^o \rightarrow \alpha^o$. Using the inhabitation machines, we enumerate all closed $\beta\eta$-normal forms of this type. (Here, as is usual in type theory, the normal forms for η are the "long" normal forms, where every subterm of type $A_1 \rightarrow \cdots \rightarrow A_n \rightarrow \alpha$ begins with n abstractions.)

Using [BDS13, 2.3] we get the diagram:

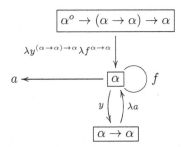

The paths through the above diagram terminating in a leaf node correspond to finite $\beta\eta$-normal forms of the given type, while infinite paths correspond to infinite $\beta\eta$-normal forms. From the diagram, we see that the general form of a term of type $\alpha^o \rightarrow \alpha^o$ is

$$\lambda y^{\alpha^o} \lambda f^{\alpha\rightarrow\alpha}.f^{n_0}(y(\lambda a_1.f^{n_1}(y(\lambda a_2.f^{n_2}(\ldots y(\lambda a_k.f^{n_k}a_i)\cdots)$$

Let $\mathcal{G}$ be the collection of such terms, and let $G \in \mathcal{G}$. We shall now investigate under what conditions G is an fpc generator.

Let us note immediately that n_0 must be positive, for otherwise the head variable of the term is its first abstracted variable, and an application of a fixed point combinator to such a term always results in an unsolvable.

Notice also that a_i occurs in G for exactly one i. So we can write

$$G = \lambda y f.f^{1+n_0'}(y(\mathsf{K}(f^{n_1}(\cdots y(\lambda a.f^{n_i}(y\cdots \mathsf{K}(f^{n_k}a)\cdots)$$

where $a = a_i$ and $n_0' = n_0 - 1$.

Proposition 22. *Let Y be a (w)fpc and $Y_G = YG$. Then*

$$Y_G f = f^m(Y_G f^n)$$

where $m = n_1 + \cdots + n_{i-1}$, and $n = n_i + \cdots + n_k$.

Proof. We are going to show that

$$Y_G f = f^{\sum_{j=0}^{i-1} n_j}(Y_G(\lambda a. f^{\sum_{j=i}^{k} n_j} a))$$
$$= f^{n_1 + \cdots + n_{i-1}}(Y_G(\lambda a. f^{n_i + \cdots + n_k} a))$$

by the following five steps.

1. For any number n_j, we have

$$Y_G(\mathsf{K}(f^{n_j} a)) = G Y_G(\mathsf{K}(f^{n_j} a))$$
$$= (\mathsf{K}(f^{n_j} a))^{1 + (n_0 - 1)}(Y_G(\mathsf{K} \cdots)))$$
$$= \mathsf{K}(f^{n_j} a) \left((\mathsf{K}(f^{n_j} a))^{n_0 - 1}(Y_G \cdots)\right)$$
$$= f^{n_j} a$$

2. By induction, we have, for $j \leq j'$

$$Y_G(\mathsf{K}(f^{n_j}(\cdots Y_G(\mathsf{K}(f^{n_{j'}} a)) \cdots))$$
$$= Y_G(\mathsf{K}(f^{n_j} a))[a := Y_G(\mathsf{K}(f^{n_{j+1}}(\cdots Y_G(\mathsf{K}(f^{n_{j'}} a)) \cdots))]$$
$$=_1 f^{n_j}(Y_G(\mathsf{K}(f^{n_{j+1}}(\cdots Y_G(\mathsf{K}(f^{n_{j'}} a)) \cdots))$$
$$=_{IH} f^{n_j}(f^{n_{j+1} + \cdots + n_{j'}} a)$$
$$= f^{n_j + \cdots + n_{j'}} a$$

3. In particular, we have

$$Y_G(\mathsf{K}(f^{n_i + 1}(\cdots Y_G(\mathsf{K}(f^{n_k} a)) \cdots)) = f^{n_{i+1} + \cdots + n_k} a \qquad (2)$$

$$Y_G(\mathsf{K}(f^{n_1}(\cdots Y_G(\mathsf{K}(f^{n_{i-1}} A) \cdots)) = Y_G(\mathsf{K}(f^{n_1}(\cdots Y_G(\mathsf{K}(f^{n_{i-1}} a) \cdots))[a := A]$$
$$= f^{n_1 + \cdots + n_{i-1}} A \qquad (3)$$

4. Using (2), we get

$$\lambda a. f^{n_i}(Y_G(\cdots \mathsf{K}(f^{n_k} a))) = \lambda a. f^{n_i + \cdots + n_k} a \qquad (4)$$

5. Putting it all together gives

$$Y_G f = f^{n_0}(Y_G(\mathsf{K}(f^{n_1}(\cdots Y_G(\lambda a. f^{n_i}(\cdots Y_G(\mathsf{K}(f^{n_k} a) \cdots))$$
$$=_{(4)} f^{n_0}(Y_G(\mathsf{K}(f^{n_1}(\cdots Y_G(\lambda a. f^{n_i + \cdots + n_k} a) \cdots))$$
$$=_{(3)} f^{n_0}(f^{n_1 + \cdots + n_{i-1}}(Y_G(\lambda a. f^{n_i + \cdots + n_k} a) \cdots))$$
$$= f^{n_0 + \cdots + n_{i-1}}(Y_G f^{n_i + \cdots + n_k})$$

being what was required to show.

What conclusions can be drawn from this proposition? We know that a generic member of $\mathcal{G}$ is determined by the numbers $(k, i, n_1, \ldots, n_k)$, $1 \le i \le k$. While it seems likely that all these generators are "unique" – in the sense that when $G \neq G'$, there can be no finite conversion between Y_G and Y'_G – their behaviors nevertheless collapse to the 2-parameter family

$$g_{m,n} = \lambda y f . f^m (y f^n)$$

We can now consider two pre-generators $G, G' \in \mathcal{G}$ to be equivalent, if their "reduced pump" $\lambda y f . f^m (y f^n)$ is the same.

Let us observe the execution of such a reduced generator:

$$
\begin{aligned}
Y_G f &= f^m (Y_G f^n) \\
&= f^m (f^{mn} (Y_G f^{n^2})) \\
&= f^m (f^{mn} (f^{mn^2} (Y_G f^{n^3}))) \\
&= \vdots \\
&= f^{m(1+n+\cdots+n^k)} (Y_G f^{n^{k+1}}) \\
&= \vdots \\
&= \begin{cases} \bot & m = 0 \\ f^m \bot & n = 0 \\ f^\omega & m, n > 0 \end{cases}
\end{aligned}
$$

Thus, every such generator $g_{m,n}$ with $m, n > 0$ leads to a wfpc-generator. Conversely, the previous inhabitation argument shows that every finite simply typed wfpc-generator is of this form.

Simple intuition now tells us that, in order that $G = g_{m,n}$ be an fpc-generator, it must transpire that $m = n = 1$. Indeed, thinking of a given (w)fpc Y as a single "motor", we are poised to measure its clock velocity by counting how many fs it produces at each step, as well as how quickly it speeds itself up, by changing f to an n-fold composition of it. If $n > 1$, then the clock perpetually speeds itself up, so that Y_G cannot be an fpc. If $n = 1$ but $m > 1$, then the clocks are indeed the same, but they are "de-synced" between the terms $Y_G f$ and $f(Y_G f)$, because at k-th iteration the former will have km occurrences of f at the head, while the latter will have $km + 1$, which cannot be synchronized.

To complete the classification, it remains to ask which elements of $\mathcal{G}$ are equivalent to $g_{1,1}$. The answer brings us to the following result.

Theorem 23. *Let G be a finite simply-typed fpc-generator. There are integers $l, m, n \ge 0$ such that*

$$G = \lambda y \lambda f . f (y \circ \mathsf{K})^l (y (\lambda a . (y \circ \mathsf{K})^m (f((y \circ \mathsf{K})^n a))))$$

Remark 24. After the first iteration, it is seen that such a G exhibits the same behavior as the simplified term $g_{1,1} = \delta = \lambda y f . f(y f)$. It is precisely in this sense that this generator, discovered by Corrado Böhm and being the first term to be described as such, is unique. The uniqueness is with respect to the clocked behavioral equivalence of fpc 1-generators. It is the minimal representative of this equivalence class, being the only class of solutions that are candidate fpc-generators.

Interestingly, the inhabitation problem also generates infinite solutions:

$$G = \lambda y^{\alpha^{\circ}} \lambda f^{\alpha \to \alpha} . f^{n_0}(y(\lambda a_1 . f^{n_1}(y(\lambda a_2 . \cdots) \cdots)$$

with no occurrences of a_i.

Clearly, if $n_i = 0$ for all $i > 0$, then G is not an fpc-generator, because

$$Y_G f = G Y_G f = f^{n_0} Z$$

where $f \notin \mathsf{FV}(Z)$. Then $\mathsf{BT}(Y_G f) \neq f^{\omega}$.

Similarly, if $n_i = 0$ for $i > i_0$, then we can apply Step 2 of the above proposition to get

$$Y_G(\mathsf{K}(f^{n_0}(Y_G(\mathsf{K}(f^{n_1} \cdots (Y_G(\mathsf{K}(f^{n_{i_0}} Z) \cdots) = f^{\Sigma} Z$$

where $\Sigma = n_1 + \cdots + n_{i_0}$. But $f \notin \mathsf{FV}(Z)$. So

$$Y_G f = f^{n_0}(Y_G(\mathsf{K}(f^{n_1} \cdots) \cdots) = f^{\Sigma} Z \neq f^{\omega}$$

(In this example, as well as the previous one, the term Z can be given explicitly: $Z = Y_G(KZ) = (Y_G \circ K)^{\omega}$.)

Conversely, if $n_i \neq 0$ for infinitely many i, we have that

$$Y_G f = f^M(\cdots)$$

for M larger than any given number. Thus Y_G is indeed a weak fixed point combinator.

8   Further Questions

In this final section we discuss some important questions. In particular we point to a conjecture which could have several deep consequences (see Section 8.3). The conjecture connects the simply typed $\lambda\beta\mu^{\to}$-calculus with the untyped $\lambda\beta$-calculus. If it is true, it would be a striking example of how simple types can be used to obtain results in the pure untyped $\lambda\beta$-calculus.

8.1 Decidability of Fixed Point Combinators

The simultaneous restriction–extension of $\lambda\beta\mu^{\rightarrow}$ presents us with a more abstract, high level view on fixed point combinators. For, the simple types restriction disallows much of the possible complexity that fpc's may possess – spurious complexity one might say. In particular self-application in subterms is removed, at least between subterms of the same type. Thus the formerly simplest fpc's of Curry and Turing, respectively

$$\lambda f.(\lambda x.f(xx))(\lambda x.f(xx)) \qquad \text{and} \qquad (\lambda ab.b(aab))(\lambda ab.b(aab))$$

are ruled out, and in $\lambda\beta\mu^{\rightarrow}$ are replaced by the simpler

$$\lambda x.\mu y.xy \qquad \text{and} \qquad \mu x.\delta x \ ,$$

respectively.

At this point, it is interesting to speculate how complicated fpc's can be in $\lambda\beta\mu^{\rightarrow}$. Is the notion of fpc still undecidable? Does Scott's theorem used to show the undecidability of the notion of fpc's in pure lambda calculus still hold?

What number theoretic functions are definable in this calculus, when one restricts to working with the Church numerals (of type $\alpha \rightarrow (\alpha \rightarrow \alpha) \rightarrow \alpha$)?

8.2 Comparison with PCF

When we extend the calculus to its infinitary version (see Figure 1), similar questions can be asked. At present the meta-theory of the calculus $\lambda\beta\mu^{\rightarrow}$ is not fully clear to us, in particular its relation to PCF where the native type of natural numbers leads to Turing-completeness.

8.3 Completeness of μ-Reduction

The $\lambda\beta\mu^{\rightarrow}$-calculus can be interpreted in the untyped $\lambda\beta$-calculus by instantiating the μ-constructor with any fixed point combinator Y.

Definition 25. Let Y be an fpc. For a simply typed $\lambda\mu$-term t, its Y-*translation* $|t|_Y$ is defined by induction on t, as follows:

t	$|t|_Y$
x	x
st	$|s|_Y|t|_Y$
$\lambda y^A.t$	$\lambda y.|t|_Y$
$\mu z^A.t$	$Y(\lambda z.|t|_Y)$

The following is a deep conjecture about fixed point combinators.

Conjecture 26. For any fpc Y and simply typed s, t we have:

$$|s|_Y =_\beta |t|_Y \iff s =_{\beta\mu} t .$$

Remark 27. (i) The direction $\Leftarrow$ of the conjecture is trivial (soundness). The interesting part is completeness, $\Rightarrow$.

(ii) It is essential that the right-hand side involves types. Otherwise we have the following 'chiasm' counterexample:

$$s = \lambda z.z(\mu x.x)(Y(\lambda x.x)) \qquad\qquad t = \lambda z.z(Y(\lambda x.x))(\mu x.x)$$

Then $s \neq_{\beta\mu} t$ but $|s|_Y \equiv |t|_Y$.

(iii) It is also interesting to give the equivalent reformulation of the conjecture for the $\lambda\beta Y^{\rightarrow}$-calculus.

To illustrate the fundamental importance of this conjecture, we show that its positive resolution would yield immediate answers to questions posed by Plotkin, Statman and Klop.

Question 28. (Plotkin) Does there exist an fpc Y such that $|\mu x.\mu y.fxy|_Y = |\mu x.fxx|_Y$?

The question of Plotkin has been answered in [EHKP12] using clocked Böhm Trees. A positive answer to Conjecture 26 would yield this result immediately.

Corollary 29. *If the conjecture holds, the answer to Plotkin's question is "no".*

Proof. For Plotkin's question, consider the terms $s \equiv \mu x.\mu y.fxy$ and $t \equiv \mu x.fxx$. As we noted before, these terms have the same infinitary normal form. However, they are not finitely convertible (every reduct of s has nesting of μ's whereas no reduct of t has). Hence for no fpc Y are their images under the $|\cdot|_Y$ map convertible, yielding a negative answer to Plotkins question.

Question 30. (Statman) Is it the case that for *no* fpc Y we have $Y\delta = Y$?

A proof of this conjecture given by Intrigila [Int97] turned out to contain a serious gap, see [EHKP13]. Thus the answer to this conjecture remains open. A positive answer to Conjecture 26 would immediately imply Statman's conjecture as follows.

Corollary 31. *If the conjecture holds, the answer to the conjecture of Statman is "yes".*

Proof. Suppose there exists an fpc Y convertible with $Y\delta$. Then $Y\delta =_\beta Y\delta\delta$. Let

$$s \equiv (\lambda f.\mu x.fx)\delta \qquad\qquad t \equiv (\lambda f.\mu x.fx)\delta\delta$$

It is not difficult to see that s and t are typable, and $(*)$ $s \neq_{\beta\mu} t$ since the terms have different clocks, see further the Böhm sequence in [EHKP12]. We have

$$|s|_Y = (\lambda f.Y(\lambda x.fx))\delta =_\beta Y(\lambda x.\delta x) =_\beta Y\delta \qquad |t|_Y =_\beta Y\delta\delta$$

If $Y\delta =_\beta Y\delta\delta$, then we have $|s|_Y =_\beta |t|_Y$. However, then by Conjecture 26 we get $s =_{\beta\mu} t$, contradicting $(*)$.

We briefly indicate that this method has much wider applicability, namely establishing a conjecture by Klop [EHK10, EHKP12], generalizing Statman's conjecture considerably. The conjecture refers to several fpc generating schemes, of which the following are examples:

(G_1) $\Box\delta$;
(G_2) $\Box(SS)S^{\sim n}I$ for $n \in \mathbb{N}$;
(G_3) $\Box(AAA)A^{\sim n}II$ for $n \in \mathbb{N}$.

Note that (G_2) and (G_3) are schemes of generating vectors. There are actually infinitely many of such fpc-generating schemes, but we will stick with the three as mentioned. They enable us to build fpcs in a modular way by repeatedly adding a vector as given by one of the schemes, starting with some arbitrary fpc Y.

Question 32. (Klop) Constructing fpcs in this way is a 'free construction' in that never non-trivial identifications will arise: Let Y, Y' be fpc's and let $B_1 \ldots B_n$, $C_1 \ldots C_k$ be picked from the fpc-generating vectors (i),(ii),(iii) above. Then we have:

(i) $YB_1 \ldots B_n =_\beta Y'B_1 \ldots B_n$ iff $Y = Y'$;
(ii) $YB_1 \ldots B_n =_\beta YC_1 \ldots C_k$ iff $B_1 \ldots B_n \equiv C_1 \ldots C_k$.

Already the restriction to (G_1), the generating vector δ, is a generalization of Statman's conjecture, stating that $Y\delta^n \neq Y\delta^m$ for any fpc Y and $n \neq m$ (instead of $Y \neq Y\delta$). This indicates how non-trivial this conjecture is for the general case. For the particular fpc Y_0 we have partial results:

(i) The sequence $Y_0, Y_0\delta, Y_0\delta\delta, \ldots$ is known as the Böhm sequence, and is known to not contain any duplicates.
(ii) For Y_0 in combination with the set of all generating vectors (G_2), the conjecture has been proven in [EHKP12].

Both results can easily be extended to the setting of $\lambda\beta\mu^{\rightarrow}$. We therefore think that there is hope to prove freeness of the construction for all generating vectors (G_1), (G_2), (G_3) for the $\lambda\beta\mu^{\rightarrow}$ calculus. Then a positive answer to Conjecture 26 would immediately yield a positive answer to Klop's conjecture.

In view of the strong consequences of the Conjecture 26 one must expect that the conjecture is indeed difficult to prove. Also a counterexample would be very interesting. Even if the conjecture fails, or as a partial result towards the conjecture, it would be interesting to determine a class of fixed point combinators for which the conjecture holds.

References

[AK95]   Ariola, Z.M., Klop, J.W.: Equational Term Graph Rewriting. Technical Report IR-391, Vrije Universiteit Amsterdam (1995),
ftp://ftp.cs.vu.nl/pub/papers/theory/IR-391.ps.Z

[Bar84]   Barendregt, H.P.: The Lambda Calculus. Its Syntax and Semantics, re-
            vised edition. Studies in Logic and The Foundations of Mathematics,
            vol. 103. North-Holland (1984)
[BDS13]   Barendregt, H.P., Dekkers, W., Statman, R.: Lambda Calculus with
            Types. Perspectives in Logic. Cambridge University Press (2013)
[Ber85]   Bercovici, I.: Unsolvable Terms in Typed Lambda Calculus with Fix-Point
            Operators. In: Parikh, R. (ed.) Logic of Programs 1985. LNCS, vol. 193,
            pp. 16–22. Springer, Heidelberg (1985)
[BKdV00]   Bethke, I., Klop, J.W., de Vrijer, R.C.: Descendants and Origins in Term
            Rewriting. Information and Computation 159(1-2), 59–124 (2000)
[BN98]   Baader, F., Nipkow, T.: Term Rewriting and All That. Cambridge
            University Press (1998)
[CC96]   Coquand, C., Coquand, T.: On the Definition of Reduction for Infi-
            nite Terms. Comptes Rendus de l'Académie des Sciences. Série I 323(5),
            553–558 (1996)
[dMJB⁺]   de Mast, P., Jansen, J.-M., Bruin, D., Fokker, J., Koopman, P., Smetsers,
            S., van Eekelen, M., Plasmeijer, R.: Functional Programming in Clean
[EGKvO11]   Endrullis, J., Grabmayer, C., Klop, J.W., van Oostrom, V.: On Equal
            μ-Terms. Theoretical Computer Science 412(28), 3175–3202 (2011)
[EHH⁺13]   Endrullis, J., Hansen, H.H., Hendriks, D., Polonsky, A., Silva, A.: A Coin-
            ductive Treatment of Infinitary Term Rewriting (submitted, 2013)
[EHK10]   Endrullis, J., Hendriks, D., Klop, J.W.: Modular Construction of Fixed
            Point Combinators and Clocked Böhm Trees. In: Proc. Symp. on Logic in
            Computer Science (LICS 2010), pp. 111–119 (2010)
[EHK12]   Endrullis, J., Hendriks, D., Klop, J.W.: Highlights in Infinitary Rewriting
            and Lambda Calculus. Theoretical Computer Science 464, 48–71 (2012)
[EHKP12]   Endrullis, J., Hendriks, D., Klop, J.W., Polonsky, A.: Discriminating
            Lambda-Terms using Clocked Böhm Trees. Logical Methods in Computer
            Science (in print, 2012)
[EHKP13]   Endrullis, J., Hendriks, D., Klop, J.W., Polonsky, A.: Clocked Lambda
            Calculus. Mathematical Structures in Computer Science (accepted for
            publication, 2013)
[EP13]   Endrullis, J., Polonsky, A.: Infinitary Rewriting Coinductively. In: Proc.
            Types for Proofs and Programs (TYPES 2012). LIPIcs, vol. 19, pp. 16–27.
            Schloss Dagstuhl (2013)
[HS08]   Hindley, J.R., Seldin, J.P.: Lambda-Calculus and Combinators. Cambridge
            University Press (2008)
[Hut07]   Hutton, G.: Programming in Haskell. Cambridge University Press (2007)
[Int97]   Intrigila, B.: Non-Existent Statman's Double Fixed Point Combinator
            Does Not Exist, Indeed. Information and Computation 137(1), 35–40
            (1997)
[KdV05]   Klop, J.W., de Vrijer, R.C.: Infinitary Normalization. In: We Will Show
            Them: Essays in Honour of Dov Gabbay, vol. 2, pp. 169–192. College Publ.
            (2005), Techn. report:
            http://www.cwi.nl/ftp/CWIreports/SEN/SEN-R0516.pdf
[KS09]   Ketema, J., Simonsen, J.G.: Infinitary Combinatory Reduction Systems:
            Confluence. Logical Methods in Computer Science 5(4), 1–29 (2009)

[NI89]   Naoi, T., Inagaki, Y.: Algebraic Semantics and Complexity of Term Rewriting Systems. In: Dershowitz, N. (ed.) RTA 1989. LNCS, vol. 355, pp. 311–325. Springer, Heidelberg (1989)

[Pla84]   Platek, R.A.: Foundations of Recursion Theory. University Microfilms (1984)

[Plo77]   Plotkin, G.D.: Lcf considered as a programming language. Theor. Comput. Sci. 5(3), 223–255 (1977)

[Smu85]   Smullyan, R.: To Mock a Mockingbird, and Other Logic Puzzles: Including an Amazing Adventure in Combinatory Logic. Alfred A. Knopf, New York (1985)

[Sta02]   Statman, R.: On The Lambda Y Calculus. In: Proc. Symp. on Logic in Computer Science (LICS 2002), pp. 159–166. IEEE (2002)

[Ter03]   Terese. Term Rewriting Systems. Cambridge Tracts in Theoretical Computer Science, vol. 55. Cambridge University Press (2003)

Declarative Natural Language Specifications

Pascal Serrarens

Abstract. Natural languages are often used for specification because they can easily be understood by non-technical people. The downside is the inherent ambiguity of the language, which makes natural languages unsuitable for specifications. When declarative language concepts are applied for natural language specifications it will reduce ambiguity and the cost of writing specifications.

1 Specification

Specifications record the requirements a system shall fulfil in order to be accepted. The difficulty in writing good specification is that a varied group of people need to work with it: apart from the designers, programmers this also involves customers including users, testers, project managers and system managers. Many of them do not have a technical programming background and find it difficult to read technical code. Natural language is therefore preferred and used for most systems. It is therefore no surprise that specifications are often extensive but still incomplete.

1.1 Defining Specification

Specifications exist on many levels, from technical to abstract. The use of (pseudo) formal specification techniques is more widespread in the former, as people who work with them are more technically educated. Natural languages are used often in the latter as they are often also part of a call for tender and more non-technically educated people are involved.

In this article we focus on system specifications forming the bridge between the customer needs and the designers input. This immediately shows the problem: the specification's target audience is diverse. On the customer's side technical knowledge is often limited as their main focus is on business domain. On the other hand designers lack the business knowledge and focus on technical issues.

The goal is therefore a specification which can be evaluated by the customer and still covers all technical/functional topics needed by the designers to make a good design.

2 Related Work

Most work on improving natural language specifications is based around text patterns. But like with programming we see that imperative language constructions

P. Achten and P. Koopman (Eds.): Plasmeijer Festschrift, LNCS 8106, pp. 127–132, 2013.

are used most often. See for instance [CD03], where language patterns consist of traditional constructions like if-then, while and for loops.

2.1 Legal Codes (Laws)

Probably the oldest form of specifications are laws. Written laws are first recorded around 2100 BC [Tie05]. Codified Cival Law is always written in natural languages. One reason for this is that it shares a common (idealistic) goal with specifications:

> "The aim was to state the law so clearly that an ordinary citizen could read the code and determine what his rights and responsibilities were." [Tie05]

In our case we want to write down the behaviour such that ordinary users can read the specifications and determine whether the system will support his needs.

A beautiful aspect of laws is their declarative nature. Take for instance the first article in the Dutch Constitution:

> "All persons in the Netherlands shall be treated equally in equal circumstances. Discrimination on the grounds of religion, belief, political opinion, race, or sex or on any other grounds whatsoever shall not be permitted." [Dut]

Although the text is imperative ("all persons ... shall"), it is a rule which is independent of context (referential transparent) and not sequential. Note that this article in itself is defined twice: the second sentence is in fact a clarification by example of the first.

Next to the laws themselves, an extensive system of explaining and interpreting them, which is called jurisdiction. The often interesting cases coming forward in this are great examples of the drawbacks of using natural languages for specification. 4000 years of experience has not produced a way to avoid this.

3 Functional Properties

Most functional specifications use an imperative style. Especially the if-then language construct is used often. In relation to that, a large part of the specifications are case based: in case A, the system should be performing X. The use of these language constructs is caused by the process in which specifications are produced. It merely is a collection of specific cases which should be covered by the system.

The drawback of this approach is that the cases in the specifications are not covering the whole system and as cases may (and therefore, will) overlap: the specification can contradict itself.

A good specification is therefore not case based, but generic, defining the universal behaviour of the system. Another advantage of this is that the resulting system is more predictable, as the behaviour is defined for any case, not just some cases.

In this section we will discuss how specific declarative properties help to achieve such a generic specification.

3.1   Declarative

Many specifications use imperative language constructs like if-then-else and for-loop constructs. Using these constructs limit the implementer greatly, as it forces an order of evaluation and specifications often quickly transform into natural language programs.

Declarative statements stay very close to the rule: want does one want to ensure, instead of how to ensure this. Although the difference seems small, it has a huge effect on clarity:

1. If it begins to rain, the umbrella shall be opened
2. The umbrella shall be open when it is raining

The second line is much more powerful than the first. Not only does it state when the umbrella needs to be opened, but also when to close it. In fact, the second is more concise: as the umbrella is needed to protect us from the rain, it needs to be open when it starts raining. If one starts opening the umbrella when the first raindrops fall, we are in fact too late. Of course the second is harder to implement, but that is an issue which should not be solved by the specification, but by the implementer. The implementation may be more complex, but will produce the right results.

As an example we give a specification for where trains are allowed to stop. Because of safety issues, trains are only allowed to stop on certain areas on the track: not on a crossing, before (and not just behind) signalling lights, completely along the platform, not covering any switches etc.

The first attempts to write a specification for this were imperative, using pseudo-code to define an algorithm checking for each piece of track whether the train was allowed to stop there. The problem was that the train length had to be taken into account as well, which made the algorithm complex. Multiple attempts therefore failed. Using a declarative approach showed that the specification is actually quite simple:

1. The length of the train may not stand still within *non stopping zones*.
2. The following areas a defined as *non stopping zones*
   - Railway crossings
   - A stretch of 1m on either side of the platform
   - ...

Actually, it is the same description as in the paragraph above, but now written in a concise way.

Of course, this does not solve the problem how this should be implemented, but that is exactly what a specification is not supposed to do: it should not limit the party realizing the system to a specific implementation, but instead give them the freedom to choose the best implementation as long as it fulfils the specification.

3.2 Referential Transparency

Universal requirements are the best to work with: they define the system behaviour in any situation, independent from the system status at any moment. This results in clearer and predictable system behaviour and simplifies the specification as a whole. It also provides a better baseline for the implementers, because they do not have to work through the whole specification to determine a specific desired system behaviour.

For this reason requirements shall be side-effect free: its meaning should not change by any other requirement hanging around somewhere or which may be added later on. This is in contrast to the case-by-case specification where cases may overlap.

The way to achieve this is to use definitions are much as possible. In the example above, *non stopping zones*, is defined as a term to specify the places where a train is not allowed to stop. The complete definition is found there and should not be altered by other requirements. In a section on weather conditions one may specify that in dry and hot conditions, tracks close by vegetation are also non stopping zones, because of the fire hazard from sparks coming from the brakes of trains. Constructions like that have to be prevented by the author, as it breaks referential transparency. Of course, there is nothing to prevent the author of the specification to extend the definition somewhere else: it is up to the author to know and apply this rule.

3.3 Lazy

A specification is not evaluated of course, but when writing a requirement, one does not need to understand a specific term to understand the full requirement. This helps in understanding the requirement more quickly.

In the example above on the non stopping zones, requirement 1 specifies that there is a limitation to where a train is allowed to stop, but it does not specify where. One can understand requirement 1 on its own and only when one needs to know where a train is not allowed to stop, he should look at requirement 2.

Furthermore, the definition of requirement 1 is not dependent on the actual definition of the non stopping zones. It is possible to replace the definition in requirement 2 by something completely different. It is even possible to leave out the definition of the non-stopping zone during the writing of the specification, as it may not be available yet. This still does not invalidate the specifications.

4   Advantages

4.1   Speed of Writing

Specifications written in Functional English are quicker to produce, because of the declarative style and referential transparency. One case tackles every aspect one by one and not get tangled in a complex text with dependencies throughout the whole document.

4.2   Expressive Power

A declarative specification style takes significantly less text to describe the requirements than traditional specification. It really forces the author to focus on what the system should ensure, leaving the implementation issues to the implementer. Imperative specifications make it easy to include implementation aspects because of their similarity to programming languages.

5   Limitations

5.1   Overall System Behaviour

Although Functional English helps to reduce the ambiguity of natural language specifications, it does not suffice alone. The major shortcoming is that it fails to draw a complete picture of the whole system: how will the result behave when implemented? Functional programming languages do not have this drawback, as they can be executed, which shows the behaviour of the whole system.

For this reason, specifications written in a declarative style should always be accompanied with illustrating descriptions. Use cases are well suited for this, as they are equally accessible for various people as natural language specifications.

5.2   Enforcing the Declarative Style

Writing specifications in a declarative style is not enforced in any way. Functional programming languages force the program into declarative constructs as imperative elements are not available. Type and other checking mechanisms prevent the programmer to violates against the declarative rules.

On the other hand there is nothing to prevent the author to deviate from these rules when writing declarative specifications. Peer review may improve the use of the declarative style, but in most cases the peers are not available. Other reviewers often have a tendency to direct the author to writing imperative requirements, as that is the common practice. Therefore there is a need for distributing and teach the knowledge about writing declarative specifications.

6   Conclusion

The declarative way of writing specifications improves the quality and effort needed. Language constructs from declarative languages can be applied well in natural language specifications, resulting in clearer and more compact specifications, while retaining the advantage of a specification which can be read by non-technical people.

While it works well as a specification, an additional illustration is needed to show the workings of the system as a whole, as the specifications cannot be executed. Additionally, without a language environment enforcing writing good declarative specifications, the possibilities to check against the declarative rules are limited.

This should not prevent requirements engineers using these rules, as every time it is applied, the quality of the specification will increase. For this reason we should spread the word and improve system specifications using a declarative style.

References

[CD03]   Denger, E.K.C., Berry, D.M.: Higher quality requirements specifications through natural language patterns. In: Proceedings of the IEEE International Conference on Software - Science, Technology & Engineering, SwSTE 2003 (2003)

[Dut]   The Constitution of the Kingdom of the Netherlands 2008. Ministry of the Interior and Kingdom Relations, Consitutional Affairs and the Legislation Division in collaboration with the Translation Departument of the Ministry of Foreign Affairs

[Tie05] Tiersma, P.: Writing, text and the law. This paper can be downloaded without charge from the Social Science Research Network (SSRN) (November 2005), electronic library at: http://ssrn.com/abstract=850305

Clean Up the Web!
Rapid Client-Side Web Development with Clean

László Domoszlai and Tamás Kozsik

Department of Programming Languages and Compilers
Eötvös Loránd University, Budapest, Hungary
{dlacko,kto}@pnyf.inf.elte.hu

Abstract. Programming in Clean is much more appealing than programming in JavaScript. Therefore, solutions that can replace JavaScript with Clean in client-side web development are widely welcomed. This paper describes a technology for the cross-compilation of Clean to JavaScript and for the tight integration of the generated code into a web application. Our solution is based on the iTask framework and its extension, the so-called Tasklets. The application server approach provides simple and easy deployment, thus supporting rapid development. Examples are shown to illustrate how communication between the Clean and JavaScript code can be established.

1   Introduction

Using JavaScript for the development of client-side web applications displeases the Clean programmer and former web developer writing these words. JavaScript, even despite it has some functional features, creates a hostile environment compared to Clean. Consider, for example, the lack of type safety, the ugly and sometimes unnecessarily verbose syntax, and the productivity loss caused by these. One can also miss very much the elegance of a well-designed and mature functional language, and the programmers' self-confidence enhanced by the strong type system and referential transparency.

Still, JavaScript, as the only language of the platform for browser development, is inevitable. As a consequence, several attempts have been made for cross-compiling all kinds of languages to JavaScript. It is a well-established technique considering imperative languages, but the picture is not that clear when the subject of compilation is a functional language. Even worse, compiling a *lazy* functional language, such as Clean, to JavaScript is definitely a delicate job.

The main problem is the limitation of the available resources in the browser: the run-time system imposes severe constraints on heap and stack usage. As iteration in functional languages is accomplished via recursion, stack limitation seems to be the most serious issue. A standard technique to overcome this is trampolining [16], but, as it increases the memory footprint and the running time of the application, usually it does not perform effectively enough in the case of lazy functional languages. The reason for the higher memory footprint in these languages is the need to maintain thunks, i.e. delayed computations.

P. Achten and P. Koopman (Eds.): Plasmeijer Festschrift, LNCS 8106, pp. 133–150, 2013.

As for Clean, a mature JavaScript compilation technique is available which solves these problems to an extent which is applicable for most practical tasks [5]. However, this is only half the job. Compiling a Clean program to JavaScript still involves numerous steps which hampers the development of client side web applications in Clean: (1) the Clean program must be transformed to an intermediate language using the Clean compiler, (2) this intermediate must be compiled to JavaScript using a standalone application, and (3) the generated JavaScript code must be integrated into the web application. This complex and mundane process can nullify the advantages of non-JavaScript development.

In this paper an extension to iTask and Tasklets is presented, to make the above mentioned deployment process transparent. With this extension, iTask becomes a rapid development environment, or even an application server for client side web applications written in Clean. Furthermore, this extension does not only solve the aforementioned deployment problem, but it also enables complex information interchange between the Clean and JavaScript code in a type safe manner.

The rest of the paper is structured as follows. Section 2 gives a brief introduction to the iTask system and Tasklets. Section 3 presents what contributions the present paper makes. To that end, it illustrates the approach and some of the technical issues through three carefully selected examples. Section 4 discusses type correspondence between the JavaScript and Clean side of the code. Related work is described in section 5. Finally, section 6 concludes. The system as well the examples presented here can be downloaded from the web.[1]

2   Preliminaries

The iTask system [10] is a framework for programming workflow supporting applications in Clean using a new programming paradigm built around the concept of *tasks* [15]. A task is an abstract description of an interactive persistent unit of work which delivers a value when it is executed. From a practical point of view, a task can be anything from a system call to some interaction to be performed in a web browser by a user.

iTask provides a combinator-based embedded domain specific language to specify compositions of such interdependent tasks. A complete multi-user web application can be generated from the specification of the workflow and of the different data types involved – all the details (including the web user interface, client-server communication, state management etc.) are automatically taken care of by the framework itself.

Developing web applications such a way is straightforward in the sense that the programmers are liberated from these cumbersome and error-prone jobs, such that they can concentrate on the essence of the application. The iTask system makes it very easy to develop interactive multi-user applications. The down side is that one has only limited control over the customization of the generated user

---

[1] http://people.inf.elte.hu/dlacko/papers/rapmix/

interface. Sometimes, even if the functional web design is satisfactory, custom building blocks may be required for the purpose of user-friendliness.

Tasklets, a recent extension to iTask, are introduced to overcome this short-coming [6]. Tasklets enable the development of interactive web components directly in Clean. A tasklet consists of an inner state, user interface, and behavior provided by non-pure event handler functions. The user interface can be defined in any abstract or concrete way that enables HTML code generation. The event handlers are written in Clean, but compiled to JavaScript and executed in the browser where they have unrestricted access to client-side resources. Using browser resources, the tasklet can create custom appearance and exploit functionality available only in the browser; utilizing the event-driven architecture the tasklet can achieve interactive behavior.

From a technical point of view, tasklets are defined by the means of the `Tasklet st val` record type. It has two type parameters: one of the parameters denotes the type of the internal state of the tasklet (`st`) while the other gives the type of its observable state (`val`):

```
:: Tasklet st val = { generatorFunc :: (*World → *(TaskletGUI st, st, *World))
                    , resultFunc    :: (st → Maybe val)
                    }
```

During initialization, `generatorFunc` is executed on the server to provide the user interface and the initial state of the tasklet. Its only argument, a value of the unique type `*World`, allows access to the external environment. Whenever needed, the current observable value of the tasklet can be computed from the internal state by calling `resultFunc`. This value is optional (`Maybe`). The user interface and its behavior are defined by the `TaskletHTML` structure:

```
:: TaskletGUI st  = TaskletHTML (TaskletHTML st) | ...
:: TaskletHTML st = { html          :: HtmlDef
                    , eventHandlers :: [HtmlEvent st]
                    }
:: HtmlDef = ∃a: HtmlDef a & toHtml a

:: HtmlEvent st = HtmlEvent HtmlElementId EventType (EventHandlerFunc st)
:: EventType     = OnClick | OnMouseOver | OnMouseOut | ...
:: EventHandlerFunc st :== (st HtmlObject *HtmlDocument → *(*HtmlDocument, st))
```

The actual user interface (`html` field) can be given by any data structure provided that it has an instance of the function class `toHtml`.

The run-time behavior of a tasklet is encoded in a list of event handler functions (`eventHandlers` field). Event handlers are defined using the `HtmlEvent` type. Its only data constructor has three arguments: the identifier of an HTML element, the type of the event and the event handler function. During the instantiation of the tasklet on the client, the event handler function is attached to the given HTML element to catch events of the given type.

The event handler functions work on the JavaScript event object (a value of type `HtmlObject` in Clean) and on the current internal state of the tasklet. They also have access to the HTML Document Object Model (DOM) to maintain their appearance. The DOM is a shared object from the point of event handlers, therefore it can be manipulated only the way as IO is done in Clean, through unique types. That is, accessing the DOM is possible only using library functions controlled by the unique *HtmlDocument type.

Following the tasklet definition, a wrapper task must be created to hide the behavior of the tasklet behind the interface of a task (tasks are represented by the opaque type Task a, where a denotes the type of the value of the task):

```
mkTask :: (Tasklet st a) → Task a
```

The life cycle of a tasklet starts when the value of the wrapper task is requested. First, generatorFunc is executed on the server to provide the initial state and user interface of the tasklet. Then, the initial task state and the event handlers defined in Clean are on the fly compiled to JavaScript and, along with the UI definition, shipped to the browser. In the browser, the HTML markup is injected into the page and the event handlers are attached. As events are fired, the related event handlers catch them, and may modify the state of the tasklet and the DOM. If the state is changed, resultFunc is called to create a new result value that is sent to the server immediately. The life cycle of the tasklet is terminated by the framework when the result value is finally taken by another task.

3   Rapid Development with iTask

In iTask, the deployment process during development is fairly straightforward. Given an iTask task, aTask, by adding the following main function and running the application, an embedded web server is started, which publishes the task on the local host.

```
Start :: *World → *World
Start world = startEngine aTask world
```

When the page is requested in the browser, first a client-side run-time environment is loaded, which manages the user interface (UI) of the tasks. The actual task is published on a special URL where it provides the abstract description of its UI as a JSON encoded descriptor object. The run-time environment can load and display such abstract UI descriptions.

A tasklet is self-contained in the sense that its UI description contains all the JavaScript code necessary to run the tasklet in the browser. Thus, to turn an iTask application into an application server for non-iTask applications, all we have to do is to provide, as a standalone JavaScript library, a small part of the aforementioned run-time environment: a part which is able to load and create a tasklet. On the server side, a list of tasklets can be published all at once:

```
Start world = startEngine [{ PublishedTask
                           | url  = "/test"
                           , task = TaskWrapper (const testTasklet)
                           , defaultFormat = JSONGui}]
                          world
```

This overloaded version of function startEngine enables the specification of a list of tasks together with the URLs where they will be published (in the example above the list had only one element).

On the client side, loading the published tasklet is this simple:

```html
<html>
    <head>
        <script type="text/javascript" src="tasklet-runtime.js"/>
        <script type="text/javascript">

            loadTasklet("http://localhost/test", function(tasklet){
                tasklet.display(document.getElementById("out"));
            });

        </script>
    </head>
    <body>
        <div id="out"/>
    </body>
</html>
```

The JavaScript library tasklet-runtime.js is less than 10 kB compressed. It contains the logic for loading and instantiating tasklets, as well as the run-time environment of the Clean to JavaScript compiler. Function loadTasklet tries to load a tasklet from the URL given in its first argument. Since the loading mechanism is implemented with an asynchronous AJAX request, a call-back function must also be provided as a second argument; this will be called when the tasklet is loaded and created in the browser.

An instantiated tasklet is represented as a JavaScript object with the predefined prototype Tasklet. It encapsulates and hides all the properties of a tasklet (the user interface, the state and the behavior), and exposes only the display method which injects the UI of the tasklet into a given point in the HTML DOM.

Using the above method, an arbitrary tasklet can be included into a non-iTask application. However, it is still a foreign element in the application, as it runs independently and has no way for information exchange. In the following sections our solution is presented to this problem. We propose a mixed-language programming model where different parts of a web-application are written in either Clean or JavaScript, making the best use of the two languages. Each functionality can be coded in the language which suits better to the given task, and interaction is made easy between fragments written in the two languages. Rapid application deployment is supported by the concept of an application server for client-side web applications. Tasklets run embedded in a lightweight application server, which generates and supplies the JavaScript code through a standard web socket; the client side support library automatically injects this JavaScript code into the web page. At the end of program development, the application server can be eliminated: the JavaScript code generated from the tasklets can be saved into a .js or .html file, and deployed on a web server.

Our approach will be demonstrated step-by-step in the following sections through a series of example applications. What these examples have in common is the lack of a user interface and observable state of tasklets. According to the principle that in a mixed language environment both languages should be used at their best, we chose to implement control and user interaction in JavaScript, and stress pure style in the Clean code. This approach results in a very special, unconventional use of iTask and Tasklets. To indicate that a given tasklet does not encapsulate a GUI, a new data constructor NoGUI for the type TaskletGUI is introduced. Moreover, as it is used for task-to-task communication in proper iTask applications only, no return value (observable state) for tasklets are needed here. Therefore, in the forthcoming examples, for the creation of tasklets, we use the initially function which specifies the initial internal state only.

```
initially :: st → Tasklet st Void
initially st = { generatorFunc   =   λworld = (NoGUI, st, world)
               , resultFunc      =   const Nothing
               }
```

3.1 Writing the Logic of a Web Application in Clean

One day the need to display Clean source code in a web application, as part of a source code repository, has emerged. Many Clean developers use the integrated Clean development environment, CleanIDE, for programming. This environment provides excellent syntax highlighting, and Clean developers have really got used to it. Therefore the same style to present Clean code seemed highly desirable for our web application. Reprogramming the functionality in JavaScript would have been a fairly complex task. However, with our tasklet-based framework it has proven to be relatively easy. We decided to use the modules responsible for syntax highlighting in the CleanIDE, which meant more than 1000 lines altogether. We had to add a main module containing a tasklet definition (which mimics the CleanIDE for calling in the syntax highlight module) and a Start rule: 30 effective lines of code. Furthermore, 18 effective lines of JavaScript and 13 effective lines of HTML code had to be written only. The Clean to JavaScript compiler generated 136 kB of JavaScript from the 33 kB of Clean code, and the source code viewer was up and running. Now we take a closer look at the code.

```
:: Color :== String

highlight :: [String] → [[(String, Color)]]    // definition omitted

annotateI (Just dynArg) st eventqueue = (res, st, eventqueue)
    where res   =   case dynArg of (lines :: [String]) = highlight lines

highlighter = mkInterfaceTask (initially Void) [InterfaceFun "annotate" annotateI]
Start world = startEngine [{PublishedTask | url = "/highlighter"
                                          , task = TaskWrapper (const highlighter)
                                          , defaultFormat = JSONGui}]
                world
```

The unnecessary technical details have been omitted, as well as the body of the `highlight` function, which can be written as the composition of some functions defined already in the CleanIDE.

In the case of this simple tasklet, not only the GUI and the result value, but also the internal state is absent, i.e. Void. The only way to interact with the highlighter tasklet is to call its single *interface function*, `annotateI`, from the JavaScript code. When a tasklet is created with `mkInterfaceTask` (defined in the tasklet library), a list of interface functions can be passed. In this case, this list has a single entry: whenever the JavaScript code calls the `annotate` method of the tasklet, the code generated from the `annotateI` function is executed. This `annotateI` takes the current (Void) state of the tasklet and an event queue (explained in section 3.3), and returns them unmodified. Information from JavaScript to Clean is received through the second parameter, which is of type `Maybe Dynamic`. Dynamics provide dynamic typing facilities in a statically typed language [1,14].) We expect here that a list of strings is stored in the `Dynamic`, namely the lines of some Clean source code. If the dynamic pattern matching fails, the run-time engine triggers an exception to inform the caller. The `highlight` function will be called with the lines found in the dynamic: it splits each line into tokens, and annotates each token with its colour. The token and its colour is represented as a pair of strings, a list of pairs corresponds to a line, and the list of lists is the whole program text syntax highlighted. This list of lists of pairs of strings is sent back to the JavaScript side as a component of the triple returned by `annotateI`.

To understand how types are handled in our Clean to JavaScript compiler, consider below the interesting part of the JavaScript side in our mixed-language application.

```
function onLoadTasklet(tasklet){
    var lines = prepareLines();
    var tokens = tasklet.intf.annotate(lines);

    for(var i=0; i<tokens.length; i++){
        for(var j=0; j<tokens[i].length; j++){
        var token = tokens[i][j][0];
        var color = tokens[i][j][1];
        appendToken(token, color);
        }
        appendNewLine();
    }
}


loadTasklet("http://localhost/highlighter", onLoadTasklet);
```

When the page is loaded, the function `loadTasklet` is executed by the browser. The tasklet is loaded from the specified URL, instantiated, and `onLoadTasklet` is called with it. This latter function first creates an array of strings (i.e. `lines`), which is passed to the `annotate` interface function of the tasklet (the interface functions are created under the `intf` namespace to avoid possible name collisions with the original properties of the Tasklet prototype). Note that this array of strings corresponds to a `Dynamic` containing a list of strings in the Clean side (the details of the type correspondence algorithm are explained in section 4). Function `annotate` returns an array of arrays of arrays of strings, `tokens`, which is processed in a straightforward way in the `for`-loop.

Communication between JavaScript and Clean sources is, therefore, accomplished in the following way. Primitive types of Clean are represented with similar primitive types in JavaScript, while lists and tuples are represented by arrays (an n-tuple is represented as an array of length n, e.g. 2 in our example). Algebraic types are also represented by arrays – the name of a data constructor is stored in the first element of such an array. Values from JavaScript correspond to `Dynamic` in Clean, so that pattern matching on types in the Clean side facilitates type-safe programming. This has been an example of an interface function with a single argument. Interface functions with no arguments receive a `Nothing`, and those with multiple arguments will find a tuple in the `Dynamic`.

3.2   Adding State and Interaction

Suppose you must write some interactive presentation logic to be executed in a browser. For example, you want to display the bibliographic data of your publications in a searchable, filterable way on the web (Fig. 1). The application should receive a BibTeX file as input, and parse, filter and pretty-print the entries found in this file. To write a client-server application for this, and implement parsing and filtering on the server would be too much hassle. It is more reasonable to send over the data to the browser all at once, parse it, and then let an interactive client side application filter the data and display the selected items. Coding all these activities in JavaScript is not what you would like to do on a rainy

Entry type: In Proceedings ▾

Author: Plasmeijer

Year:

Keyword: iTask

[Search]

[1] Rinus Plasmeijer and Bas Lijnse and Steffen Michels and Peter Achten and Pieter W. M. Koopman. Task-oriented programming in a pure functional language. In *PPDP*, 2012. [DOI]

[2] Rinus Plasmeijer and Bas Lijnse and Peter Achten and Steffen Michels. Getting a grip on tasks that coordinate tasks. In *LDTA*, 2011. [DOI]

[3] Rinus Plasmeijer and Peter Achten and Pieter W. M. Koopman and Bas Lijnse and Thomas van Noort and John H. G. van Groningen. iTasks for a change: type-safe run-time change in dynamically evolving workflows. In *PEPM*, 2011. [DOI]

Fig. 1. Web application for filtering bibliographic data

Friday afternoon. Contrarily, much of the functionality is fairly straightforward to develop in Clean, using higher order functions. To implement parsing, for instance, the Parser Combinator library of Clean may prove useful. It turns out that tasklets are a valuable tool for building this application.

The main difference between this and the syntax highlighter application is that interaction with the user is required, and that there is some state that should be preserved between user interactions. We suggest that the state should be stored in the JavaScript side of the code, and state-to-state functions should be written in Clean. The following fragments present the interesting parts from the JavaScript side of the code.

```
var entries;
var tasklet;

function onLoadTasklet(aTasklet){
    tasklet = aTasklet;
    entries = tasklet.intf.init();

    var refs = prepareReferences();

    for( var i=0; i<refs.length; i++ )
        entries = tasklet.intf.parse(entries, refs[i]);

    display_bibitems(entries);
}
```

The state of the application, stored in the global variable **entries**, represents all the entries of the BibTeX file. Right after the page is loaded and the tasklet is created, function **onLoadtasklet** will be called, which parses the bibliography items. First, it creates the initial state by calling the **init** interface function, then the bibliography items are parsed and added to the state one by one using the **parse** interface function of the tasklet. Parsing is performed in such a "per item" basis as a precaution only – otherwise, in the case of a long bibliography list, like that of Rinus Plasmeijer, parsing might run out of stack.

Whenever the user interacts with our application, namely when the search button on the web page is pressed, function **search** will be called. It filters the bibliography items, again using interface functions of the tasklet.

```
function search(){
    var selected = entries;

    var year = document.getElementById("year").value;
    if( year != "" ) selected = tasklet.intf.filter(selected,"year",year);
    // similarly for entry type and author

    var keyword = document.getElementById("keyword").value;
    if( keyword != "" ) selected = tasklet.intf.search(selected, keyword);

    display_bibitems(selected);
}
```

Similarly to the syntax highlighter, this tasklet is also stateless and provides no GUI. It does not make use of `eventqueue` either.

```
bibtex  =  mkInterfaceTask (initially Void)
                [ InterfaceFun     "init"  initI
                , InterfaceFun     "parse" parseI
                , InterfaceFun "toString"  toStringI
                , InterfaceFun   "filter"  filterI
                , InterfaceFun   "search"  keywordI]
```

The interface functions of the tasklet have a similar structure to that of `annotateI` in the previous example. The only argument they use is the one of type `Maybe Dynamic`, on which they pattern match. The `filter` method calls in the JavaScript code, for instance, has three actual arguments, therefore the dynamic in the corresponding Clean function, `filterI`, should be a triple.

```
filterI (Just dynArg) st eventqueue = (dynamic res, st, eventqueue)
    where res = case dynArg of
                ((entries,tag,value) :: ([Entry],String,String))
                    = filterEntries entries tag value
```

Section 4 will explain why `res`, the result from filtering is wrapped in a `dynamic`.

3.3 Even More State and Even More Interaction

In the BIBTEX example, the state of the application was stored in the code written in JavaScript, and the internal state of the tasklet was Void. Our next challenge is to write a game for solving Rubik's cube – but now in this application a stateful tasklet will be used. Similarly to the previous examples, the tasklet will have neither a GUI nor an observable state, and it will provide interface functions available for the controlling JavaScript side of the code.

The level of interactivity is much higher in this example than in the previous one. The Rubik cube is controlled by moving the mouse and by pressing some keys; the cube is rendered (Fig. 2) on-the-fly by the Clean side of the code when its state is changed. Another interesting issue in this example is how information flows between the pure Clean side of the code and the impure JavaScript side.

Fig. 2. Rubik's cube rendered in Clean, drawn by JavaScript

Although the tasklet depends on information from the outer environment (the browser), and has an impact on its environment as well, referential transparency is not violated.

This is achieved by using a technique we call *the method of the blind chess player*. A blind chess player cannot observe the chessboard in any way, only possesses a mental picture, an inner representation of the board. The blind chess player depends on an independent observer to announce the movements. The blind chess player cannot even move the pieces directly, but can ask someone to carry out the movement. The first sign of using this technique is that from the nine interface functions of the tasklet, eight are merely used to delegate events. When such an event is delivered, the inner state of the tasklet is updated, the cube is re-rendered, and finally displayed.

```
rubik = mkInterfaceTask (initially (State standard (pi/10.0,pi/10.0,0.0) Nothing))
                [ InterfaceFun    "display" displayI
                , InterfaceFun "mouseDown" mouseDownI
                , InterfaceFun   "mouseUp" mouseUpI
                , InterfaceFun "mouseMove" mouseMoveI
                , InterfaceFun  "turnLeft" (turnI fst left)
                , InterfaceFun "turnRight" (turnI fst right)
                , InterfaceFun    "turnUp" (turnI snd up)
                , InterfaceFun  "turnDown" (turnI snd down)
                ]

:: R3    :== (Real,Real,Real)
:: Color :== String
:: Cube  :== (R3 -> Color)
:: State  = State Cube R3 (Maybe (Int,Int))
```

The internal state of the tasklet will keep track of the actual configuration of the cube (initially it is the "standard" configuration, explained a bit later), an angle describing the viewpoint of the user (R3), and the mouse coordinates if the mouse is pressed (initially it is not). Note that the second and the third components in the internal state of the tasklet describe the state of the user interface.

To model Rubik's cube, we follow Péter Diviánszky.[2] The cube is placed in such a way that its size is $3 \times 3 \times 3$, its middle point is the origin of the Cartesian coordinate system and its edges are parallel to the axes. The representation is given as a partial function R3 $\to$ Color, which assigns a color to the middle point of each of the 6×9 small faces of the cube. The operations, namely rotating the cube and twisting one of the 6 layers, can be implemented by composing functions that describe coordinate transformations, for instance left (x,y,z) = (z,y,~x). The initial, standard configuration can be given in the following way.

---

[2] http://pnyf.inf.elte.hu/fp/Rubik_en.xml

```
standard (x,y,z)
   | abs x > abs y && abs x > abs z  = if (x < 0.0) "green"  "blue"
   | abs y > abs x && abs y > abs z  = if (y < 0.0) "yellow" "white"
   | otherwise                       = if (z < 0.0) "orange" "red"
```

Now we come to an essential question, namely how to display this cube from a pure environment. A trivial solution would be to return the list of polygons from an interface function and let the JavaScript side to display it. However, that would clutter the interface of the tasklet and would move a substantial part of the algorithm from Clean to JavaScript. Therefore, another solution was chosen: the tasklets are allowed to fire events just as arbitrary JavaScript objects can do. In the JavaScript side, functions can be subscribed to these events.

```
tasklet.addListener("draw", function(event){

    var v = event.value;
    var color = v[1];
    var p1 = v[0][0];
    ...

    drawPolygon(p1,p2,p3,p4,color);
}
```

The `displayI` interface function computes a 2D projection of the cube from the viewpoint of the user (`polygons`), asks the JavaScript side to clear the display, and asks it again and again to draw each polygon with the appropriate color. To achieve this, the function fires events `clear` and `draw`.

```
displayI :: (Maybe Dynamic) State *EventQueue → *(Void, State, *EventQueue)
displayI Nothing st=:(State cube angle _) eventqueue
   # eventqueue = fireEvent eventqueue "clear" Void
   # eventqueue = foldl (λq p → fireEvent q "draw" p) eventqueue polygons
   = (Void, st, eventqueue)
   where polygons = project cube angle
```

In Clean unique types (`*EventQueue` here) are used to thread effectful computations in a pure functional way. Since `fireEvent` interacts with the outside world, namely with the user interface of our application, a "new event queue" is formed after each invocation of `fireEvent`, and the previous event queue is "consumed". However, this is not enough to preserve referential transparency. What is missing is that events are not allowed to interfere with the interface function that triggers them. No return value is coming back to the Clean side from the JavaScript function(s) triggered by an event, and there is no means to access the outside world from the Clean side other than through the parameters of the interface functions. Type `*EventQueue` is abstract; it can only be used to ensure that events are delivered, and to define the order of event delivery. Due to this mechanism, the meaning of an interface function does not depend on *when* the event handlers are executed in the JavaScript side. They can be executed either interleaved with the Clean side of the code (i.e. by synchronous method calls) or asynchronously, after the completion of the interface function.

The division of labour described above is advantageous: pure definitions are written in Clean, while in JavaScript only the control and the effectful user interactions are implemented. In this application, for example, the JavaScript side is responsible for drawing polygons (it is straightforward in JavaScript using its browser-independent primitives), for capturing pressed keys and mouse events, and for doing some hacks to make the application work with different browsers. Altogether the JavaScript side is made up of a few dozens of effective lines of code here, such as the one catching key events.

```
function key(event){
    switch(event.charCode){
        case 119: tasklet.intf.turnUp();    break;
        case  97: tasklet.intf.turnLeft();  break;
        case 115: tasklet.intf.turnDown();  break;
        case 100: tasklet.intf.turnRight(); break;
    }
}
```

Most of the application, that is, roughly 200 effective lines of code, is written in Clean. All the decisions, all the difficult parts are in the Clean side. For instance, those interface functions of the tasklet which are partial applications of turnI make decisions on what to do with the key events based on the tasklet state, viz. whether rotate the cube (if the mouse button is not pressed) or twist a layer (if the mouse button is pressed over a polygon which belongs to the 2D projection of a layer of the cube).

```
turnI _ rotation Nothing st=:(State cube angle Nothing) eventqueue
    = displayI Nothing (State (cube o rotation) angle Nothing) eventqueue
turnI selector rotation Nothing st=:(State cube angle (Just coord)) eventqueue
    = displayI Nothing (State new_cube angle (Just coord)) eventqueue
    where polygons = project cube angle
          new_cube = case (select_layer polygons coord) of
                          Nothing     = cube
                          Just layer  = twist cube layer selector rotation
```

Some details of the definition are left uncovered here, and some other details were left out completely in order to increase readability – for the precise definitions the Reader can look up the code of the example on the web.[3]

4   Type Correspondence in Parameter Passing

The communication between the JavaScript side and the Clean side of the code is bidirectional. The JavaScript side calls the interface functions of tasklets, passing arguments and expecting results. Moreover, the Clean side fires events, with parameters attached, and the JavaScript side may observe these events and receives their attached parameters. In both cases information exchange between the two sides is achieved through pass-by-value parameters and, in the first case,

---

[3] http://people.inf.elte.hu/dlacko/papers/rapmix/rubiksource.html

through pass-by-value return values. The proper transmission of data requires a consequent correspondence between Clean types and JavaScript types. Certain types carry over between the two languages quite straightforwardly, others need special encoding.

It must be emphasized, however, that when we talk about the Clean side of the code, we actually mean some JavaScript code that was generated from Clean code by our cross-compiler. For clarity, we will refer here to the JavaScript side of the application as JS code, and to the code generated from the Clean side as JS* code. JS* uses a special run-time encoding of Clean types. For details on this encoding, the Reader is referred to [5].

To facilitate information exchange between Clean and JavaScript, a conversion from the JS* encoded values to JS is provided. The programmer could use the JS* encoded values in the JS code directly, but the structure of the encoded values is quite unnatural. Therefore, our runtime environment converts JS* values to JS values that are easier to use. As the examples in section 3 revealed, (1) during conversion primitive types are preserved; (2) the encoding of lists and tuples of Clean are converted to arrays; (3) algebraic types are also represented by arrays, where the name of a data constructor is stored in the first element of such an array. The conversion of functions in JS* to JS is not supported in the current version of the system. Handling partially applied functions and lazy arguments would demand special care of these values on the JS side, which, in our opinion, is not worth the effort.

The opposite direction, however, is not that simple. Clean has a much richer type system than JavaScript, thus JS values cannot be converted to JS* unequivocally. A further problem is that JavaScript is dynamically typed, and thus special care must be taken to avoid passing values of wrong type from JS to JS* and prevent run-time errors. Due to laziness, these run-time errors would emerge in the most unexpected moments.

A solution to overcome these problems is based on the *dynamics* feature of Clean. A value of an arbitrary Clean type can be converted to the special type `Dynamic`, then later the value of such a dynamic can be extracted by run-time pattern matching on the enclosed type using an algorithm called *type unification*.

When a value is passed from JS to JS*, the run-time environment tries to convert it to a `Dynamic` first. Obviously, this cannot be done in every case, but using the following (conservative) unification rules the most frequently occurring cases are covered.

1. JS booleans can be unified with Clean `Bool`s.
2. Although JS has no special character type, strings of one length can be unified with `Char` in Clean.
3. There are no separate integer and floating point types in JS, a JS integer value can be unified with both `Int` and `Real` in Clean.
4. Non-integer numbers can be unified with Clean `Real`s only.
5. JS strings can be unified with the `String` type of Clean.
6. An array of JS values can be unified with a Clean list type, if

(a) all of its elements can be determined by the preceding rules,

(b) they have the same type, and

(c) this type is equivalent with the type parameter of the Clean list.

7. In all other cases type unification fails.

Finally, there is one more important case to consider. As the BibTeX example revealed, it can be very useful to allow passing JS* values of some intricate type to JS as a state. Such a value is not supposed to be used directly by the JS code, it is only to be passed around between interface calls. Unfortunately, the JS* to JS to JS* conversion of such an intricate value would destroy the original type. In this case we allow the JS* code to pass a Clean `Dynamic` to JS. The run-time environment detects whether a value has type `Dynamic` and does not convert it into a JS value. When such a `Dynamic` is passed from JS to JS*, the run-time detects again its special nature, and does not try to recognize the type of the JS value, but uses its original Clean type (generated by the `dynamic` keyword) for type unification.

5   Related Work

Compilation of traditional programming languages to JavaScript has drawn much attention in the last few years as client-side processing for Internet applications has been gaining importance. Virtually every modern language has some kind of technology which allows its client-side execution – see [2] for an overview.

An interesting approach to avoid the usage of JavaScript, is the so called single-language compilation technique. Single-language systems allow the development of all tiers of a whole client-server application in the same language. Those parts of the application which are needed on the client are automatically transformed to JavaScript, while the other parts are compiled to some server-side binary. Communication between the client and the server can be transparent. The most mainstream example is GWT [9] for Java. As for functional languages, the prominent representatives of this approach are Links [3] and Hop [11]. A notable advantage of single-language systems is that the whole application can be type checked. However, mixed-languages solutions, like ours, are also advantageous: one can use the best of all languages. GWT, for instance, also makes it possible to export libraries as well [12].

In this section we are particularly interested in compiler technologies for lazy functional languages, paying special attention to the deployment process and the possibilities of interacting with JavaScript.

UHC-JS is the JavaScript backend of the Utrecht Haskell Compiler [4]. Although it is still in beta stage, it can already successfully compile a fair amount of Haskell programs. Its main advantage is that the generated JavaScript code is acceptably small, albeit relatively slow. Compilation can either proceed in a per-module basis or the modules can be linked together using source code level linking. Unfortunately, in the second case the whole application has to be compiled, and the start expression cannot be specified. Its abilities to interact with

JavaScript are very limited. In fact, they are restricted to a standard foreign function interface (FFI) and some DOM manipulation libraries implemented above it.

The Fay language [7] has a unique approach – namely, it does not utilize a Haskell compiler for preprocessing, but directly parses Haskell source code using third party libraries, and generates JavaScript code from the abstract syntax tree. As a consequence, Fay supports only a limited subset of the Haskell language, which makes it less appealing for us. JavaScript interoperability is enabled through a trivial foreign function interface.

GHCJS [13] is the most promising compiler technology among those discussed here. However, it has a rather heavyweight approach compared to our solution. It compiles most Haskell libraries without a problem, but suffers from a relatively slow engine (an advanced engine is under development) and huge code footprint. It uses GHC as a front end, and JavaScript code is generated from the resulting STG. Complete interactive applications can be developed using GHCJS through non-standard support libraries, such as WebKit, bindings for WebKitGTK+, which provide a low level DOM interface, and different low and high level interfaces for JavaScriptCore. Unfortunately, due to the use of these libraries, even the most trivial application will consist of several hundred kB (or even MB) of JavaScript. On the other hand, these libraries enable the most advanced JavaScript interoperability among the compilers of study. Besides the ubiquitous FFI support, GHCJS enables callbacks to the Haskell code as well. Type safety of these calls are ensured, but limited to primitive types, like Numbers, Booleans and Strings. Furthermore, GHCJS utilizes an algebraic data type to deal with JavaScript values – this is highly limited compared to our Dynamic-based approach. The deployment process is overcomplicated, several JavaScript files are generated, and have to be included in the final application along with numerous pre-compiled libraries.

Finally, the Haste compiler [8] is a relatively new approach aiming at small code footprint and a fast engine. Currently it compiles only full applications, which sets a limit on its applicability. Haste supports calling JavaScript functions from Haskell through a standard foreign function interface.

In summary, the cross-compilers studied in this section stress the quality of compilation and the compiler infrastructure, but place no particular emphasis on deployment, and on integration of the generated code into a larger application. None of them provide a simple way for the inclusion of the generated JavaScript code into a web application as a library, and only one of them, the GHCJS, enables callbacks to the Haskell code through a type safe, albeit limited, interface.

6   Conclusions

In this paper an extension to iTask and Tasklets has been presented, which enables rapid client-side web development with Clean. The solution is basically an unorthodox application of the iTask system, which in this way becomes an application server for client-side web applications. The presented method, in terms of deployment and integration, makes web development in Clean a competitive alternative to development directly in JavaScript. In terms of productivity, the balance is clearly tilted towards programming in Clean.

A mixed-language programming model has been proposed, where different parts of a web-application are written partly in Clean, and partly in JavaScript, making the best use of the two languages. Bidirectional communication between the two languages was a major concern. A particular strength of the ideas presented here is that instead of compiling a whole application to JavaScript, we propose to compile libraries (call-in) or components (call-in/call-out) only – the latter is achieved through events triggered by the Clean side of the applications.

Our approach enables the use of special interface and event handler functions. Furthermore, the communication interface is well typed from the point of view of the Clean code, which is achieved by the Dynamic feature of the Clean language. The applicability of the proposal has been proven through a series of carefully selected non-trivial examples.

The technology described here can be generalized in at least two ways. First, languages other than Clean can be used for writing the main body of applications. Our Clean to JavaScript compiler uses Sapl [5] (one of the core languages of Clean) as an intermediate language. A Haskell to Sapl compiler is currently under development. Besides writing a small server-side application for run-time source code level linking of Sapl and the compilation of the result to JavaScript, one technical problem must be solved: to obtain dynamically the Sapl source code of an arbitrary expression. This would make Haskell a proper replacement for Clean here.

The second option for generalization is due to the loosely-coupled communication interface between the Clean-side and the control-side of the applications. One could use platforms other than the web as a run-time environment, i.e. platforms supporting JavaScript. Such platforms are, for instance, Android and iOS, where the control logic could be implemented in Java or Objective-C, respectively; the JavaScript code generated from Clean could be used without any modifications.

References

1. Abadi, M., Cardelli, L., Pierce, B., Plotkin, G.: Dynamic typing in a statically-typed language. In: Proceedings of the 16th ACM SIGPLAN-SIGACT Symposium on Principles of Programming Languages, POPL 1989, pp. 213–227. ACM, New York (1989)
2. Ashkenas, J.: List of languages that compile to JavaScript, https://github.com/jashkenas/coffee-script/wiki/List-of-languages-that-compile-to-JS
3. Cooper, E., Lindley, S., Yallop, J.: Links: Web programming without tiers. In: de Boer, F.S., Bonsangue, M.M., Graf, S., de Roever, W.-P. (eds.) FMCO 2006. LNCS, vol. 4709, pp. 266–296. Springer, Heidelberg (2007)
4. Dijkstra, A.: The Utrecht Haskell Compiler JavaScript Backend, http://uu-computerscience.github.com/uhc-js/

5. Domoszlai, L., Bruël, E., Jansen, J.M.: Implementing a non-strict purely functional language in JavaScript. Acta Univ. Sapientiae. Informatica 3(1), 76–98 (2011)
6. Domoszlai, L., Plasmeijer, R.: Tasklets: Client-side evaluation for iTask3 (2012), http://people.inf.elte.hu/dlacko/papers/tasklets.pdf
7. Done, C.: The FAY language, http://fay-lang.org/
8. Ekblad, A.: Towards a DeclarativeWeb. Master's thesis, University of Gothenburg, Göteborg, Sweden (August 2012)
9. The Google Web Toolkit site, http://code.google.com/webtoolkit/
10. Lijnse, B., Plasmeijer, R.: iTasks 2: iTasks for end-users. In: Morazán, M.T., Scholz, S.-B. (eds.) IFL 2009. LNCS, vol. 6041, pp. 36–54. Springer, Heidelberg (2010)
11. Loitsch, F., Serrano, M.: Hop client-side compilation. In: Proc. 7th Symposium on Trends in Functional Programming, TFP 2007 (2007)
12. Moñino, M.C.: The Google Web Toolkit site, http://code.google.com/webtoolkit/
13. Nazarov, V.: The GHCJS Haskell to Javascript translator, https://github.com/ghcjs/ghcjs
14. Pil, M.: Dynamic types and type dependent functions. In: Hammond, K., Davie, T., Clack, C. (eds.) IFL 1998. LNCS, vol. 1595, pp. 169–185. Springer, Heidelberg (1999)
15. Plasmeijer, R., Lijnse, B., Michels, S., Achten, P., Koopman, P.: Task-oriented programming in a pure functional language. In: Proceedings of the 14th Symposium on Principles and Practice of Declarative Programming, PPDP 2012, pp. 195–206. ACM, New York (2012)
16. Tarditi, D., Lee, P., Acharya, A.: No assembly required: compiling standard ML to C. ACM Lett. Program. Lang. Syst. 1(2), 161–177 (1992)

A Duality of Sorts

Ralf Hinze, José Pedro Magalhães, and Nicolas Wu*

Department of Computer Science, University of Oxford
{ralf.hinze,jose.pedro.magalhaes,nicolas.wu}@cs.ox.ac.uk

Abstract. Sorting algorithms are one of the key pedagogical foundations of computer science, and their properties have been studied heavily. Perhaps less well known, however, is the fact that many of the basic sorting algorithms exist as a pair, and that these pairs arise naturally out of the duality between folds and unfolds. In this paper, we make this duality explicit, by showing how to define common sorting algorithms as folds of unfolds, or, dually, as unfolds of folds. This duality is preserved even when considering optimised sorting algorithms that require more exotic variations of folds and unfolds, and intermediary data structures. While all this material arises naturally from a categorical modelling of these recursion schemes, we endeavour to keep this presentation accessible to those not versed in abstract nonsense.

1 Introduction

Sorting, described in great detail by Knuth (1998), is one of the most important and fundamental concepts in computer science. In one form or another, sorting appears in nearly every domain of computer science. As such, there are many different implementations of sorting algorithms, with varying performance and complexity.

One of the simplest sorting algorithms is insertion sort, which revolves around the idea of inserting a single element in an already sorted list. To sort a list of elements using this strategy, we take the next element in the list that is to be considered, insert it into an accumulated sorted list that is initially empty, and proceed recursively until all elements have been inserted. In Haskell (Peyton Jones et al. 2003), insertion sort is concisely expressed using the *foldr* operation on lists, defining it as the application of the *insert* operation to each element of the input list, producing a result starting with the empty list:

$$insertSort :: [Integer] \rightarrow [Integer]$$
$$insertSort = foldr\ insert\ [\,]$$

The *insert* function takes one element and inserts it in an already sorted list. It does this using *span* to break the sorted list into two segments according to the pivot element we want to insert, which is then introduced in between the two parts:

$$insert :: Integer \rightarrow [Integer] \rightarrow [Integer]$$
$$insert\ y\ ys = xs \mathbin{+\!\!+} [y] \mathbin{+\!\!+} zs$$
$$\textbf{where}\ (xs, zs) = span\ (\leqslant y)\ ys$$

---

* This work has been funded by EPSRC grant number EP/J010995/1.

P. Achten and P. Koopman (Eds.): Plasmeijer Festschrift, LNCS 8106, pp. 151–167, 2013.
© Springer-Verlag Berlin Heidelberg 2013

The use of *span* relies on the fact that the list *ys* is already sorted.

Another basic sorting algorithm, selection sort, can be easily expressed in terms of an unfold. Unfolds are a recursion scheme dual to folds, and are used to produce data, instead of consuming data. Unfolds are often given less attention than folds (Gibbons and Jones 1998), but that is not the case in this paper: we assure the reader that we will maintain proportional representation, and show an unfold for every fold. In Haskell, the unfold operation on lists is defined as *unfoldr*:

$$unfoldr :: (b \rightarrow Maybe\ (a, b)) \rightarrow (b \rightarrow [a])$$

The first argument to *unfoldr* defines how to produce lists from a seed: the *Nothing* case corresponds to the empty list, whereas *Just* (a, b) corresponds to a list with element *a* and new seed *b*. Using this function, and a starting seed, *unfoldr* produces a complete list.

Selection sort works on a list by recursively picking the smallest element of the input list and adding this element to the result list. It can be defined as the unfold of a *select* operation:

$$selectSort :: [Integer] \rightarrow [Integer]$$
$$selectSort = unfoldr\ select$$

This *select* operation picks the smallest element from the input list using *minimum*, removes it using *delete*, and continues recursively by returning the smallest element together with the remaining list.

$$select :: [Integer] \rightarrow Maybe\ (Integer, [Integer])$$
$$select\ [\ ] = Nothing$$
$$select\ xs = Just\ (x, xs')$$
$$\mathbf{where}\ x\ = minimum\ xs$$
$$xs' = delete\ x\ xs$$

For practical reasons, the types of *foldr* and *unfoldr* in Haskell are not clearly dual. This contributes to obscuring the inherent duality in our *insert* and *select* functions. The purpose of this paper is to explicitly highlight the duality in sorting algorithms, so that we can provide a unified definition for both *insertSort* and *selectSort*. We do this by exploring a type-directed approach to algorithm development, where the types dictate most of the behaviour of functions.

The remainder of this paper is structured as follows. We first introduce a framework of functors, folds, and unfolds in Section 2, which we use in Section 3 to implement two exchange sorts in one go. To define more efficient insertion and selection sorts, we start by introducing more exotic variants of folds and unfolds, called paramorphisms and apomorphisms, in·Section 4. We use these morphisms in Section 5, revisiting the two sorting algorithms shown in this introduction. In Section 6 we turn our attention to mergesort, in order to show how these recursion schemes can be applied to create more efficient sorting algorithms. We conclude our discussion in Section 7.

This paper is built on our earlier work on this same subject (Hinze et al. 2012), but we have rewritten the exposition entirely, simplifying many aspects and removing all the category theory jargon. The theoretically-inclined reader is referred to the earlier work for a deeper understanding of bialgebras and distributive laws in sorting, but this is not required for the comprehension of this paper; the entire development arises naturally out of a type-directed approach to programming, without need for appealing to category theory for the justification of design choices.

2 Functors, Folds, and Unfolds

In this paper we focus on the duality of folds and unfolds, and how these recursion schemes can be used in sorting. The standard functions *foldr* and *unfoldr* are particularly useful since they allow us to express a whole class of recursive functions. Their utility draws from the fact that folds and unfolds allow us to abstract away from using functions with direct recursion. In the case of folds, the exact site of the recursive step is handled by the *foldr* function, and the non-recursive component is described by its parameters, which constitute a so-called algebra. Dually, unfolds are considered in terms of a corecursive step and a non-recursive coalgebra.

This pattern is mirrored at the level of data and is not unique to lists, where recursive datatypes are described as two-level types (Sheard and Pasalic 2004): one level describes the fact that the data is recursive, and the other is non-recursive and describes the shape of the data. Using this representation we can decompose the list datatype into two parts. First, consider the non-recursive component:

data *List list* = *Nil* | *Cons Integer list*

We call a datatype such as *List* the *base functor* of the recursive type. For simplicity we consider lists of elements of type *Integer*; our development generalises readily to polymorphic lists with an *Ord* constraint on the element type.

Note that the type of *List* is intrinsically not recursive, but instead uses a parameter where one might expect the recursive site. We can retrieve the usual lists from our non-recursive *List* datatype using the fixed-point combinator *Fix*, which builds recursion into datatypes:

newtype *Fix f* = *In* { *out* :: *f* (*Fix f*) }

Combining these two parts into a two-level type yields *Fix List*, which is isomorphic to the predefined type of integer lists [*Integer*].

The recursive component of this data structure is marked by the *Functor* instance of the base functor, and is key to providing a generalised definition of a fold:

instance *Functor List* **where**
    fmap f Nil   = *Nil*
    fmap f (*Cons k x*) = *Cons k* (*f x*)

Note that this is not the same functoriality as the one typically used to express a mapping over the elements in a list.

The advantage of representing lists by their base functor becomes evident when we define the fold and unfold operations. Datatypes defined by abstracting over the recursive positions, like *List*, enjoy a single fold operator:

$$fold :: (Functor f) \Rightarrow (f\ a \rightarrow a) \rightarrow (Fix f \rightarrow a)$$
$$fold\ a = a \cdot fmap\ (fold\ a) \cdot out$$

The *fold* function takes an argument *a*, called the algebra, that is able to crush one level of the data structure. The definition works by first exposing the top level of the structure by using *out*, which is then crushed at its recursive sites using *fmap*, and finally crushed at the top level using *a*.

There is also a single, generic definition of unfold, which is now clearly dual to fold:

$$unfold :: (Functor f) \Rightarrow (a \rightarrow f\ a) \rightarrow (a \rightarrow Fix f)$$
$$unfold\ c = In \cdot fmap\ (unfold\ c) \cdot c$$

The first argument to *unfold*, the coalgebra *c*, defines how to expand a seed into some functorial type *f* with seeds at the leaves. The coalgebra is applied by *unfold* recursively until a complete structure is built. Again the recursive site is marked by the *Functor* instance of the structure in question.

Unlike Haskell lists, which have *foldr* and *unfoldr* operations specialised to their type, our *fold* and *unfold* operations work on any datatype with a *Functor* instance, and we will soon make use of this generality. We have only sketched the details of base functors and their recursive morphisms; a more detailed presentation, including relevant category theory background, can be found in Meijer et al. (1991). Another categorical treatment that generalises folds and unfolds to operate on an even wider class of recursive types can be found in Hinze (2011).

3   Sorting by Swapping

In this section we will look at our first sorting algorithms expressed in terms of the generalised folds and unfolds introduced in the previous section, and show how duality naturally arises in this setting. To ease the understanding of the algebras and coalgebras that we will see, which generally perform "one step" of sorting, we introduce a datatype of sorted lists, together with its *Functor* instance:

data *List* *list* = *Nil* | *Cons* *Integer* *list*

instance *Functor* *List* **where**
   fmap f *Nil*   = *Nil*
   fmap f (*Cons* *k* *list*) = *Cons* *k* (*f* *list*)

Note that *List* is entirely isomorphic to *List*. The only difference lies in the names used: the fact that a list is sorted is indicated by the underlining on its type and constructor names. The compiler will not be able to enforce the condition that *List* always represents sorted lists for us, but we keep this invariant throughout our development.

A sorting algorithm, in general, takes arbitrary lists to sorted lists:

$$sort :: Fix\ List \rightarrow Fix\ \underline{List}$$

By looking at its type, we can interpret *sort* as either a fold, that consumes a value of type *Fix List*, or as an unfold that produces a value of type *Fix List*. If *sort* is a *fold*, its algebra will have type *List* (*Fix List*) → *Fix List*. This algebra can then be defined as an *unfold* which produces a value of type *Fix List*. These observations are summarised in the following type signatures:

$$fold\ (unfold\ c) :: Fix\ List \to Fix\ \underline{List}$$
$$unfold\ c\ :: List\ (Fix\ \underline{List}) \to Fix\ \underline{List}$$
$$c\ :: List\ (Fix\ \underline{List}) \to \underline{List}\ (List\ (Fix\ \underline{List}))$$

Using this approach brings an additional benefit: the analysis of the complexity of our algorithms can be framed in terms of the cost of the *fold* and *unfold* functions. The running time of a fully evaluated result of a *fold* is proportional to the depth of its input structure multiplied by the cost of one step of the algebra. Dually, the running time of an *unfold* is proportional to the depth of its output structure multiplied by the cost of one step of the coalgebra. This property will become useful when evaluating the performance of our algorithms.

Let us then write a sorting function as a fold of an unfold:

```
naiveInsertSort :: Fix List → Fix List
naiveInsertSort = fold (unfold naiveInsert)
naiveInsert :: List (Fix List) → List (List (Fix List))
naiveInsert Nil              = Nil
naiveInsert (Cons a (In Nil)) = Cons a Nil
naiveInsert (Cons a (In (Cons b x)))
   | a ⩽ b      = Cons a (Cons b x)
   | otherwise = Cons b (Cons a x)
```

Most of the behaviour of *naiveInsert* follows naturally from its type. The empty and single element unsorted lists are trivially converted into sorted variants. For an unsorted list with at least two elements, we compare the elements, reordering if necessary. What we obtain is a form of "naive" insertion sort, since it does not make use of the fact that the list where an element is being inserted in is already sorted. Instead, the traversal is continued, even though there is no more work to be done. Indeed, the analysis of the time complexity of this algorithm is simple: the input size of the fold is linear, and the output size of the inner unfold is also linear, so we should expect quadratic behaviour. We will see how to make use of the fact that the inner list is already sorted in Section 5.

Recall now that we can also see a sorting function as an unfold of a fold. In that case, the type of the inner algebra can be derived as in the following type signatures:

$$unfold\ (fold\ a) :: Fix\ List \to Fix\ \underline{List}$$
$$fold\ a\ :: Fix\ List \to \underline{List}\ (Fix\ List)$$
$$a\ :: List\ (\underline{List}\ (Fix\ List)) \to \underline{List}\ (Fix\ List)$$

The sorting algorithm that we obtain as an unfold of a fold is a version of bubble sort:

```
bubbleSort :: Fix List → Fix List
bubbleSort = unfold (fold bubble)
```

$$bubble :: List\ (\underline{List}\ (Fix\ List)) \rightarrow \underline{List}\ (Fix\ List)$$
$$bubble\ Nil \qquad\quad = \underline{Nil}$$
$$bubble\ (Cons\ a\ \underline{Nil}) = \underline{Cons}\ a\ (In\ Nil)$$
$$bubble\ (Cons\ a\ (\underline{Cons}\ b\ x))$$
$$\quad |\ a \leqslant b \qquad = \underline{Cons}\ a\ (In\ (Cons\ b\ x))$$
$$\quad |\ otherwise = \underline{Cons}\ b\ (In\ (Cons\ a\ x))$$

This algorithm proceeds by continually comparing adjacent elements, swapping them if they are in the wrong order, which is the principal idea behind a bubble sort. The similarity between *bubble* and *naiveInsert* is striking; they differ only in the placement of the fixed-point constructor *In*. This becomes clear if we look at their types, after expanding one definition of *Fix* in each of them:

$$naiveInsert :: List\ (\underline{List}\ (Fix\ \underline{List})) \rightarrow \underline{List}\ (List\ (Fix\ \underline{List}))$$
$$bubble \qquad :: List\ (\underline{List}\ (Fix\ List)) \rightarrow \underline{List}\ (List\ (Fix\ List))$$

The only difference is in the inner type of lists at the third level of depth. However, this third level is in some sense redundant, since these algorithms only inspect elements in the first two levels. It is this observation that allows *naiveInsert* and *bubble* to be safely generalised to a *step function* of the following type:

$$swap :: List\ (\underline{List}\ x) \rightarrow \underline{List}\ (List\ x)$$

Such a step function is sometimes called a *distributive law*, since it captures an abstract notion of distributivity. The definition of this new function, which we call *swap* since it simply swaps adjacent elements based on their order, is entirely similar to the definitions of both *naiveInsert* and *bubble*:

$$swap\ Nil \qquad\quad = \underline{Nil}$$
$$swap\ (Cons\ a\ \underline{Nil}) = \underline{Cons}\ a\ Nil$$
$$swap\ (Cons\ a\ (\underline{Cons}\ b\ x))$$
$$\quad |\ a \leqslant b \qquad\quad = \underline{Cons}\ a\ (Cons\ b\ x)$$
$$\quad |\ otherwise \qquad = \underline{Cons}\ b\ (Cons\ a\ x)$$

The *swap* function can be understood as a distributive law between the types *List* and *List*, and is a generalisation that captures the essence of both *naiveInsert* and *bubble*. We can use *swap* to define both *naiveInsertSort'* and *bubbleSort'*:

$$naiveInsertSort', bubbleSort' :: Fix\ List \rightarrow Fix\ \underline{List}$$
$$naiveInsertSort' = fold \quad (unfold\ (swap \cdot fmap\ out))$$
$$bubbleSort' \qquad = unfold\ (fold \quad (fmap\ In \cdot swap))$$

The use of *fmap out* in *naiveInsertSort'*, and, dually, *fmap In* in *bubbleSort'*, reflects our expansion of the *Fix* datatype in the type of the (co)algebra. What we have obtained is a single definition for two conceptually distinct sorting algorithms, in terms of a function that expresses how to perform one step of the computation.

At this point it is worth reinforcing our intuition for how these algorithms work. The duality of these sorting algorithms can be seen visually when we assume a call-by-value evaluation order of the definitions. The diagrams below emphasise that the actual comparisons performed by *swap* are the same, and that the algorithms only differ in the order in which these comparisons are performed:

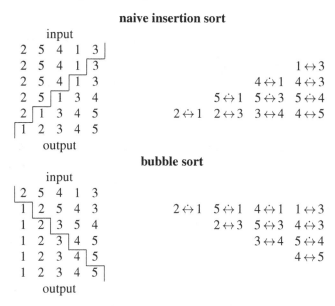

naive insertion sort

bubble sort

For both of these algorithms, it is the outer recursion scheme that drives the computation. In the case of *naiveInsertSort'* this is a *fold*, and the progression is depicted by the vertical line that separates sorted from unsorted data working its way from the end of the unsorted list until only a sorted list remains. Since *bubbleSort'* is expressed as an *unfold*, the corresponding diagram is pleasingly dual. The computation starts from the beginning of a sorted list, beginning with an empty list and gradually bubbling values to the front. Notice how for *naiveInsertSort'*, the input remains stable, whereas the output does not, whereas for *bubbleSort'*, it is the output that remains stable, whereas the input does not.

On the right side of these diagrams we have presented the comparisons that take place in the *swap* function, which are effectively determined by the inner recursion. The arrows correspond to comparisons that are made between two elements, and dotted arrows indicate comparisons that result in a swap (this is the case when the element on the left is greater than that on the right). The arrows that correspond to each line of *naiveInsertSort'* show the comparisons that are needed to insert the element immediately to the left of the vertical line, and should be read from left to right. On the other hand, the swaps that correspond to each line of *bubbleSort'* show the comparisons that are needed to select the value to the left of the vertical line, and should be read from right to left.

4   Paramorphisms and Apomorphisms

In the previous section we defined two sorting algorithms with performance $\Theta(n^2)$, where both work in quadratic time regardless of the input. In particular, the unfolding step in the insertion sort will continue to traverse a sorted structure long after a new element has been inserted into its appropriate place. This is unfortunate, as it fails to make use of the fact that the output that has already been constructed is sorted. If this information was taken into consideration, the inner traversals could be interrupted for better performance. However, using folds and unfolds as recursion schemes prohibits us from meddling with the recursion, and no such interruption is possible. In order to gain explicit control of when an unfold should stop traversing a structure, we turn to a slightly more exotic version of unfold, namely the apomorphism (Vene and Uustalu 1998), which gives us the required ability to abort recursion. Dually, we will also make use of paramorphisms (Meertens 1992), which give us the power to use a part of the input data in an algebra. Paramorphisms and apomorphisms can be understood as the counterparts to folds and unfolds, and enjoy aspects of duality.

Before diving into the details of these recursion schemes, however, it is informative to first consider the duality that exists between so-called product and sum types. The *product* of types is simply a synonym for a pair of values, and the *sum* of types is a synonym for the *Either* type (a choice between two values):

type $a \times b = (a, b)$
type $a + b = Either\ a\ b$

In a sense, these operators encode a form of arithmetic on types. Assuming a is a type with m inhabitants, and b a type with n inhabitants, the product type $a \times b$ is inhabited by $m \times n$ values, as we can choose one element of b for each element of a. Similarly, the sum type $a + b$ has $m + n$ inhabitants, as we have to pick either an element from a or an element from b.

The duality between these types can be understood in terms of two operators: one which constructs products, and another which deconstructs sums. The operator $\triangle$, or *split*, constructs a pair by applying two functions with a common source type:

$(\triangle) :: (x \rightarrow a) \rightarrow (x \rightarrow b) \rightarrow (x \rightarrow a \times b)$
$(f \triangle g)\ x = (f\ x, g\ x)$

The dual operator $\triangledown$, or *join*, deconstructs a sum by applying two functions with a common target type:

$(\triangledown) :: (a \rightarrow x) \rightarrow (b \rightarrow x) \rightarrow (a + b \rightarrow x)$
$(f \triangledown g)\ (Left\ \ \ a) = f\ a$
$(f \triangledown g)\ (Right\ b) = g\ b$

Using these operators, we can extend the duality that folds and unfolds enjoy, and define paramorphisms and apomorphisms.

A paramorphism is defined as a variation on *fold* which makes use of a product in the source of its algebra. The product is used to "remember" the original *Fix f* structure:

$para :: (Functor f) \Rightarrow (f\ (Fix f \times a) \rightarrow a) \rightarrow (Fix f \rightarrow a)$
$para\ f = f \cdot fmap\ (id \triangle para\ f) \cdot out$

The first argument to *para* now has access to both the original *Fix f* structure and the computed result for this same structure. This argument is not an algebra in the categorical sense, but we shall name it so for simplicity, since it serves essentially the same purpose. We will render the product constructor of two elements a and b as $a \doteq b$, to remind us that the first element is the precomputed result of the second.

A typical example of a paramorphism on lists is the function that calculates all *proper* suffixes of a list:

$$suffixes :: Fix\ List \rightarrow [Fix\ List]$$
$$suffixes = para\ suf$$
$$suf :: List\ (Fix\ List \times [Fix\ List]) \rightarrow [Fix\ List]$$
$$suf\ Nil \qquad\qquad = []$$
$$suf\ (Cons\ \_n\ (l \doteq ls)) = l : ls$$

Although it may seem like paramorphisms are more powerful than folds, this is not the case. They simply make certain algorithms more convenient to express by providing direct access to the original structure. This behaviour can also be expressed in a fold; in fact, we can define *para* as a fold:

$$para' :: (Functor\ f) \Rightarrow (f\ (Fix\ f \times a) \rightarrow a) \rightarrow (Fix\ f \rightarrow a)$$
$$para'\ f = snd \cdot fold\ ((In \cdot fmap\ fst) \triangle f)$$

Dually, an apomorphism is a variation of an unfold which makes use of a sum in the target of its first argument. As before, we abuse terminology, and name this argument a coalgebra. This sum is used to encode the choice between stopping the apomorphism with a concrete value of type *Fix f*, or going on with a new seed of type *a*:

$$apo :: (Functor\ f) \Rightarrow (a \rightarrow f\ (Fix\ f + a)) \rightarrow (a \rightarrow Fix\ f)$$
$$apo\ f = In \cdot fmap\ (id\ \triangledown\ apo\ f) \cdot f$$

Here the coalgebra uses its source value to produce either a final result, or an intermediate step. If a final result is given then the recursion no longer continues; otherwise, values are produced just as in an unfold. For mnemonic reasons, we will render the *Left* constructor as *Stop*, as it encodes stopping the recursion, and *Right* as *Go*, as it encodes continuing the traversal.

Note that the power to improve the running time of our sorting algorithms relies on the use of apomorphisms. Paramorphisms are mostly a cosmetic improvement; the resulting traversal still consumes the entire input linearly. Apomorphisms, on the other hand, allow for early termination of the computation, so their running time is no longer necessarily linear on the size of the resulting structure.

4.1 Folds of Apomorphisms, Unfolds of Paramorphisms

As before, we use a type-directed approach to guide the development of a sorting algorithm, except this time we replace the inner recursions with *apo* and *para*, since we are aiming for a more efficient algorithm. Deriving the appropriate algebra and coalgebra yields the following:

$$fold\ (apo\ c) :: Fix\ List \rightarrow Fix\ \underline{List}$$
$$apo\ c \ :: List\ (Fix\ \underline{List}) \rightarrow Fix\ \underline{List}$$
$$c \ :: List\ (Fix\ \underline{List}) \rightarrow \underline{List}\ (Fix\ \underline{List} + List\ (Fix\ \underline{List}))$$

$$unfold\ (para\ a) :: Fix\ List \rightarrow Fix\ \underline{List}$$
$$para\ a\ ::\ Fix\ List \rightarrow \underline{List}\ (Fix\ List)$$
$$a\ ::\ List\ (Fix\ List \times \underline{List}\ (Fix\ List)) \rightarrow \underline{List}\ (Fix\ List)$$

The duality is somewhat hidden by some noise in the types, but can be easily recovered by introducing some synonyms for what are sometimes called *pointed* and *copointed* types, and unrolling some fixpoints:

type $f_+\ a = a + f\ a$
type $f_\times\ a = a \times f\ a$

After unrolling one layer of the fixed point, we obtain the following types for our (co)algebras:

$$c \cdot fmap\ In\ :: List\ (\underline{List}\ \ (Fix\ \underline{List})) \rightarrow \underline{List}\ (List_+\ (Fix\ \underline{List}))$$
$$fmap\ out \cdot a :: List\ (\underline{List}_\times\ (Fix\ List)) \rightarrow \underline{List}\ (List\ \ (Fix\ List))$$

From this it is clear that the (co)algebras are almost of the same form, except that the coalgebra should be modified to consume a copointed type in its source, and the algebra should be modified to produce a pointed type in its target.

This suggests that we can combine the (co)algebras into a single step function with a more general type:

$$b\ ::\ List\ (\underline{List}_\times\ x) \rightarrow \underline{List}\ (List_+\ x)$$

For convenience, we shall abuse terminology, and occasionally call such step functions distributive laws, since they serve almost the same purpose as the distributive laws introduced in Section 3. With some gentle massaging, we can use such a step function in the context of either an apomorphic coalgebra or a paramorphic algebra:

$$c = b \cdot fmap\ (id \vartriangle out) :: List\ (Fix\ \underline{List}) \qquad \rightarrow \underline{List}\ (List_+\ (Fix\ \underline{List}))$$
$$a = fmap\ (id \triangledown In) \cdot b\ :: List\ (\underline{List}_\times\ (Fix\ List)) \rightarrow \underline{List}\ (Fix\ List)$$

Once again, the step function crucially depends on parametricity for unifying algebras and coalgebras.

5   Insertion and Selection Sort

Now that we have apomorphisms, which allow us to stop recursion, we can write a non-naive version of insertion sort that adequately stops traversing the result list once the element has been inserted. Insertion sort is the *fold* of an *apo*:

$$insertSort :: Fix\ List \rightarrow Fix\ \underline{List}$$
$$insertSort = fold\ (apo\ insert)$$

The coalgebra *insert* is similar to *naiveInsert*, but with the essential difference that it stops creating the list (with *Stop*) if no swapping is required. Otherwise, it continues traversing (with *Go*):

$insert :: List\ (Fix\ \underline{List}) \rightarrow \underline{List}\ (List_+\ (Fix\ \underline{List}))$
$insert\ Nil \qquad\qquad\quad = \underline{Nil}$
$insert\ (Cons\ a\ (In\ \underline{Nil})) = \underline{Cons}\ a\ (Stop\ (In\ \underline{Nil}))$
$insert\ (Cons\ a\ (In\ (\underline{Cons}\ b\ x')))$
$\quad |\ a \leqslant b \qquad = \underline{Cons}\ a\ (Stop\ (In\ (\underline{Cons}\ b\ x')))$
$\quad |\ otherwise = \underline{Cons}\ b\ (Go \quad (Cons\ a\ x'))$

Because we are using apomorphisms, *insertSort* will run in linear time on a list that is already sorted, as the inner traversal is immediately terminated each time it is started. This behaviour is crucial for the best case behaviour of *insertSort*.

As before, we can find a dual algorithm to *insertSort* that is defined as an *unfold* of a *para*. Instead of writing a specialised algebra, we will directly write the distributive law that can be used both as argument to *apo* and *para*. Its type, as explained in Section 4, is the following:

$swop :: List\ (\underline{List}_\times\ x) \rightarrow \underline{List}\ (List_+\ x)$

We nickname this function *swop* as it "swaps and stops"; its type indicates that it has access to the sorted list as its argument, and that it can decide to abort recursion when producing a result. Its definition is an unsurprising generalisation of *insert*:

$swop\ Nil \qquad\qquad\qquad = \underline{Nil}$
$swop\ (Cons\ a\ (x \doteq \underline{Nil})) = \underline{Cons}\ a\ (Stop\ x)$
$swop\ (Cons\ a\ (x \doteq \underline{Cons}\ b\ x'))$
$\quad |\ a \leqslant b \qquad\qquad = \underline{Cons}\ a\ (Stop\ x)$
$\quad |\ otherwise \qquad\quad = \underline{Cons}\ b\ (Go \quad (Cons\ a\ x'))$

Having defined *swop*, we can use it to define an alternative version of *insertSort*, which does not use *insert*:

$insertSort' :: Fix\ List \rightarrow Fix\ \underline{List}$
$insertSort' = fold\ (apo\ (swop \cdot fmap\ (id \vartriangle out)))$

However, being a distributive law, *swop* can also be used to construct the algebra of a paramorphism .The sorting algorithm that we then obtain is selection sort:

$selectSort :: Fix\ List \rightarrow Fix\ \underline{List}$
$selectSort = unfold\ (para\ (fmap\ (id \triangledown In) \cdot swop))$

Unlike bubble sort (the dual of "naive" insertion sort), selection sort uses the accumulated result x in the $a \leqslant b$ case, meaning the smallest element has been placed in the correct location. We again get two, entirely dual sorting algorithms for the price of one step function.

6   Mergesort

The work in the previous section brought us a slight boost in performance over the naive version of insertion sort. However, its time complexity is still on average $O(n^2)$, which is bound by the fact that we use folds and unfolds over *lists*: only the lower bound was improved to $\Omega(n)$. To improve on the average bound we must move to a different algorithm where an intermediate data structure with sublinear depth is built from the input list, and then used to produce the output list. This two-phase approach was used in our previous work to synthesise versions of quicksort and heapsort (Hinze et al. 2012). In this section we show the development of mergesort, which improves the average case complexity to $\Theta(n \log n)$.

These two phases can be seen in a typical implementation of mergesort in Haskell, where the recursive nature of the algorithm is expressed directly, rather than through an intermediary datastructure:

```
mergeSort :: [Integer] → [Integer]
mergeSort as = merge (mergeSort bs) (mergeSort cs)
    where (bs, cs) = split as

split :: [Integer] → ([Integer], [Integer])
split []        = ([],   [])
split [a]       = ([a],  [])
split (a : b : cs) = (a : as, b : bs)
    where (as, bs) = split cs

merge :: [Integer] → [Integer] → [Integer]
merge as     [] = as
merge []     bs = bs
merge (a : as) (b : bs)
    | a ⩽ b    = a : merge as    (b : bs)
    | otherwise = b : merge (a : as) bs
```

In the first phase, *split* is called at each recursive step of *mergeSort*, and recursively splits the input list in two by uninterleaving the elements. The *merge* function performs the second phase of the algorithm, and recursively merges the lists generated in the first phase. In this section we will see how to expose the recursive structure of *mergeSort* as an explicit intermediate data structure, and each phase as a recursive morphism with an associated distributive law. We stress that this structure serves only to turn the recursion into data, allowing for more explicit control of computation, an idea that is echoed in our description of two level types, where recursion in a data structure is decomposed.

When considering which data structure with sublinear depth to use for sorting, one natural choice is the type of balanced binary trees, since these have logarithmic depth in the number of elements they contain. This tree must faithfully represent the structure of the sorting algorithm in question; for quicksort, which picks a pivot element and splits the list in two halves, we would use trees with elements in the branches, where the element would be the pivot, and each branch a fragment of the list. Mergesort, on the other hand, works by merging lists at each recursive step. A tree structure with elements at the leaves is appropriate to encode this behaviour:

```
data Tree tree = Tip | Leaf Integer | Fork tree tree
instance Functor Tree where
    fmap f Tip      = Tip
```

$$fmap\,f\,(Leaf\ a)\ = Leaf\ a$$
$$fmap\,f\,(Fork\ l\ r) = Fork\ (f\ l)\ (f\ r)$$

We include a *Tip* constructor in our datatype that correspond to the empty lists that can be observed in the output of *split*. As before, this is a two-level type, and the recursive site is denoted by the *Functor* instance.

6.1   First Phase: Growing a Tree

Using the same type directed approach as before, we begin by defining a step function that relates our two structures. The type of the function we seek is therefore:

$$grow :: List\ (Tree_\times\ x) \rightarrow Tree\ (List_+\ x)$$

Defining such a function for the first few cases is unproblematic, but alas, this line of development turns out to be in vein, where our best efforts to deal with the following case are always thwarted:

$$grow\ (Cons\ a\ (t \doteq Leaf\ b)) = Fork\ (Go\ (Cons\ a\ ?))\ (Stop\ t)$$

The goal in this case is to create a *Fork* that contains the element a in one branch, and b in the other. The type of *Tree* demands that the branches in this fork are of type $List_+\ x$. Embedding the b in one branch is a simple matter of making use of *Stop t*, since t refers to the *Leaf b* construct. The problem arises in that we cannot provide a suitable second parameter to *Cons*, since the only value of appropriate type x in scope is the t that refers to the *Leaf b* constructor. While this is correctly typed, using this value as a parameter is incorrect for two reasons: first, this would result in a duplication of the value b, and second, it leads to infinite recursion, since in the next step the value *Case a t* would considered again. Possible alternative definitions are either merely variations on this theme, or satisfy the types by dropping data, which is manifestly unsatisfactory for a sorting function.

The heart of the problem lies in the fact that the constructors of *List* offer no way of signaling the existence of a singleton that should terminate the recursion. In a sense, there is no constructor in a *List* that is the counterpart to a *Leaf*. To recover a step function that can build trees, the list representation needs a means of expressing singletons as a primitive constructor. One solution is to lift existing lists so that there is a a new constructor *Single Integer*:

data *List list* = *Nil* | *Single Integer* | *Cons Integer list*

This type gives us everything we need to build the distributive law that relates lists and trees. The first few cases fall naturally from the types, and there is very little choice in how to proceed:

$$grow :: List\ (Tree_\times\ x) \rightarrow Tree\ (List_+\ x)$$
$$grow\ Nil \qquad\qquad = Tip$$
$$grow\ (Single\ a) \qquad\quad = Leaf\ a$$

$$grow \ (Cons \ a \ (t \doteq Tip)) \qquad = Leaf \ a$$
$$grow \ (Cons \ a \ (t \doteq Leaf \ b)) = Fork \ (Go \ (Single \ a)) \ (Stop \ t)$$

Note that here the problem encountered previously has been circumvented by embedding the value a in a *Single* constructor in the left hand branch of the *Fork*. In a later step, this *Single a* value will be turned into a *Leaf a* as desired.

The remaining final case where the list contains a *Fork* can be implemented in a number of ways. We can arbitrarily insert the element a in either the left or the right side of the *Fork* that is produced. Once this choice is established we have another, more interesting, decision to make with regards to the subtrees given by l and r. One option is to preserve their order:

$$grow \ (Cons \ a \ (t \doteq Fork \ l \ r)) = Fork \ (Go \ (Cons \ a \ l)) \ (Stop \ r)$$

However, this solution leads to trees that are unbalanced in that new elements are always inserted on the left side of the tree. The only other option is to reverse the two subtrees when inserting an element:

$$grow \ (Cons \ a \ (t \doteq Fork \ l \ r)) = Fork \ (Go \ (Cons \ a \ r)) \ (Stop \ l)$$

In so doing, we have rediscovered Braun's method of producing perfectly balanced trees (Braun and Rem 1983). In fact, this trick can also be seen in an alternative defintion of *split* that considers only empty and non-empty lists, and rotates lists as it recurses.

Since we have described a distributive law, two methods for producing trees emerge:

$$makeTree, makeTree' :: Fix \ List \rightarrow Fix \ Tree$$
$$makeTree \ = fold \quad (apo \ (grow \cdot fmap \ (id \vartriangle out)))$$
$$makeTree' = unfold \ (para \ (fmap \ (id \triangledown In) \cdot grow))$$

The first method, *makeTree*, encodes the standard way of building a tree by repeated insertion, using Braun's method for keeping the tree balanced. The second method, *makeTree'*, encodes the slightly more unusual process of generating a tree by repeatedly uninterleaving a list. This uninterleaving of the list has the same swapping behaviour as Braun's method on trees.

6.2 Second Phase: Merging Trees

Once the tree is constructed, the second phase of the algorithm reduces the tree until a sorted list is produced. The distributive law falls out naturally from the types:

$$merge :: Tree \ (\underline{List}_\times \ x) \rightarrow \underline{List} \ (Tree_+ \ x)$$
$$merge \ Tip \qquad\qquad\qquad\qquad\qquad\qquad = \underline{Nil}$$
$$merge \ (Leaf \ a) \qquad\qquad\qquad\qquad\qquad = \underline{Cons} \ a \ (Go \ Tip)$$
$$merge \ (Fork \ (l \doteq \underline{Nil}) \qquad\quad (r \doteq \underline{Nil})) \qquad = \underline{Nil}$$
$$merge \ (Fork \ (l \doteq \underline{Nil}) \qquad\quad (r \doteq \underline{Cons} \ b \ r')) = \underline{Cons} \ b \ (Stop \ r')$$
$$merge \ (Fork \ (l \doteq \underline{Cons} \ a \ l') \ (r \doteq \underline{Nil})) \qquad = \underline{Cons} \ a \ (Stop \ l')$$
$$merge \ (Fork \ (l \doteq \underline{Cons} \ a \ l') \ (r \doteq \underline{Cons} \ b \ r'))$$

$$\begin{aligned}
&\mid a \leqslant b \quad = \underline{Cons}\ a\ (Go\ (Fork\ l'\ r)) \\
&\mid otherwise = \underline{Cons}\ b\ (Go\ (Fork\ l\ r'))
\end{aligned}$$

Empty trees give rise to empty lists, and a single element tree produces a single element list. When we have two subtrees, we inspect the list contained in each subtree. If both lists are empty, we return the empty list. In case only one of the lists is non-empty, the element is added to the front of the output sorted list, and the recursion stops with the tail in hand. In the most general case, we have one element in each branch. We compare the two elements, picking the smallest one and recursing using the appropriate subtrees.

Note that for this phase, lists do not need to be extended with a *Single* constructor, since in the case of *Leaf a* the fact that the *Cons a* should terminate is signalled by embedding a *Tip* in the tail. This *Tip* is later turned into a *Nil* as desired.

As before, we obtain two methods for merging a tree into a list:

$$\begin{aligned}
&mergeTree, mergeTree' :: Fix\ Tree \rightarrow Fix\ \underline{List} \\
&mergeTree\ = fold \quad (apo\ (merge \cdot fmap\ (id \triangle out))) \\
&mergeTree' = unfold\ (para\ (fmap\ (id \triangledown In) \cdot merge))
\end{aligned}$$

An operational understanding of how these algorithms work helps develop our understanding of the sense in which duality expresses itself here.

The first of these two variations uses a *fold* in the outer recursion, and this drives the deconstruction of the tree of values from the bottom until a single list remains. The controlling *fold* has an algebra of type:

$$Tree\ (Fix\ \underline{List}) \rightarrow Fix\ \underline{List}$$

Here, the algebra is in fact an apomorphism that starts working at the bottom of the tree. When a *Tip* is encountered, the *merge* will simply produce a *Nil*, and control is passed back to the *fold*. Otherwise, each *Leaf a* is initially turned into a *Cons a (Go Tip)*, and the apomorphism continues to unfold the remaining *Tip* resulting in a remaining structure that is *Cons a Nil*. When the *fold* encounters a *Fork*, the contents of each branch are analysed by the apomorphism. In the case where both lists are empty, they become a single *Nil*. When only one contains data, that branch is turned into a *Cons* with this payload, and the apomorphism is signalled to continue using the appropriate tail with a *Stop*. The more interesting case is when both branches contain data. In this case, the *merge* function is used to collapse the fork so that the least value is placed at the beginning of the new *List*. The apomorphism is then signalled with *Go* to continue merging the remaining tail of the list that contained the least element, and the whole of the other list that contained the greater element. This control is directed by constructing a new *Fork* that contains these two lists that must be merged, and the *Go* constructor signifies that the apomorphism must continue merging. Once the apomorphism has finished merging the lists, control is given back to the *fold*, which will continue bottom-up, collapsing the tree using the apomorphism, until a single list remains.

The second variation makes use of an *unfold* that focuses on producing the ensuing sorted list. The *unfold* has a coalgebra that has the type:

$$Fix\ Tree \rightarrow \underline{List}\ (Fix\ Tree)$$

To determine the next element of the ordered list that is to be produced, the *unfold* must apply a paramorphism to its seed tree. The work of this paramorphism can be thought of as collapsing the tree into either a *Nil* when the tree is empty and the work is finished, or a *Cons* *a t*, where *a* is the least value in the tree, and *t* is the tree that is to be used as the next seed. The tree is collapsed from the bottom, where the paramorphism is applied recursively at each *In Fork* until either an *In Tip* or *In* (*Leaf a*) is reached. *In Tip* values are turned into *Nil* values, and *In* (*Leaf a*) values are turned into *Cons a* (*In Tip*) values. These intermediate results are then combined bottom-up at each *Fork* by the function *merge*, which maintains the invariant that *Cons a t* contains the least element *a*, and *t* is the remaining tree. When two such *Cons* constructors meet at a fork, the least value is kept, and the seed tree is built out of a new *Fork* and the appropriate subtrees.

While these two algorithms certainly share many characteristics, their operation differs significantly. The behaviour of *mergeTree* is closer to the traditional merge-sort, where lists are successively merged together until only one remains. In contrast, *mergeTree'* behaves much more like a weak kind of heap sort, where the least element is floated out of the tree structure, but no heap property is maintained on the remaining tree.

6.3 Merging After Growing

Combining these two phases, we can write four variations of mergesort, where simple functional composition combines the various functions we have already discussed:

$$mergeSort, mergeSort', mergeSort'', mergeSort''' :: Fix\ List \to Fix\ \underline{List}$$
$$mergeSort\ \ = mergeTree \cdot makeTree$$
$$mergeSort'\ = mergeTree \cdot makeTree'$$
$$mergeSort''\ = mergeTree' \cdot makeTree$$
$$mergeSort''' = mergeTree' \cdot makeTree'$$

In this section we have used the *Tree* structure as a concrete representation of the implicit way mergesort works. Generally, however, these intermediate representations are inefficient, and can be fused away in a process called deforestation (Wadler 1988). A deforested version of the above algorithms would look similar to *mergeSort*, as shown in the beginning of this section. In the fused version, the *Tree* data structure disappears, instead becoming implicit from the recursive structure of the function.

7   Conclusion

In this paper we have revisited our previous work on sorting with bialgebras and distributive laws (Hinze et al. 2012), recasting it in a more applied setting without use of category theory. Due to the structure of recursive morphisms, and through the use of a type-directed approach for program construction, we have not lost the intuition behind our development; the duality is obvious in each sorting method, giving us "algorithms for free", and helping to understand the relations between different sorting methods.

Even though we have chosen Haskell as the presentation language for this paper, our developments readily generalise to other functional programming languages. In particular, all the code shown compiles with the "exchanging sources" version of the Clean compiler (Van Groningen et al. 2010) (after some minor refactoring to remove symbolic operators). This reinforces the argument that sorting algorithms become more clean and elegant when expressed as distributive laws in recursive morphisms.

References

Braun, W., Rem, M.: A logarithmic implementation of flexible arrays. Memorandum MR83/4, Eindhoven University of Technology (1983)

Gibbons, J., Jones, G.: The Under-Appreciated Unfold. In: Proceedings of the International Conference on Functional Programming, ICFP 1998, pp. 273–279. ACM (1998), doi:10.1145/289423.289455

van Groningen, J., van Noort, T., Achten, P., Koopman, P., Plasmeijer, R.: Exchanging sources between Clean and Haskell: A double-edged front end for the Clean compiler. In: Proceedings of the Third ACM Haskell Symposium on Haskell, Haskell 2010, pp. 49–60. ACM (2010), doi:10.1145/1863523.1863530

Hinze, R.: Generic programming with adjunctions. In: Gibbons, J. (ed.) Generic and Indexed Programming. LNCS, vol. 7470, pp. 47–129. Springer, Heidelberg (2012)

Hinze, R., James, D.W.H., Harper, T., Wu, N., Magalhães, J.P.: Sorting with bialgebras and distributive laws. In: Proceedings of the 8th ACM SIGPLAN Workshop on Generic Programming, WGP 2012, pp. 69–80. ACM (2012), doi:10.1145/2364394.2364405

Knuth, D.E.: The Art of Computer Programming, 2nd edn. Sorting and Searching, vol. 3. Addison-Wesley (1998)

Meertens, L.: Paramorphisms. Formal Aspects of Computing 4(5), 413–424 (1992), doi:10.1007/BF01211391

Meijer, E., Fokkinga, M., Paterson, R.: Functional programming with bananas, lenses, envelopes and barbed wire. In: Hughes, J. (ed.) FPCA 1991. LNCS, vol. 523, pp. 124–144. Springer, Heidelberg (1991)

Peyton Jones, S., et al.: Haskell 98, Language and Libraries. The Revised Report. Cambridge University Press (2003), A special issue of JFP

Sheard, T., Pasalic, T.: Two-level types and parameterized modules. Journal of Functional Programming 14(5), 547–587 (2004)

Vene, V., Uustalu, T.: Functional programming with apomorphisms (corecursion). Proceedings of the Estonian Academy of Sciences: Physics, Mathematics 47(3), 147–161 (1998)

Wadler, P.: Deforestation: Transforming programs to eliminate trees. In: Ganzinger, H. (ed.) ESOP 1988. LNCS, vol. 300, pp. 344–358. Springer, Heidelberg (1988)

Programming in the λ-Calculus: From Church to Scott and Back

Jan Martin Jansen

Faculty of Military Sciences,
Netherlands Defence Academy,
Den Helder, The Netherlands
jm.jansen.04@nlda.nl

Abstract. Although the λ-calculus is well known as a universal programming language, it is seldom used for actual programming or expressing algorithms. Here we demonstrate that it is possible to use the λ-calculus as a comprehensive formalism for programming by showing how to convert programs written in functional programming languages like Clean and Haskell to closed λ-expressions. The transformation is based on using the Scott-encoding for Algebraic Data Types instead of the more common Church encoding. In this way we not only obtain an encoding that is better comprehensible but that is also more efficient. As a proof of the pudding we provide an implementation of Eratosthenes' prime sieve algorithm as a self-contained, 143 character length, λ-expression.

1 The Church and Scott Encodings for Algebraic Data Types

The λ-calculus can be considered as the mother of all (functional) programming languages. Every course or textbook on λ-calculus (e.g. [1]) spends some time on showing how well-known programming constructs can be expressed in the λ-calculus. It commonly starts by explaining how to represent For natural numbers, in almost all cases the Church numerals are chosen as the leading example. The definition of Church numerals and operations on them shows that it is possible to use the λ-calculus for all kinds of computations and that it is indeed a universal programming language. The Church encoding can be generalized for the encoding of general Algebraic Data Types (see [2]). This encoding allows for a straightforward implementation of iterative (primitive recursive) or fold-like functions on data structures, but often requires complex and inefficient constructions for expressing general recursion.

It is less commonly known that there exist an alternative encoding of numbers and algebraic data structures in the λ-calculus. This encoding is relatively unknown, and independently (re)discovered by several authors (e.g. [9,8,10] and the author of this paper[6]), but originally attributed to Scott in an unpublished lecture which is cited in Curry, Hindley and Seldin ([4], page 504) as:
Dana Scott, A system of functional abstraction. Lectures delivered at University

P. Achten and P. Koopman (Eds.): Plasmeijer Festschrift, LNCS 8106, pp. 168–180, 2013.

of California, Berkeley, Cal., 1962/63. Photocopy of a preliminary version, issued by Stanford University, September 1963, furnished by author in 1968.[1] We will therefore call it the *Scott* encoding. The encoding results in a representation that is very close to algebraic data types as they are used in most functional programming languages.

The goal of this paper is not to introduce a new (functional) programming language, but to show how the λ-calculus itself can be used as a concise programming formalism.

This paper starts with a discussion on Algebraic Data Types in Section 2. In Section 3 it discusses how the Scott and Church encoding can be used to encode Algebraic Data Types as λ-terms and how these approaches differ. Section 4 focusses on the encoding of recursive functions as λ-terms. In Section 5 the focus is on the conversion of a complete Haskell or Clean program to a singe λ-term. The paper ends with a discussion in Section 7 and some conclusions in Section 8.

2   The Nature of Algebraic Data Types

Consider Algebraic Data Type (ADT) definitions in languages like Clean or Haskell such as tuples, booleans, temperature, maybe, natural (Peano) numbers and lists:

```
data Boolean      = True | False
data Tuple a b    = Tuple a b
data Temperature  = Fahrenheit Int | Celsius Int
data Maybe a      = Nothing | Just a
data Nat          = Zero | Suc Nat
data List t       = Nil  | Cons t (List t)
```

A type consists of one or more alternatives. Each alternative consist of a name, possibly followed by a number of arguments. Algebraic Data Types are used for several purposes:

- to make enumerations, like in Boolean;
- to package data, like in Tuple;
- to unite things of different kind in one type, like in MayBe and Temperature;
- to make recursive structures like in Nat and List (in fact to construct new types with an infinite number of elements).

The power of the ADT construction in modern functional programming languages is that one formalism can be used for all these purposes.

If we analyse the construction of ADT's more carefully, we see that constructor names are used for two purposes. First, they are used to distinguish the different cases in a single type definition (like True and False in Boolean, Nothing and Just in Maybe and Fahrenheit and Celsius in Temperature). Second, we need them for recognizing them as being part of a type and making type inferencing possible.

---

[1] I would like to thank Matthew Naylor for pointing me at this reference.

Therefore, all constructor names must be different in a single functional program (module). For distinguishing the different cases in a function definition, pattern matching on constructor names is used.

3 Representing Algebraic Data Types in the λ-Calculus

In this section it is shown how to represent ADT's in the λ-calculus. First, we focus on non-recursive data types for which the Scott and Church encodings are the same and thereafter on recursive types for which the encodings differ.

3.1 Named λ-Expressions

First, some remarks about the notation of λ-expressions. For convenience we will give λ-expressions sometimes names:

True ≡ λt f . t

These names can be used as macro's in other λ-expressions. They are always written in italics:

True (λf g . f g) (λf g . g f)

is a short-hand for:

(λt f . t) (λf g . f g) (λf g . g f)

Note that these macro names may not be used recursively, because this will lead to an infinite substitution process. Later on we discuss how to represent recursion in λ-expressions.

3.2 Expressing Enumeration Types in the λ-Calculus

The simplest example of such a type is Boolean. We already noted that we use pattern matching for recognizing different cases (constructors). So we are actually looking for an alternative for pattern matching using λ-expressions. The simplest boolean pattern matching example is if-then-else:

ifte True t f = t
ifte False t f = f

But the same effect can easily be achieved by making True and False functions of two variables, selecting the first or second argument respectively and by making ifte the identity function. Therefore, the λ-calculus solution for this is straightforward:

True ≡ λt f . t
False ≡ λt f . f
ifte ≡ λi   . i

This is also the standard encoding used for booleans that can be found in λ-calculus courses and text books. Both Church and Scott use this encoding.

3.3   Expressing a Simple Container Type in the λ-Calculus

Tuple is the simplest example of a container type. If we group data into a container, we also need constructions to get data out of it (projection functions). For Tuple this can be realized by pattern matching or by using the selection functions fst and snd. These functions are defined in Haskell as:

```
fst (Tuple a b) = a
snd (Tuple a b) = b
```

Containers can be expressed in the λ-calculus by using closures (partial applications). For Tuple the standard way to do this is:

$$Tuple \equiv \lambda a\ b\ f\ .\ f\ a\ b$$

A tuple is a function that takes 3 arguments. If we supply only two, we have a closure. This closure can take a third argument, which should be a 2 argument function. This function is then applied to the first two arguments. The third argument is therefore called a continuation (the function with which the computation continues). It is now easy to find out what the definitions of fst and snd should be:

$$fst \quad \equiv \lambda t\ .\ t\ (\lambda a\ b\ .\ a)$$
$$snd \quad \equiv \lambda t\ .\ t\ (\lambda a\ b\ .\ b)$$

If applied to a tuple, they apply the tuple to a two argument function, that selects either the first (fst) or second (snd) argument.

Again, this definition of tuples is the standard one that can be found in λ-calculus text books and courses. Also for this case the Church and Scott encoding are the same.

3.4   Expressing General Non-recursive Multi-case Types in the λ-Calculus

It is now a straightforward step to come up with a solution for arbitrary non-recursive ADT's. Just combine the two solutions from above. Let us look at the definition of the function warm that takes a Temperature as an argument:

```
warm :: Temperature → Boolean
warm (Fahrenheit f) = f > 90
warm (Celsius c)    = c > 30
```

We have to find encodings for (Fahrenheit f) and (Celsius c). The enumeration example tells that we should make a λ-expression with 2 arguments that returns the first argument for Fahrenheit and the second argument for Celsius. The container solution (as used for Tuple) tells us that we should feed the argument of Fahrenheit or Celsius to a continuation function. Combining these two solutions we learn that Fahrenheit and Celsius should both have 3 arguments. The first one to be used for the closure and the second and third as continuation arguments. Fahrenheit should choose the first continuation argument and apply it to its first argument and Celsius should do the same with the second continuation argument:

```
Fahrenheit   ≡ λt f c .  f t
Celsius      ≡ λt f c .  c t
```

Using this encoding the definition of warm becomes:

$warm \equiv \lambda t . t (\lambda f . f > 90) (\lambda c . c > 30)$

In the body the first argument of t represents the Fahrenheit case and the second one the Celsius case.

Also in this non-recursive case the Scott and Church approach do not differ.

3.5   Recursive Types in the λ-Calculus: The Scott Encoding

In the Scott Encoding the previous strategy, as used for Temperature, is also applied to recursive types. As a matter of fact, the Scott Encoding ignores the fact that we deal with a recursive type! Let us look for example at Nat and List. Applying the strategy we used for Temperature for Nat we obtain the following definitions:

$Zero \equiv \lambda z\ s\quad . z$
$Suc \equiv \lambda n\ z\ s\quad . s\ n$

Applying the same strategy for List, we obtain:

$Nil \equiv \lambda n\ c . n$
$Cons \equiv \lambda x\ xs\quad n\ c . c\ x\ xs$

Functions like predecessor, head and tail can now easily be defined:

$pred \equiv \lambda n . n\ undef\ (\lambda m . m)$

$head \equiv \lambda xs . xs\ undef\ (\lambda x\ xs . x)$
$tail \equiv \lambda xs . xs\ undef\ (\lambda x\ xs . xs)$

Note that *pred* and *tail* have constant time complexity!

As another example we give the Scott Encoding of the fold functions for Nat and List. The Haskell definition foldNat is given by:

```
foldNat f x Zero     = x
foldNat f x (Suc n)  = f (foldNat f x n)
```

The conversion for the Scott encoding of Nat is straightforward, the bodies of the two cases simply appear as the first and second argument of n (later on we show how to remove the recursive call for foldNat):

$foldNat \equiv \lambda f\ x\ n . n\ x\ (\lambda n . f\ (foldNat\ f\ x\ n))$

For foldList, the Haskell definition is:

```
foldList f d []    = d
foldList f d (h:t) = f h (foldList f d t)
```

Using the Scott encoding for lists this becomes:

$foldList \equiv \lambda f\ d\ xs . xs\ d\ (\lambda h\ t . f\ h\ (foldList\ f\ d\ t))$

The Scott encoding of ADT's is completely equivalent to their counterparts in Haskell and Clean. Functions acting on them can be straightforwardly converted to their Scott versions.

3.6   Recursive Types in the λ-Calculus: The Church Encoding

Church uses an entirely different approach for the encoding of recursive data types.

The Church definitions of natural numbers are:

$Zero \equiv \lambda f\ x\quad .\ x$
$Suc\ \equiv \lambda n\ f\ x\ .\ f\ (n\ f\ x)$

If we compare this to the Scott approach we see that, instead of feeding only n to the continuation function f, the result of n f x is fed to it. But this is exactly the same thing as what happens in the fold function. The definition of foldNat for Church encoded numerals can therefore be given by:

$foldNat\ \equiv \lambda f\ x\ n\ .\ n\ f\ x$

In [5] Hinze states that Church numerals are actually folds in disguise. As a consequence only primitive recursive functions on numbers can be easily expressed using the Church encoding. For functions that need general recursion (or functions for which the result for suc n cannot be expressed using the result for n) we run into troubles. Church himself was not able to solve this problem, but Kleene found a way out during a visit to the dentist (as described by Barendregt in [2]). A nice example of his solution is the predecessor function, which could be easily expressed using the Scott encoding, as we saw earlier. To define it using the Church encoding Kleene used a construction with pairs (Tuple):

$pred\ \equiv\ \lambda n\ .\ snd(n\ (\lambda p\ .\ Tuple\ (Suc\ (fst\ p))\ (fst\ p))\ (Tuple\ Zero\ Zero))$

Each pair combines the result of the recursive call with the previous element. A disadvantage of this solution, besides that it is hard to comprehend, is that it has complexity $O(n)$ while the Scott version has constant complexity.

The Church encoding for lists together with the function tail is given by:

$Nil\quad \equiv \lambda f\ x\quad .\ x$
$Cons \equiv \lambda h\ t\ f\ x\ .\ f\ h\ (t\ f\ x)$

$tail\ \equiv \lambda xs\ .\ snd\ (xs\ (\lambda x\ rs\ .\ Tuple\ (Cons\ x\ (fst\ rs))\ (fst\ rs))\ (Tuple\ Nil\ Nil))$

Also here the definition of Cons behaves like a fold (a foldr actually). Again, we need the pair construction from Kleene for tail. The definition of foldList for Church encoded lists is given by:

$foldList\ \equiv \lambda f\ d\ xs\ .\ xs\ f\ d$

3.7   The Scott Encoding: The General Case

In general the mapping of an ADT to λ-expressions using the Scott encoding is defined as follows. Given an ADT definition in Haskell or Clean:

```
data type_name t₁ ... tₖ = C₁ t₁,₁ ... t₁,ₙ₁ | ... | Cₘ tₘ,₁ ... tₘ,ₙₘ
```

Then this type definition with m constructors can be mapped to m λ-expressions:

$$C_1 \equiv \lambda v_{1,1} \ldots v_{1,n_1} \ \mathbf{f_1} \ldots \mathbf{f_m} \ . \ \mathbf{f_1} \ v_{1,1} \ldots v_{1,n_1}$$

$\ldots$

$$C_m \equiv \lambda v_{m,1} \ldots v_{m,n_m} \ \mathbf{f_1} \ldots \mathbf{f_m} \ . \ \mathbf{f_m} \ v_{m,1} \ldots v_{m,n_m}$$

Consider the (multi-case) pattern-based function `f` in Haskell or Clean defined on this type:

```
f (C₁ v₁,₁ ... v₁,ₙ₁) = body₁
...
f (Cₘ vₘ,₁ ... vₘ,ₙₘ) = bodyₘ
```

This function is converted to the following λ-expression (of course, the bodies should also be encoded):

$$f \equiv \lambda \mathbf{x} \ . \ \mathbf{x}$$
$$(\lambda v_{1,1} \ldots v_{1,n_1} \ . \ \mathbf{body_1})$$
$$\ldots$$
$$(\lambda v_{m,1} \ldots v_{m,n_m} \ . \ \mathbf{body_m})$$

3.8   From Church to Scott and Back

It is straightforward to convert Church and Scott encoded numerals into each other. Because a fold replaces constructors by functions and Church numerals are actually folds, we can obtain the Scott representation by substituting back the Scott versions of the constructors:

$$toScott \quad \equiv \lambda \mathbf{n} \ . \ \mathbf{n} \ Suc_s \ Zero_s$$

To go from Scott to Church we should use the Scott version of $foldNat$:

$$toChurch \equiv \lambda \mathbf{n} \ \mathbf{f} \ \mathbf{x} \ . \ foldNat \ \mathbf{f} \ \mathbf{x} \ \mathbf{n}$$

The conversions between the Church and Scott encoding for lists are given by:

$$toScottList \quad \equiv \lambda \mathbf{xs} \ . \ \mathbf{xs} \ Cons_s \ Nil_s$$
$$toChurchList \equiv \lambda \mathbf{xs} \ \mathbf{f} \ \mathbf{d} \ . \ foldList \ \mathbf{f} \ \mathbf{d} \ \mathbf{xs}$$

The list definitions are completely equivalent to those for numbers. They only use a different fold function in $toChurchList$ and different constructors in $toScottList$. For other recursive ADT's similar transformations can be defined.

In the remainder of this paper we will concentrate on defining algorithms in the λ-calculus using the Scott encoding.

4   Defining Functions Using the Scott Encoding

Now we know how to represent ADT's we can concentrate on functions. We already gave some examples of them above (`ifte`, `fst`, `snd`, `head`, `tail`, `pred`, `warm`, `foldNat`, `foldList`). The more interesting examples are the recursive functions. The standard technique for defining a recursive function in the λ-calculus is to use a fixed point operator. Let us look for example at addition for Peano numbers in Haskell:

```
add Zero     m = m
add (Suc n) m = Suc (add n m)
```

Using the Scott encoding, this becomes:

$add_0 \equiv \lambda$n m . n m (λn . Suc (add_0 n m))

We now have to get rid of the recusrsive macro add_0 in this definition. The standard way to do this is with the use of the Y fixed point combinator:

$add_Y \equiv Y$ (λadd n m . n m (λn . Suc (add n m)))
$Y \quad \equiv \lambda$h . (λx . h (x x)) (λx . h (x x))

There is, however, another way to represent recursion. Instead of using a fixed point operator we can also give the recursive function itself as an argument (like this is done in the argument of Y in add_Y):

$add \equiv \lambda$add n m . n m (λn . Suc (add add n m))

The price to pay is that each call of add should have add as an argument. The gain is that we do not need the fixed point operator any more. This definition is also more efficient, because it uses fewer reduction steps during reduction than the fixed-point version. The following example shows how add should be used to add one to one (note the double add in the call):

(λadd . add add ($Suc\ Zero$) ($Suc\ Zero$)) add

4.1   Mutually Recursive Functions

For mutually recursive functions, we have to add all mutually recursive functions as arguments for each function. An example to clarify this:

```
isOdd Zero      = False
isOdd (Suc n)  = isEven n
isEven Zero     = True
isEven (Suc n) = isOdd n
```

This can be represented by λ-expressions as:

$isOdd \equiv \lambda$isOdd isEven n . n $False$ (λn . isEven isOdd isEven n)
$isEven \equiv \lambda$isOdd isEven n . n $True$ (λn . isOdd isOdd isEven n)

5   Converting Algorithms to the λ-Calculus

We now have all ingredients ready for converting complete programs. The last step to be made is combining everything into a single λ-expression. For example, if we take the add 1 1 example from above, and substitute all macros, we obtain:

(λadd . add add ((λn z s.s n)(λz s. z)) ((λn z s.s n) (λz s. z)))
        (λadd n m . n m (λn . (λn z s.s n) (add add n m)))

Using normal order (outermost) reduction this reduces to:

λz s. s (λz s. s (λz s. z))

which indeed represents the desired value 2. We can improve the readability by introducing explicit names for zero and suc by abstracting out their definitions:

```
(λzero suc .
   (λadd   .
         add add (suc zero) (suc zero))
   (λadd n m . n m (λn . suc (add add n m)))
(λz s.z) (λn z s.s n)
```

Here we applied a kind of inverted λ-lifting. We have used smart indentation to make the expression better readable. Note the nesting in this definition: the definition of add is inside the scope of the variables suc and zero, because its definition depends on their definitions. In this way the macro reference *Suc* in the definition of add can be replaced by a variable suc.

As another example, the right hand side of the Haskell function:

main = isOdd (Suc (Suc (Suc Zero)))

can be written as:

(λisOdd isEven . isOdd isOdd isEven (*Suc* (*Suc* (*Suc* *Zero*)))) *isOdd* *isEven*

and after substituting all macro definitions and abstracting out definitions:

```
(λtrue false zero suc .
         (λisOdd isEven .
              isOdd isOdd isEven (suc (suc (suc zero))))
         (λisOdd isEven n . n false (λn . isEven isOdd isEven n))
         (λisOdd isEven n . n true  (λn . isOdd isOdd isEven n)))
(λt f.t) (λt f.f) (λz s.z) (λn z s.s n)
```

Which reduces to:

λt f . t

Which shows that 3 is indeed an odd number.

5.1   Formalizing the Conversion

Above we mentioned the operation of abstracting out definitions. Here we make this more precise. The conversion of a program into a closed λ-expression proceeds in a number of steps:

1. Remove all syntactic sugar like zf-expressions, where and let expressions.
2. Eliminate algebraic data types by converting them to their Scott encoding.
3. Eliminate pattern-based function definitions by using the Scott encoding.
4. Remove (mutually) recursion by the introduction of extra variables.

5. Make a dependency sort of all functions, resulting in an ordered collection of sets. So the first set contains functions that do not depend on other functions (e.g. the Scott encoded ADT's). The second set contains functions that only depend on functions in the first set, etc. We can do this because all possible cycles are already removed in the previous step.
6. Construct the resulting λ-expression by nesting the definitions from the different dependency sets. The outermost expression consists of an application of a λ-expression with as variables the names of the functions from the first dependency set and as arguments the λ-definitions of these functions. The body of this expression is obtained by repeating this procedure for the remainder dependency sets. The innermost expression is the main expression.

The result of this process is:

```
(λfunction_names_first_set .
  (λfunction_names_second_set .
    ...
      (λfunction_names_last_set .
        main_expression)
      function_definitions_last_set)
    ...
  function_definitions_second_set)
function_definitions_first_set
```

6   Eratosthenes' Prime Sieve as a Single λ-Expression

As a last, more convincing example, we convert the following Haskell version of the Eratosthenes prime sieve algorithm to a single λ-expression:

```
data Nat              = Zero | Suc Nat
data Inflist t        = Cons t (Inflist t)
nats n                = Cons n (nats (Suc n))
sieve (Cons Zero xs)  = sieve xs
sieve (Cons (Suc k) xs) = Cons (Suc k) (sieve (rem k k xs))
rem p Zero    (Cons x xs) = Cons Zero (rem p p xs))
rem p (Suc k) (Cons x xs) = Cons x    (rem p k xs)

main = sieve (nats (Suc (Suc Zero)))
```

Here we use infinite lists for the storage of numbers and the resulting primes. sieve filters out the zero's in a list and calls rem to set multiples of prime numbers to zero. Applying the first four steps of the conversion procedure results in:

$$
\begin{aligned}
&Zero \equiv \lambda z\ s\quad .\ z \\
&Suc\ \equiv \lambda n\ z\ s\ .\ s\ n \\
&Cons\ \equiv \lambda x\ xs\ c\ .\ c\ x\ xs \\
&nats\ \equiv \lambda nats\ n\ .\ Cons\ n\ (nats\ nats\ (Suc\ n)) \\
&sieve \equiv \lambda sieve\ ls\ .\ ls\ (\lambda x\ xs\ .\ x\ (sieve\ sieve\ xs) \\
&\qquad\qquad\qquad\qquad\qquad (\lambda k\ .\ Cons\ x\ (sieve\ sieve\ (rem\ rem\ k\ k\ xs))))
\end{aligned}
$$

rem ≡ λrem p k ls . ls (λx xs . k (*Cons Zero* (rem rem p p xs))
                                   (λk . *Cons* x (rem rem p k xs)))
main ≡ *sieve sieve* (*nats nats* (*Suc* (*Suc Zero*)))

The dependency sort results in:

[{zero,suc,cons},{rem,nats},{sieve},{main}]

Putting everything into a single λ-expression this becomes:

```
(λzero suc cons .
 (λrem nats    .
  (λsieve      .
    sieve sieve (nats nats (suc (suc zero))))
  sieve)
 rem  nats)
Zero Suc Cons
```

And after substituting the λ-definitions for all macros:

```
(λzero suc cons .
 (λrem nats    .
  (λsieve      .
    sieve sieve (nats nats (suc (suc zero))))
  (λsieve ls  . ls (λx xs . x (sieve sieve xs)
                              (λk . cons x (sieve sieve (rem rem k k xs)))))))
 (λrem p k ls . ls (λx xs . k (cons zero (rem rem p p xs))
                              (λk . cons x (rem rem p k xs))))
 (λnats n . cons n (nats nats (suc n))))
(λz s . z) (λn z s . s n) (λx xs c . c x xs)
```

Which reduces to an infinite λ-expression starting with:

λc. c (λz s. s (λz s. s (λz s. z))) (λc. c (λz s. s (λz s. s (λz s. s (λz s. z))))
(λc. c (λz s. s (λz s. s (λz s. s (λz s. s (λz s. s (λz s. z)))))) ...

One can recognize the start of a list containing: 2, 3 and 5. Using single character names the expression reduces to a 143 character length definition:

(λzsc.(λrf.(λe.ee(ff(s(sz))))(λel.lλht.h(eet)λk.ch(ee(rrkkt)))))
(λrpkl.lλht.k(cz(rrppt))λk.ch(rrpkt))(λfn.cn(ff(sn))))(λzs.z)(λnzs.zn)(λhtc.cht)

This λ-term can also be considered as a constructive definition of what prime numbers are. An even shorter defintion of a prime number generator in the λ-calculus can be found in Tromp [11].

7   Discussion

We already indicated that the Scott encoding just combines the techniques used for encoding booleans and tuples in the Church encoding as described in standard λ-calculus text books and courses. The Scott and Church encodings only differ for recursive types. A Church encoded type just defines how functions should be folded over an element of the type. A fold can be characterized as a function that replaces constructors by functions. The Scott encoding just packages information into a closure. Recursiveness of the type is not visible at this level. Of course, this is also the case for ADT's in functional languages, where recursiveness is only visible at the type level and not at the element level.

The representation achieved using the Scott encoding is equivalent to that of ADT definitions in modern functional programming languages and allows for an similar realization of functions defined on ADT's. Also the complexity (efficiency) of these functions is similar to their equivalents in functional programming languages. This in contrast to their counterparts using the Church encoding that sometimes have a much worse complexity. Therefore, from a programmers perspective the Scott encoding is better than the Church encoding.

An interesting question now is: Why is the Scott encoding relatively unknown and almost never mentioned in textbooks on the λ-calculus? The encoding is simpler than the Church encoding and allows for a straightforward implementation of functions acting on data types. Of course, the way ADT's are represented in modern functional programming languages is rather new and dates from languages like ISWIM [7], HOPE [3] and SASL [13,12] and this was long after the Church numerals were invented. Furthermore, ADT's are needed and defined by programmers, who needed an efficient way to define new types, which is rather irrelevant for mathematicians and logicians studying the λ-calculus.

In [6] it is shown that this representation of functional programs can be used to construct very efficient, simple and small interpreters for lazy functional programming languages. These interpreters only have to implement β-reduction and no constructors nor pattern matching.

Altogether, we argue that the Scott encoding also should have its place in λ-calculus textbooks and courses and in λ-calculus courses for computer scientist this encoding should have preference over the Church encoding.

8   Conclusions

In this paper we showed how the λ-calculus can be used to express algorithms and Algebraic Data Types in a way that is close to the way this is done in modern functional programming languages. To achieve this, we used a rather unfamiliar encoding of ADT's attributed to Scott. We showed that this encoding can be considered as a logical combination of the way how enumerations (like booleans) and containers (like tuples) are normally encoded in the λ-calculus. The encoding differs from the Church encoding and the connecting element between them is the fold function.

For recursive functions we did not use the standard fixed-point combinators, but instead used a simple technique where an expression representing a recursive function is given (a reference to) itself as an argument. In this way the recursion is made more explicit and this also results in a more efficient implementation using fewer reduction steps.

We also sketched a systematic method for converting Haskell or Clean like programs to closed λ-expressions.

Altogether we have shown that it is possible to express a functional program in a concise way as a λ-expression and demonstrated that the λ-calculus is indeed a universal programming language in a convincing way.

References

1. Barendregt, H.: The lambda calculus, its syntax and semantics, revised edition. Studies in Logic, vol. 103. North-Holland (1984)
2. Barendregt, H.: The impact of the lambda calculus in logic and computer science. The Bulletin of Symbolic Logic 3(2), 181–215 (1997)
3. Burstall, R.M., MacQueen, D.B., Sannella, D.T.: Hope: An experimental applicative language (1980)
4. Curry, H., Hindley, J., Seldin, J.: Combinatory Logic, vol. 2. North-Holland Publishing Company (1972)
5. Hinze, R.: Theoretical pearl Church numerals, twice? Journal of Functional Programming 15(1), 1–13 (2005)
6. Jansen, J., Koopman, P., Plasmeijer, R.: Efficient interpretation by transforming data types and patterns to functions. In: Nilsson, H. (ed.) Revised Selected Papers of the 7th Trends in Functional Programming 2006, vol. 7, pp. 73–90. Intellect Books, Nottingham (2006)
7. Landin, P.J.: The next 700 programming languages. Commun. ACM 9(3), 157–166 (1966)
8. Mogensen, T.A.: Efficient Self-Interpretation in Lambda Calculus. Journal of Functional Programming 2, 345–364 (1994)
9. Steensgaard-Madsen, J.: Typed representation of Objects by Functions. ACM Transactions on Programming Languages and Systems 11(1), 67–89 (1989)
10. Stump, A.: Directly reflective meta-programming. Journal of Higher Order and Symbolic Computation (2008)
11. Tromp, J.: John's lambda calculus and combinatory logic playground (2012), http://homepages.cwi.nl/ tromp/cl/cl.html
12. Turner, D.: Some History of Functional Programming Languages. In: Invited talk, Trends in Functional Programming 2012, TFP 2012, St. Andrews, United Kingdom (2012)
13. Turner, D.A.: A new implementation technique for applicative languages. Softw., Pract. Exper. 9(1), 31–49 (1979)

Modelling Unique and Affine Typing Using Polymorphism

Edsko de Vries

Well-Typed LLP

Abstract. Uniqueness typing and affine (or linear) typing are dual type systems. Uniqueness gives a *guarantee* that an term *has not* been shared, while affinity imposes a *restriction* that a term *may not* be shared. We show that we can unify both concepts through polymorphism.

1 Introduction

Side effects in modern pure functional languages such as Clean or Haskell are modelled as functions that transform the world. For instance, a function that reads a character from the keyboard might have type

$$\texttt{getChar} :: \texttt{World} \to (\texttt{World}, \texttt{Char})$$

The return type of `getChar` makes it clear that c_1 and c_2 can have different values in

$$\lambda world \cdot \text{let } (c_1, world') = \texttt{getChar } world$$
$$(c_2, world'') = \texttt{getChar } world'$$
$$\text{in } (c_1, c_2, world'')$$

They are read in different worlds, after all. Of course, this is a symbolic representation of the world only, which means we somehow need to outlaw programs such as

$$\lambda world \cdot \text{let } (c_1, world') = \texttt{getChar } world \qquad (1)$$
$$(c_2, world'') = \texttt{getChar } world$$
$$\text{in } (c_1, c_2, world'')$$

One way to do this is to define an opaque wrapper type

$$\texttt{IO } a \mathrel{\hat{=}} \texttt{World} \to (\texttt{World}, a)$$

together with two operations

$$\texttt{return} :: a \to \texttt{IO } a$$
$$\texttt{bind} \quad :: \texttt{IO } a \to (a \to \texttt{IO } b) \to \texttt{IO } b$$

That is, define `IO` to be a *monad*. Since the plumbing of the `World` happens inside `bind` "reusing" the same world cannot happen. This is the approach taken in Haskell.

P. Achten and P. Koopman (Eds.): Plasmeijer Festschrift, LNCS 8106, pp. 181–192, 2013.

An alternative approach is to use a type system to outlaw programs such as (1). For instance, we can use Clean's *uniqueness typing* to give getChar the type

$$\texttt{getChar :: World}^{\bullet} \to (\texttt{World}^{\bullet}, \texttt{Char})$$

The annotation on World$^{\bullet}$ means that getChar requires a *unique*—or non-shared—reference to the world and in turn promises to return a unique reference.

An advantage of this approach over the use of monads is that it is more compositional. For example, we can easily define a function that modifies two arrays *in place*

$$\texttt{modifyArrays :: (Array}^{\bullet}, \texttt{Array}^{\bullet}) \to (\texttt{Array}^{\bullet}, \texttt{Array}^{\bullet})$$
$$\texttt{modifyArrays} = \ldots$$

without specifying in which order these two updates should happen (indeed, they could happen in parallel).

Uniqueness typing is a *substructural* logic. We will explain this in more detail in Sect. 2. Probably the most well-known substructural logic is affine (or linear) logic. Affine logic can be regarded as *dual* to uniqueness typing; we discuss it in more detail in Sect. 3. In Sect. 4 we observe that we can simplify and unify both type systems through a familiar typing construct: polymorphism. We show that there is a sound translation from unique and affine typing into the unified system, and argue that although the translation is not complete, the loss is outweighed by the benefits of unifying the two systems. Finally, we wrap in Sect. 6.

2   Uniqueness Typing

The type syntax that we will use throughout this paper is given by

$\alpha ::= \bullet \mid \times$	(type attribute)
$\tau ::= c \mid \sigma \xrightarrow{\alpha} \sigma'$	(base type)
$\sigma ::= \tau^{\alpha}$	(attributed type)
$c \in \texttt{Unit}, \texttt{Bool}, \texttt{Array}, \ldots$	(constants)

where we will write $(\sigma_1 \xrightarrow[\alpha']{} \sigma_2)^{\alpha}$ as $\sigma_1 \xrightarrow[\alpha']{\alpha} \sigma_2$, and we will occasionally follow Clean convention and use the absence of a type annotation to mean non-unique (i.e., we might write $\tau^{\times}$ as τ). The reason for the additional attribute on the function arrow will become clear in Sect. 2.3.

In the context of uniqueness typing the attribute "$\bullet$" is read as "unique" (guaranteed not shared), and the attribute "$\times$" is pronounced "non-unique" (possibly shared). The typing rules for uniqueness typing are shown in Figure 1.

2.1   Contraction

Typing environments (here and elsewhere in this paper) are *bags* of pairs of identifiers and types, *not sets*. That is, the typing environment $\{x : \sigma, x : \sigma\}$ with

Logical Rules

$$\frac{}{x : \sigma \vdash x : \sigma}\text{VAR}$$

$$\frac{\Gamma, x : \sigma_1 \vdash e : \sigma_2}{\Gamma \vdash \lambda x \cdot e : \sigma_1 \xrightarrow[\sup \Gamma]{\alpha} \sigma_2}\text{ABS} \qquad \frac{\Gamma_1 \vdash e_1 : \sigma_1 \xrightarrow[\alpha']{\alpha} \sigma_2 \quad \Gamma_2 \vdash e_2 : \sigma_1 \quad \alpha \subseteq \alpha'}{\Gamma_1, \Gamma_2 \vdash e_1 \, e_2 : \sigma_2}\text{APP}$$

with $\alpha \subseteq \alpha$, $\times \subseteq \bullet$, and (sup) the corresponding supremum (least upper bound)

Subtyping

$$\frac{\Gamma \vdash e : \tau^\bullet}{\Gamma \vdash e : \tau^\times}\text{UNIQUE}$$

for simplicity we treat the function space as invariant

Structural Rules

$$\frac{\Gamma, x : \tau^\times, x : \tau^\times \vdash e : \sigma}{\Gamma, x : \tau^\times \vdash e : \sigma}\text{CONTR} \qquad \frac{\Gamma \vdash e : \sigma}{\Gamma, x : \sigma' \vdash e : \sigma}\text{WEAK}$$

Fig. 1. Uniqueness Typing

Logical Rules

$$\frac{}{x : \sigma \vdash x : \sigma}\text{VAR}$$

$$\frac{\Gamma, x : \sigma_1 \vdash e : \sigma_2 \quad \alpha \subseteq \sup \Gamma}{\Gamma \vdash \lambda x \cdot e : \sigma_1 \xrightarrow[\sup \Gamma]{\alpha} \sigma_2}\text{ABS} \qquad \frac{\Gamma_1 \vdash e_1 : \sigma_1 \xrightarrow[\alpha']{\alpha} \sigma_2 \quad \Gamma_2 \vdash e_2 : \sigma_1}{\Gamma_1, \Gamma_2 \vdash e_1 \, e_2 : \acute{\sigma}_2}\text{APP}$$

Subtyping

$$\frac{\Gamma \vdash e : \tau^\times}{\Gamma \vdash e : \tau^\bullet}\text{AFFINE}$$

Structural rules as above.

Fig. 2. Affine Typing

Logical Rules

$$\frac{}{x : \sigma \vdash x : \sigma}\text{VAR}$$

$$\frac{\Gamma, x : \sigma_1 \vdash e : \sigma_2 \quad \alpha \subseteq \sup \Gamma}{\Gamma \vdash \lambda x \cdot e : \sigma_1 \xrightarrow[\sup \Gamma]{\alpha} \sigma_2}\text{ABS} \qquad \frac{\Gamma_1 \vdash e_1 : \sigma_1 \xrightarrow[\alpha']{\alpha} \sigma_2 \quad \Gamma_2 \vdash e_2 : \sigma_1 \quad \alpha \subseteq \alpha'}{\Gamma_1, \Gamma_2 \vdash e_1 \, e_2 : \sigma_2}\text{APP}$$

Generalization and Instantiation

$$\frac{\Gamma \vdash e : \sigma\{^\bullet/_a\} \quad \Gamma \vdash e : \sigma\{^\times/_a\}}{\Gamma \vdash e : (\forall a \cdot \sigma)^{\sup \Gamma}}\text{GEN} \qquad \frac{\Gamma \vdash e : (\forall a \cdot \sigma)^\alpha}{\Gamma \vdash e : \sigma\{^{\alpha'}/_a\}}\text{INST}$$

Structural rules as above.

Fig. 3. Unified using Polymorphism

two (identical) assumptions for x is a different typing environment to $\{x : \sigma\}$ containing a single assumption. Moreover, in rule APP we *union* the typing environment used to type the function with the typing environment used to type the argument, rather than using the same environment for both.

This means that we must be explicit about *structural* operations on the typing environment. Rule CONTR allows us to *contract* two typing assumptions, while rule WEAK allows us to weaken a typing derivation by introducing an additional (unused) assumption. Importantly, CONTR applies only to non-unique terms, so that we can derive

$$
\cfrac{
  \cfrac{
    \cfrac{
      \vdots
    }{f : \tau^\times \to \tau^\times \to \sigma, x : \tau^\times \vdash f\,x : \tau^\times \to \sigma} \quad x : \tau^\times \vdash x : \tau^\times
  }{
    \cfrac{
      \cfrac{f : \tau^\times \to \tau^\times \to \sigma, x : \tau^\times, x : \tau^\times \vdash f\,x\,x : \sigma}{
        \cfrac{f : \tau^\times \to \tau^\times \to \sigma, x : \tau^\times \vdash f\,x\,x : \sigma}{f : \tau^\times \to \tau^\times \to \sigma \vdash \lambda x \cdot f\,x\,x : \tau^\times \to \sigma}\ \text{CONTR}
      }{\varnothing \vdash \lambda f \cdot \lambda x \cdot f\,x\,x : (\tau^\times \to \tau^\times \to \sigma) \to \tau^\times \to \sigma}\ \text{ABS}
    }{}
  }\ \text{APP}
}{}
$$

but, crucially, we cannot find any derivation for

$$\varnothing \vdash \lambda f \cdot \lambda x \cdot f\,x\,x : (\tau^\bullet \to \tau^\bullet \to \sigma) \to \tau^\bullet \to \sigma$$

The restriction on the structural rule CONTR is what makes uniqueness typing a *substructural* logic.

2.2 Subtyping

Uniqueness is a *guarantee* that a term is not shared; however, it is safe to ignore that guarantee. For instance, we can find a term with type

$$(\tau^\times \to \tau^\times \to \sigma) \to \tau^\bullet \to \sigma$$

(exercise: what is it?). For an example use case, consider a type Array of integer arrays with corresponding in-place updates

```
update :: Int → Int → Array• → Array•
sort :: Ascending → Array• → Array•
  . . .
```

Once we are done with updating the array we can apply subtyping to get an Array$^\times$ which we can freely share but no longer update.

The combination of the restriction on CONTR with subtyping (UNIQUE) justifies reading "•" as "non-shared".

2.3 Closure Typing

Consider a term such as

$$\lambda arr \cdot \lambda asc \cdot \text{sort } asc\ arr :: \text{Array}^\bullet \to \text{Ascending} \xrightarrow{\alpha}_{\bullet} \text{Array}^\bullet$$

When we partially apply this function to a unique array, we get a function of type

$$\text{Ascending} \xrightarrow[\bullet]{\alpha} \text{Array}^\bullet$$

the annotation underneath the function arrow here means that this function has a unique term in its closure. It is important that this term is still unique when we (fully) apply the function, which is why rule APP requires that when we apply a function with unique terms in its closure it must itself be unique. This is called uniqueness *propagation*, and is important whenever terms contain other terms (function closures, tuples, algebraic data types, etc.).

3 Affine Typing

Affine typing is a close cousin of uniqueness typing; the typing rules are shown in Fig. 2. Where "unique" can be interpreted as a *guarantee* that a term *has not* not shared, "affine" can be interpreted as a *restriction* that a term *may not* be shared, or, equivalently but more conventionally, can only be used once.

> *Aside.* Affine typing is closely related to linear typing, in which the weakening rule (WEAK) is also limited to non-affine types. It is often claimed that such a type system guarantees that a term of linear type will be used "exactly" once; however, since linear type systems rarely guarantee the absence of divergence, this is a dubious claim. We will use "affine" throughout this paper as the more general term.

This duality between uniqueness typing and affine typing is evident in the typing rules too, in two ways. First, the subtyping relation is inverse (rule AFFINE). Where a guarantee of uniqueness can be forgotten but not invented, an affine restriction may be self-imposed but not ignored.

Second, like in uniqueness typing, when a closure contains a restricted term then that closure itself must be restricted; but unlike in uniqueness typing, that restriction must be enforced at the *definition* site (ABS) rather than the usage site (APP). (Exercise: why is it unsafe to combine UNIQUE subtyping with definition-site propagation, or AFFINE subtyping with usage-site propagation?)

For an example use case, consider a concurrent, impure (not referentially transparent) functional language with a type Channel of communication channels with corresponding functions

$$\text{send} :: \text{Int} \to \text{Channel}^\bullet \to \text{Unit}$$
$$\text{newChannel} :: \text{Unit} \to \text{Channel}^\times$$

We can pass a channel of type Channel$^\bullet$ to a thread, meaning that it can only send a single signal on the channel; a "master" thread can create a new channel using newChannel, spawn a number of slave threads, use subtyping to pass in an affine reference to this channel, and is then guaranteed that each slave thread will write at most once to the channel.

4 Polymorphism

Consider again the type of array update:

$$\texttt{update} :: \texttt{Int} \rightarrow \texttt{Int} \rightarrow \texttt{Array}^{\bullet} \rightarrow \texttt{Array}^{\bullet}$$

The *input* array must certainly be unique, but **update** does not itself care that the result is unique; that is, we could also provide

$$\texttt{update}' :: \texttt{Int} \rightarrow \texttt{Int} \rightarrow \texttt{Array}^{\bullet} \rightarrow \texttt{Array}^{\times}$$

Similarly, in the channel example, **send** took a restricted channel, but we could also provide

$$\texttt{send}' :: \texttt{Int} \rightarrow \texttt{Channel}^{\times} \rightarrow \texttt{Unit}$$

Using uniqueness subtyping we can define **update'** in terms of **update**; using affine subtyping we can define **send'** in terms of **send**. However, since the subtyping relation in both cases is so shallow, there is a more obvious generalization of both functions:

$$\texttt{update} :: \forall a \cdot \texttt{Int} \rightarrow \texttt{Int} \rightarrow \texttt{Array}^{\bullet} \rightarrow \texttt{Array}^{a}$$
$$\texttt{send} :: \forall a \cdot \texttt{Int} \rightarrow \texttt{Channel}^{a} \rightarrow \texttt{Unit}$$

We only need a *single* construct to capture *both* subtyping relations, and thus we arrive at the central thesis of this paper: we can use polymorphism to combine uniqueness typing and affine typing within a single system. The only difference whether we use polymorphism in the codomain (**update**) or the domain of the function (**send**), once more establishing the duality between uniqueness and affine typing.

4.1 The Polymorphic Type System

We extend the systems of types with

$$\tau ::= c \mid \sigma \xrightarrow{\alpha} \sigma' \mid \forall a \cdot \sigma$$
$$\sigma ::= \tau^{\alpha} \qquad\qquad \text{(as before)}$$

A function of type $\tau_1^{\bullet} \xrightarrow{\bullet} \tau_2^{\times}$ is a *unique* function from a unique τ_1 to a non-unique τ_2; the attribute on the function is distinct from the attributes on its domain and codomain. Similarly, a value of type, say, $(\forall a.\texttt{Array}^{a})^{\bullet}$ is a *unique* polymorphic value that can be instantiated to a unique or non-unique array. The uniqueness on the polymorphic value itself means that it can only be instantiated once. The analogy with functions is appropriate: a polymorphic value can be interpreted as a function that takes a type argument; and like functions, polymorphic values must be unique themselves if they have any unique elements in their "closure".

The rules for the polymorphic type system are shown in Fig. 3. The structural rules are as they were in uniqueness typing and affine typing. We no longer have subtyping, however; this means that the "•" annotation means "has *and* may never be shared", thus no longer distinguishing between "unique" and "affine"; we can choose either interpretation based on the application we have in mind. Rule GEN embodies the propagation we described in the previous section. Rule INST is the familiar instantiation rule, where we ignore the attribute on the polymorphic value itself.

Propagation for functions is now enforced in *both* definition *and* usage sites (ABS and APP). This is overkill; it would suffice to enforce propagation in ABS (and do away with closure typing completely): after all, in the absence of sub-typing if a function is unique when it is created it must still be unique when it applied. Formally proving that this simpler type system is equivalent to the one we have presented, however, is slightly non-trivial and non-essential to the central message of this paper. We chose the representation in Fig. 3 to aid the comparison to the uniqueness and affine typing systems; we do not necessarily suggest to use the type system in this particular form.

When introducing a new type system, two questions arise:

- Is the new type system *sound*? That is, are there any programs accepted by the type system that should not be?
- Is the new type system *complete*? That is, are there any programs not accepted by the type system that should be?

We will show in Sect. 4.2 that the polymorphic system is *relatively sound*: it does not accept any more programs than the intersection of uniqueness typing and affine typing does. Few type systems can claim to be complete, and ours is no exception. In fact, even relative completeness fails, but we will argue in Sect. 4.3 that the loss is outweighed by the benefits.

4.2 Soundness

We show that if a program e is accepted by the polymorphic type system (i.e., there exists Γ, σ such that $\Gamma \vdash e : \sigma$) then it is also accepted by both the unique and affine systems. We show this by providing a translation $\lfloor \sigma \rfloor$ from the polymorphic type system to the unique or affine type system. We consider the case for the unique type system first. We translate polymorphism to uniqueness:

Definition 1 (Translation from polymorphic to unique types)

$$\lfloor c^\alpha \rfloor \quad = c^\alpha$$
$$\lfloor \sigma_1 \xrightarrow[\alpha']{\alpha} \sigma_2 \rfloor = \lfloor \sigma_1 \rfloor \xrightarrow[\alpha']{\alpha} \lfloor \sigma_2 \rfloor$$
$$\lfloor (\forall a \cdot \sigma)^\alpha \rfloor \ = \lfloor \sigma \{ {}^\bullet\!/_a \} \rfloor$$

This translation extends in the obvious manner to typing environments.

Proposition 1 (Soundness wrt to uniqueness typing)
If $\Gamma \vdash e : \sigma$ then $\lfloor \Gamma \rfloor \vdash e : \lfloor \sigma \rfloor$.

Proof. By induction on $\Gamma \vdash e : \sigma$. The logical and structural rules are straightforward. For GEN the conclusion follows from the induction hypothesis at the first premise. For INST it follows from UNIQUE (or immediately). □

As expected, the case for the affine type system is similar, but dual: we translate polymorphism to unrestricted (non-affine).

Definition 2 (Translation from polymorphic to affine types)

$$\begin{aligned}
\lfloor c^\alpha \rfloor &= c^\alpha \\
\lfloor \sigma_1 \xrightarrow[\alpha']{\alpha} \sigma_2 \rfloor &= \lfloor \sigma_1 \rfloor \xrightarrow[\alpha']{\alpha} \lfloor \sigma_2 \rfloor \\
\lfloor (\forall a \cdot \sigma)^\alpha \rfloor &= \lfloor \sigma \{ ^\times\!/_a \} \rfloor
\end{aligned}$$

Proposition 2 (Soundness wrt to affine typing)
If $\Gamma \vdash e : \sigma$ *then* $\lfloor \Gamma \rfloor \vdash e : \lfloor \sigma \rfloor$.

Proof. Like the proof of Prop. 1, but using the *second* premise of GEN and using AFFINE instead of UNIQUE. □

4.3   Completeness

In uniqueness typing we can create non-unique functions with unique elements in their closure, even though we can no longer *apply* those functions. Likewise, in affine typing we can apply non-unique functions with unique elements in their closure, even though we can never create such functions. Neither is possible in the polymorphic system, which means that the polymorphic system is not relatively complete with respect to either the uniqueness or affine type systems.

We can give a partial completeness result, however. Define the following lifting from the monomorphic types into the polymorphic type system:

Definition 3 (Lifting types)

$$\begin{aligned}
\lceil c^\alpha \rceil &= c^\alpha \\
\lceil \sigma_1 \xrightarrow[\alpha'']{\alpha'} \sigma_2 \rceil &= \lceil \sigma_1 \rceil \xrightarrow{\alpha} \lceil \sigma_2 \rceil \quad \textit{where } \alpha = \sup\{a', a''\}
\end{aligned}$$

Proposition 3 (Partial completeness). *If* $\Gamma \vdash^{unique} e : \sigma$ *or* $\Gamma \vdash^{affine} e : \sigma$ and the typing derivation does not rely on subtyping *then* $\Gamma \vdash^{poly} e : \sigma$.

Proof. Two separate straightforward induction proofs. □

In other words, programs that do not rely on subtyping will be accepted by the polymorphic type system, too. Most applications of subtyping can be replaced by use of polymorphism, as we saw at the start of Section 4. That is, for uniqueness typing we can translate

$$[\![\sigma \to \tau^\bullet]\!]_{\text{unique}} = \forall a \cdot [\![\sigma]\!] \to [\![\tau^a]\!]$$

Similarly, for affine typing we can translate

$$[\![\tau^\times \to \sigma]\!]_{\text{affine}} = \forall a \cdot [\![\tau^a]\!] \to [\![\sigma]\!]$$

(note again the duality: • *vs* ×, codomain *vs* domain). In both cases subtyping can then be replaced by instantiation.

This translation is not entirely uniform, however. As we mentioned at the start of this section, the following types are not inhabited, even though their corresponding unique or affine types are:

$$[\![\tau_1^\bullet \to \tau_2^\times \xrightarrow{\bullet} \tau_1^\bullet]\!]_{\text{unique}} \qquad = \forall a \cdot \tau_1^\bullet \to \tau_2^\times \xrightarrow{a} \tau_1^\bullet$$

$$[\![(\sigma_1 \xrightarrow{\times} \sigma_2) \to \sigma_1 \to \sigma_2]\!]_{\text{affine}} = \forall a \cdot (\sigma_1 \xrightarrow{a} \sigma_2) \to \sigma_1 \to \sigma_2$$

Note that the use of subtyping is not essential for dealing with "observing" terms at non-unique types; instead, we need a special typing rule for strict-let, and preferably some way of making sure that these non-unique terms don't escape the strict-let. See [10, Section 2.8.9] for more details.

4.4 Example Application

In Sect. 3 we used affine types to restrict how often a thread could write to a channel. We mentioned that this was in the context of an "impure" language, because affine types cannot be used to model side effects[1] (we need uniqueness typing, instead). However, now that we have both, we could define[2]

$$\texttt{withNewChannel} :: \texttt{World}^\bullet \to (\texttt{World}^\bullet \to (\forall a \cdot \texttt{Channel}^a)^\times \to \sigma) \xrightarrow{\bullet} \sigma$$

$$\texttt{send} :: \forall a \cdot \texttt{Int} \to \texttt{World}^\bullet \to \texttt{Channel}^a \xrightarrow{\bullet} \texttt{World}^\bullet$$

If we applied the translation from Sect. 4.3 indiscriminately we would have used a unique world in negative position ("input") and a polymorphic world in positive position ("output"). However, realistically we never want to share the world so we can simplify the types and not use polymorphism.

The situation for channels is a little different. We have used a polymorphic value in negative position, since we can send on channels we are allowed use once just as well as we can send on unrestricted channels. In `withChannel` we use a value of type $(\forall a \cdot \texttt{Channel}^a)^\times$ in positive position; the continuation (the "master thread") can use this polymorphic value as often as it wants to create "affine" (use-once) channels for the slave threads and then instantiate it at an unrestricted value itself to read the values written by all the slave threads.

---

[1] Wadler, one of the big proponents of linear logic, states [14]: "Does this mean that linearity is useless for practical purposes? Not completely. Dereliction [subtyping] means that we cannot guarantee *a priori* that a variable of linear type has exactly one pointer to it. But if we know this by other means, then linearity guarantees that the pointer will not be duplicated or discarded".

[2] We could return a pair instead of using continuation passing style, but we have not covered products in this paper.

We thus switch back and forth between the two interpretations at will, and use instantiation in the place of subtyping: we use polymorphism to model unique and affine typing.

5   Related Work

Uniqueness typing was introduced in [2] and implemented in the pure functional programming language Clean [7]; variations have been implemented in SAC [8] and Mercury [5,6].

The version we presented in Fig. 1 differs significantly from the Clean type system, however. Clean does not use closure typing, which was introduced in the context of uniqueness typing in [12]. Instead, Clean regards some unique types (in particular, function types) as *necessarily* unique: subtyping does not apply to them. This makes it possible to enforce propagation at definition site, rather like in our polymorphic system. However, this non-uniformity of the subtyping relation results in a loss of principal types. For instance, we have

$$\lambda x \cdot (x, x) :: \texttt{Array}^\bullet \to (\texttt{Array}^\times, \texttt{Array}^\times)$$

and

$$\lambda x \cdot (x, x) :: (\sigma_1 \xrightarrow{\times} \sigma_2) \to (\sigma_1 \xrightarrow{\times} \sigma_2, \sigma_1 \xrightarrow{\times} \sigma_2)$$

but no more general type that can be instantiated to both. Note that the polymorphic system in Fig. 3 does not satisfy principal types either. For instance, given a function $f :: \forall a, a' \cdot \tau^a \to \tau^{a'} \xrightarrow{a} \sigma$, we have

$$\lambda x \cdot \lambda y \cdot \lambda z \cdot f\ x\ y :: \tau^\times \xrightarrow{\times} \tau^\times \xrightarrow{\times} \sigma' \xrightarrow{\times} \sigma$$

$$\lambda x \cdot \lambda y \cdot \lambda z \cdot f\ x\ y :: \tau^\times \xrightarrow{\times} \tau^\bullet \xrightarrow{\times} \sigma' \xrightarrow{\bullet} \sigma$$

$$\lambda x \cdot \lambda y \cdot \lambda z \cdot f\ x\ y :: \tau^\bullet \xrightarrow{\times} \tau^\times \xrightarrow{\bullet} \sigma' \xrightarrow{\bullet} \sigma$$

and

$$\lambda x \cdot \lambda y \cdot \lambda z \cdot f\ x\ y :: \tau^\bullet \xrightarrow{\times} \tau^\bullet \xrightarrow{\bullet} \sigma' \xrightarrow{\bullet} \sigma$$

but no more general type that captures all four; in particular, although we have

$$\lambda x \cdot \lambda y \cdot \lambda z \cdot f\ x\ y :: \forall a, a' \cdot \tau^a \xrightarrow{\times} \tau^{a'} \xrightarrow{a} \sigma' \xrightarrow{\bullet} \sigma$$

the annotation on the final arrow must be "•" because we cannot express within the type system that it must be unique if either a or a' is and thus we must be conservative. One way to solve this problem is introduce boolean expressions as annotations [13]; this is a nice approach because boolean unification is well-understood and hence can we use standard type inference algorithms for such a type system (it might also be possible to lift the "sup" operation we used to the type level).

Linear logic was introduced by Girard [3]; its use as a type system was pioneered by Wadler [14,9]. Several authors have proposed type systems that explicitly combine uniqueness typing and linear typing [4,1,11]. All of these systems however have *explicit* notions of uniqueness and affinity, rather than using one concept to model both.

The author's PhD thesis contains a detailed review of these and other papers [10].

6   Conclusions

Uniqueness typing and affine or linear typing are dual type systems. Uniqueness gives a *guarantee* that an term *has not* been shared, thus enabling destructive update and modelling of side effects in a pure functional language. Affinity imposes a *restriction* that a term *may not* be shared, thus enabling more precise APIs (a continuation that can be invoked at most once, a channel that can be sent on at most once, etc.). Both type systems have different purposes and indeed it is useful to combine them.

In this paper we have shown that when we introduce polymorphism—a useful construct in its own right—we do not need to distinguish explicitly between uniqueness and affinity anymore, but enable the programmer to choose between either interpretation by introducing polymorphism in negative or positive positions. For instance, we saw that we might type destructive array updates as

$$\texttt{update} :: \forall a \cdot \texttt{Int} \to \texttt{Int} \to \texttt{Array}^\bullet \to \texttt{Array}^a$$

Other API choices are possible too, of course. For instance, if non-updatable arrays have a more efficient representation in memory then we might want to change the API to

$$\texttt{update} :: \texttt{Int} \to \texttt{Int} \to \texttt{Array}^\bullet \to \texttt{Array}^\bullet$$
$$\texttt{freeze} :: \texttt{Array}^\bullet \to \texttt{Array}^\times$$

By replacing subtyping with polymorphism we place this choice in the hands of the API designer.

The particular type system that we presented was designed to aid the comparison with "traditional" uniqueness and affine type systems. It can be simplified and extended in various ways. At the very least one might want universal quantification over base types (τ) as well as type attributes (α); it is possible to use a kind system to use a single construct for both [13]. As mentioned in Sect. 5, we can introduce boolean expressions as type attributes in order to obtain principal types. Chapter 8 of [10] contains many more avenues for future work.

Acknowledgements. This paper is a follow-up from the author's PhD thesis on uniqueness typing, which Rinus Plasmeijer mentored. Rinus, your support and enthusiasm was greatly appreciated.

References

1. Ahmed, A., Fluet, M., Morrisett, G.: A step-indexed model of substructural state. In: Proceedings of the 10th ACM SIGPLAN International Conference on Functional Programming (ICFP), pp. 78–91. ACM (2005)
2. Barendsen, E., Smetsers, S.: Uniqueness typing for functional languages with graph rewriting semantics. Mathematical Structures in Computer Science 6, 579–612 (1996)
3. Girard, J.Y.: Linear logic. Theoretical Computer Science 50(1), 1–102 (1987)
4. Hage, J., Holdermans, S., Middelkoop, A.: A generic usage analysis with subeffect qualifiers. In: Proceedings of the 12th ACM SIGPLAN International Conference on Functional Programming (ICFP), pp. 235–246. ACM (2007)
5. Henderson, F.: Strong modes can change the world! honours Report, Department of Computer Science, University of Melbourne (November 1992)
6. Overton, D.: Precise and expressive mode systems for typed logic programming languages. Ph.D. thesis, The University of Melbourne (December 2003)
7. Plasmeijer, R., van Eekelen, M.: Clean Language Report (version 2.1) (November 2002)
8. Scholz, S.B.: Single assignment C: efficient support for high-level array operations in a functional setting. Journal of Functional Programming 13(6), 1005–1059 (2003)
9. Turner, D.N., Wadler, P., Mossin, C.: Once upon a type. In: Proceedings of the 7th International Conference on Functional Programming Languages and Computer Architecture (FPCA), pp. 1–11. ACM (1995)
10. de Vries, E.: Making Uniqueness Typing Less Unique. Ph.D. thesis, Trinity College Dublin (2008)
11. de Vries, E., Francalanza, A., Hennessy, M.: Uniqueness typing for resource management in message-passing concurrency. Journal of Logic and Computation (2012)
12. de Vries, E., Plasmeijer, R., Abrahamson, D.M.: Uniqueness typing redefined. In: Horváth, Z., Zsók, V., Butterfield, A. (eds.) IFL 2006. LNCS, vol. 4449, pp. 181–198. Springer, Heidelberg (2007)
13. de Vries, E., Plasmeijer, R., Abrahamson, D.M.: Uniqueness typing simplified. In: Chitil, O., Horváth, Z., Zsók, V. (eds.) IFL 2007. LNCS, vol. 5083, pp. 201–218. Springer, Heidelberg (2008)
14. Wadler, P.: Is there a use for linear logic? In: Proceedings of the 2nd ACM SIGPLAN Symposium on Partial Evaluation and Semantics-based Program Manipulation (PEPM), pp. 255–273. ACM (1991)

Evolution of a Parallel Task Combinator

Bas Lijnse

Radboud University Nijmegen
b.lijnse@cs.ru.nl

Abstract. The development of experimental software is rarely straightforward. If you start making something you don't understand yet, it is very unlikely you get it right at the first try. The iTask system has followed this predictably unpredictable path. In this system, where combinator functions are used to construct interactive workflow support systems, the core set of combinator functions has changed along with progressed understanding of the domain. Continuous work on this system led to the emergence of a new programming paradigm for interactive systems: Task-Oriented Programming (TOP). In this paper we reconstruct the evolution of one of the core iTasks combinators to catch a glimpse of this emergence. The combinator is the `parallel` combinator that facilitates the composition of multiple concurrent tasks into a single one. We reconstruct its evolution from the written record in the form of published papers and discuss this reconstruction and what it tells about the progressed understanding of programming with tasks.

1 Introduction

If you don't know where you are going, you don't know where you will end up. Making research software based on ideas that you don't yet fully understand is inherently different from "production" software where you assume that you can clearly scope the requirements, and you can draw up designs based on understood principles. Although you cannot reliably work towards a defined product, it does not mean that you are just randomly doing something. By trying to embody little understood ideas in a software system, and trying to make things of which you don't know if they are even possible you learn what is possible and you get a better understanding of your initial ideas. You have, of course, ideas about what you consider important and expectations of what you might find, but you have to try to keep an open mind and be prepared to change course midway. In the process you may find that your hypotheses about properties of your system don't hold or you end up with something different than you imagined.

The iTask System (iTasks) is a system that followed this uncertain path and has been changing ever since it was first conceived [9]. This system started out as a modest experiment to express workflow in the functional language Clean [16], but that was just the beginning. In the past years it evolved and eventually became a general-purpose framework for making interactive web-based multi-user applications, supporting a new programming paradigm: Task-Oriented Programming (TOP). In this paradigm, multi user systems are expressed by composing

P. Achten and P. Koopman (Eds.): Plasmeijer Festschrift, LNCS 8106, pp. 193–210, 2013.
© Springer-Verlag Berlin Heidelberg 2013

tasks. The evolution of iTasks was driven primarily by two desires. The first driver was the quest to find a minimal, yet complete, core set of primitives to express task patterns with. The second driver was the wish to not be limited to work with little variation, modeled by rigid workflows, but be able to capture a wide range of dynamic real-world tasks. These desires pushed the scope of the iTask system beyond what is usually considered workflow, and into a general purpose framework for any interactive system. At some point we realized that programming applications with iTasks had drifted so far away from workflow specification and traditional functional programming, that it could be considered a separate new paradigm. The present day iTask system provides a combinator based embedded domain specific language that implements the basic TOP constructs for defining and composing tasks. It consists of generic user interaction primitives, combinators for sequential and parallel composition of tasks and primitives for sharing data between tasks.

Some iTask combinators have remained relatively stable, such as the monadic "bind" for sequential compositions. Others however, changed more often. One of the combinators that changed a lot was the `parallel` core combinator for concurrent execution of multiple tasks. This combinator originally was not even a single combinator but a set of specialized combinators that were more or less related to each other. At some point it seemed that there was a new version of this combinator in every published paper. When students who used iTasks for their research projects asked for a paper they could read as introduction, we almost always had to answer that there was of course something they could read, but that the latest version was already different from that paper.

Now that we have arrived at the TOP paradigm, it is interesting to look back and see how we got here. We usually focus on the future, and aim to improve the status quo, but sometimes looking back can provide valuable insights too. A festschrift such as this provides a good opportunity to do so. In this paper we reconstruct the evolution of the `parallel` combinator as angle on the emergence of TOP. Because we cannot rely on memory, we turn to the accumulated publications about iTasks as written record of the evolution of the system, and to keep the scope manageable, we focus on the "parallel" combinator in particular. In the remainder of this paper, we see how we can reconstruct the history of the parallel combinator (Section 2), walk through its evolution (Section 3), and reflect on it (Section 4).

2   Methodology

To reconstruct the evolution of the `parallel` combinator, we have two sources at our disposal. There is a written record of milestone versions in the form of publications that contain an explanation of the iTask system. The advantage of these publications is that they do provide an explanation along with the definitions. The disadvantage of publications is that it is hard to reconstruct the time frame in which the published definition was used due to the delays of the publication process. Fortunately, since the majority of the publications were published in conference proceedings, the submission deadlines of those conferences are mentioned in their calls for papers. These calls are easily retrievable through public archives of mailing lists to which they were posted. The submission deadlines provide a reasonable estimation of the date the paper was finalized.

The second source we can use is the logging provided by the public Subversion (version control) repository of the iTask system. This record is more fine grained than the publication record, because not all small changes are immediately worthy of publication. Finding out when changes were made is very easy for this source, because all commits to the repository are automatically timestamped. The disadvantage of this source is that changes are often only accompanied by short log messages, such that we need to study the source code of the system at critical points in time to understand the interface and semantics of the combinator in that time frame.

In this paper we limit ourselves to the publication record because these are milestone versions and we aim to reconstruct the complete history. The Subversion log is simply too fine grained for such a global overview. To make our reconstruction we simply collect all publications about the iTask System that mention the parallel combinator or its specialized predecessors. We then organize them chronologically and isolate those sections of the papers that explain parallel composition.

3   Evolution of the Parallel Combinator

In this section we present the history of the `parallel` as reconstructed from publicly available sources. Other than grouping the chronology in related periods, we do not yet interpret anything. We only collect and organize what is said about the combinators and postpone discussion to the next section.

3.1   The 'AND' and 'OR' Period

The `parallel` combinator did not start out as a single construct for all possible parallel patterns of combining tasks. It started out as a set of combinators for specific patterns. The first iTasks paper, "iTasks: Executable Specifications of Interactive Work Flow Systems for the Web" [9] presented at ICFP 2007 (October 1-3, 2007), defined two combinators for parallel composition. They are explained as follows:

> The infix operator (t1 -&&- t2) activates subtasks t1 and t2 and ends when both subtasks are completed; the infix operator (t1 -||- t2) also activates two subtasks t1 and t2 but ends as soon as one of them terminates, but it is biased to the first task at the same time. In both cases, the user can work on each subtask in any desired order. A subtask, like any other task, can consist of any composition of iTasks.

The paper also shows the implementations of these combinators. In this code we can already see that both combinators are very similar.

```
(-&&-) infixr 4 :: (Task a) (Task b) → Task (a,b) | iCreate a & iCreate b
(-&&-) taska taskb = doTask and
where and tst=:{tasknr}
        # (a,tst=:{activated=adone}) = mkParSubTask 0 tasknr taska tst
        # (b,tst=:{activated=bdone}) = mkParSubTask 1 tasknr taskb tst
        = ((a,b),set_activated (adone && bdone) tst

(-||-) infixr 3 :: (Task a) (Task a) → Task a | iCreate a
(-||-) taska taskb = doTask or
where or tst=:{tasknr}
        # (a,tst=:{activated=adone}) = mkParSubTask 0 tasknr taska tst
        # (b,tst=:{activated=bdone}) = mkParSubTask 1 tasknr taskb tst
        = ( if adone a (if bdone b createDefault)
          , set_activated (adone || bdone) tst
          )
mkParSubTask :: Int TaskID (Task a) → Task a
mkParSubTask i tasknr task = task o newSubTaskNr o set_activated True o subTaskNr i
```

In the lecture notes of the CEFP 2007 summer school [8], which included a
course on iTasks, we find the exact same code and accompanying explanations
as in the ICFP 2007 paper. This summer school was held the same summer, so
this is not surprising.

The next publication that mentions the parallel iTask combinator is "Declarative Ajax and Client Side Evaluation of Workflows using iTasks" presented at
PPDP 2008 (July 15,17 2008) [13]. This paper gives type definitions for the same
two parallel combinators:

```
(-||-) infixr 3 :: (Task a) (Task a) → Task a | iData a
(-&&-) infixr 4 :: (Task a) (Task b) → Task (a,b) | iData a & iData b
```

The only difference between these signatures and the previous ones is the context of iData instead of iCreate. The difference between these restrictions is that
the iData class also contains generic storage and visualization in addition to default value creation provided by iCreate. The paper provides explanations of the
combinators by examples that reveal that the semantics of the combinators did
not change:

> The expression t-||-u offers tasks t and u simultaneously. As soon as
> either one is finished first, t-||-u is also finished. Any work in the other
> task is discarded. The -||- combinator is very useful to express work
> that can be aborted by other workers or external circumstances. In
>
> ot = yt -||- nt -||- et
>
> the iTasks system offers the task yt, nt, and et simultaneously. Any edit
> work in et is discarded when the user presses one of the buttons labeled
> Yes or No.

And for the -&&- combinator:

> If one really needs both results of tasks t and u, then this is expressed by
> t -&&- u, which runs both tasks to completion and returns both results.
> For instance, if we need a string and an integer (with default value 5)
> we can use the task:

```
at :: Task (String, Int)
at = ot -&&- editTask "Done" 5
```

The next mention of the parallel combinators is in the lecture notes of the
AFP 2008 summer school [10] (May 19-24, 2008). In this publication, the iTask
system is explained following a case study. The combinators are initially only
explained in so far they are relevant to that case. Therefore initially only the
"OR" combinator is defined:

```
(-||-) infixr 3 :: (Task a) (Task a) → Task a | iData a
```

And explained only briefly as:

> The left-biased task t -||- u is finished as soon as either t or u has fin-
> ished, or both.

In a later section that explains the semantics of the iTask system using a simplified model, the 'AND' combinator is introduced together with its equivalent
in the model:

> We introduce the iTask combinator t -&&- u, and represent it by t .&&. u.
> In the case study in Section 2 we did not use this combinator, but it
> belongs to the basic repertoire of the iTask system, therefore we in-
> clude it here. In the task t -&&- u, both subtasks t and u are available
> to the user. The composite task is finished as soon as both subtasks
> are finished. Hence, it differs from -||- in which termination is con-
> trolled by the first subtask that finishes. Also, its type is more gen-
> eral, because the types of the return values of the subtasks are al-
> lowed to be different, the type of this operator in the iTask system is
> (Task a) (Task b) → Task (a,b) | iData a & iData b.

The full semantic model is too lengthy to quote here, but the reduction of the
modeled combinators .||. and .&&. that represent the 'OR' and 'AND' combi-
nators is defined to exhibit the behaviour that has been explained in the various
papers so far.

This semantic model is worked out in full in the next publication that mentions the parallel combinators. In "An Executable and Testable Semantics for
iTasks" [5] presented at IFL 2008 (September 10-12) we find the now familiar
type signatures and the following explanation.

> The expression t -||- u indicates that both iTasks can be executed in
> any order and interleaved, the combined task is completed as soon as
> any subtask is done. The result is the result of the task that completes

first, the other task is removed from the system. The expression t -&&- u states that both iTasks must be done in any order (interleaved), the combined task is completed when both tasks are done. The result is a tuple containing the results of both tasks.

The most notable thing here is that the interleaving semantics of the combinators is mentioned explicitly for the first time.

3.2 Lists of Parallel Tasks

In the next publication, "Web Based Dynamic Workflow Systems and Applications in the Military Domain" [2], in the 2008 issue of NL ARMS, we see additional parallel combinators for the first time. The 'OR' and 'AND' combinators are generalized to versions that use lists of tasks that are executed in parallel. The combinators are explained by example:

The AND (-&&-) operator generates two tasks that both have to be finished before the results can be used.

```
simpleAndMU :: Task Int
simpleAndMU
=       (0  @:: editTask "Number entered" 0)
  -&&- (1  @:: editTask "Number entered" 0)
  =>> λ(v,w) → 2 @:: editTask "Sum" (v+w)
```

For AND also a multi-version 'andTasks' exists, which handles a list of tasks. The task completes when all subtasks are completed.
The OR (-||-) operator generates two tasks in parallel. As soon as one of them finishes the result of that task is available. The result of the other task is ignored.

```
simpleOrMU :: Task Int
simpleOrMU
=       (0   @:: editTask "A number" 0)
  -||- (1   @:: editTask "A number" 0)
  =>> λv → 2 @:: editTask "First number" v
```

Also for OR a multi-version 'orTasks' exists, which handles a list of tasks. The task completes as soon as one of the tasks completes.

Additionally, an important new concept is reported for the first time: a general parallel combinator with which other combinators can be expressed:

In iTasks a special version of 'andTasks' exists: 'andTasksCond'. A number of tasks can be started in parallel. Each time one of the tasks is finished a condition is applied to all completed tasks. If the condition is met, 'andTasksCond' is finished and the completed results are returned in a list.

This combinator is also explained by example:

```
simpleAndTaskCond :: Task Int
simpleAndTaskCond
=  andTasksCond pred [("User" +++ toString u,
                       u @:: editTask "Number entered" 0) \\ u ← [1..4]]
⇒> λxs → [Txt "Their sum is"] !>> return_D (sum xs)
where pred xs = sum xs > 3
```

Here a parallel task for 4 users is started. They all have to enter a number.
Here the condition checks if the sum of the already entered numbers is
greater than 3. As soon as this is the case this task stops and the results
are passed to another task where they are displayed.

What is more, the paper shows how this 'andTasksCond' can be used to express
other combinators:

This is a very powerful combinator because many other combinators
can be expressed using it. For example the definitions of 'andTasks' and
'orTasks' can be given by:

```
andTasks xs = andTasksCond (λys = length ys==length xs) xs
orTasks  xs = andTasksCond (λys = length ys==1) xs
```

The next publication that mentions the parallel combinators is "Tasks 2:
iTasks for End-users" [6] presented at IFL 2009 (September 23-25, 2009). Although it reports on a new implementation of the iTask system, the combinator
language has not changed as can be seen in the signatures that are mentioned
without further explanation.

```
// Execute two tasks in parallel
(-&&-) infixr 4 :: (Task a) (Task b) → Task (a,b)
// Execute two tasks in parallel, finish as soon as one yields a result
(-||-) infixr 3 :: (Task a) (Task a) → Task a
// Execute all tasks in parallel
allTasks :: ([Task a] → Task [a])
// Execute all tasks in parallel, finish as soon as one yields a result
anyTask :: ([Task a] → Task a)
```

The new combinators introduced here, 'allTasks' and 'anyTask' appear to be just
variations of the 'andTasks' and 'orTasks' combinators in the NL ARMS paper.

This apparent variation is confirmed in the next publication, "Embedding a
Web-Based Workflow Management System in a Functional Language" [4] presented at LDTA 2010 (March 27-28, 2010). The signatures with an explanation
of these combinators are given.

```
// Splitting-joining any number of arbitrary tasks:
anyTask  :: [Task a] → Task a | iTask a
allTasks :: [Task a] → Task [a] | iTask a
```

Any number of tasks ts $= [t_1...t_n](n >= 0)$ can be performed in parallel and synchronized (also known as splitting and joining of workflow expressions): anyTasks ts and allTasks ts both perform all tasks ts simultaneously, but anyTasks terminates as soon as one task of ts terminates and yields its value, whereas allTasks waits for completion of all tasks and returns their values.

In this paper the fully generalized parallel combinator is presented for the first time. Unlike the 'andTasksCond combinator, which could not express 'anyTask' for example because its type is always Task [a], this combinator is capable of expressing all parallel patterns.

As a final example, iTask provides a core combinator function, parallel that is used in the system to define many other split-join combinators such as anyTask and allTasks that were shown earlier. Its type signature is:

```
parallel :: ([a] → Bool) ([a] → b) ([a] → b) [Task a] → Task b
                                                |iTask a & iTask b
```

parallel c f g ts performs all tasks within ts simultaneously and collects their results. However, as soon as the predicate c holds for any current collection of results, then the evaluation of parallel is terminated, and the result is determined by applying f to the current list of results. If this never occurs, but all tasks within ts have terminated, then parallel terminates also, and its result is determined by applying g to the list of results.

The paper after this one reinforces the idea of a single general parallel combinator to express multiple patterns without going into details. This paper, "Web Based Dynamic Workflow Systems for C2 of Military Operations" [3], presented at ICCRTS 2010 (June 22-24, 2010) stresses the use of a single general concept and gives 'anyTask' and 'allTasks' as examples.

An important combinator for executing a number of tasks in parallel is the parallel combinator. Where other workflow formalisms contain a large number of patterns for executing tasks in parallel, iTask needs only one combinator for this. Using the power of the functional host language, one can construct all other patterns (and more) using this single combinator. This is hard to do in other workflow languages because these lack the right abstraction mechanism for realizing this. With the parallel combinator one can start the execution of several tasks in parallel and stop this execution as soon as a user specified condition is fulfilled. For example, one can stop when one task (or-parallelism) is finished:

anyTask [task_1,task_2,task_3,task_n]

When all tasks (and-parallelism) are finished:

allTasks [task_1,task_2,task_3,task_n]

Or when the results of the finished tasks satisfy a certain condition (ad-hoc parallelism):

`conditionTasks condition [task_1,task_2,task_3,task_n]`

These different combinators are all shorthands for the same generic `parallel` combinator instantiated with different parameters.

The next paper, "iTask as a New Paradigm for Building GUI Applications" [7] presented at IFL2010 (September 1-3, 2010), is concerned mostly with the additional concepts needed to make GUI programs with iTasks. It explains the iTasks combinators only to the extent necessary for the leading example of the paper. Regarding parallel combinators this is just the familiar 'AND' combinator.

Finally, we need a combinator to compose tasks in parallel: `-&&-` performs both tasks and returns their combined result when both are terminated.

`(-&&-) infixr 4 :: (Task a) (Task b) → Task (a,b) | iTask a & iTask b`

Similarly, the next paper also explains the combinators only to the extent necessary for the purpose of the paper. This paper, "iTasks for a Change: Type-Safe Run-Time Change in Dynamically Evolving Workflows" [11] presented at PEPM2011 (January 24-25, 2011), ignores that the 'AND' and 'OR' combinators are expressed using a general '`parallel`' combinator. It defines their semantics directly such that their behaviour during run-time change can be explained.

`(-||-) infixr 3 :: (Task a) (Task a) → Taska | iTaska`
`(-&&-) infixr 4 :: (Task a) (Task b) → Task (a, b) | iTask a & iTask b`

To compose tasks in parallel, the combinators `-||-` and `-&&-` are provided. A task constructed using `-||-` is finished as soon as either one of its subtasks is finished, returning the result of that task. The combinator `-&&-` is finished as soon as both subtasks are finished, and pairs their results.

The semantics of these combinators is defined in a separate semantic domain. The paper gives definitions for `-||-` as well as `-&&-`, but we will limit ourselves to the definition of `-||-`.

The semantic function of `-||-` is defined as follows:

```
(-||-) infixr 3 :: (STaska) (STaska) → STaska
(-||-) ta ua = λ i p e s →
  case ta (subIds i !! 0) p e s of
    (NF va, s) → (NF va, s)
    (Redex nta, s) →
      case ua (subIds i !! 1) p e s of
      (NFwa, s) → (NFwa, s)
      (Redex nua, s) → (Redex (nta -||- nua), s)
```

From the formal definition of the behaviour of the 'AND' and 'OR' combinators in this paper we can see that the semantics of these combinators have not changed since the original definitions three and a half year earlier.

3.3   Towards Dynamically Extensible Parallel Tasks

The next paper covers the overall design of the iTask system again. This paper, "Getting a Grip on Tasks that Coordinate Tasks" [14] was an invited paper at the LDTA 2011 Workshop (March 26-27, 2011). It both explains the status quo of the iTask system and discusses future needs. This paper starts by giving the familiar definitions for the basic 'AND' and 'OR' combinators. When discussing the expressiveness of the combinator language, the general `parallel` combinator is explained and definitions for 'AND' and 'OR' are given.

The need for more functionality does not necessarily imply that more combinators are required. By using higher order functions, Swiss-Army-Knife combinators can be defined, that strongly reduce the number of needed core combinators. In the current iTask system, the parallel combinator is one such example:

```
parallel :: ([a] → Bool) ([a]→b) ([a]→b) [Task a] → Task b
                                               | iTask a & iTask b
```

For instance, the core combinators `-||-` and `-&&-` can be replaced by suitable parametrization of `parallel`. The function `parallel predOK someDone allDone taskList` takes a list of tasks (`taskList`) to be executed in parallel, a predicate (`predOK`), and two conversion functions (`someDone` and `allDone`). Whenever a member of `taskList` is finished, its result is collected in a list `results` of type `[a]`, maintaining the order of tasks. Now `predOK results` is computed to determine whether `parallel` should complete, in which case the result is computed by `someDone results`. When all parallel tasks have run to completion, and `predOK` is still not satisfied, then `parallel` also completes, but now with result `allDone results`. We can define `-||-` and `-&&-` as follows:

```
(-||-) infixr 3 :: (Task a) (Task a) → Task a | iTask a
(-||-) ta1 ta2 = parallel (not o isEmpty) first undef [ta1, ta2]
where
 first [a] = a

(-&&-) infixr 4 :: (Task a) (Task b) → Task (a, b) | iTask a & iTask b
(-&&-) ta tb = parallel (const False) undef all
                       [ta >>= Left, tb >>= Right]
where
 all [Left a,Right b] = (a,b)
```

Although a Swiss-Army-Knife combinator such as `parallel` can be used to define many different kinds of parallel behaviours, there is room for improvement here as well. With `predOK` one can freely define when the parallel tasks can be stopped, but perhaps one also needs to be able to start new tasks dynamically, because more work is required.

So far the paper provides little new information. However in the section that addresses future needs, it is revealed that big changes to the `parallel` combinator are afoot.

The workflow engineer should be able to specify the means of control as (arbitrarily many) additional tasks that coordinate these tasks. We hypothesize that these forms of parallel behaviour can be captured with a single, more general combinator. The combinator needs to meet the following criteria:

1. The number of tasks in the current **parallel** combinator remains constant, and **parallel** can only enforce early termination, not the extension of new tasks. The number of tasks in a parallel setting should not be fixed once and for all, but should adapt to the needs of the current situation.

2. The tasks within the current parallel combinator simply perform their duty and as such do not interfere with each other (except of course when using shared communication). Next to these regular tasks we introduce control tasks. These are also tasks, but, being control tasks, they edit the collection of parallel tasks. In this way, we can replace the predefined behaviour of task delegation and instead leave it to the workflow engineer whether or not to use a predefined control delegation-task or introduce a (number of) custom control task(s).

3. Because the number of both regular and control tasks varies during the evaluation of a parallel group, we need to share information about the state of the parallel group. Access to this state is restricted to control tasks only, which is easily achieved using the strong type system.

4. In the current **parallel** combinator, control is limited to either early completion (computed by **predOK**) in which case the final task result was computed by **someDone** or full completion in which case the final result was computed by **allDone**. In the more general case, we need to decide how to continue whenever a regular or control task runs to completion. Again, this should not be computed by the regular tasks. Instead, we need a function that knows which task has completed, and hence has a result value that needs to be accumulated in the shared state. In addition, this function can decide what should happen with the group of parallel (control and regular) tasks: tasks can be suspended and resumed, they can be removed, replaced, and new (control and regular) tasks can be added to the group of parallel tasks. It is clear that this functionality subsumes the current behaviour of parallel, and adds behaviour that was inexpressible before.

5. The final part that should be abstracted from is the arrangement, or layout, of the generated GUIs of the (control and regular) tasks. In the current iTask system a distinction is made between a parallel form for tasks that can, in principle, each be delegated to other workers and a parallel form for tasks which GUI should be merged into one single presentation. In order to abstract from this, it is better to parameterize the new parallel combinator with a function that describes how the component GUIs of (control and regular) tasks should merged.

We are currently experimenting with a single `parallel` combinator that meets the above criteria. With this combinator we hope to express all other task combinators as special cases.

These five points illustrate that all aspects of parallel combination are considered. Even the visual representation (layout) of parallel combinations, which we have not encountered in the publications so far, is taken into account.

In the next publication, "Defining Multi-user Web Applications with iTasks" [12] in the lecture notes of the CEFP 2011 summer school (June 14-24, 2011), we can see that the proposed changes to the parallel combinator have found their way into the system. In this paper two sections (8 & 9) are devoted to the parallel combinator. The first of those presents a far more complex `parallel` combinator:

> The iTask system provides a single, swiss army knife combinator for this purpose, called parallel. In this section we explain how to use this versatile combinator for an arbitrary, yet constant, number of users. In Section 9 we continue our discussion and show how it can be used to accommodate a dynamic number of users. The signature of parallel is:

```
parallel :: d s (ResultFun s a) [TaskContainer s] → Task a
                                             | iTask s & iTask a
                                             & descr d
```

We briefly discuss its parameters first. The first parameter is the usual description argument that we have encountered many times so far. It plays the same role here: a description to the user to inform her about the purpose of this particular parallel task in the workflow. The second argument is the initial value of the state of the parallel task: the state is a shared data that can be inspected and altered only by the tasks that belong to this parallel task. The third argument is a function of type:

```
:: ResultFun s a :== TerminationStatus s → a
:: TerminationStatus = AllRunToCompletion | Stopped
```

The purpose of the `ResultFun` function is to turn the value of the state of the parallel task at termination into the final value of the parallel task itself. They need not have the same type, so the state is converted to the final value when the parallel task is finished. The `parallel` combinator can terminate in two different ways. It can be the case that all subtasks are finished (`AllRunToCompletion`). But, as we will see later, a subtask can also explicitly kill the whole parallel construction (`Stopped`). This information can be used to create a proper final value of parallel. Finally, the fourth argument is the initial list of task (container)s that constitute the parallel task. A task container consists of two parts: a task type representation (`ParallelTaskType`) defining how the subtask relates to its super-task, and the subtask itself (defined on shared state s) to be run in parallel with the others (`ParallelTask s`):

```
:: TaskContainer s :== (ParallelTaskType, ParallelTask s)
:: ParallelTaskType = Embedded
                    | Detached ManagementMeta
```

The `ParallelTaskType` is either one of the following:
- `Embedded` basically 'inlines' the task in the current task.
- `Detached` meta displays the task computed by the function as a distinct new task for the user identified in the worker field of meta. `ManagementMeta` is a straightforward record type that enumerates the required information:

```
:: ManagementMeta =
    { worker           :: Maybe User
    , role             :: Maybe Role
    , startAt          :: Maybe DateTime
    , completeBefore   :: Maybe DateTime
    , notifyAt         :: Maybe DateTime
    , priority         :: Maybe TaskPriority
    }
:: TaskPriority = HighPriority | NormalPriority | LowPriority
```

It should be noted that the u @: combinator is simply expressed as a parallel combination of two tasks. One of type `Detached` with the worker set, and another of type `Embedded` that displays progress information.

```
:: ParallelTask s :== (TaskList s) → Task ParallelControl
:: TaskList s
:: ParallelControl = Stop | Continue
```

The task creation function takes as argument an abstract type, `TaskList s`, where s is the type of the data the subtasks share. Every subtask has to yield a task of type `ParallelControl` to tell the system, when the subtask is finished, whether the parallel task as a whole is also finished (by yielding `Stop`) or not (by yielding `Continue`.) As will be explained in Section 9, the number of subtasks in the task list can change dynamically. One can enquire its status, using the following functions on the abstract type `TaskList s`:

```
taskListState      :: (TaskList s) → Shared s | TC s
taskListProperties :: (TaskList s) → Shared [ParallelTaskInfo]
```

With the function `taskListState` one can retrieve the data shared between the tasks of the **parallel** combinator. As discussed in Section 5, you can use `get`, `set`, and `update` to access its value. There is another function, `taskListProperties`, which can be used to retrieve detailed information about the current status of the parallel tasks created. This can be used to control the tasks, and is explained in more detail in the next section.

The second section devoted to the **parallel** combinator in this paper covers dynamically adding and removing tasks from a parallel set:

> In this section it is shown how the `taskList` can be used to dynamically alter the number of subtasks running in parallel. The following operations are offered to the programmer.

```
appendTask :: (TaskContainer s) (TaskList s) → Task Int | TC s
removeTask :: Int (TaskList s) → Task Void → TC s
```

Tasks can be appended to the list of tasks running under this parallel construction using appendTask. In a similar way, removeTask terminates the indicated task from the list of tasks, even if it has not run to completion.

The publication after this large change concerns itself with the more friendly derived parallel combinators only. In this paper, "GiN: A Graphical Language and Tool for Defining iTask Workflows" [1] presented at TFP 2011 (May 16-18, 2011), only the following familiar signatures and explanation are presented:

```
(-||-) infixr 3 :: (Task a) (Task a) → Task a       | iTask a
(-&&-) infixr 4 :: (Task a) (Task b) → Task (a,b)   | iTask a & iTask b
anyTask         :: [Task a]          → Task a        | iTask a
allTasks        :: [Task a]          → Task [a]      | iTask a
```

Tasks can be composed in parallel. Either the result of the first completed task is returned (-||- and anyTask combinators) or the results of all parallel tasks are collected and returned as a whole (-&&- and allTasks)

In the final and most recent publication that covers the parallel combinator we see a new definition again. In this publication, "Task-Oriented Programming in a Pure Functional Language" [15] presented at PPDP2012 (May 31, 2012), the parallel combinator is presented as follows:

Tasks can often be divided into parallel sub tasks if there is no specific predetermined order in which the sub tasks have to be done. It might not even be required that all sub tasks contribute sensibly to a stable result. All variants of parallel composition can be handled by a single parallel combinator:

```
parallel:: d → [(ParallelTaskType,ParallelTask a)]
             → Task [ (TimeStamp, Value a) ] | descr d & iTask a

:: ParallelTaskType = Embedded | Detached ManagementMeta
:: ManagementMeta = { worker :: Maybe User
                    , role   :: Maybe Role
                    , ...
                    }
:: ParallelTask    a == SharedTaskLista → Taska
:: SharedTaskList a == ROShared (TaskList a)
:: TaskList a = { state :: [Value a]
                , ...
                }
```

We distinguish two sorts of parallel sub-tasks: Detached tasks get distributed to different users and Embedded tasks are executed by the current user. The client may present these tasks in different ways. Detached tasks need a window of their own while embedded tasks may by visualized in an existing window. With the `ManagementMeta` structure properties can be set such as which worker must perform the sub-task, or which role he should have. Whatever its sort, every parallel sub-task can inspect each others progress. Of each parallel sub-tasks its current task value and some other system information is collected in a shared task list. The parallel sub-tasks have read-only access to this task list. The `parallel` combinator also delivers all task values in a list of type [(`TimeStamp`,`Value a`)]. Hence, the progress of every parallel sub-task can also be monitored constantly from the "outside".

The paper does not go into details of adding and removing tasks but mentions that it is still possible.

For completeness, we remark that the shared task list is also used to allow dynamic creation and deletion of parallel sub-tasks. We do not discuss this further in this paper.

3.4 Summary

Because the chronology given in this section may be too much to take in at once, Table 1 summarizes the results presented in this section. It dates the publications which are identified by the conference or journal acronym, it indicates which parallel combinators are covered in that paper, and some of the properties the parallel combinator(s) had according to that paper. These properties are: The use of parameters to make derived combinators easier, whether the `parallel` has a variable number of tasks, and if there is data sharing between branches in a parallel combination.

4   Reflections

Now that we have reconstructed the history of the parallel combinator, we can discuss the developments it went through in the five years worth of publications in which it is mentioned.

4.1   Towards a Unified Parallel

The parallel combinator in the last publication we examined [15] is something completely different than the simple orginal 'AND' and 'OR' [9]. Yet as we read through the history, the changes are mostly gradual. The semantics of the 'AND' and 'OR' remain unchanged for a long time, but with the introduction of the `andTasksCond` combinator [2] and later the `parallel` combinator [4], a single unified combinator emerges that aims to capture *all* parallel constructs. Once this unified combinator is established it is clear that there can be a single core combinator for all possible task combinations.

Table 1. Parallel definitions in publications

Paper	Date (Deadline date)	AND,OR	ANY,ALL	parallel	Parameters	Var # tasks	Data sharing
	The 'AND' and 'OR' Period						
ICFP2007 [9]	October 1-3, 2007 (April 6, 2007)	X	-	-	-	-	-
CEFP2007 [8]	June 23-30, 2007	X	-	-	-	-	-
PPDP2008 [13]	July 15-17, 2008 (April 10, 2008)	X	-	-	-	-	-
AFP2008 [10]	May 19-24, 2008	X	-	-	-	-	-
IFL2008 [5]	September 10-12 2008 (November 14, 2008)	X	-	-	-	-	-
	Lists of Parallel Tasks						
NLARMS2008 [2]	September 2008	X	X	-	X	-	-
IFL2009 [6]	September 23-25, 2009 (November 1, 2009)	X	X	-	X	-	-
LDTA2010 [4]	March 27-28, 2010 (December 4, 2009)	-	X	X	X	-	-
ICCRTS2010 [3]	June 22-24 2010 (April 21, 2010)	-	X	X	X	-	-
IFL2010 [7]	September 1-3, 2010 (October 25, 2010)	X	-	-	-	-	-
PEPM2011 [11]	January 24-25, 2011 (October 22, 2010)	X	-	-	-	-	-
	Towards Dynamic Extensible Parallel Tasks						
LDTA2011 [14]	March 26-27, 2011 (December 22, 2010)	X	-	X	X	-	-
CEFP2011 [12]	June 14-24, 2011	-	-	X	X	X	X
TFP2011 [1]	May 16-18, 2011 (June 24, 2011)	X	X	-	-	-	-
PPDP2012 [15]	September 19-21, 2012 (May 31, 2012)	-	-	X	-	X	X

4.2 Safe Experiments

The convergence of the parallel combinators to a single core combinator that can be used to express specific parallel patterns, does not mean we no longer see the 'AND' and 'OR' combinators. An interesting observation is that the publications can be divided in two categories. Papers that report on overall progress of the system ([9,8,10,2,6,4,3,14,12,15]), and papers that focus on a single experimental extension or a specific issue ([13,5,7,11,1]). In the second category of papers we often see the 'AND' and 'OR' combinators still being used. These easier to explain combinators are used to provide context of the iTask system, in favor of the more accurate but more complex generalized combinator.

4.3 The Paradigm Shift

After the introduction of the single `parallel` we can see a new tension building fueled by the drive to capture real-world dynamic tasks. The original iTask system was based on tasks that always completed. Only when a task was completed its result was available for further computation of the workflow. For parallel sets of tasks, this meant that they always had to terminate as full set in order to deliver a result. In [14] we see the first signs of dissatisfaction with this model when the need for more dynamic parallel sets is discussed. Tasks in a parallel composition should be able to be monitored, and if necessary extended if additional work is needed. In [12] we see the first attempt to realize these goals, but the notion of terminating tasks is still maintained. This leads to a powerful, yet complicated swiss-army-knife combinator that can express more parallel constructs, but is quite difficult to use. Only when in [12] the TOP paradigm had fully emerged, the **parallel** combinator was simplified again. By then it was clear that treating tasks as units of work that have to be completed before you can use their results, was making compositions more difficult than necessary. Defining tasks as units of work that continuously produce (temporary) results that can be observed made it possible to fully reduce the **parallel** combinator to its essence: just executing a set of tasks in parallel.

4.4   The Future?

By following the path of the **parallel** combinator we have seen the emergence of the TOP paradigm as an incremental interaction between the ideas about programming with tasks, and their concrete embodyment in the implementation of the iTask system. A process that eventually led to a new definition of the notion of tasks to provide the basis for a new way of programming interactive systems. With a major change in the **parallel** definition in the last publication we examined, it is too soon to tell whether this is the final one. For now at least it looks like the pieces of the puzzle have fallen into place and we have found a simple, yet powerful unified parallel construct.

References

1. Henrix, J., Plasmeijer, R., Achten, P.: GiN: A graphical language and tool for defining iTask workflows. In: Peña, R., Page, R. (eds.) TFP 2011. LNCS, vol. 7193, pp. 163–178. Springer, Heidelberg (2012)
2. Jansen, J., Koopman, P., Plasmeijer, R.: Web based dynamic workflow systems and applications in the military domain. In: Hupkens, T., Monsuur, H. (eds.) Netherlands Annual Review of Military Studies - Sensors, Weapons, C4I and Operations Research, pp. 43–59 (2008)
3. Jansen, J., Lijnse, B., Plasmeijer, R., Grant, T.: Web based dynamic workflow systems for C2 of military operations. In: Revised Selected Papers of the 15th International Command and Control Research and Technology Symposium, ICCRTS 2010, Santa Monica, CA, USA (June 2010)
4. Jansen, J., Plasmeijer, R., Koopman, P., Achten, P.: Embedding a web-based workflow management system in a functional language. In: Brabrand, C., Moreau, P. (eds.) Proceedings 10th Workshop on Language Descriptions, Tools and Applications, LDTA 2010, Paphos, Cyprus, March 27-28, pp. 79–93 (2010)
5. Koopman, P., Plasmeijer, R., Achten, P.: An executable and testable semantics for iTasks. In: Scholz, S.-B., Chitil, O. (eds.) IFL 2008. LNCS, vol. 5836, pp. 212–232. Springer, Heidelberg (2011)
6. Lijnse, B., Plasmeijer, R.: iTasks 2: iTasks for end-users. In: Morazán, M.T., Scholz, S.-B. (eds.) IFL 2009. LNCS, vol. 6041, pp. 36–54. Springer, Heidelberg (2010)
7. Michels, S., Plasmeijer, R., Achten, P.: iTask as a new paradigm for building GUI applications. In: Hage, J., Morazán, M.T. (eds.) IFL 2010. LNCS, vol. 6647, pp. 153–168. Springer, Heidelberg (2011)

8. Plasmeijer, R., Achten, P., Koopman, P.: An introduction to iTasks: Defining interactive work flows for the web. In: Horváth, Z., Plasmeijer, R., Soós, A., Zsók, V. (eds.) CEFP 2007. LNCS, vol. 5161, pp. 1–40. Springer, Heidelberg (2008)

9. Plasmeijer, R., Achten, P., Koopman, P.: iTasks: executable specifications of interactive work flow systems for the web. In: Hinze, R., Ramsey, N. (eds.) Proceedings of the International Conference on Functional Programming, ICFP 2007, Freiburg, Germany, pp. 141–152. ACM Press (2007)

10. Plasmeijer, R., Achten, P., Koopman, P., Lijnse, B., van Noort, T.: An iTask case study: A conference management system. In: Koopman, P., Plasmeijer, R., Swierstra, D. (eds.) AFP 2008. LNCS, vol. 5832, pp. 306–329. Springer, Heidelberg (2009)

11. Plasmeijer, R., Achten, P., Koopman, P., Lijnse, B., van Noort, T., van Groningen, J.: iTasks for a change - Type-safe run-time change in dynamically evolving workflows. In: Khoo, S., Siek, J. (eds.) Proceedings of the Workshop on Partial Evaluation and Program Manipulation, PEPM 2011, Austin, TX, USA, pp. 151–160. ACM Press (2011)

12. Plasmeijer, R., Achten, P., Lijnse, B., Michels, S.: Defining multi-user web applications with iTasks. In: Zsók, V., Horváth, Z., Plasmeijer, R. (eds.) CEFP 2011. LNCS, vol. 7241, pp. 46–92. Springer, Heidelberg (2012)

13. Plasmeijer, R., Jansen, J., Koopman, P., Achten, P.: Declarative Ajax and client side evaluation of workflows using iTasks. In: Proceedings of the 10th International Conference on Principles and Practice of Declarative Programming, PPDP 2008, Valencia, Spain, July 15-17, pp. 56–66 (2008)

14. Plasmeijer, R., Lijnse, B., Achten, P., Michels, S.: Getting a grip on tasks that coordinate tasks. In: Proceedings Workshop on Language Descriptions, Tools, and Applications (LDTA), Saarbrücken, Germany, March 26-27 (2011)

15. Plasmeijer, R., Lijnse, B., Michels, S., Achten, P., Koopman, P.: Task-Oriented Programming in a Pure Functional Language. In: Proceedings of the 2012 ACM SIGPLAN International Conference on Principles and Practice of Declarative Programming, PPDP 2012, Leuven, Belgium, pp. 195–206. ACM (September 2012)

16. Plasmeijer, R., van Eekelen, M.: Clean language report, version 2.1 (2002), http://clean.cs.ru.nl

Beautiful Workflows: A Matter of Taste?

Wil M.P. van der Aalst[1,2,3], Michael Westergaard[1,2], and Hajo A. Reijers[1,4]

[1] Architecture of Information Systems, Eindhoven University of Technology,
P.O. Box 513, NL-5600 MB, Eindhoven, The Netherlands
{w.m.p.v.d.aalst,m.westergaard,h.a.reijers}@tue.nl
[2] International Laboratory of Process-Aware Information Systems,
National Research University Higher School of Economics (HSE),
33 Kirpichnaya Str., Moscow, Russia
[3] Business Process Management Discipline, Queensland University of Technology,
GPO Box 2434, Brisbane QLD 4001, Australia
[4] Perceptive Software,
Piet Joubertstraat 4, 7315 AV Apeldoorn, The Netherlands

Abstract. Workflows can be specified using different languages. Mainstream workflow management systems predominantly use procedural languages having a graphical representation involving AND/XOR splits and joins (e.g., using BPMN). However, there are interesting alternative approaches. For example, case handling approaches are data-driven and allow users to deviate within limits, and declarative languages based on temporal logic (where everything is allowed unless explicitly forbidden). Recently, Rinus Plasmeijer proposed the iTask system (iTASKS) based on the viewpoint that workflow modeling is in essence a particular kind of functional programming. This provides advantages in terms of expressiveness, extendibility, and implementation efficiency. On the occasion of his 61st birthday, we compare four workflow paradigms: *procedural*, *case handling*, *declarative*, and *functional*. For each paradigm we selected a characteristic workflow management system: YAWL (procedural), BPM|ONE (case handling), DECLARE (declarative), and iTASKS (functional). Each of these systems aims to describe and support business processes in an elegant manner. However, there are significant differences. In this paper, we aim to identify and discuss these differences.

Keywords: Workflow Management, Business Process Management, Case Handling, Declarative Languages, Functional Programming.

1 Demand Driven Workflow Systems

Functional programming and process modeling are related in various ways. For example, well-known Petri nets tools such as CPN TOOLS [14] and EXSPECT [6] use functional languages to describe the consumption and production behaviors of transitions in the Petri net. However, the different communities focusing on process modeling and analysis are largely disconnected from the functional programming community (and vice versa). Business Process Management (BPM),

P. Achten and P. Koopman (Eds.): Plasmeijer Festschrift, LNCS 8106, pp. 211–233, 2013.
© Springer-Verlag Berlin Heidelberg 2013

Workflow Management (WFM), and concurrency-related (e.g., Petri nets) communities are rarely using concepts originating from functional languages. Therefore, the groups of Rinus Plasmeijer and Wil van der Aalst submitted the joint project proposal "Controlling Dynamic Real Life Workflow Situations with Demand Driven Workflow Systems" to STW in 2006. The project was accepted in 2007 and started in 2008. The project completed successfully in 2012.

In the STW project different styles of workflow modeling and enactment were used. A new style of functional programming, called *Task-Oriented Programming* (TOP), was developed by Rinus and his team [39]. The *iTask* system (ITASKS), an implementation of TOP embedded in the well-known functional language CLEAN, supports this style of workflow development [37, 39]. ITASKS workflows consist of typed tasks that produce results that can be passed as parameters to other tasks. New combinators can be added to extend the ITASKS language. At Eindhoven University of Technology, Maja Pesic and Michael Westergaard worked on an alternative approach based on the DECLARE system. The DECLARE language is based on the notion of constraints, grounded in LTL, and also extendible. Moreover, previously we worked on procedural workflow languages like YAWL and collaborated with Pallas Athena on the case handling paradigm.[1]

In the project we could experience the enthusiasm, dedication, an persistence of Rinus when it comes to functional programming and beautiful code. Therefore, it is an honor to be able to contribute to this festschrift devoted to the 61st birthday of Rinus Plasmeijer!

In the remainder, we report on insights obtained in our joint STW project. In Section 2 we discuss four different workflow paradigms using four representative examples: YAWL (procedural), BPM|ONE (case handling), DECLARE (declarative), and ITASKS (functional). Section 3 compares the different paradigms and reflects on the current BPM/WFM market. Section 4 concludes our contribution to this festschrift.

2   Four Workflow Paradigms

Business Process Management (BPM) is the discipline that combines knowledge from information technology and knowledge from management sciences and applies this to operational business processes [1, 3, 46]. It has received considerable attention in recent years due to its potential for significantly increasing productivity and saving costs. Moreover, today there is an abundance of BPM systems. These systems are *generic software systems that are driven by explicit process designs to enact and manage operational business processes* [3].

BPM can be seen as an extension of *Workflow Management* (WFM). WFM primarily focuses on the automation of business processes [8, 28, 30], whereas BPM has a broader scope: from process automation and process analysis to operations management and the organization of work. BPM aims to improve operational business processes, with or without the use of new technologies.

---

[1] Pallas Athena was also involved in the User Committee of our joint STW project.

For example, by modeling a business process and analyzing it using simulation, management may get ideas on how to reduce costs while improving service levels. Moreover, BPM is often associated with software to manage, control, and support operational processes. This was the initial focus of WFM. However, traditional WFM technology aimed at the automation of business processes in a rather mechanistic manner without much attention for human factors and management support.

In the remainder we use the terms WFM and BPM interchangeably as we focus on the modeling and enactment of business processes, i.e., the emphasis will be on process automation rather than management support.

We identify four very different styles of process automation: procedural workflows (YAWL), case handling workflows (BPM|ONE), declarative workflows (DECLARE), and functional workflows (ITASKS). In the remainder of this section, these are introduced and subsequently compared in Section 3.

2.1   Procedural Workflows (YAWL)

Procedural programming (also referred to as imperative programming) aims to define sequences of commands for the computer to perform in order to reach a predefined goal. Procedural programming can be seen as the opposite of more declarative forms of programming that define *what* the program should accomplish without prescribing *how* to do it in terms of sequences of actions to be taken. Despite criticism, procedural programming is still the mainstream programming paradigm. A similar observation can be made when looking at the modeling, analysis, and enactment of business processes. Almost all BPM/WFM languages and tools are procedural (see also Section 3.4). Examples are BPMN (Business Process Modeling Notation), UML activity diagrams, Petri nets, process calculi like CSP and CCS, BPEL (Business Process Execution Language), and EPCs (Event-driven Process Chains).

Figure 1(a) describes a simple diagnosis process in terms of Petri, a *WF-net* (WorkFlow net) to be precise [13, 26, 46]. Tasks are modeled by labeled transitions and the ordering of these tasks is controlled by places (represented by circles). A transition (represented by a square) is enabled if each of its input places contains a token. An enabled transition may occur thereby consuming a token from each input place and producing a token for each output place. The process in Figure 1(a) starts with a token in place *in* (depicted by a black dot). Transition *a* (*admit patient*) can occur if there is a token in place *in*. Firing *a* corresponds to removing the token from place *in* and producing a token for place *p1*. After admitting the patient (modeled by transition *a*), vital signs may be checked (*b*) or not (modeled by the silent transition). Then the physical examination (*c*) is conducted. Subsequently, the blood is tested (*d*), an X-ray is taken (*e*), and an ECG is made (*f*) (any ordering is allowed). In the last step, the diagnosis is finalized (*g*). The process instance terminates when place *out* is marked. Figure 1(c) shows an event log describing some example traces of the model. The WF-net allows for 12 different executions: *d*, *e* and *f* can be executed in any order and *b* may be skipped.

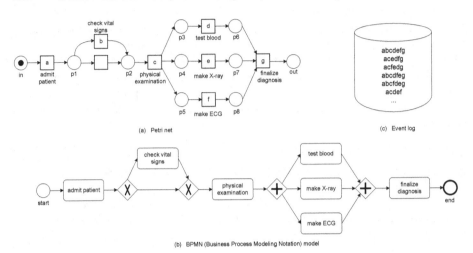

Fig. 1. A Petri net (a) and BPMN model (b) describing a simple medical diagnosis process. Example traces are shown in the event log (c), $a = admit\ patient$, etc.

BPMN, EPCs, UML ADs, and many other business process modeling notations have in common that they all use *token-based semantics* [3, 13, 21, 26, 46]. Therefore, there are many techniques and tools to convert Petri nets to BPMN, BPEL, EPCs and UML ADs, and vice versa. As a result, the core concepts of Petri nets are often used indirectly, e.g., to enable analysis, to enact models, and to clarify semantics. For example, Figure 1(b) shows the same control-flow modeled using the *Business Process Modeling Notation* (BPMN) [34]. BPMN uses activities, events, and gateways to model the control-flow. In Figure 1(b) two types of gateways are employed: exclusive gateways are used to model XOR-splits and joins and parallel gateways are used to model AND-splits and joins. BPMN also supports other types of gateways corresponding to inclusive OR-splits and joins, deferred choices, etc. [21, 26, 46].

In an effort to gain a better understanding of the fundamental concepts underpinning business processes, the *Workflow Patterns Initiative*[2] was conceived in the late nineties with the goal of identifying the core architectural constructs inherent in workflow technology [10]. The original objective was to delineate the fundamental requirements that arise during business process modeling on a recurring basis and describe them in an imperative way. The main driver for the Workflow Patterns Initiative was the observation that WFM/BPM languages and tools differed markedly in their expressive power and the range of concepts that they were able to capture. The initial set of 20 patterns provided a basis for valuable comparative discussions on the capabilities of languages and systems. Later the original set of 20 patterns was extended into a set of 43 control-flow patterns supported by additional sets of patterns, e.g., 40 data patterns and 43 resource patterns [26].

---

[2] See www.workflowpatterns.com

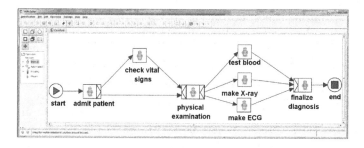

Fig. 2. Screenshot of YAWL editor while modeling the process described using Figure 1

The workflow patterns provided the conceptual basis for the YAWL language [9] and YAWL workflow system [26].[3] YAWL supports most workflow patterns directly, i.e., no workarounds are needed to model and support a wide variety of imperative process behaviors. Petri nets were taken as a starting point for YAWL and extended with dedicated constructs to deal with patterns that Petri nets have difficulty expressing, in particular patterns dealing with cancelation, synchronization of active branches only, and multiple concurrently executing instances of the same task. The screenshot in Figure 2 shows the YAWL variant of the diagnosis process introduced using earlier. The YAWL model allows for the same 12 traces as allowed by the WF-net and BPMN model in Figure 1. None of the advanced features of YAWL are needed to model this simple diagnosis process. Note that compared to the Petri net there are no explicit places. In YAWL one can connect two tasks directly without inserting a place. However, internally the places are added to model states. Moreover, for workflow patterns such as the *deferred choice* pattern (the decision is not made automatically from within the context of the process but is deferred to an entity in the operational environment) and the *milestone* pattern (the additional restriction that a task can only proceed when another concurrent branch of the process has reached a specific state), places need to be represented explicitly to model the desired behavior. The aim of YAWL is to offer direct support for many patterns while keeping the language simple. It can be seen as a reference implementation of the most important workflow patterns. Over time, the YAWL language and the YAWL system have increasingly become synonymous and have garnered widespread interest from both practitioners and the academic community alike. Over time YAWL evolved into one of the most widely used open-source workflow systems.

Most mainstream WFM/BPM languages are procedural and use a token-based semantics. The same holds for *analysis techniques* relevant for WFM/BPM efforts. Most model-based analysis techniques ranging from verification to performance analysis are tailored towards procedural models. *Verification* is concerned with the correctness of a system or process. *Performance analysis* focuses

---

[3] YAWL can be downloaded from www.yawlfoundation.org

on flow times, waiting times, utilization, and service levels. Also *process mining* techniques driven by event data typically assume procedural models. For example, *process discovery* techniques can be used to learn procedural models based on event data. *Conformance checking* techniques compare procedural models (modeled behavior) with event data (observed behavior).

There is an abundance of analysis techniques developed for Petri nets ranging from verification and simulation [13] to process mining [2]. Procedural languages such as BPMN, UML activity diagrams, BPEL, and EPCs can be converted to Petri nets for verification, performance analysis, and conformance checking. Petri nets can be mapped onto mainstream notations to visualize processes discovered using process mining.

2.2 Case Handling Workflows (BPM|one)

Mainstream procedural languages are often criticized for being inflexible. *Case handling* is a paradigm for supporting *flexible* and *knowledge intensive* business processes [15]. It is strongly based on data as the typical product of these processes. Unlike traditional WFM systems, which use predefined process control structures to determine what should be done during a workflow process, case handling focuses on what can be done to achieve a business goal. In case handling, the knowledge worker in charge of a particular case actively decides on how the goal of that case is reached, and the role of a case handling system is assisting rather than guiding her in doing so. The core features of case handling are:

- *avoid context tunneling* by providing all information available (i.e., present the case as a whole rather than showing just bits and pieces),
- decide which tasks are *enabled on the basis of the information available* rather than the tasks already executed,
- *allow for deviations* (without certain bounds) that are not explicitly modeled (skip, redo, etc.),
- *separate* work distribution from authorization,
- allow workers to *view and add/modify data* before or after the corresponding tasks have been executed (e.g., information can be registered the moment it becomes available).

The central concept for case handling is the *case* and not the tasks or the ordering of tasks. The case is the "product" which is manufactured, and at any time workers should be aware of this context. For knowledge-intensive processes, *the state and structure of a case can be derived from the relevant data objects*. A data object is a piece of information which is present or not present and when it is present it has a value. In contrast to existing workflow management systems, the state of the case is not determined by the control-flow status but by the presence of data objects. This is truly a paradigm shift: case handling is also driven by data-flow and not just by control-flow.

In a procedural workflow, workers need to execute all tasks offered by the system and there is no way to later correct errors if not modeled explicitly. Case

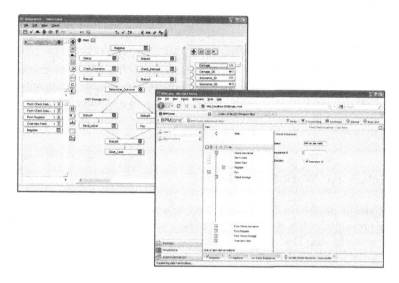

Fig. 3. Screenshot showing the BPM|ONE designer and worklist handler

handling allows for deviations within certain bounds. For a task at least three types of roles can be specified:

- The *execute* role is the role that is necessary to carry out the task or to start a process.
- The *redo* role is necessary to undo tasks, i.e., the case returns to the state before executing the task. Note that it is only possible to undo a task if all following tasks are undone as well.
- The *skip* role is necessary to bypass tasks, e.g., a check may be skipped by a manager but not by a regular employee.

Case handling is supported by only a few vendors. The best-known example is BPM|ONE which is now part of the Perceptive Platform (Lexmark).[4] BPM|ONE is the successor of FLOWER [15] both developed by Pallas Athena. In turn, FLOWER was inspired by the ECHO (Electronic Case-Handling for Offices) system whose development started in 1986 within Philips and later moved to Digital. BPM|ONE supports all of the concepts mentioned (see Figure 3). The system is much more flexible than most WFM/BPM systems. This is achieved without forcing end-users to adapt process models (which is typically infeasible).

Consider the process described in Figure 1. Using BPM|ONE one could make some tasks "skipable", e.g., task *make ECG* may be skipped by the department chief even though this is not modeled. Similarly, some tasks may be "redo-able", e.g., after doing the blood test, the process may be rolled-back to the task *physical examination*. Moreover, tasks may be data driven. If a recent X-ray is

---

[4] See http://www.perceptivesoftware.com/products/perceptive-process/
business-process-management

available, task *make X-ray* is completed automatically without actually making a new X-ray.

Recently, the terms Adaptive Case Management (ACM) and Dynamic Case Management (DCM) received quite some attention. These terms are used to stress the need for workflows to be more human-centric, flexible, and content and collaboration driven. Unfortunately, the different vendors interpret these terms in different ways and the actual case-handling functionality described before is often missing.

2.3   Declarative Workflows (Declare)

The procedural paradigm focuses on *how* to accomplish a goal. At any point a user is presented with a relatively limited selection of possible tasks based on explicit decisions. Declarative workflows instead focus on the *relationship* between tasks, such as one task cannot be executed together with another or one task has to be followed by another [12]. For example, in a medical treatment, one type of medicine may be incompatible with another and cannot be used together, or surgery must be followed up by retraining.

Declarative workflows therefore focus on two things, *tasks* to be executed and *constraints* between the tasks, stating properties the aforementioned [12]. In Fig. 4, we see an example of a simple medical process for treating wounds modeled using DECLARE.[5] Tasks are represented as rectangles, e.g., Disinfect Wound and constraints are either represented as arcs between tasks (for binary constraints) or as annotations of tasks (for unary constraints). For example, we have a init constraint on the Receive Patient task, and a precedence constraint from Disinfect Wound to Stitch Wound. We also have a response constraint from Stitch Wound to Prescribe Antibiotics, a non co-existence constraint between Prescribe Antibiotics and Give Tetanus Vaccine, and a second precedence constraint from Disinfect Wound to Give Tetanus Vaccine.

Constraints have informal descriptive semantics and formal semantics. The informal semantics suffice for users and the formal semantics are only used by

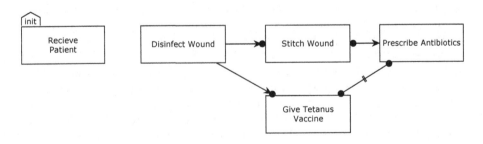

Fig. 4. DECLARE model of simple medical treatment

---

[5] DECLARE can be downloaded from www.win.tue.nl/declare/

Table 1. Selected DECLARE constraints

Name	Parameters	Representation	Semantics	
			Informal	Formal
init	(A)	[init] [A]	start with A	$\bar{\mathbf{X}}A$
precedence	(A, B)	[A]———•[B]	no B before A	$A\mathbf{R}\neg B$
response	(A, B)	[A]•——→[B]	after A must execute B	$\mathbf{G}(A \rightarrow \mathbf{F}B)$
not no-existence	(A, B)	[A]•—#—•[B]	not both A and B	$\neg\mathbf{F}A \vee \neg\mathbf{F}B$

implementers and for reasoning about processes. We have summed up the formal semantics of four example DECLARE constraints in Table 1. DECLARE comes with many more constraints, but these suffice here for understanding the basic idea. We first consider the informal semantics for these constraints. The init constraint models that any execution has to start with this task, and in our example this means that the first thing to do in any execution is to receive a patient. The precedence constraint models that it is not legal to execute the target before executing the source of the constraint. In the example, we model that we may not stitch a wound (nor give a tetanus vaccine) before disinfecting the wound. This does not mean that after disinfection we have to stitch a wound (for example, if it is not severe), but only that we may not stitch before disinfection. The response constraint on the other hand means that after executing the source, we have to execute the target. In our example, we must prescribe antibiotics after stitching a wound. It is perfectly acceptable to execute the source multiple times and the target only once, for example stitching a wound two or more times and only prescribe antibiotics once. The non co-existence constraint models that only one of the connected tasks can be executed (but none of them has to be). In our example, we cannot both give a tetanus vaccine and prescribe an antibiotics, maybe because the effect of the vaccine is diminished or voided by the antibiotics.

We notice that we can rely on the informal semantics to understand local aspects of a model. We also see that at no point do we talk about any explicit execution order: *anything not explicitly forbidden is allowed.* A DECLARE model with no constraints allows any execution of any task in the model. In the example in Fig. 4, after performing patient registration and wound disinfection, the process allows executing any task in the model. This allows a lot of freedom, which is often useful in a highly dynamic process, such as a medical process, or in a process which is not very well-known. The dynamic behavior is present in processes where a lot of possibilities are available and there is no obvious best choice. Processes can be partially unknown either because they are so complex nobody fully understands the entire process, or because they are early in the specification phase. Using a declarative approach allows modelers to only specify known constraints, such as incompatibilities between two treatments or a required follow-up to one treatment, and not worry about concrete global execution order.

The formal semantics of DECLARE is given using (finite) linear temporal logic (LTL). This yields a compact syntax, and an abstract and well-understood semantical foundation. More interesting is the fact that finite LTL can be translated into finite automata [24, 47]. These automata can be used to analyze the process and to provide enactment. As the modeler does not explicitly specify an execution order, the system has to figure out what constitutes a legal execution. This is done by instantiating a constraint template for each constraint. Instantiation comprises of taking the formal semantics for each constraint (Table 1) and replacing the parameters with actual tasks, obtaining for example $\overline{X}$(Receive Patient) for the init constraint. We can get a specification of the full semantics of the entire system by taking the conjunction of all instantiations of constraint templates, and translating it to a finite automaton with task names as transition labels. We can use this automaton to enact the system by following states in the automaton and only allowing tasks that lead to states from which an accepting state is reachable.

The translation from LTL to automata is exponential in the size of the formula given, so it may seem it would be better to consider each constraint in isolation. This is not sufficient, however, because DECLARE models may have implicit choices that are not immediately obvious. In our example in Fig. 4 we have an explicit choice between Prescribe Antibiotics and Give Tetanus Vaccine, but we actually have an implicit choice in that system as well. If we consider the trace Receive Patient;Disinfect Wound;Give Tetanus Vaccine;Stitch Wound, we see that we do not irreparable violate any constraint, but neither is it possible to arrive at a situation where all constraints are satisfied at the same time. After executing the trace, the response from Stitch Wound to Prescribe Antibiotics is not satisfied, because we have stitched the wound without prescribing antibiotics yet. We can satisfy this constraint by prescribing antibiotics, but this would violate the non co-existence between Give Tetanus Vaccine and Prescribe Antibiotics. The DECLARE system does this analysis and will not allow an execution trace with both Stitch Wound and Give Tetanus Vaccine. In [31] we describe how this can be efficiently represented in a single automaton, which keeps track of the status of individual constraints and of the entire process, and in [47] we give an efficient means of constructing this automaton.

A very strong point about declarative workflows is that models are less concerned with the actual execution, and hence more modular. In our previous execution trace, we said that the DECLARE system would prevent executing both Give Tetanus Vaccine and Stitch Wound. This can be overridden by the user, however. For example maybe an initial assessment concludes that stitches are not necessary and instead gives a tetanus shot. This is subsequently readdressed and now stitching is deemed necessary. The system can then say that either the non co-existence constraint or the response will be violated by this action, and authorized personnel can choose to proceed, ignoring a constraint in the process. This effectively is a migration from one model to another (with fewer constraints). As removing constraints never removes allowed behavior, this is guaranteed to be successful. We can also do migration in cases where we add new constraints as long as the added constraint is not violated and in conflict with another constraint (or the conflicting constraints are removed). This means that a declarative model not only allows flexibility by naturally producing permissive models, but also by allowing deviations from the model and even changing the model on-the-fly [35].

The automaton can obviously also be used a-posteriori to do conformance checking of models with respect to historical data, or to check for and remove dead parts of models [29, 33]. DECLARE models can be mined automatically by systematically instantiating all constraint templates and checking them against the historical log [32].

2.4 Functional Workflows (iTasks)

Functional workflow specifications arise from functional programming. This means that functional workflows automatically inherit properties of functional languages, importantly explicit flow of data and ability to efficiently execute the resulting specifications in complicated computing environments, including parallel and distributed execution.

The iTask system (ITASKS) augments a standard functional programming language, CLEAN [36], with connectives useful for workflow specification [37, 39].[6] The basic unit in an ITASKS process is a *task*, which is a basic type describing a process to be executed. ITASKS builds on the functional idea of inductively defining values in terms of basic values and composite values. A basic task value would be inputting an integer into a field and a composite task could be sequencing tasks or making a choice. The sequence is already well-known to procedural programmers but used less in functional programming. The choice is similar to a conditional in traditional programming, but ITASKS has a general choice operator, which can be specialized (and is by default) to provide semantics of XOR, AND, OR, and parallel splits as well as more specialized splits, for example a 2-out-of-3 split.

An ITASKS process consists of specification of the data types used and a process specification. In Listing 1, we see a simple patient registration process for a hospital. The example illustrates both the major weakness and major strength of the paradigm: the code is very verbose for a simple descriptive model, but compact for a full-features implementation of a system for executing the process. The process comprises data definitions (ll. 4-15), helper functions (ll. 17-23), and a process description (ll. 25-53). The data definitions describe a patient record (ll. 4-8) and an insurance record (ll. 10-13). In addition, we have an instruction to the system to generate a full implementation of these from the data specification (l. 15). The returnV function (ll. 17-18) is used for technical reasons, and the hasName and isInsured functions (ll. 20-23) are simple predicates on patients. Lines 25-28 set up the main process, which consists of starting the task handlePatient (ll. 44-53) which is a composite task using the primitive tasks in lines 30-42. The primitive tasks comprises two tasks for inputting information

---

[6] ITASKS and CLEAN can be downloaded from `itasks.cs.ru.nl`

Listing 1. ITASKS model of patient registration

```
1   implementation module PatientRegistration
2   import iTasks

4   :: Patient =
5       { name          :: String
6       , dateOfBirth    :: Maybe Date
7       , insurance      :: Bool
8       }

10  :: InsuranceInfo =
11      { company         :: String
12      , insuranceNumber :: Int
13      }

15  derive class iTask Patient, InsuranceInfo

17  returnV :: (TaskValue a) -> Task a | iTask a
18  returnV (Value v _) = return v

20  hasName (Value { name, dateOfBirth, insurance } _) = name <> ""
21  hasName _ = False

23  isInsured { name, dateOfBirth, insurance } = insurance

25  Start :: *World -> *World
26  Start world = startEngine (manageWorklist [mainProcess]) world

28  mainProcess = workflow "New_Patient" "Handle_a_patient" handlePatient

30  enterPatient :: Task Patient
31  enterPatient = enterInformation "Enter_patient_information" []

33  enterInsurance :: Task InsuranceInfo
34  enterInsurance = enterInformation "Enter_insurance_information" []

36  treat :: Patient -> (Task Patient)
37  treat patient =
38      viewInformation ("Treat_Patient", "Treating_Patient") [] patient

40  showInsurance :: InsuranceInfo -> (Task InsuranceInfo)
41  showInsurance insurance =
42      viewInformation ("Insurance", "Insurance_Details") [] insurance

44  handlePatient :: Task (Patient, Maybe InsuranceInfo)
45  handlePatient =
46      enterPatient
47      >>* [OnAction (Action "Continue") hasName returnV]
48      >>= \patient ->
49              if (isInsured patient)
50              ((treat patient &&
51               (enterInsurance >>= showInsurance))
52               >>= \(p, i) -> return (p, Just i))
53              (treat patient >>= \p -> return (p, Nothing))
```

for each of the two defined data types (ll. 30-34) and two tasks for displaying information (ll. 36-42). The treat task is a simplified placeholder version of a full treatment. The handlePatient task is by far the more complicated one and shows some of the task combinators supported by ITASKS. First we enter patient information (l. 46). The >>* combinator allows us to add ways to proceed the workflow; line 47 produces a Continue button that is enabled when the hasName predicate holds for the patient record entered. In that case, the patient record is passed on. The >>= combinator allows us to pass a result from one task to the next in a sequence. The combinator expects a function taking the result of the previous task as the first parameter, so we make an anonymous function (l. 48). We then use a common if statement (ll. 49-53) to branch according to whether the patient has an insurance or not. If the patient does (ll. 50-52) we start treating them (l. 50) in parallel (-&&-) with inputting and subsequently showing insurance information (l. 51). Finally, we return the treated patient and their insurance information (l. 52). If a patient does not have insurance, they are treated and returned without insurance information (l. 53).

We notice that ITASKS is very explicit about data flow and types. We explicitly type all tasks. This is used by the system to automatically generate a (web-based) user interface. We need to explicitly pass and compute data, and a strong type system prevents errors. The explicit passing of information is more verbose than the previously discussed paradigms, but the process oriented combinators makes it very simple to do things that are normally very complicated in programming, such as the parallel split in ll. 50-51 of Listing 1. We can easily change that to an XOR split, OR split, or sequence as long as we preserve the types. Similarly, the treat task (ll. 36-38) is very abstract and would be detailed further in a more elaborate implementation. As long as types are preserved, we can do that without changing the rest of the model. Finally, it is possible to change the type of, e.g., the patient record (ll. 4-8) and add new fields if necessary without changes to most of the tasks; for example, the enterPatient task (ll. 30-31) explicitly state the type but polymorphism and introspection makes the user-interface automatically adapt to the changed type. In our example we need to change the signature of the hasName and isInsured functions (ll. 20-23), but this can be avoided by using a slightly more verbose syntax we have avoided here for simplicity.

The fact that ITASKS *is realized as a combinator library in a real programming language, makes it possible to easily extend with features not normally available in workflow languages.* For example, modeled processes can natively communicate over the network, making it possible to easily invoke remote services. Another advantage is that there is no gap between the model and the implementation; they are really one and the same in ITASKS. Using a general-purpose functional language also makes it possible to use traditional functional techniques, such as making higher-order tasks. In fact, ITASKS combinators are just higher order tasks and can be used to create new composite tasks. This makes it easy to add new combinators as needed. An elegant consequence of this is that the process of choosing a task to work on and maintaining a work-list can be considered tasks as well, and in ITASKS they are realized as such.

The manageWorklist used in line 26 is actually just a task taking a list of (wrapped) tasks and allowing a user to pick which to execute. This makes it possible to customize how tasks are presented and chosen.

3   Comparison and Market Analysis

After presenting the distinguishing features of YAWL, BPM|ONE, DECLARE, ITASKS, and the corresponding paradigms, we aim to identify differences and commonalities. Table 2 shows our main findings. The characteristics used in Table 2 are based on topics frequently discussed in BPM literature. See for example the survey paper [3] which identifies twenty main BPM use cases based on an analysis of all 289 papers published at the main BPM conference series in a ten year period [7], [11], [19], [5], [22], [17], [20], [18], [27], and [42]. The list of characteristics used in Table 2 is far from complete. Nevertheless, we feel that the list is representative for our high-level comparison and discussion of the four different paradigms. In the remainder we discuss these findings and also provide an analysis of the BPM/WFM market.

3.1   Basic Characteristics of the Different Paradigms

Table 2 characterizes the four workflow paradigms and tools using three characteristics: *focus*, degree of *coupling*, and *extendibility*. Procedural languages like YAWL are driven by control-flow [9]. Case handling systems like BPM|ONE are data driven, i.e., the moment a data element gets a value or changes value, the state of the process instance is recomputed [15]. DECLARE allows for any behavior unless forbidden through constraints [12]. ITASKS specifies the desired behavior in terms of a functional program extended with special workflow operators [39]. YAWL and DECLARE use service-orientation and a clear separation between data and control-flow to decouple different perspectives. In ITASKS and BPM|ONE these are deliberately coupled, e.g., control-flow and data are intertwined to provide additional support and expressiveness. DECLARE and ITASKS are extendible, i.e., the language can be extended by adding new constraint templates [12] or combinators [39]. This is not possible in contemporary procedural workflow and case handling systems.

3.2   Flexibility Support

Table 2 list four types of flexibility. These originate from the classification in [44].

Flexibility by definition is the ability to incorporate alternative execution paths within a process definition at design time such that selection of the most appropriate execution path can be made at runtime for each process instance. For example, an XOR-split defined at design time adds the ability to select one or more activities for subsequent execution from a set of available activities. Parallelism defined at design time leaves the actual ordering of activities open and

Table 2. Comparison of paradigms

	Procedural (YAWL)	Case Handling (BPM|ONE)	Declarative (DECLARE)	Functional (ITASKS)
Characteristics				
Focus	control-flow[a]	data dependencies[b]	tasks and constraints[c]	functional program[d]
Coupling of perspectives	decoupled	tight	decoupled	tight
Extendible			√[e][12]	√[37, 39]
Flexibility				
Definition	√[f][9, 26]	√[g][15]	√[h][12]	√[i][37, 39]
Deviation		√[j][15]	√[k][12, 35]	
Underspecification	(√)[l][4, 16, 26]		(√)[m][4, 12]	√[n][37, 39]
Change	(√)[o]		√[p][35]	√[q][38]
Analysis				
Verification	√[13, 26]		√[12, 47]	(√)[r]
Performance analysis	√[13, 14, 26]		√[s]	
Process discovery	√[2, 26]		√[32]	
Conformance checking	√[2]		√[29, 31]	

[a] Token-based semantics (like playing the token game on a Petri net).

[b] Available data objects and their values determine the state.

[c] Anything that is not explicitly forbidden through some combination of constraints is allowed.

[d] Extendible set of combinator functions are used to specify the flow of work.

[e] Can be achieved by adding a template and LTL semantics.

[f] Supports XOR/AND/OR-splits and joins, cancelation regions, deferred choice, multiple instance tasks, etc.

[g] Supports XOR/AND/OR-splits and joins next to data-driven behavior.

[h] Anything is allowed unless explicitly forbidden.

[i] Core combinators can be used to express basic workflow patterns.

[j] Authorized users can deviate by skipping and redoing tasks.

[k] Users can choose to ignore non-mandatory constraints.

[l] Supported using worklets in YAWL but not a common feature for procedural languages.

[m] Can defer the task execution to other tools.

[n] Selecting a task is itself a task.

[o] Not supported by YAWL, but there are systems like ADEPT that support such changes [40, 41].

[p] Possible to migrate cases that do not violate constraints in the new model. Migration is postponed if needed.

[q] Change is viewed as a type-safe replacement of one task function by another one.

[r] Static analysis and common program analysis.

[s] Under development (combining DECLARE and CPN TOOLS).

thus provides more flexibility than sequential routing. All WFM/BPM systems support this type of flexibility. However, declarative languages make it easier to defer choices to runtime.

The classical workflow patterns mentioned earlier [10] can be viewed as a classification of "flexibility by definition" mechanisms for procedural languages. For example, the "deferred choice" pattern [10] leaves the resolution of a choice to the environment at runtime. Note that a so-called "flower place" in a Petri net, i.e., a place with many transitions that have this place as only input and output place, provides a lot of flexibility.

Flexibility by deviation is the ability for a process instance to deviate at runtime from the execution path prescribed by the original process without altering the process definition itself. The deviation can only encompass changes to the execution sequence for a specific process instance, and does not require modifications of the process definition. Typical deviations are *undo*, *redo*, and *skip*.

The BPM|ONE system of Perceptive Software is a system that provides various mechanisms for deviations at runtime. The case handling paradigm [15] supported by BPM|ONE allows the user to skip or redo activities (if not explicitly forbidden and assuming the user is authorized to do so). Moreover, data can be entered earlier or later because the state is continuously recomputed based on the available data. DECLARE supports flexibility by deviation through *optional* constraints.

Flexibility by underspecification is the ability to execute an incomplete process specification, i.e., a model that does not contain sufficient information to allow it to be executed to completion. An incomplete process specification contains one or more so-called *placeholders*. These placeholders are nodes which are marked as underspecified (i.e., "holes" in the specification) and whose content is specified during the execution of the process. The manner in which these placeholders are ultimately enacted is determined by applying one of the following approaches: *late binding* (the implementation of a placeholder is selected from a set of available process fragments) or *late modeling* (a new process fragment is constructed in order to complete a given placeholder). For late binding, a process fragment has to be selected from an existing set of fully predefined process fragments. This approach is limited to selection, and does not allow a new process fragment to be constructed. For late modeling, a new process fragment can be developed from scratch or composed from existing process fragments.

In the context of YAWL [9], the so-called *worklets* approach [16] has been developed which allows for late binding and late modeling. Late binding is supported through so-called "ripple-down rules", i.e., based on context information the user can be guided to selecting a suitable fragment. In [43] the term "pockets of flexibility" was introduced to refer to the placeholder for change. In [25] an explicit notion of "vagueness" is introduced in the context of process modeling. The authors propose model elements such as arc conditions and task ordering to be deliberately omitted from models in the early stages of modeling. Moreover, parts of the process model can be tagged as "incomplete" or "unspecified". In ITASKS selecting a task is itself a task [37, 39]. This can be used to support late binding.

Flexibility by change is the ability to modify a process definition at run-time such that one or all of the currently executing process instances are migrated to a new process definition. Changes may be introduced both at the process instance and the process type levels. A *momentary change* (also known as change at the instance level) is a change affecting the execution of one or more selected process instances. An example of a momentary change is the postponement of registering a patient that has arrived to the hospital emergency center: treatment is started immediately rather than spending time on formalities first. Such a momentary change performed on a given process instance does not affect any future instances. An *evolutionary change* (also known as change at the type level) is a change caused by modification of the process definition, potentially affecting all new process instances. A typical example of the evolutionary change is the redesign of a business process to improve the overall performance characteristics by allowing for more concurrency. Running process instances that are impacted by an evolutionary or a momentary change need to be handled properly. If a running process instance is transferred to the new process, then there may not be a corresponding state (called the "dynamic change bug" in [23]).

Flexibility by change is challenging and has been investigated by many researchers. In the context of the ADEPT system, flexibility by change has been examined in detail [40, 41]. This work shows that changes can introduce all kinds of anomalies (missing data, deadlocks, double work, etc.). For example, it is difficult to handle both momentary changes and evolutionary changes at the same time, e.g., an ad-hoc change made for a specific instance may be affected by a later change at the type level. The declarative workflow system DECLARE has been extended to support both evolutionary and momentary changes [35] thus illustrating that a declarative style of modeling indeed simplifies the realization of all kinds of flexibility support. In [38] it is shown that replacing a task can be seen as a type-safe replacement of one pure function by another one. The ITASKS type system ensures that the values passed between task have the correct type in the initial workflow as well as after any number of changes in this workflow. Note that such changes are more restrictive than in some of procedural and declarative approaches, e.g., the degree of concurrency can not be changed other than by replacing the whole subprocess. Moreover, there should be a dedicated user interface to support such changes. Otherwise, it is unrealistic to assume that end-users can define new functions on-the-fly. However, this holds also for most other approaches.

3.3 Analysis Support

Table 2 illustrates that procedural and declarative approaches are supported by a range of analysis techniques. For example, procedural workflow languages benefit from the verification [1, 13, 26], simulation [13, 14, 26], and process mining techniques [2, 26] developed for Petri nets. To apply these results to industry-driven languages such as BPMN, UML activity diagrams, EPCs, and BPEL conversions are needed. Sometimes there conversions need to make abstractions (e.g., ignoring data or time). Nevertheless, it is fair to say that most analysis techniques are tailored towards these procedural workflow languages.

In recent years, various analysis techniques have been developed for declarative languages like DECLARE [12, 24, 29, 31–33, 35, 47]. These techniques heavily rely on the fact that the semantics of DECLARE are defined in terms of LTL and that there are various ways to translate DECLARE constraints into automata.

BPM|ONE and ITASKS are more implementation-oriented providing hardly any dedicated analysis support.[7]

3.4   Overview of BPM/WFM Market

Given the very different styles of process automation that we distinguished and explained in the previous sections, it seems worthwhile to reflect on their use in practice. One way of doing so is to consider what the dominating paradigms are that commercial vendors of BPM systems have adopted in their products. There are more than 100 BPM vendors active at this point of writing, which makes a full consideration of all existing products infeasible. Instead, we will rely on a subset of these as they are listed in the so-called Magic Quadrant on BPM systems provided by Gartner [45]. Gartner is a market analyst that has been following the BPM market space for a number of years and its reports are highly influential in how companies decide on their selection of products in the BPM domain. Specifically, we will rely on their 2010 version of this quadrant; it is provided in Figure 5.

In the diagram, 27 BPM suites of 25 different vendors are displayed. While a BPM suite arguably encompasses more functionality than a BPM system does, it is safe to say that process automation is at its core.[8]

Two dimensions are used to differentiate the various offerings in the Magic Quadrant. The 'ability to execute' refers to the presence of a particular product in the market place, while the 'completeness of vision' reflects the analyst's view on the innovation and breadth of the offering. Gartner evaluated over 60 BPM vendors to select the top performers with respect to these criteria [45]. For these reasons, we consider this overview as useful for profiling both popular and best-in-class BPM systems.

We conducted a light-weight evaluation of all the products that are described in the Magic Quadrant, which comprised of the following steps. First, we checked whether the products were still available in the market place and in what form. By doing so, we established that various offerings changed hands because of acquisitions. Also, vendors decided to integrate multiple solutions they offered. Specifically, OpenText acquired both Metastorm and Global 360, Perceptive Software acquired Pallas Athena, Singularity is now Kofax, and Polymita is acquired by Red Hat. OpenText integrated its two BPM products into one offering; IBM integrated its Lombardi and WDPE offerings (its Filenet product is

---

[7] Note that simulation and process discovery are supported for the procedural parts of BPM|ONE, but not for the parts specific for case handling.

[8] Note that for this reason we have not used Gartner's 2012 Magic Quadrant on intelligent BPM suites in which the analytical capabilities play a much bigger role.

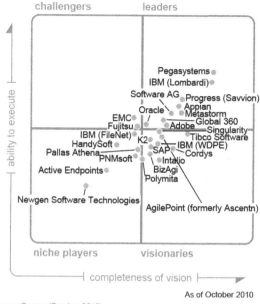

challengers   leaders

Pegasystems ●
IBM (Lombardi) ●
Software AG ● ● Progress (Savvion)
● Appian
Oracle ● ● Metastorm
EMC ● Global 360
Fujitsu ● ● Adobe Singularity
IBM (FileNet) ● Tibco Software
HandySoft ● K2 ● ● IBM (WDPE)
Pallas Athena SAP ● Cordys
PNMsoft ● Intalio
Active Endpoints ● BizAgi
Polymita

Newgen Software Technologies   AgilePoint (formerly Ascentn)

niche players   visionaries

ability to execute

completeness of vision ▶

As of October 2010

Source: Gartner (October 2010)

Fig. 5. Gartner's Magic Quadrant on the market of BPM Suites

still a separate product). As a result, of the original 27 products in the Magic Quadrant, 25 can still be considered to be active.

The second step consisted of the actual evaluation. We consulted the on-line document information of each of the vendors on their products, specifically related to their modeling approach and tool set. We also studied the samples that vendors provided of actual models of business processes as specified with their tools. This approach is light-weight in the sense that there was no interaction with experts of the vendors and that no hands-on use of these tools took place.

The evaluation led to the insight that *of all 25 products, 23 of these dominantly follow a procedural approach for specifying and enacting workflows.* Two of the 25 products can be said to adhere to the case management paradigm, i.e. Perceptive Software's BPM|ONE and OpenText's BPM solution. No products can be clearly said to support declarative or functional workflows.

There are two interesting side-notes to make. First of all, the adherence to the procedural approach to workflow modeling seems closely aligned with the widely prevalent support among vendors for BPMN [34]. As discussed in Section 2.1, the BPMN notation essentially supports a procedural approach, in which explicit paths are modeled in a sequential manner. The BPMN standard does cover a so-called *Ad Hoc Process*, in which the relations between activities is less prescribed. The current development efforts by OMG to specify the Case Management and Modeling Notation (CMNN) seems to head towards the use declarative rules and constraints to pinpoint the semantics of this element. As such, the popularity of BPMN among BPM vendors may pave the way to the uptake of more declarative aspects in workflow specifications, although this is a tentative development.

Secondly, case management is a paradigm that is claimed by many vendors as a feature of their offerings, despite their dominant adherence to the procedural paradigm. Such claims mostly build on the notion that workflows provide a lifecycle of a particular type of case and that a *document-centric view* on such cases is provided with their products. Despite the value of this idea, it is a far cry from the paradigm that we described in Section 2.2. Closely related to the previous observation is that both the products that adhered to case management as the dominant paradigm also fully support a procedural approach.

In conclusion, the procedural paradigm can be said to be the overly dominant one in the marketplace. In second place, but a long way behind, is the case management paradigm. Interestingly, case management is perceived as an attractive idea by many vendors although it is never offered as a fully stand-alone approach (i.e. totally ruling out the use of procedural workflows). Declarative and functional approaches are not spotted in the marketplace. Since the different approaches are complementary, we hope to see combined approaches in commercial systems in the future.

4   A Matter of Taste?

In this paper we compared different workflow paradigms that all played a role in the STW project "Controlling Dynamic Real Life Workflow Situations with Demand Driven Workflow Systems" where we collaborated with Rinus Plasmeijer and his team. In our view none of the four paradigms (procedural, case handling, declarative, and functional) is superior (or inferior). All emphasize different aspects. For example, analysis techniques ranging from verification and performance analysis to process discovery and conformance checking are best developed for procedural languages (e.g., Petri nets). However, recently, also many analysis techniques have been developed for DECLARE. Case handling systems like BPM|ONE and functional language extensions like ITASKS provide little support for analysis. Instead, these approaches concentrate on the development of data- and process-centric information systems. Both BPM|ONE and DECLARE focus on offering flexibility to end-users. ITASKS provides a different kind of flexibility: workflows can be reused and changed easily. In fact, new combinators can be added making the language extensible (like DECLARE). The ITASKS language would benefit from a graphical front-end to make it more understandable. However, such a graphical front-end could reduce expressiveness and limit flexibility at design time. ITASKS is very fast compared to existing systems; it has the pro's and con's of a programming language.

Each of the four approaches is beautiful in its own way and has a different appeal to it (analysis, reuse, flexibility, maintainability, etc.). For example, different forms of flexibility are possible and it is not realistic to assume a single language that suits all purposes. Partly, the choice of language is also a matter of taste. Fortunately, one can combine different approaches as discussed in [4]. A task in one language may correspond to a subprocess in another language. This way different styles of modeling and enactment may be mixed and nested in any way appropriate.

Acknowledgements. This work was supported by the Basic Research Program of the National Research University Higher School of Economics (HSE).

References

1. van der Aalst, W.M.P.: Business Process Management Demystified: A Tutorial on Models, Systems and Standards for Workflow Management. In: Desel, J., Reisig, W., Rozenberg, G. (eds.) ACPN 2003. LNCS, vol. 3098, pp. 1–65. Springer, Heidelberg (2004)
2. van der Aalst, W.M.P.: Process Mining: Discovery, Conformance and Enhancement of Business Processes. Springer, Berlin (2011)
3. van der Aalst, W.M.P.: Business Process Management: A Comprehensive Survey. ISRN Software Engineering, Article ID 507984, 1–37 (2013), doi:10.1155/2013/507984
4. van der Aalst, W.M.P., Adams, M., ter Hofstede, A.H.M., Pesic, M., Schonenberg, H.: Flexibility as a Service. In: Chen, L., Liu, C., Liu, Q., Deng, K. (eds.) DASFAA 2009. LNCS, vol. 5667, pp. 319–333. Springer, Heidelberg (2009)
5. van der Aalst, W.M.P., Benatallah, B., Casati, F., Curbera, F. (eds.): BPM 2005. LNCS, vol. 3649. Springer, Heidelberg (2005)
6. van der Aalst, W.M.P., de Crom, P.J.N., Goverde, R.R.H.M.J., van Hee, K.M., Hofman, W.J., Reijers, H.A., van der Toorn, R.A.: ExSpect 6.4 An Executable Specification Tool for Hierarchical Colored Petri Nets. In: Nielsen, M., Simpson, D. (eds.) ICATPN 2000. LNCS, vol. 1825, pp. 455–464. Springer, Heidelberg (2000)
7. van der Aalst, W.M.P., Desel, J., Oberweis, A. (eds.): Business Process Management. LNCS, vol. 1806. Springer, Heidelberg (2000)
8. van der Aalst, W.M.P., van Hee, K.M.: Workflow Management: Models, Methods, and Systems. MIT Press, Cambridge (2004)
9. van der Aalst, W.M.P., ter Hofstede, A.H.M.: YAWL: Yet Another Workflow Language. Information Systems 30(4), 245–275 (2005)
10. van der Aalst, W.M.P., ter Hofstede, A.H.M., Kiepuszewski, B., Barros, A.P.: Workflow Patterns. Distributed and Parallel Databases 14(1), 5–51 (2003)
11. van der Aalst, W.M.P., ter Hofstede, A.H.M., Weske, M. (eds.): BPM 2003. LNCS, vol. 2678. Springer, Heidelberg (2003)
12. van der Aalst, W.M.P., Pesic, M., Schonenberg, H.: Declarative Workflows: Balancing Between Flexibility and Support. Computer Science - Research and Development 23(2), 99–113 (2009)
13. van der Aalst, W.M.P., Stahl, C.: Modeling Business Processes: A Petri Net Oriented Approach. MIT Press, Cambridge (2011)
14. van der Aalst, W.M.P., Stahl, C., Westergaard, M.: Strategies for Modeling Complex Processes Using Colored Petri Nets. In: Jensen, K., van der Aalst, W.M.P., Balbo, G., Koutny, M., Wolf, K. (eds.) ToPNoC VII. LNCS, vol. 7480, pp. 6–55. Springer, Heidelberg (2013)

15. van der Aalst, W.M.P., Weske, M., Grünbauer, D.: Case Handling: A New Paradigm for Business Process Support. Data and Knowledge Engineering 53(2), 129–162 (2005)
16. Adams, M., ter Hofstede, A.H.M., Edmond, D., van der Aalst, W.M.P.: Worklets: A Service-Oriented Implementation of Dynamic Flexibility in Workflows. In: Meersman, R., Tari, Z. (eds.) OTM 2006. LNCS, vol. 4275, pp. 291–308. Springer, Heidelberg (2006)
17. Alonso, G., Dadam, P., Rosemann, M. (eds.): BPM 2007. LNCS, vol. 4714. Springer, Heidelberg (2007)
18. Dayal, U., Eder, J., Koehler, J., Reijers, H. (eds.): BPM 2009. LNCS, vol. 5701. Springer, Heidelberg (2009)
19. Desel, J., Pernici, B., Weske, M. (eds.): BPM 2004. LNCS, vol. 3080. Springer, Heidelberg (2004)
20. Dumas, M., Reichert, M., Shan, M.-C. (eds.): BPM 2008. LNCS, vol. 5240. Springer, Heidelberg (2008)
21. Dumas, M., La Rosa, M., Mendling, J., Reijers, H.: Fundamentals of Business Process Management. Springer, Berlin (2013)
22. Dustdar, S., Fiadeiro, J.L., Sheth, A.P. (eds.): BPM 2006. LNCS, vol. 4102. Springer, Heidelberg (2006)
23. Ellis, C.A., Keddara, K., Rozenberg, G.: Dynamic Change within Workflow Systems. In: Comstock, N., Ellis, C., Kling, R., Mylopoulos, J., Kaplan, S. (eds.) Proceedings of the Conference on Organizational Computing Systems, Milpitas, California, pp. 10–21. ACM SIGOIS, ACM Press, New York (1995)
24. Giannakopoulou, D., Havelund, K.: Automata-Based Verification of Temporal Properties on Running Programs. In: Proceedings of the 16th IEEE International Conference on Automated Software Engineering (ASE 2001), pp. 412–416. IEEE Computer Society (2001)
25. Herrmann, T., Hoffmann, M., Loser, K.U., Moysich, K.: Semistructured Models are Surprisingly Useful for User-Centered Design. In: De Michelis, G., Giboin, A., Karsenty, L., Dieng, R. (eds.) Designing Cooperative Systems (Coop 2000), pp. 159–174. IOS Press, Amsterdam (2000)
26. ter Hofstede, A.H.M., van der Aalst, W.M.P., Adams, M., Russell, N.: Modern Business Process Automation: YAWL and its Support Environment. Springer, Berlin (2010)
27. Hull, R., Mendling, J., Tai, S. (eds.): BPM 2010. LNCS, vol. 6336. Springer, Heidelberg (2010)
28. Jablonski, S., Bussler, C.: Workflow Management: Modeling Concepts, Architecture, and Implementation. International Thomson Computer Press, London (1996)
29. de Leoni, M., Maggi, F.M., van der Aalst, W.M.P.: Aligning Event Logs and Declarative Process Models for Conformance Checking. In: Barros, A., Gal, A., Kindler, E. (eds.) BPM 2012. LNCS, vol. 7481, pp. 82–97. Springer, Heidelberg (2012)
30. Leymann, F., Roller, D.: Production Workflow: Concepts and Techniques. Prentice-Hall PTR, Upper Saddle River (1999)
31. Maggi, F.M., Montali, M., Westergaard, M., van der Aalst, W.M.P.: Monitoring Business Constraints with Linear Temporal Logic: An Approach Based on Colored Automata. In: Rinderle-Ma, S., Toumani, F., Wolf, K. (eds.) BPM 2011. LNCS, vol. 6896, pp. 132–147. Springer, Heidelberg (2011)
32. Maggi, F.M., Bose, R.P.J.C., van der Aalst, W.M.P.: Efficient Discovery of Understandable Declarative Process Models from Event Logs. In: Ralyté, J., Franch, X., Brinkkemper, S., Wrycza, S. (eds.) CAiSE 2012. LNCS, vol. 7328, pp. 270–285. Springer, Heidelberg (2012)

33. Montali, M., Pesic, M., van der Aalst, W.M.P., Chesani, F., Mello, P., Storari, S.: Declarative Specification and Verification of Service Choreographies. ACM Transactions on the Web 4(1), 1–62 (2010)

34. OMG. Business Process Model and Notation (BPMN). Object Management Group, formal/2011-01-03 (2011)

35. Pesic, M., Schonenberg, M.H., Sidorova, N., van der Aalst, W.M.P.: Constraint-Based Workflow Models: Change Made Easy. In: Meersman, R., Tari, Z. (eds.) OTM 2007, Part I. LNCS, vol. 4803, pp. 77–94. Springer, Heidelberg (2007)

36. Plasmeijer, R.: CLEAN: A Programming Environment Based on Term Graph Rewriting. Electronic Notes in Theoretical Computer Science 2, 215–221 (1995)

37. Plasmeijer, R., Achten, P., Koopman, P.: iTasks: Executable Specifications of Interactive Workflow Systems for the Web. SIGPLAN Notices 42(9), 141–152 (2007)

38. Plasmeijer, R., Achten, P., Koopman, P., Lijnse, B., van Noort, T., van Groningen, J.: iTasks for a change: Type-safe run-time change in dynamically evolving workflows. In: Proceedings of the 20th ACM SIGPLAN Workshop on Partial Evaluation and Program Manipulation, pp. 151–160. ACM, New York (2011)

39. Plasmeijer, R., Lijnse, B., Michels, S., Achten, P., Koopman, P.: Task-Oriented Programming in a Pure Functional Language. In: Proceedings of the 14th Symposium on Principles and Practice of Declarative Programming, pp. 195–206. ACM, New York (2012)

40. Reichert, M., Dadam, P.: ADEPTflex: Supporting Dynamic Changes of Workflow without Loosing Control. Journal of Intelligent Information Systems 10(2), 93–129 (1998)

41. Rinderle, S., Reichert, M., Dadam, P.: Correctness Criteria For Dynamic Changes in Workflow Systems: A Survey. Data and Knowledge Engineering 50(1), 9–34 (2004)

42. Rinderle-Ma, S., Toumani, F., Wolf, K. (eds.): BPM 2011. LNCS, vol. 6896. Springer, Heidelberg (2011)

43. Sadiq, S., Sadiq, W., Orlowska, M.: Pockets of Flexibility in Workflow Specification. In: Kunii, H.S., Jajodia, S., Sølvberg, A. (eds.) ER 2001. LNCS, vol. 2224, pp. 513–526. Springer, Heidelberg (2001)

44. Schonenberg, H., Mans, R., Russell, N., Mulyar, N., van der Aalst, W.M.P.: Process Flexibility: A Survey of Contemporary Approaches. In: Dietz, J., Albani, A., Barjis, J. (eds.) Advances in Enterprise Engineering I. LNBIP, vol. 10, pp. 16–30. Springer, Heidelberg (2008)

45. Sinur, J., Hill, J.: Magic Quadrant for Business Process Management Suites, Gartner RAS Core Research Note G00205212 (2010), http://www.gartner.com

46. Weske, M.: Business Process Management: Concepts, Languages, Architectures. Springer, Berlin (2007)

47. Westergaard, M.: Better Algorithms for Analyzing and Enacting Declarative Workflow Languages Using LTL. In: Rinderle-Ma, S., Toumani, F., Wolf, K. (eds.) BPM 2011. LNCS, vol. 6896, pp. 83–98. Springer, Heidelberg (2011)

Parse Your Options

Doaitse S. Swierstra and Atze Dijkstra

Dept. of Computer Science, O.O. Box 80.089, 3508 TB Utrecht, The Netherlands
http://www.cs.uu.nl

Abstract. We describe the development of a couple of combinators which can be used to run applicative style parsers in an interleaved way. In the presentation we advocate a scheme for choosing identifier names which clearly shows the types of the values involved, and how to compose them into the desired result. We finish with describing how the combinators can be used to parse command line arguments and files containing options.

Keywords: Parser combinators, Haskell, Parallel parsing, Option processing, Permutation parsing.

1 Introduction

In the original version of the uulib[1] parsing combinator library we introduced two modules, providing combinators for parsing more complicated input structures than those described by context free languages: one for recognising permuted structures and one for recognising merged lists. In this paper we present an *interleave* combinator which generalises these two patterns. As we will see this library can almost completely be constructed using the basic *Applicative* and *Alternative* parser interfaces as e.g. provided by the uu-parsinglib package, without having to deal with the intricate internals of the parsing process itself. We only require that it is possible to split a parser into two components: one which recognises the empty sequence in case the original parser can do so and one which takes care of the non-empty cases. Of course, a direct consequence of choosing a feature rich library as uu-parsinglib is that the parsers constructed out of it inherit all its nice properties: returning results in an online way, providing informative error messages, and adapting the input where parsing cannot proceed.

Before we introduce our new library we introduce some common definitions and give an example of parsing permuted and merged structure in Section 2, followed by a motivating example for our new combinators in Section 3. Section 4 forms the core of the paper describing the internals of the new library, whereas in Section 5 we develop a small library using the new combinators for processing command line options. We will see that there is not much more work left for the programmer than just enumerating the possible options and the way they are to be denoted. We conclude in Section 6.

---

[1] http://hackage.haskell.org/package/uulib

P. Achten and P. Koopman (Eds.): Plasmeijer Festschrift, LNCS 8106, pp. 234–249, 2013.

2   Common Definitions and Background

We start out by repeating the definition some familiar classes, and give applications of the previously introduced combinators. The class *Applicative* introduces a combinator <*> that combines two side-effecting functions into a single function. The important observation is that the results of the two functions are combined by applying the result of the first to that of the second. In this paper such functions will be referred to as parsers, as this is the way we will instantiate the interface. The <*> operator is a function which runs its two parser arguments sequentially on the input: i.e. the second parser takes off in with the input state in which the first one has finished. The class *Alternative* introduces the companion operator <|> which runs either one of its operands, but not both. Its unit element is *empty*; this is not, as its name suggests, the parser which recognises the empty string but instead the parser which always fails. For the sake of completeness we also introduce the *Functor* class.

> **class** *Functor f* **where**
> $\quad$ *fmap* :: $(b \rightarrow a) \rightarrow f\ b\ \rightarrow f\ a$
>
> **class** *Applicative f* **where**
> $\quad$ (<*>) :: $f\ (b \rightarrow a) \rightarrow f\ b \rightarrow f\ a$
> $\quad$ *pure* :: $a \qquad\qquad\quad \rightarrow f\ a$
>
> **class** *Alternative f* **where**
> $\quad$ (<|>) :: $f\ a \rightarrow f\ a \rightarrow f\ a$
> $\quad$ *empty* :: $f\ a$

Next we introduce some helper functions that may be used to modify the result of a parser, or to throw away a result in which we are not interested:

> (<$>) :: *Functor f* $\Rightarrow (b \rightarrow a) \rightarrow f\ b \rightarrow f\ a$
> (<$>) $\quad$ = *fmap*
> p <* q $\quad$ = *const* $\quad$ <$> p <*> q
> f <$ p $\quad$ = *const f* $\quad$ <$> p
> p *> q $\quad$ = *flip const* <$> p <*> q
> p 'opt' a = p <|> *pure a*

In addition to the operator for sequential composition <*> we defined [1] a permuting combinator, with a similar type (the precise definition of the g does not matter here):

> <||> :: $g\ (b \rightarrow a) \rightarrow g\ b \rightarrow g\ a$

This operator also recognises both its operands, but irrespective of the order in which they occur in the input stream, i.e. we may either run its left operand and have its right operand take off where the first one finished or the other way around. Actually it is even more expressive in the sense that if either of its g-operands is again built using <||> the elements of the other operand may intervene. Using this combinator we can construct parsers which recognise input in which the components are possibly permuted. Examples of such uses abound: the order of the fields in a BIBTEX entry is not fixed, nor is the order of the specification of the field values in a Haskell record fixed. Consider the data type:

$$\textbf{data } Cart = Cart \ \{x \quad :: Float; y \quad :: Float\}$$
$$| \ Polar \ \{rho :: Float; phi :: Float\}$$

Now one might want to be able to read both `Cart{x=1,y=2}` as well as `Cart{y=2,x=1}` from the input; if a Haskell compiler accepts both representations, why shouldn't we be able to read both these representations from the input? Using the `<||>` parser this is easily achieved (*mkG* and *sepBy* are helper functions to which we will come back later):

$$pTwoFloats \ op \ constr \ s1 \ s2$$
$$= \quad pToken \ constr \ \text{*>} \ pCurly \ ((op \ \text{<\$>} \ pField \ s1 \ pFloat$$
$$\text{<||>} \ pField \ s2 \ pFloat)$$
$$\text{`}sepBy\text{`} \ pSym \ \text{'},\text{'}$$
$$)$$
$$pField \ s \ p = mkG \ (pToken \ s \ \text{*>} \ pSym \ \text{'}=\text{'} \ \text{*>} \ p)$$
$$pCurly \quad p = pSym \ \text{'}\{\text{'} \ \text{*>} \ p \ \text{<*} \ pSym \ \text{'}\}\text{'}$$
$$pCart = \quad pTwoFloats \ Cart \quad \text{"Cart"} \quad \text{"x"} \quad \text{"y"}$$
$$\text{<|>} \ pTwoFloats \ Polar \quad \text{"Polar"} \ \text{"rho"} \ \text{"phi"}$$

We [3] furthermore defined a combinator `<+>` which makes it possible to construct parsers which recognise merged lists. In parser *int_low* the *listOf* function converts a parser to a parser which may run interleaved with other parsers and recognises a list of values accepted by its argument parser, the function `<+>` runs both arguments in an interleaved mode, and *pMerged* converts its argument back to a normal parser again:

$$int\_low :: Parser \ ([Int], [Char])$$
$$int\_low = pMerged \ (listOf \ pInt \ \text{<+>} \ listOf \ pLower)$$

The function *int_low* accepts the input string `"a1bc2"` and returns the nested pair $([1, 2], \text{"abc"})$; the input is split into two sub-streams which are each accepted by one of the two operands of `<+>`.

On closer inspection we see that the list merging parsers are a generalisation of the permuting parsers: just make sure that each of the merged lists has precisely length 1 and list merging degenerates to permuting. This made us also realise that the merging of lists was just a special case of *merging any collection of structured sequences*, which in its turn raised the question whether we can define combinators which make it possible to describe this process, thus generalising the two libraries just mentioned into a single one.

3   Parsing Log Files

As a motivation for our new combinators we start with a simple example of their use. It deals with unraveling a file which was created by several concurrent processes writing entries into it: each process indicates its start by writing out the character 's' followed by its unique identity (numbers in the example), next it will emit a couple of work entries each consisting of the character 'w' followed by its process identity and a space. The rest of the line contains log information. A process indicates its termination by closing its sequence of entries with a line consisting of the character 'c' gaian followed by its process identity. So all entries generated by a single proces will be labeled with the same process identity, which we assume to be unique throughout the log file. Given e.g. a log file containing the following lines:

s2	-- start of process 2
s1	-- start of process 1
w1 a1	-- first work entry of process 1
w2 b	-- first work entry of process 2
w1 a2	-- second work entry of process 1
c1	-- process 1 closes
s3	-- start of process 3
w3 c	-- first work entry of process 3
c2	-- process 2 closes
c3	-- process 3 closes

we want to produce the following table, where each process is associated with the contents of its work entries:

$$[("2",["b"]),("1",["a1","a2"]),("3",["c"])]$$

In the code we use names starting with a g to bind to parsers which can run in an interleaved way (which we will refer to as *grammars* from now on), whereas names starting with a p refer to conventional parsers which recognise a consecutive segment of input. The function *mkG* converts a conventional parser to a grammar; the result will still recognise a consecutive part of the input, but once it has done so it may pass control on to a competing parser.

We start out by defining the grammar *gProcess* recognising the sequence of events for a single process, using some of the basic parsers provided by common combinator libraries providing an applicative interface, and subsequently use the function *gmList* to concurrently run as many of them as needed. We have used a monadic bind to use the process identity retrieved from the starting line in constructing the parsers for the subsequent lines of this process.

$$
\begin{aligned}
gProcess = \mathbf{do}\ i \leftarrow &&& mkG\ \ pStart \\
& w \leftarrow pMany \circ mkG\ \$\ pWork\ i \\
& \_ \leftarrow && mkG\ \$\ pClose\ i \\
& return\ (i, w) \\
gLog\ \ \ = gmList\ gProcess
\end{aligned}
$$

Next we define the parsers recognising the various kinds of log entries. The function *pMunch* accepts the longest prefix of the input which passes the predicate parameter.

$pStart$ $= pToken$ "s" $*> pMunch$ ($\neq$ '\n') $<* pToken$ "\n"
$pWork\ i =$ $pToken$ ('w' $: i +\!\!+$ " ")
              $*> pMunch$ ($\neq$ '\n') -- read the rest of the line
              $<* pToken$ "\n"
$pClose\ i = pToken$ ('c' $: i +\!\!+$ "\n")

Note that the order in which the work comes out is determined by the order of their first entry in the log file.

4 Merging Parsers

4.1 Representing Parsers for Merged Input Structures

As we have seen in the example, what we are looking for is the possibility to interleave parsers; one can think of this as associating a separate colour with each parser and splitting up the input in a series of coloured segments, such that the concatenation of segments of the same colour is accepted by its correspondingly coloured parser.

The question to answer is how to split the input into uniformly coloured segments, i.e. how to find the points in the input where colour switching may take place and what colour to give to the segments. In order to be able to do so efficiently we have decided to construct our interleaving parsers out of *basic* parsers, which are conventional parsers which recognise a *consecutive part* of the input. We rephrase our use of the word *grammar* to stand for a *description of* a parser which can pause at a colour switch and continue when the input switches back to its colour again. Such grammars can thus be run in a competing fashion. From this point on we will use the word *parser* to refer to a conventional parser which recognises a segment of the input.

Once a parser gets hold of the input, and has successfully started parsing, we will let this parser run until completion. Once it has completed, all pending grammars (including the grammar for which the parser which just ran forms a constituent) can try to continue to parse. A consequence of this is that at any point in the input where we may switch between grammars each of the competing grammars should present its *first-parsers*, i.e. the candidates for accepting the next uniformly coloured segment. These presented first-parsers play a similar role as the *first* sets resulting from an $LL(1)$ grammar analysis; the only difference is that we dynamically compute the collection of first-parsers instead of statically a the set of first symbols.

A very important issue we have to take care of is the avoidance of unwanted ambiguity as the following example shows. Suppose we have the following permuting parser:

$pMaybe\ s = pToken\ s$ 'opt' ""
$pAmb = (,) <\$> pMaybe$ "A" $<|\!|> pMaybe$ "B"

and our input consists of the string "A", then there are two different ways in which the empty string "" can be seen as part of the input: "" $+\!\!+$ "A" and

"A" $+\!\!+$ "". Thus when running the parser *pAmb* on the input string "A" there are two possible parses, both returning the same result. Unless our underlying parsing library somehow knows how to deal with this we will eitherget an error message, a rather arbitrary choice of one of the possible parses or, when this happens more than once, and exponnetial number of results. Even if the library could handle ambiguity it may not be able to discover that both results are the same. This problem has already been described in the development of the permuting combinators [1] and the solution we take here is based on a similar assumption as we have chosen there: we assume that we are able to split a parser in a part recognising the non-empty part and one recognising the possibly empty part. The latter will be represented by the value that is to be returned as as a witness in case the parser accepts the empty input (denoted as ϵ from now on). In order to make this explicit in our interface we introduce a class:

> **class** *Splittable f* **where**
>   *getNonPure* :: $f\ a \to Maybe\ (f\ a)$
>   *getPure*   :: $f\ a \to Maybe$ a

where we will assume the following equality to hold for any *Alternative* functor *f* we want to use for our basic parsers:

$$f \equiv maybe\ empty\ id\ (getNonPure\ f)\ \texttt{<|>}\ maybe\ empty\ pure\ (getPure\ f)$$

We are now ready to define the data type *Gram* representing *grammars*. It allows us to compute, at each possible splitting point in the input, the collection of first-parsers that may try to continue at that point. We start out by defining a data type *Alt* which has a constructor *Seq* which explicitly represents the splitting of the grammar into in a first-parser and "the rest of the work to be done". Since we also want our grammars to have a monadic interface we equip our data type *Alt* a *Bind* alternative, which again explcitly contains the first-parser to be run:

> **data** *Alt f a* = *forall c.*$(f\ (c \to a))$ '*Seq*' (*Gram f c*)
> | *forall c.*$(f\ c)$ '*Bind*' $(c \to Gram\ f\ a)$

Based on the data type *Alt* we now define the data type *Gram*. It contains two components: a value of type $[Alt\ f\ a]$ which is the alternation (choice) of all non-empty parts jointly accepting a non-empty sequence of symbols, and a *Maybe a* value representing the value to be returned in case ϵ is accepted:

> **data** *Gram f a* = *Gram* $[Alt\ f\ a]\ (Maybe\ a)$

The type parameter *f* corresponds to the conventional, non-interruptible parsers, which we use as building blocks for our grammars.

4.2   Defining the Various Class Instances for *Gram*

We now define the instances for these newly introduced data types for the classes *Functor*, *Applicative*, *Alternative* and *Monad*.

Gram Is a Functor. We start with the instances for *Functor* for both the data type *Gram* and *Alt*. The code is straightforward:

> **instance** *Functor f* ⇒ *Functor* (*Gram f*) **where**
> $\quad$ *fmap b2a* (*Gram l_b m_b*) = *Gram* (*map* (*b2a*<$>) l_b) (*b2a* <$> m_b)
>
> **instance** *Functor f* ⇒ *Functor* (*Alt f*) **where**
> $\quad$ *fmap b2a* (*f_{c2b}* `Seq` *g_c* $\quad$) = ((*b2a*∘) <$> *$f_{c2b}$*) `Seq` *$g_c$*
> $\quad$ *fmap b2a* (*f_c* `Bind` *$c2g_b$*) = *f_c* `Bind` (λ*c* → *b2a* <$> *$c2g_b$* *c*)

Here we have chosen a naming convention which makes the types of the values involved explicitly visible in the program text: *b2a* holds a function value of the type $b \to a$, *m_b* stands for a value of type *Maybe b*, *l_a* stands for a list of *Alt f a* values, *f_{c2b}* is bound to a value of type *f* (*c* → *b*), *g_c* is bound to a value of type *Gram f c* and *$c2g_b$* to a value of type *c* → *Gram b*. Now it is easy to see that *fmap b2a* (*fc* `Bind` *$c2g_b$*) should result in a value of type *Gram a*, etc. Note that applying *fmap* maintains the invariant that the first-parser can be easily recognised for each *Alt* intact. We have chosen to use <$> as an alias for *fmap* in this code wherever possible, since this makes the names chosen even more helpful in the representation of the code.

Gram Is an Applicative Functor. We want to construct our merging parsers in just the same way as we construct normal parsers, using the well known *Applicative* and *Alternative* interfaces [4]. Since our data types enforce the property that we can easily identify the first-parser to be used, this is where the real work takes place. The pattern we follow however is common, and well known from various process algebras and given in Figure 1. The first-parsers in the *Seq* and *Bind* constructs of the left-hand side operand are "rotated" out. The hard work is done by the function *fwdby* which combines the remaining part of the *Seq* and *Bind* constructs to form the new right-hand side of the *Seq* and *Bind* construct in the result. The *g_c* and *g_b* grammars of a *Seq* are ran returning a value of type (*c, b*). We modify the value returned by the first-parser –by applying *uncurry* to it– to accept this pair of values instead of getting passed the two arguments individually. If the left-hand side parser can recognise the empty input then also the first-parsers of the right-hand side grammar are first-parsers of the resulting grammar; they can start to accept part of the input too. This explains the second component in the definition of the *Alts f b* in the right-hand side of the <*> definition, where we use the witness value of type $b \to a$ to update the result of the right-hand side parser. The definition of *pure* speaks for itself: we have no non-empty alternatives, and the parser can recognise ϵ with a witness of type *a*.

A subtle point is that we had to add an irrefutable pattern match (∼) to the right-hand side operand of <*>, since otherwise the pattern matching creates an endless loop in situations like the definition of *pMany* when *f* is instantiated with some *Gram g*:

> *pMany p* :: *f a* → *f* [*a*]
> *pMany p* = **let** *result* = (:) <$> *p* <*> *result* `opt` [] **in** *result*

instance $Functor\ f \Rightarrow Applicative\ (Gram\ f)$ **where**
 $pure\ a = Gram\ [\ ]\ (Just\ a)$
 $Gram\ l_{b2a}\ m_{b2a}\ \texttt{<*>}\ {\sim}g_b@(Gram\ l_b\ m_b)$
  $= Gram\ (\ map\ (\text{`}fwdby\text{`}\ g_b)\ l_{b2a}$
    $\mathbin{+\!\!\!+}$
    $[\,b2a\ \texttt{<\$>}\ f_b\ |\ Just\ b2a \leftarrow [m_{b2a}], f_b \leftarrow l_b]$
   $)\ (\ m_{b2a}\ \texttt{<*>}\ m_b)$
 $fwdby :: Functor\ f \Rightarrow Alt\ f\ (b \to a) \to Gram\ f\ b \to Alt\ f\ a$
 $(f_{c2b2a}\ \text{`}Seq\text{`}\ \ \ g_c)\ \ \ \ \text{`}fwdby\text{`}\ g_b = (uncurry\ \texttt{<\$>}\ f_{c2b2a})\ \text{`}Seq\text{`}\ ((,)\ \texttt{<\$>}\ g_c\ \texttt{<*>}\ g_b)$
 $(f_c\ \ \ \ \text{`}Bind\text{`}\ c2g_{b2a})\ \text{`}fwdby\text{`}\ g_b = f_c\ \text{`}Bind\text{`}\ (\lambda c \to c2g_{b2a}\ c\ \texttt{<*>}\ g_b)$
 $uncurry\ f\ (x, y) = f\ x\ y$

instance $Functor\ f \Rightarrow Alternative\ (Gram\ f)$ **where**
 $empty = Gram\ [\ ]\ Nothing$
 $Gram\ ps\ pe\ \texttt{<|>}\ Gram\ qs\ qe = Gram\ (ps \mathbin{+\!\!\!+} qs)\ (pe\ \texttt{<|>}\ qe)$

Fig. 1. $Gram$ is a member of the $Applicative$ and $Alternative$ classes

---

Here $\texttt{<*>}$ does not have access to the top-level constructor in its right-hand side, since this constructor is produced by this very call to $\texttt{<*>}$. Note that the call to $\texttt{<*>}$ is evaluated lazily, so we have no problems with recursive grammars. The unrolling of these definitions is done on a by-demand basis during the actual parsing process. This technique resembles the parallel parsing strategy as developed by Claessen [2] and code also bears close resemblance to the computation of the $firsts$ set, as described by Swierstra and Duponcheel [5].

In case the left-hand side is a monadic construct we just use the original first-parser f_c, and again move the right-hand side $c2g_{b2a}$ of the left operator to the right-hand side of the result, where it is composed with the original right hand side using $\texttt{<*>}$.

***Gram* Is an *Alternative* Functor.** The instance for $Alternative$ is almost trivial: we concatenate the list of alternatives from both operands. This leaves the question what to do if the grammar is ambiguous, caused by both alternatives to be able to accept ϵ. We have chosen to use the left-biasedness of $\texttt{<*>}$ as defined for $Maybe$ to choose the left value to return. The code is again given in figure 1.

***Gram* Is a *Monad*.** The next thing we want to do is to equip our grammars with a monadic interface, which we again achieve by "rotating" all but the first-parser to the right so the first-parser again is presented at the top level constructor. In the case of a `}Seq\text{` construct as the left argument of $\ggg$ we split its monadic effect into two steps: in the first step we make the first part if the left-hand side operand explicitly visible in the resulting `}Bind\text{` construct, whereas the corresponding right-hand side g_c of the `}Seq\text{` part is, once it has been combined using $\lambda c2b \to c2b\ \texttt{<\$>}\ g_c$ with the result $c2b$ of the left-hand side of the '*Seq*' in another call to ⋙ in the right-hand side of the resulting top level '*Bind*' constructs.

When the left-hand side accepts ϵ we have to take some extra precautions, since in this case the first-parsers created by a call to right-hand side compete for input too, since they too may accept input at this point. Since we have the witness of this empty left-hand side available, we can use it to compute the *Gram a* value returned by the right-hand side of ⋙, and with this its first-parsers become available too and can take part in the competition:

instance *Functor f* ⇒ *Monad* (*Gram f*) **where**
    return a = *Gram* [] (*Just a*)
    Gram l_b m_b ⋙ $b2g_a$ = **case** m_b **of**
        Nothing → *Gram* (*map* ('*bindto*'$b2g_a$) l_b) *Nothing*
        Just b   → **let** *Gram* l_a m_a = $b2g_a$ b
                      in *Gram* (*map* ('*bindto*'$b2g_a$) l_b ⧺ l_a) m_a
    bindto :: *Functor f* ⇒ *Alt f b* → (*b* → *Gram f a*) → *Alt f a*
    (f_{c2b} '*Seq*' g_c)   '*bindto*' $b2g_a$ = f_{c2b} '*Bind*' $\lambda c2b$ → $c2b$ <$> g_c ⋙ $b2g_a$
    (f_c '*Bind*' $c2g_b$) '*bindto*' $b2g_a$ = f_c '*Bind*' λc → $c2g_b$ c ⋙ $b2g_a$

Constructing Elementary *Gram* Values. The last thing we have to do is to show how we can lift a parser into an equivalent *Gram*

    mkG :: (*Splittable f*, *Functor f*) ⇒ *f a* → *Gram f a*
    mkG p = *Gram* (*maybe* [] (λp → [(*const* <$> p) '*Seq*' *pure* ()]) (*getNonPure p*))
              (*getPure p*)

At first sight this code looks more complicated than strictly needed; this is caused by our choice of the *Alt* data type. We could have easily added a third case *Single* (*f a*) to this data type, and have used this *Single* constructor here. We have chosen for the current, minimalistic approach, in which this *Single* data type is encoded as a parser which is to be followed by an ϵ parser returning () the result of which is subsequently discarded. This adds a small constant-time overhead to our parsers, which we think is acceptable in return for the increased simplicity of the code.

4.3   <||> and <<||>

In the previous subsections we have defined the data type *Gram f a*, have shown how to lift elementary parsers to this structure, and have defined instances for this type for the *Functor*, *Applicative*, *Alternative* and *Monad* classes. As a final step we now define the <||> combinator, which describes the "interleaved" composition of two grammars. We will however express this combinator in terms of an even more primitive combinator <<||>:

    infixl 4 <||>
    infixl 4 <<||>

$$(<||>), (<<||>) :: Gram\ (b \to a) \to Gram\ b \to Gram\ a$$

Note that we have given these operators the same type as the conventional `<*>` combinator, since we very much like the applicative interface for describing how to combine the two accepted values into the result. The reason, of course, that we cannot use the `<*>` combinator is that it has already been used to express the more conventional sequential composition of two *Gram* values.

The idea of the `<<||>` combinator is that it will run one of the first-parsers of its left-hand side operand on the input first, and from that point on will behave like `<||>`, which does not have a preference for either of its operands to start accepting input. We can easily define `<||>` in terms of `<<||>`:

$$g_{b2a} <||> g_b = \qquad\qquad g_{b2a} <<||> g_b$$
$$<|> flip\ (\$) <\$> g_b \quad <<||> g_{b2a}$$

Here we see that the resulting parser will either run one of the first-parsers from its left-hand side operand or one of the first-parsers of its right-hand side operand. In case both grammars can accept ϵ we get the same witness value twice, and in principle our grammar becomes ambiguous; the biased choice of the *Maybe* instance of *Alternative* throws away one of these two (equal) values.

So all we have to do now is to define `<<||>`. We construct a new grammar which has as its first-parsers all the first-parsers of its left-hand side operand:

$$(<<||>) :: Functor\ f \Rightarrow Gram\ f\ (b \to a) \to Gram\ f\ b \to Gram\ f\ a$$
$$g_{b2a}@(Gram\ l_{b2a}\ m_{b2a}) <<||> {\sim}g_b@(Gram\ \_\ m_b)$$
$$= Gram\ (map\ (`fwdby`\ g_b)\ l_{b2a})\ (m_{b2a} <*> m_b)$$
$$(f_{c2b2a}\ `Seq`\ g_c) \quad `fwdby`\ g_b = (uncurry <\$> f_{c2b2a})\ `Seq`\ ((,) <\$> g_c <||> g_b)$$
$$(f_c\ `Bind`\ c2g_{b2a})\ `fwdby`\ g_b = f_c\ `Bind`\ (\lambda c \to c2g_{b2a}\ c <||> g_b)$$

Notice that this code is almost the same as that for the definition of `<*>`; only have the occurrences of `<*>` in the right-hand sides of the *fwdby* function been replaced by `<||>`, thus indicating that thus constructed parsers should run interleaved instead of sequentially.

4.4   Converting Grammars into Parsers

The only thing left to do now it to show how to construct a real parser from a *Gram* structure. We will require that the parameter f we have carried around thus far has instances for the usual *Applicative*, *Alternative* and *Monad* interfaces, so we can use the functions available from these classes in this process. For each of the alternatives we select the first-parser from it, use `<|>` to select one of these to run, and after that either combine its result using `<*>` with the parser generated from the corresponding *Gram* value in the case of a `Seq`, or use it as an argument to the right-hand side operand in the case of a `Bind` and convert this result again into a proper parser.

$$mkP :: (Monad\ f, Applicative\ f, Alternative\ f) \Rightarrow Gram\ f\ a \to f\ a$$
$$mkP\ (Gram\ l_a\ m_a) = foldr\ (<|>)\ (maybe\ empty\ pure\ m_a)$$

$$(map\ mkP\_Alt\ l_a)$$
$$\mathbf{where}\ mkP\_Alt\ (f_{b2a}\ 'Seq'\ g_b)\quad = f_{b2a}\ \texttt{<*>}\ mkP\ g_b$$
$$mkPrAlt\ (f_b\quad 'Bind'\ b2g_a) = f_b\quad \ggg (mkP \circ b2g_a)$$

4.5 Inserting Separators

As we have seen in the *pCart* example it is a common case that the elements which we want to recognise, and which occur in a permuted order are separated by e.g. a ' ; ' or a ' , '. For these cases we have introduced a special version of *mkP*, which takes an additional argument telling how to parse a separator. The hard work is done by a function *insertSep* which prefixes each parser, except the first one, in the *Gram* parameter by the parser that recognises the separator:

$$sepBy :: Applicative\ f \Rightarrow Gram\ f\ a \to f\ b \to f\ a$$
$$sepBy\ g\ sep = mkP\ (insertSep\ sep\ g)$$
$$insertSep :: (Applicative\ f) \Rightarrow f\ b \to Gram\ f\ a \to Gram\ f\ a$$
$$insertSep\ sep\ (Gram\ l_a\ m_a :: Gram\ f\ a) = Gram\ (map\ insertSepInAlt\ l_a)\ m_a$$
$$\mathbf{where}$$
$$\quad insertSepInAlt\ (f_{b2a}\ 'Seq'\ g_b) = f_{b2a}\ 'Seq'\ prefixSepInGram\ g_b$$
$$\quad insertSepInAlt\ (f_b\ 'Bind'\ b2g_a) = f_b\ 'Bind'\ (insertSep\ sep \circ b2g_a)$$
$$\quad prefixSepInGram\ (Gram\ l_a\ m_a) = Gram\ (map\ prefixSepInAlt\ l_a)\ m_a$$
$$\quad prefixSepInAlt :: Alt\ f\ b \to Alt\ f\ b$$
$$\quad prefixSepInAlt\ (f_{b2a}\ 'Seq'\ g_b) = (sep\ \texttt{*>}\ f_{b2a})\ 'Seq'\ prefixSepInGram\ g_b$$

Because we are making use of polymorphic recursion we had to insert a few type annotations in the code.

4.6 Parsing Merged Lists

Although the combinators follow the common interfaces, there are a few tricky points one has to keep in mind when using them. The fact that the interleaved parsers compete for input may lead to some complications one should be aware of. We take a look at the traditional definition of *pMany*, which converts a parser into a parser which recognises a list of elements recognised by its argument parser:

$$pList\ p = \mathbf{let}\ pmp = (:)\ \texttt{<\$>}\ p\ \texttt{<*>}\ pmp\ 'opt'\ [\,]\ \mathbf{in}\ pmp$$

In this definition the recursive call to *pmp* only starts to play a role once the first instance of *p* has succeeded. If we however replace the *<*>* operator by a *<||>* operator, then the recursive *pmp* can start to parse immediately too, and will spawn yet another instance of *p* which starts to compete for the input and so on recursively; apparently changing sequential execution by interleaved execution has deeper implications than is directly visible from the code. Fortunately this problem can be solved rather easily: we decide to only start with a new instance of *pmp* competing for the input, once *p* has started its work and has comsumed a bit of input. Hence we define:

$$gmList\ p = \textbf{let}\ pmp = (:) <\$> p <<||> pmp\ `opt`\ [\ ]\ \textbf{in}\ pmp$$

We see here that the availability of `<<||>` plays an essential role in this definition; in that sense it is more primitive than `<||>`, which was expressed in terms of `<<||>`.

5   Applications

In this section we will give two examples of the use of the introduced merging combinators.

5.1   Parsing Options

One of the most boring tasks in writing an application is the processing of the options passed on the command line. Although there are some packages and tools to make one's life a bit easier, there always remains a lot of work to be done. Usually conversion from the strings which were passed to the kind of values one is really interested in has to be done explicitly, for optional arguments defaults have to be provided, for required arguments we have to check that they have actually been provided, and there are many conventions for passing the options, be it in short form as in `ls -l`, in long form as in `haddock --enable-documentation`, in a kind of key-value pair as in `process -o outputfile` or `process -o=outputfile`, etc. We will now present a small collection of combinators which completely takes away this burden from the programmer, using the introduced merging parser combinators.

We start out by assuming that in our program we want to put our recognised options in a record with named fields. Using Template Haskell we generate lenses to give us access to the individual fields. As an example we define the following data types and example record:

```
import Data.Lenses
import Data.Lenses.Template
data Prefers = Clean | Haskell deriving Show
data Address = Address { city_ :: String, room_ :: String }
             deriving Show
data Name    = Name { name_ :: String, prefers_ :: Prefers, ints_ :: [Int]
                    , address_ :: Address }
             deriving Show
$ (deriveLenses ' ' Name)
$ (deriveLenses ' ' Address)
$ (deriveLenses ' ' Prefers)
defaults = Name "Doaitse" Haskell [] (Address "Utrecht" "BBL517")
```

The *deriveLenses* calls to template Haskell generate code which will give us read and write access to the fields which a name which ends in an '_'. What is precisely generated does not matter too much here, but what is important is that the imported packages provide amongst others a function *alter* which can be used to update a field of type a pointed at by the first parameter in a record of type r by applying the passed function of type $a \to a$ to it:

$$alter :: MonadState \ a \ m \Rightarrow (m \ () \to StateT \ r \ Identity \ b) \to (a \to a)$$
$$\to (r \to r)$$

Now we can update the record at say the field *prefers* as follows:

```
print ((prefers 'alter' (const Clean)) defaults)
Name { name_ = "Doaitse", prefers_ = Clean, ints_ = [],
       address_ = Address {city_ = "Utrecht", room_ = "BBL517"}}
```

So the important thing to remember is that an expression a `'alter'` f applies the function f to a field pointed at by the lens a.

The first thing we do is to define a function oG (*optionGrammar*), which takes a normal parser p which parses a single option and modifies the parser such thatits result is applied to the field pointed at by the lens:

$$oG \ p \ a = mkG \ ((a \text{'}alter\text{'}) \texttt{<\$>} \ p)$$

Using this code we can define an option parser which recognises a required option that takes a single extra parameter, such as e.g. filename.

$$required\_ \ a \ (string, p)$$
$$= \quad oG \ (pSymbol \ (\texttt{"-"} +\!\!\!+ [head \ string])) \texttt{*>} lexeme \ p) \ a$$
$$\texttt{<|>} \ oG \ (pSymbol \ (\texttt{"--"} +\!\!\!+ string +\!\!\!+ \texttt{" "}) \texttt{*>} lexeme \ p) \ a$$
$$\texttt{<|>} \ oG \ (pSymbol \ (\texttt{"--"} +\!\!\!+ string +\!\!\!+ \texttt{"="}) \texttt{*>} lexeme \ p) \ a$$
$$required \ a \ (string, p) = required\_ \ a \ (string, const \ \texttt{<\$>} \ p)$$

The call *inp* `'required'` (`"filename"`, *pFileName*) will construct a grammar which is able to recognise one occurrence of the three possible forms of passing an option: `-f inputfile`, `--filename inputfile` and `--filename=inputfile`, and will update the field with name *inp* in the record which will hold our recognised options. The parser *pFilename* recognises the file name part of the option.

Using this basic parser for a single option we can now define special versions of it. The function *option* makes the required field optional, as its name suggests. The function *flag* recognises an option which does not read an extra argument from the input, but just sets the field to the passed value:

$$option \ a \ string\_p \quad = required \ a \ string\_p \ \text{'}opt\text{'} \ id$$
$$flag \quad a \ (string, v) = option \quad a \ (string, pure \ v)$$
$$flags \quad a \ table \quad = foldr \ (\texttt{<>}) \ (pure \ id) \ (map \ (flag \ a) \ table)$$

At this point one may say that the code we have presented thus far does not really depend on the fact that we have introduced grammars, and could have been implemented using the permutation parsers which have been available for a long time (see e.g. the `options-applicative` or the `uu-parsinglib` packages on hackage). We now come to the point where our somewhat more involved combinators will start to pay of. In the example record we see that we have a field which holds a list of integers, and wouldn't it be nice if these integers could each be specified by a separate item in the list of options? For this we define the functions:

$$
\begin{aligned}
options & \ a \ (string, p) = pFoldr \ ((\circ), id) \ (required_- \ a \ (string, (:) \ \texttt{<\$>} \ p)) \\
optionsl & \ a \ string_-p = (last\circ) \ \texttt{<\$>} \ options \ a \ string_-p \\
optionsf & \ a \ string_-p = (head\circ) \ \texttt{<\$>} \ options \ a \ string_-p
\end{aligned}
$$

Use of each of these functions will make that several settings, distributed over the total list of options, will be recognised and combined into a value for a single field, to which they will be prepended. The functions *optionsl* and *optionsf* select the last, respectively the first element of this list. They can be used in the case where the same option may be set several times and we want to use the last setting or the first one. This may come in handy when the total list of options consists of e.g. a sequence of options as typed on the command line concatenated with a list of options taken from some preferences file.

Finally we want to be able to define the options for the *Address* field which is part of our *Name* record holding the recognised options. Using lenses this is easy. We recognise a list of options, and apply these to field of the parent record pointed to by the passed lens:

$$field \ s \ opts = (s`alter`) \ \texttt{<\$>} \ opts$$

So now we are finally ready to show how the specification of the option parser for our *name* record looks like (note that the order in which we specify the options does not matter):

instance $Functor \ f \Rightarrow Monoid \ (Gram \ f \ (r \to r))$ **where**
    $mappend \ p \ q = (\circ) \ \texttt{<\$>} \ p \ \texttt{<||>} \ q$
    $mempty = empty$
$flags \ table \ a = foldr \ (\texttt{<>}) \ (pure \ id) \ [flag \ text \ val \ a \ | \ (text, val) \leftarrow table]$
$oName = \quad name \ `option` \ (\texttt{"name"}, pString)$
$\qquad\qquad \texttt{<>} \ ints \quad `options` \ (\texttt{"int"}, \ pNatural)$
$\qquad\qquad \texttt{<>} \ prefers \ `flags` \quad [(\texttt{"clean"}, \quad Clean)$
$\qquad\qquad\qquad\qquad\qquad\qquad , (\texttt{"haskell"}, Haskell)]$
$\qquad\qquad \texttt{<>} \ address \ `field` \quad (\quad city \ `option` \ (\texttt{"city"}, pString)$
$\qquad\qquad\qquad\qquad\qquad \texttt{<>} \ room \ `option` \ (\texttt{"room"}, pString)$
$\qquad\qquad\qquad\qquad\qquad)$

By making values of type $Gram \ f \ (r \to r)$ an instance of the class *Monoid*, by defining *mappend* as the merge of the two parameters, and composing the record updating functions returned by both parameters when used as parser, we can use the nice `<>` notation to combine the options. We finally run our options:

```
run (($ defaults) <$> mkP oName)
   "--name=Rinus --int=7 --city=Nijmegen -i 5 --clean -i3"
-- Result: Name { name_ = "Rinus"
                , prefers_ = Clean
                , ints_ = [7,5,3]
                , address_ = Address { street_ = "Nijmegen"
                                     , room_ = "BBL517"}}
```

Note that the specifications for the nested *Address* field appear distributed among the other options, and that all the integers we have specified end up together in the *ints* field.

In the definition of the derived combinators used for specifying specific variants of options we have chosen to use lenses, which return a function which updates an already existing structure containing the values to be collected. The advantage of this approach is that we may start with a record containing the default values and apply the result of reading a preferences file to it, and next apply on top of that the extra information parsed from the command line. Note that each of these structures can be easily parsed using the newly introduced combinators, be it using parsers described in an applicative style or using lenses, which correspond more closely to the familiar keyword-value way of specifying parameters.

5.2 Nested Options

It is not unfamiliar to pass options for a linker that is to be involved in a later stage on the command line of a compiler. One of the problems which may arise from such an option architecture is that the option specifications of otherwise rather independent programs may start to interfere; is e.g. the `--verbose` option passed to a module installer like *cabal* meant for the installer itself, or for the *haddock* program that is used to generate the associated documentation? This problem can be easily solved by requiring these options to be surrounded by `+haddock` and `-haddock` markers on the command line, and specifying the command line parser as follows:

$$pHaddock = (gList \circ mkG) \ (\ pToken \ \texttt{"+haddock"}$$
$$\texttt{*>}\ mkP\ (<haddock\ options>)$$
$$\texttt{<*}\ pToken\ \texttt{"-haddock"}$$
$$)$$

6 Conclusions

We have derived a set of very general combinators which make it possible to unravel merged input structures. The library imposes very few restrictions on the underlying parser combinators used. A distinguishing feature of our combinators is that they extend beyond the now common parsers used for permuted structures. Our new combinators have both a monadic and an applicative interface. By being able to switch between the sequential and the merging view on the input we can recognise permuted structures which are embedded inside other permuted structures. In this way we may specify options for various different subsequent program stages, where the option structures for these programs would otherwise conflict.

In deriving the library we found it very helpful to choose our identifiers in such a way that the types are explicitly represented in the chosen identifiers. As we will see his greatly helps in identifying the way we can construct the needed values out of the available values. Choosing the identifiers in the way we did greatly helped us in writing the code, and is an essential ingredient in applying the programming paradigm in which we *"Let the types do the work"*. Our experience in programming in this way helped us so much, how trivial this observation may seem, that we think it deserves being pointed at explicitly rather than just being used in the construction of this library.

Acknowledgement. We want to thank Bastiaan Heeren and members of the Software Technology reading club for commenting on earlier versions of this paper.

References

1. Baars, A.I., Löh, A., Swierstra, S.D.: Parsing permutation phrases. J. Funct. Program. 14(6), 635–646 (2004)
2. Claessen, K.: FUNCTIONAL PEARL Parallel Parsing Processes. Journal of Functional Programming 14(6), 741–757 (2004)
3. Guerra, R., Baars, A.I., Swierstra, S.D., Saraiva, J.: Preserving order in non-order preserving parsers. Tech. Rep. UU-CS-2005-025, Department of Information and Computing Sciences, Utrecht University (2005)
4. McBride, C., Paterson, R.: Applicative programming with effects. Journal of Functional Programming 18(01), 1–13 (2007),
   http://portal.acm.org/citation.cfm?id=1348940.1348941
5. Swierstra, S.D., Duponcheel, L.: Deterministic, error-correcting combinator parsers. In: Launchbury, J., Sheard, T., Meijer, E. (eds.) AFP 1996. LNCS, vol. 1129, pp. 184–207. Springer, Heidelberg (1996)

The Beauty
of Declarative Purely Functional Projections

Steffen Michels

Institute for Computing and Information Sciences
Radboud University Nijmegen, P.O. Box 9010, 6500 GL Nijmegen, The Netherlands
s.michels@science.ru.nl

Abstract. The concept of mathematical functions allows to declaratively express knowledge of how to project information to new derived information. The beauty of this approach emerges from the properties of pure functions fitting into a whole system like a piece of a jigsaw puzzle. Projections defining information in terms of other available information can be the building blocks of a system with a complex behaviour, where all details of how this complex behaviour is achieved can be completely separated from dealing with information used in the system. In this essay this is illustrated by examples of how the same projections can be used in two very different contexts.

1 Introduction

Purely functional programming has proven to be useful for distinct kinds of programming tasks including those with a more imperative flavour like I/O. This essay however deals with the most natural usage of pure functions which is working on values representing information processed by information systems.

Information systems generally deal with information that is stored, received or generated in some way. The aim is e.g. to view information, use it to update stored other information or reason about information derived from the information available. In this essay I discuss how to use purely functional projections to declaratively express the knowledge of how to obtain new information from existing information.

The essence of what I want to express is that for that purpose pure functions allow to write beautiful code. While I do not want to go into a deep discussion of what beauty is, at least I assume that it requires some kind of structure one can comprehend in order to find something beautiful. This structure allows for some kind of harmony, which requires restriction with respect to complete chaos. Indeed, functions are mathematically speaking a restricted kind of relations. This restriction however allows functional projections to harmonically fit into a whole like the individual pieces of a jigsaw puzzle and achieve the goal of separation of concerns.

The properties functions possess provide this kind of structure and are discussed in the following. Lenses [1] provide an example that in certain contexts

P. Achten and P. Koopman (Eds.): Plasmeijer Festschrift, LNCS 8106, pp. 250–257, 2013.

imposing even more restrictions on a set of functions provide a very valuable tool. Here however I focus on the properties of a single function.

The most important property functions possess is that each input is related to exactly one output, also called *right-unique* property. It is very natural to map a given input state to only a single output in cases there is no unambiguity or uncertainty. This is a very common case in most information systems. For example, one wants to give a single possible view to the user, given a current state of information available. One wants a single new state of information to store, given a request to update and the current state of information. Still functions can be used to represent non-determinism and uncertainty by mapping inputs to sets of possible outputs.

The second important property of total functions is that there is an output for all possible inputs. For each possible input there should be an output, which makes it possible to use a function without knowing anything about its structure. A function defined to derive information from existing information, must do so for all possible states of the existing information. The behaviour of the system as a whole becomes undefined otherwise, even though the function is only a tiny part of a huge complex system. Here the importance of a strong type system becomes apparent. In order to define a total function one must specify the input set, and in order to use a function one must know the possible inputs. Type systems provide a natural and powerful way to describe sets and also allow to statically check the definitions of functions.

The output set is implicitly defined by the input set and the function definition. It is still crucial to also assign an output type to a function. The reason for this is that the user of a function processes the result, by composing the function with other ones. Such composition can only provide a system with a single unambiguous behaviour, if the outputs of a function fits the input of functions it is composed with. Partial functions can be made total by for instance using a Maybe type as output, which requires to explicitly deal with the Nothing case. In this essay I assume all functions to be total with respect to their type.

Another important aspect is that types help to understand and communicate about functions. It not only makes it possible to derive certain properties about them [12], but also the intended meaning of even complex functions is often clear from its name and type signature only. An example is for this the task-oriented programming library *iTask* [9], where functions represent complex descriptions of tasks interacting with users. Still, given the name and type signature it becomes clear what the purpose of a task is. That types are helpful to think about functions, is also supported by the fact that *Hoogle* [3] supports searching for functions by type signature.

In this essay I first give simple examples of pure functional projections in Section 2. Then I shown how those projections can be used as part of a complex information system in two different contexts. These are task-oriented applications (Section 3) and probabilistic programming (Section 4). Section 5 concludes the essay.

2   Running Example

In this section very simple examples of functional projections are given. Although the essay is about beautiful programming I did not include a large amount of code. The reason for that is that the aim is not to show the beauty of the implementation of functional projections, but to show that the concept of functions allows to define projections beautifully fitting in a whole.

The example comes from the maritime domain, which is related to the work I discuss in the next two sections. The *iTask* library used as first example has been used to implement a maritime crisis management operation system [4,5]. The probabilistic programming library *Figaro* that is discussed in the second example has been used to develop a prototype model for dealing with uncertainty in the information about ships. (A version of this model based on probabilistic logics is described in a technical report [7].) For all code examples in this essay I use *Clean* notation.

The running example is about dealing with information about ships. Ships have a name, an identification number and a current position, represented by the following record type:

```
:: Ship = { name :: String
          , id   :: Int
          , pos  :: Position }
```

Furthermore, I assume that types are defined for indicating positions and areas, but abstract from their concrete representation:

```
:: Position
:: Area
```

In addition, I assume that there is a specific area one is currently interested in, called the area of interest. In general, this area would be dynamic, e.g. editable by the user, but for simplicity I assume it to be fixed for the moment:

```
areaOfInterest :: Area
```

The main concern of all examples is whether a ship is inside this area or not. Beeing inside of an area is defined by the following purely functional projection[1]:

```
within :: Position Area → Bool
```

From the name and the type of the function alone it becomes clear which kinds of relation it defines without knowing anything about its structure. This allows anybody to use it to derive another function which indicates whether a position is inside of a fixed area of interest:

```
withinAOI :: Position → Bool
withinAOI pos = within pos areaOfInterest
```

Also a projection can be defined, filtering from a set of ships the ones in the area of interest:

---

[1] In *Clean* function have arity, e.g. the following functions has two parameters.

```
filterWithinAOI :: [Ship] → [Ship]
filterWithinAOI ships = [ship \\ ship ← ships | within ship.pos areaOfInterest]
```

As discussed, the functional projections presented here are intentionally very simple. It is obvious that arbitrary complex concepts can be defined in terms of pure functions, like all ships involved in a certain incident, all ships with a risk of being involved in a collision or ships which are suspicious of doing something illegal because of their behaviour or other information.

3   Functional Projection in *iTask* GUIs

In this section I show how to use functional projections to realise web-based GUI applications using the task-oriented programming (TOP) framework *iTask* [9]. While a task definition in this style is a piece of beautiful code by itself, I focus on projecting information used in TOP programs.

I assume a set of ships is provided to the system in some way, e.g. the information could be aggregated from different sensors. In the *iTask* library the concept of *shared data sources* is used to abstract from the actual physical source of information. A data source providing the ship information, but not allowing to write to it, can be represented by:

```
ships :: ReadOnlyShared [Ship]
```

The system is able to provide an up-to-date web-based view of all ships inside the area of interest, using the previously defined projection filterWithinAOI in combination with the task viewSharedInformation, which the library provides:

```
viewSharedInformation "Ships in Area of Interest" [viewWith filterWithinAOI] ships
```

Because of the functional nature of the projection, this unambiguously defines which information to show to the user for each possible ship information provided to the system. The projection's type fits like a piece of a jigsaw puzzle between the information provided by the ships data source and other functions responsible to generate a visualisation of the information, hidden inside of the system.

Under the hood the *iTask* system performs a lot of complex operations. First, the task defined above is instantiated and performed by a user, the system has to keep track of the current state of that instantiation. Then, to come from that abstract task description to a user interface, the system has to retrieve data from a physical implementation ensuring type-safety, to project the information to what the user is supposed to see and to generate a visual representation suitable for the information's type. Finally, this representation is sent to the correct client, which renders the visualisation. To keep the view up-to-data the system additionally has to detect that the input information has changed, update the state of the current task process and send instructions to the client to update the user interface.

However, from the perspective of the projection all those nasty details do not matter. Since it declaratively defines what it means that a ship is in the area of interest, i.e. it is side-effect free, it does no matter how it is used by the system.

For me this is one example of the true magic of declarative programming: one can define what one wants to view, completely abstracting of how this is achieved.

This mechanism can be used in a realistic system showing an overview map of ships on the sea. Assuming that there is a projection `shipMap :: [Ship] → Map` and that the system knows how to properly visualise values of type `Map`, an up-to-date map visualisation can be shown to the user by the following one-liner:

```
viewSharedInformation
        "Ships in Area of Interest" [viewWith (shipMap o filterWithinAOI)] ships
```

Again a lot of details of how to generate and update such maps are hidden.

Another example of how projections are used in the *iTask* system is to compose data sources. Assume that the area of interest is not fixed, but for instance depends on the role of the user or is editable. Again it can be abstracted from how the area of interest is determined using the shared data source abstraction:

```
areaOfInterest :: ReadOnlyShared Area
```

A new data source providing all ships in the area of interest can be derived from that data source and the data source providing ship information by first combining them and then projecting the combination:

```
shipsInAOI :: ReadOnlyShared [Ship]
shipsInAOI = mapRead (λ(aoi,ships) → [ship \\ ship ← ships | within ship.pos aoi])
                    (areaOfInterest |+| ships)
```

Here `|+|` combines two read-only data sources to a new one providing a tuple of the values. The function `mapRead` allows to project the values provided by a a data source using a functional projection. Again, for the projection it does not matter how and whether the area of interest is dynamically changed or how this is detected. The same projection `within` can be used not matter whether the area of interest is dynamically changing or not. Further, the user of `shipsInAOI` only has to know that the data source provides the set of all ships in the area of interest. It can for instance just be used by `viewSharedInformation`.

4   Probabilistic Functional Programming

The example presented next shows how to use functional projections in probabilistic programming. As an example I use the *Figaro* library [8] which is written in *Scala*. Anyhow I use *Clean* notation for uniformity. Some theoretical foundations about combining functional programming and probabilistic reasoning have been introduced in [10].

I use the same example as before, but this time the position of ships is uncertain. A distribution of possible positions is used to express that uncertainty. In *Figaro* the type `Element a` indicates a distribution over values of type `a`. I first only deal with a single ship position:

```
shipPos :: Element Position
shipPos = normPosition ...
```

Here `normPosition` constructs an element representing a multivariate normal distribution of the position.

In the previous example I used the pure function `within` to determine whether a ship is in the area of interest. The same function, in combination with the library function `apply`, can be used to derive a distribution over a boolean value indicating whether a ship is in the area of interest from the distribution of its position:

```
shipWithinAOI :: Element Bool
shipWithinAOI = apply shipPos (λpos → within pos areaOfInterest)
```

Now inference can be performed on the defined program, for instance to compute the probability that the ship is in the area of interest, i.e. the value of `shipWithinAOI` is `true`. An instance of an algorithm to perform inference is represented by `alg`:

```
p :: Real
p = alg.probability shipWithinAOI True
```

This again illustrates the declarative character of pure functional projections. The example projection `within` defines what it means that a ship is in an area, abstracting from whether it is used on a single value shown in a GUI or on a distribution over values.

Different probabilistic inference algorithms can be used to derive the probabilities. Examples of such algorithms are *Variable Elimination* [13], *Importance sampling* [11] and *Metropolis-Hastings Markov chain Monte Carlo* [6,2]. The different probabilistic inference algorithms also make use of the main properties of functional projections. For instance, sampling-based algorithms are based on the assumption that each sample is generated according to the same distribution. This is only true if all projections used to define the distribution fulfil the *right-unique* property. In other words, the projection must not have any side-effects since it is called by the sampling algorithm a number of times which only depends on how good the approximation of the result should be. The projection itself should not have any notion of how often it is called or by which algorithm it is used. Also, in this context all projections should be total. Assuming a normal distribution, a ship can potentially have each possible position. For each of those positions to guarantee a consistent distribution, the random variable `shipWithinAOI` must be unambiguously defined, meaning it can only take the values `true` or `false` according to its type.

I use a *Figaro* element with values of type [`Ship`] in order to generalise again to a set of ships:

```
ships :: Element [Ship]
```

It can now be used together with the same list comprehension as in the previous example to get a list of ships in the area of interest:

```
shipsWithinAOI :: Element [Ship]
shipsWithinAOI = apply ships (λships → [ship \\ ship ← ships | within ship.pos aoi])
```

This can for example be used to infer the expected number of ships in the area
of interest:

```
n :: Real
n = alg.expectation shipsWithinAOI (toReal o length)
```

5 Conclusions

In this essay I have shown how to use the concept of mathematical functions to
declaratively express knowledge of how to project information to new derived
information. The properties of functions allowing them to beautifully fit in a
system like a piece of a jigsaw puzzle were discussed. Two examples were used
to demonstrate how purely functional projections can be used inside complex
information systems.

A general lesson learned from that is that systems should be designed in such
a way that dealing with information and expressing the knowledge of how to
derive new information, should be separated from how the system operates on
that information. The more structure the used programming languages provides,
the better the separation of those concerns can be achieved. For a wide variety
of information systems, functions, as provided by strongly-typed pure functional
programming languages, perfectly provide that structure.

References

1. Bohannon, A., Pierce, B.C., Vaughan, J.A.: Relational lenses: a language for up-
   datable views. In: PODS 2006: Proceedings of the Twenty-fifth ACM SIGMOD-
   SIGACT-SIGART Symposium on Principles of Database Systems, pp. 338–347.
   ACM, New York (2006)
2. Keith Hastings, W.: Monte carlo sampling methods using markov chains and their
   applications. Biometrika 57(1), 97–109 (1970)
3. Hoogle, http://www.haskell.org/hoogle/
4. Lijnse, B., Jansen, J.M., Nanne, R., Plasmeijer, R.: Capturing the netherlands coast
   guard's sar workflow with itasks. In: Mendonca, D., Dugdale, J. (eds.) Proceedings
   of the 8th International Conference on Information Systems for Crisis Response and
   Management, ISCRAM 2011, Lisbon, Portugal. ISCRAM Association (May 2011)
5. Lijnse, B., Jansen, J.M., Plasmeijer, R.: Incidone: A task-oriented incident co-
   ordination tool. In: Rothkrantz, L., Ristvej, J., Franco, Z. (eds.) Proceedings of
   the 9th International Conference on Information Systems for Crisis Response and
   Management, ISCRAM 2012, Vancouver, Canada (April 2012)
6. Metropolis, N., Rosenbluth, A.W., Rosenbluth, M.N., Teller, A.H., Teller, E.: Equation of state calculations by fast computing machines. The Journal of Chemical
   Physics 21, 1087 (1953)
7. Michels, S., Velikova, M., Hommersom, A., Lucas, P.J.F.: A Probabilistic Logic-
   based Model for Fusing Attribute Information of Objects Under Surveillance.
   Technical Report ICIS–R12006, Radboud University Nijmegen (December 2012),
   https://pms.cs.ru.nl/iris-diglib/src/getContent.php?id=2012-
   Michels-Fusion

8. Pfeffer, A.: Figaro: An object-oriented probabilistic programming language. Technical report, Charles River Analytics (2009)
9. Plasmeijer, R., Lijnse, B., Michels, S., Achten, P., Koopman, P.: Task-Oriented Programming in a Pure Functional Language. In: Proceedings of the 2012 ACM SIGPLAN International Conference on Principles and Practice of Declarative Programming, PPDP 2012, , Leuven, Belgium, pp. 195–206. ACM (September 2012)
10. Ramsey, N., Pfeffer, A.: Stochastic lambda calculus and monads of probability distributions. In: In 29th ACM POPL, pp. 154–165. ACM Press (2002)
11. Ripley, B.D.: Stochastic simulation, vol. 316. Wiley (2009)
12. Wadler, P.: Theorems for free? In: Proceedings of the Fourth International Conference on Functional Programming Languages and Computer Architecture, FPCA 1989, pp. 347–359. ACM, New York (1989)
13. Zhang, N., Poole, D.: A simple approach to Bayesian network computations. In: Proceedings of the Tenth Canadian Conference on Artificial Intelligence, pp. 171–178 (1994)

Finding Palindromes: Variants and Algorithms

Johan Jeuring[1,2]

[1] Department of Information and Computing Sciences, Universiteit Utrecht
[2] School of Computer Science, Open Universiteit Nederland
P.O. Box 2960, 6401 DL Heerlen, The Netherlands
J.T.Jeuring@uu.nl

Abstract. The problem of finding palindromes in strings appears in many variants: find exact palindromes, ignore punctuation in palindromes, require space around palindromes, etc. This paper introduces several predicates that represent variants of the problem of finding palindromes in strings. It also introduces properties for palindrome predicates, and shows which predicates satisfy which properties. The paper connects the properties for palindrome predicates to two algorithms for finding palindromes in strings, and shows how we can extend some of the predicates to satisfy the properties that allow us to use an algorithm for finding palindromes.

1 Introduction

Rinus Plasmeijer was born on 26-10-52, which makes him 60 on the date I start writing this paper, an excellent occasion to celebrate a productive career in functional programming!

If I turn Rinus' date of birth around, I get 25-01-62, which is close to its original, but not exactly equal. This birthdate is an example of an *approximate palindrome*, a sequence of symbols which is a *palindrome* if you are allowed a minor number of edit operations on the reverse of the original.

Palindromes have long been considered interesting curiosities used in wordplays. We now know that palindromes play an important role in DNA. If I search for the keyword palindrome in the electronic publications available at the library of Utrecht University, I get more than 500 hits. The first ten of these hits are all about palindromes in DNA. My guess is that at least 90% of these 500 publications are about palindromes in DNA. DNA stores information in palindromes amongst others to repair genes. For example, the male DNA contains huge approximate palindromes with gaps in the middle [5]. Some of these palindromes are more than a million base-pairs long. Essential genes, such as the genes for male testes, are encoded on these palindromes.

We need software to find palindromes in large pieces of text, or approximate palindromes with gaps in DNA. Algorithms for determining whether or not a string is a palindrome, and finding palindromes in strings have a long history in computer science, longer than Rinus' career. In an earlier paper [3] I describe the history of finding palindromes. The current paper discusses some of the

P. Achten and P. Koopman (Eds.): Plasmeijer Festschrift, LNCS 8106, pp. 258–272, 2013.

variants of the problem of finding palindromes, describes their properties, and gives two algorithms for finding palindromes. The main contributions of this paper are the description of the variants of palindrome finding, their properties, and the relation between these properties and algorithms for finding palindromes. The algorithms themselves are not new. The corresponding software has been implemented in Haskell, and can be found on hackage[1].

2   What Is a Palindrome?

Palindromes. How can I determine whether or not a string (a list of characters) is a palindrome? The simplest method is to reverse the string and to compare it with itself. So the string xs is a palindrome (*palindrome xs*), if xs is equal to its reverse: $xs == reverse\ xs$, where $xs == ys$ is *True* only when the strings xs and ys are exactly equal. In Haskell I write:

$$palindrome \quad :: String \rightarrow Bool$$
$$palindrome\ xs = xs == reverse\ xs$$

where *reverse* is defined in the *Prelude*. Without the type declaration, this definition would also work on lists $[a]$ instead of strings, provided we have an equality operator on the type a.

The *palindrome* predicate satisfies several properties. First, the empty list is a palindrome:

$$palindrome\ [] \hspace{8cm} (\text{EMPTY})$$

A singleton list is a palindrome, since under standard character equality, $c == c$ for all characters c.

$$\forall\ c.palindrome\ [c] \hspace{7cm} (\text{SINGLE})$$

This property doesn't hold for all kinds of palindromes, since in some cases the comparison operator used is not a real equality, and is for example not reflexive. A third property allows me to extend a palindrome at the front with a string and at the back with the reverse of this string to obtain a palindrome. This property is an equivalence: if I remove a string from the front of a palindrome, and remove its reverse from the back, I also obtain a palindrome.

$$\forall\ xs\ ys.palindrome\ ys \Leftrightarrow palindrome\ (xs + ys + reverse\ xs)\ (\text{EXTEND})$$

A consequence of this property is that once a string is not a palindrome, I cannot extend it on both the front and the back to become a palindrome. The final property I introduce is the 'palindromes in palindromes' (PALINPAL) property. This property says that if a large palindrome contains a smaller palindrome that does not appear exactly in the middle, the large palindrome contains a second

---

[1] http://hackage.haskell.org/package/palindromes

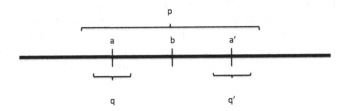

Fig. 1. The palindromes in palindromes property (PALINPAL)

copy of the smaller palindrome at the other arm of the large palindrome. Figure 1 gives an example: suppose I have a palindrome p (say "abadaba", with center b), which contains a palindrome q (say "aba", with center a). Then the string q' I get by mirroring q in p with respect to p's center is a palindrome again ("aba", with center a'). This property is essentially a consequence of the symmetry of equality: for all a, and b: $a == b \Leftrightarrow b == a$.

Text palindromes. The standard example 'A man, a plan, a canal, Panama!' is not a palindrome according to the *palindrome* definition. Reversing it gives '!amanaP ,lanac a ,nalp a ,nam A', in which it is hard to recognize the original. For this string to also pass the palindrome test, I slightly adapt the definition of what is a palindrome. I call a string a text palindrome if it is equal to its reverse after throwing away all punctuation symbols such as spaces, comma's, periods, etc, and after turning all characters into lower case characters.

$$textPalindrome :: String \rightarrow Bool$$
$$textPalindrome = palindrome \circ lowerLetter$$

$$lowerLetter \quad :: String \rightarrow String$$
$$lowerLetter \quad = map\ toLower \circ filter\ isLetter$$

where *isLetter* and *toLower* are functions from the module *Data.Char*. The predicate *textPalindrome* satisfies all palindromic properties.

Word palindromes. When looking for palindromes in a text, I often only want palindromes that start and end in complete words. For example, the longest text palindrome in the King James Bible is the string: "no man; even amon", from Isaiah 41:28. The complete verse reads

```
For I beheld, and there was no man; even among them,
and there was no counsellor, that, when I asked of them,
could answer a word.
```

Since Amon is also a biblical name, it is probably slightly confusing to list "no man; even amon" as the longest palindrome in the Bible. If I only consider palindromes that start and end in words, I get the string "war draw" in Joel 3:9 as the longest palindrome. A word palindrome is a text palindrome that is preceded and followed by non-letter symbols. To determine whether or not a string is a word palindrome, I also need the context of the input string. The type *CString* describes three tuples of strings, modelling a string (the second component) with its context before (the first) and after (the third).

type $CString = (String, String, String)$

$wordPalindrome :: CString \rightarrow Bool$
$wordPalindrome\ input@(before, string, after) =$
    $textPalindrome\ string$
    $\land\ surroundedByPunctuation\ input$

$surroundedByPunctuation\ (before, \_, after)\quad =$
    $(null\ before \lor \neg\ (isLetter\ (last\ before)))$
    $\land\ (null\ after\quad \lor \neg\ (isLetter\ (head\ after)))$

Since the predicate *wordPalindrome* fundamentally depends on its context, it doesn't satisfy the palindromic properties. Even the PALINPAL property is not satisfied, since the punctuation around a word might differ for two occurrences of a palindrome in a palindrome.

Palindromes in DNA. A sequence of DNA symbols 'A', 'T', 'C' or 'G' is a palindrome if its reverse is the *complement* of the original, where 'T' is the complement of 'A' and vice versa, and similarly for 'C' and 'G'. It follows that we cannot use the == operator anymore in the definition of what it means to be a palindrome in DNA. We define the DNA symbol comparison function =:= by

$(=:=)$ $:: Char \rightarrow Char \rightarrow Bool$
$'A' =:= 'T' = True$
$'T' =:= 'A' = True$
$'C' =:= 'G' = True$
$'G' =:= 'C' = True$
$\_\quad =:= \_\quad = False$

This operator is symmetric but not reflexive. We use the new equality operator in a definition of *dnaPalindrome* for sequences of DNA symbols. We pairwise combine the elements of an input sequence *xs* and *reverse xs* with the equality operator =:= using the *PreludeList* function *zipWith*, and fold the list we obtain to a single result using the *PreludeList* function *and*.

$dnaPalindrome$ $:: String \rightarrow Bool$
$dnaPalindrome$ $= palindromeEq\ (=:=)$

type $CharEq$ $= Char \rightarrow Char \rightarrow Bool$

$palindromeEq$ $:: CharEq \rightarrow String \rightarrow Bool$
$palindromeEq\ eq\ xs = and\ (zipWith\ eq\ xs\ (reverse\ xs))$

Note that the predicate *palindrome* can be defined in terms of *palindromeEq* by $palindrome = palindromeEq\ (==)$. Since a DNA symbol is not its own complement the SINGLE property does not hold, and all palindromes in DNA have even length. *dnaPalindrome* satisfies the EMPTY, EXTEND, and PALINPAL properties.

Approximate palindromes. Sometimes I not only want to find perfect palindromes, but also palindromes that contain a limited number of errors. A palindrome with a limited number of errors is often called an *approximate palindrome*. For example, in the book Judges in the King James Bible, verse 19:9 reads:

```
And when the man rose up to depart, he, and his
concubine, and his servant, his father in law, the
damsel's father, said unto him, Behold, now the day
draweth toward evening, I pray you tarry all night:
behold, the day groweth to an end, lodge here, that
thine heart may be merry; and to morrow get you early
on your way, that thou mayest go home.
```

The substring "draweth toward" is a text palindrome with one error: the 'e' and the 'o' don't match. This is an example of an error that is resolved by substituting one symbol by another symbol. Other errors may be resolved by inserting or deleting a symbol. The substitution, insertion, and deletion operations are the operations used in calculating the Levenshtein distance between two strings.

A string s is an approximate palindrome with k errors, if at most k substitution, deletion, or insertion operations are needed to convert the reverse of s into s. Note that this number of operations will generally be twice the number of operations necessary for turning a string into a palindrome. It follows that "draweth toward" is an approximate palindrome with two errors, substituting 'e' for 'o' and 'o' for 'e'. In the following definition we abstract from the equality operator (==), because we also want to determine approximate palindromes in DNA, for example.

$$
\begin{aligned}
&approximatePalindrome &&:: Int \to String \to Bool \\
&approximatePalindrome\ k\ s = levenshteinDistance\ (==)\ s\ (reverse\ s) \leqslant k \\[4pt]
&levenshteinDistance :: CharEq \to String \to String \to Int \\
&levenshteinDistance\ eq\ (x:xs)\ (y:ys) = \\
&\qquad\quad ((\textbf{if}\ x == y\ \textbf{then}\ 0\ \textbf{else}\ 1) + levenshteinDistance\ eq\ xs\qquad ys\quad\ ) \\
&\quad `min`\ (1 \qquad\qquad\qquad\qquad + levenshteinDistance\ eq\ (x:xs)\ ys\quad\ ) \\
&\quad `min`\ (1 \qquad\qquad\qquad\qquad + levenshteinDistance\ eq\ xs\qquad (y:ys)) \\
&levenshteinDistance\ eq\ xs\qquad ys\quad = max\ (length\ xs)\ (length\ ys)
\end{aligned}
$$

As a program, this predicate is terribly inefficient. The *approximatePalindrome* predicate satisfies the EMPTY, SINGLE, and EXTEND properties. Since it takes an integer argument, the PALINPAL property has to be slightly reformulated. Suppose I have a palindrome p satisfying *approximatePalindrome* k, which contains a palindrome q satisfying *approximatePalindrome* k'. Then the string q' I get by mirroring q in p with respect to p's center satisfies *approximatePalindrome* k'. Unfortunately, this property doesn't hold for *approximatePalindrome*. The errors in q need not appear in q', and vice versa, so I cannot make a statement about whether or not q' satisfies *approximatePalindrome* k' given that q satisfies *approximatePalindrome* k'.

Gapped palindromes. A palindrome with a gap is a palindrome in which a gap of a particular size in the middle is ignored. An example of a palindrome with a gap is found in Revelations, where verses 20:7-8 read:

```
And when the thousand years are expired, Satan shall
be loosed out of his prison, And shall go out to
deceive the nations which are in the four quarters of
the earth, Gog, and Magog, to gather them together to
battle: the number of whom is as the sand of the sea.
```

Here "Gog, and Magog" is a text palindrome with a gap of length three in the middle: the 'n' and the 'M' around the central 'd' don't match. A gapped palindrome is a special case of an approximate palindrome, where the errors occur in the middle of the palindrome, but one that occurs so often in DNA that it deserves a special category. Since the gap appears in the middle of the string, the length of the gap is odd if the length of the palindrome is odd, and even if the length of the palindrome is even. To be precise, a string s is a palindrome with a gap of length g in the middle, if it satisfies the predicate *gappedPalindrome g s*:

$$
\begin{array}{ll}
gappedPalindrome & :: Int \rightarrow String \rightarrow Bool \\
gappedPalindrome\ g\ s = palindrome\ (rmCenter\ g\ s) \\
rmCenter & :: Int \rightarrow String \rightarrow String
\end{array}
$$

$$
\begin{array}{llll}
rmCenter\ g\ s = \textbf{let } ls & & = length\ s \\
& armLength & = div\ (ls - g)\ 2 \\
& (before, rest) & = splitAt\ armLength\ s \\
& (gap, after) & = splitAt\ g\ rest \\
& sameParity\ m\ n & = even\ m\ \text{==}\ even\ n \\
\textbf{in if} & g \leqslant ls \wedge sameParity\ g\ ls \\
\textbf{then } before + after \\
\textbf{else } error\ \text{"removeCenter"}
\end{array}
$$

This predicate specifies perfect palindromes with gaps. If I want to find other kinds of palindromes with gaps, I have to replace *palindrome* with the required predicate. Provided g is at most the length of the input list, and the parity of the input list is the same as the parity of g, *gappedPalindrome g* satisfies the EMPTY, SINGLE, and EXTEND properties. Since gapped palindromes only have a gap at their center, I need to adapt the formulation of the PALINPAL property to apply it to gapped palindromes. Suppose I have a palindrome p satisfying *gappedPalindrome g*, which contains a palindrome q satisfying *palindrome*. Then the string q' I get by mirroring q in p with respect to p's center satisfies *palindrome*. This property holds for gapped palindromes.

The palindrome predicate. I have introduced six predicates for determining whether or not a string is a palindrome: besides the basic *palindrome* predicate, these are the predicates *textPalindrome*, *wordPalindrome*, *dnaPalindrome*, *approximatePalindrome*, and *gappedPalindrome*. It doesn't stop here, of course. The examples in this section show gapped text palindromes, and approximate text palindromes. The example of palindromes in male DNA requires finding gapped approximate DNA palindromes. Some DNA files use both capital and underscore letters for DNA symbols, and it follows that I have to find gapped approximate DNA text palindromes. The number of possible variants is substantial.

I redefine the *palindrome* predicate to accommodate all of the palindromic variants. The predicate now takes six arguments: two booleans denoting whether or not I want to find text or word palindromes, two integers denoting the length of the gap and the allowed number of errors, an equality operator, and a string in context.

$$palindrome :: Bool \to Bool \to Int \to Int \to CharEq \to CString \to Bool$$
$$palindrome\ text\ word\ g\ k\ eq\ (before, s, after)$$

$$
\begin{array}{ll}
|\ text & =\ palindrome\ False\ False\ g\ k\ eq\ (before, lowerLetter\ s, after) \\
|\ word & =\ surroundedByPunctuation\ (before, s, after) \\
& \wedge\ palindrome\ False\ False\ g\ k\ eq\ (before, lowerLetter\ s, after) \\
|\ g > 0 & =\ palindrome\ False\ False\ 0\ k\ eq\ (before, rmCenter\ g\ s, after) \\
|\ k > 0 & =\ levenshteinDistance\ eq\ s\ (reverse\ s) \leqslant k \\
|\ otherwise & =\ palindromeEq\ eq\ s
\end{array}
$$

Predicate *palindrome* combines the previous predicates in a single predicate, and also deals with combinations of palindromic aspects. The properties satisfied by *palindrome* are obtained by combining the properties for its components.

3   Finding Palindromes

Both versions of the *palindrome* predicate defined in the previous section can be used to determine whether or not a string is a palindrome. The first version takes a number of steps linear in the length of the input string to do so. These predicates can be used to verify that a given string is a palindrome, but they are not very useful for finding the largest palindrome in the Bible, or for finding the gapped approximate text palindromes in DNA. This section discusses first which kind of palindromes we want to find, and then gives two algorithms for finding such palindromes.

3.1   Finding Which Palindromes?

Software for finding palindromes is particularly useful for finding palindromes in large documents. For example, I analysed the human Y chromosome, consisting of almost 25 million DNA symbols, and chromosome 18, consisting of almost 75 million symbols. The typical questions about palindromes asked by geneticists are: "what are the longest palindromes occurring in this string", or "how many palindromes of length in between m and n occur in this string?" The question of where a particular palindromic string appears inside DNA is more a pattern-matching problem than a palindrome finding problem. Almost all of the palindrome-related questions can be answered relatively fast if I know the length of the longest palindrome around each position of the input string. A string of length n has $2n + 1$ *positions* (sometimes also called center position, or just center): the position before the first character, the positions of the characters, the positions in between two characters, and the position after the last character. For example, the list of the longest palindromes around each position in the string "abb" is $[$"", "a", "", "b", "bb", "b", ""$]$. The EXTEND property says that if palindrome q is the longest palindrome around its center in a string s, then all strings obtained by removing equally many symbols from the front and the back of q are also palindromes, and none of its extensions is a palindrome. I call the longest palindrome around center a in the string s the *maximal palindrome* around center a in s. The list of all maximal palindromes in a string is a concise description of all palindromes that occur in the string. For a list consisting of n copies of the same symbol, the total length of the list of maximal palindromes is quadratic in n. An even more concise description of all palindromes that occur in a string is obtained by returning the list of *lengths* of maximal palindromes in a string. Given a center position and the length of the maximal palindrome around it, I can easily reconstruct all palindromes around that center. The resulting list of lengths of maximal palindromes has length $2n + 1$ for an input list of length n. In the following sections I will develop algorithms for finding the lengths of all maximal palindromes in a string.

3.2 A Naive Algorithm for Finding Palindromes

In this subsection I will describe the obvious algorithm for finding the length of all maximal palindromes in a string.

Given a string as input, I want to find the list of lengths of maximal palindromes around all centers of the string. I use the function *maximalPalindromes* for this purpose.

$$maximalPalindromes :: String \rightarrow [Int]$$

I want to find the length of the maximal palindrome around each center in a string. I will do this by trying to extend the trivial palindromes consisting of either a single letter (for odd centers, starting counting centers with 0) or of the empty string (for even centers) around each center. This only works for *palindrome* predicates satisfying the EXTEND and SINGLE property. If the predicate doesn't satisfy the SINGLE predicate, I only look at the even centers. To extend a palindrome, I have to compare the characters before and after the current palindrome. It would be helpful if I had random access into the string, so that looking up the character at a particular position in a string can be done in constant time. Since an array allows for constant time lookup, I change the input type of *maximalPalindromes* to an array.

$$maximalPalindromes :: Array\ Int\ Char \rightarrow [Int]$$

If I change my input type from strings to arrays, I have to convert an input string into an array, for which I use the function *listArray* from the module *Data.Array*.

Function *maximalPalindromes* calculates the length of maximal palindromes by first calculating all center positions of an input array, and then the length of the maximal palindrome around each of these centers.

$$maximalPalindromes\ a = \textbf{let}\ (first, last) = bounds\ a$$
$$centers\quad = [0\mathinner{\ldotp\ldotp}2 * (last - first + 1)]$$
$$\textbf{in}\ \ map\ (lengthPalindromeAround\ a)\ centers$$

Function *lengthPalindromeAround* takes an array and a center position, and calculates the length of the longest palindrome around that position.

$$lengthPalindromeAround :: Array\ Int\ Char \to Int \to Int$$
$$lengthPalindromeAround\ a\ center$$
$$|\ even\ center\ \ = lengthPalindrome\ (first + c - 1)\ (first + c)$$
$$|\ odd\ \ center\ \ = lengthPalindrome\ (first + c - 1)\ (first + c + 1)$$
$$\textbf{where}\ c\qquad\qquad\qquad = div\ center\ 2$$
$$(first, last)\qquad\quad = bounds\ a$$
$$lengthPalindrome\ start\ end =$$
$$\textbf{if}\quad start < 0 \vee end > last - first \vee a\,!\,start \not\equiv a\,!\,end$$
$$\textbf{then}\ end - start - 1$$
$$\textbf{else}\ \ lengthPalindrome\ (start - 1)\ (end + 1)$$

For each position, this function may take an amount of steps linear in the length of the array, so this is a worst-case quadratic-time algorithm. A more precise analysis shows that this algorithm is linear in the sum of the lengths of the palindromes found. The sum of the lengths of the palindromes in the King James Bible is less than twice the length of the Bible, so for this example this function behaves like a linear-time program. For determining palindromes in DNA, the situation is similar. The Y chromosome contains huge palindromes, but they hardly overlap. Chromosome 18 contains quite a few "ATAT"-sequences, but the longest of these has length 66, and almost all are much shorter.

3.3   Efficient Algorithms for Finding Palindromes

Using the PALINPAL property, I now develop an algorithm for finding palindromes that requires a number of steps approximately equal to the length of its input. This linear-time algorithm can be used to find palindromes in documents of any size, and any content, even in very long strings consisting of the same symbol. Finding palindromes in a string of length $5,000,000$ using this algorithm requires a number of seconds on a modern laptop. It is impossible to find palindromes substantially faster, unless you have a machine with many cores, and use a parallel algorithm.

The program for efficiently finding palindromes is only about 25 lines long. Although the program is short, it is rather intricate. I guess that you need to experiment a bit with to find out how and why it works.

The reason why the algorithm for finding palindromes from the previous subsection is naive is that *lengthPalindromeAround* calculates the maximal palindrome around a center independently of the palindromes calculated previously.

I now change this by calculating the maximal palindromes from left to right around the centers of a string. In this calculation I either extend a palindrome around a center, or I move the center around which I determine the maximal palindrome rightwards because I have found a maximal palindrome around a center. So I replace the definition of *maximalPalindromes* by

$$maximalPalindromes \quad :: \ Array \ Int \ Char \rightarrow [Int]$$
$$maximalPalindromes \ a = \textbf{let} \ (first, last) = bounds \ a$$
$$\textbf{in} \ reverse \ (extendPalindrome \ a \ first \ 0 \ [\,])$$

Before I introduce and explain function *extendPalindrome*, I give an example of how the algorithm works.

An example. I want to find the maximal palindromes in the string "yabad-abadoo". The algorithm starts by finding the maximal palindrome around the position in front of the string, which cannot be anything else than the empty string. It moves the position around which to find the maximal palindrome one step to point to the 'y'. The maximal palindrome around this position is "y", since there is no character in front of it. It again moves the position around which to find palindromes one step to point to the position in between 'y' and 'a'. Since 'y' and 'a' are different, the maximal palindrome around this position is the empty string. Moving the center to 'a', it finds that "a" is the maximal palindrome around this center, since 'y' and 'b' are different. The maximal palindrome around the next center in between 'a' and 'b' is again the empty string. Moving the center to 'b', it can extend the current longest palindrome "b" around this center, since both before and after 'b' it finds an 'a'. It cannot further extend the palindrome "aba", since 'y' and 'd' are different. To determine the maximal palindrome around the center in between 'b' and 'a', the next center position, it uses the fact that "aba" is a palindrome, and that it already knows that the maximal palindrome around the center in between 'a' and 'b' is the empty string. Using the PALINPAL property, it finds that the maximal palindrome around the position in between 'b' and 'a' is also the empty string, without having to look at the 'b' and the 'a'. To determine the maximal palindrome around the next center position on the last 'a' of "aba", it has to determine if 'd' equals 'b', which it doesn't of course. Also here it uses the PALINPAL property. Since "a" is the maximal palindrome around the center of the first 'a' in "aba", and it reaches until the start of the palindrome "aba", I have to determine if the palindrome "a" around the second 'a' can be extended. I won't describe all steps *extendPalindrome* takes in detail, but only give one more detail I already described above: the second occurrence of the palindrome "aba" in "yabadabadoo" is not found by extending the palindrome around its center, but by using the PALINPAL property to find "aba" a second time in "abadaba".

Function extendPalindrome. Function *extendPalindrome* takes four arguments. The first argument is the array *a* in which we are determining maximal pa-lindromes. The second argument is the position in the array directly after the longest palindrome around the current center (the longest palindrome around the center before the first symbol has length 0, so the position directly after the empty palindrome around the first center is the first position in the array). I will call this the current *rightmost* position. The third argument is the length of the current longest palindrome around that center (starting with 0), and the fourth and final argument is a list of lengths of longest palindromes around positions before the center of the current longest tail palindrome, in reverse order (starting with the empty list []). It returns the list of lengths of maximal palindromes around the centers of the array, in reverse order. Applying function reverse to the result gives the maximal palindromes in the right order. The function *extendPalindrome* maintains the invariant that the current palindrome is the longest palindrome that reaches until the current rightmost position.

There are three cases to be considered in function *extendPalindrome*. If the current position is after the end of the array, so *rightmost* is greater than *last*, I cannot extend the current palindrome anymore, and it follows that it is maximal. It only remains to find the maximal palindromes around the centers between the current center and the end of the array, for which I use the function *finalPalindromes*. If the current palindrome extends to the start of the array, or it cannot be extended, it is also maximal, and I add it to the list of maximal palindromes found. I then determine the maximal palindrome around the following center by means of the function *moveCenter*. If the element at the current rightmost position in the array equals the element before the current palindrome I extend the current palindrome.

```
extendPalindrome a rightmost curPal curMaxPals
  | rightmost > last =
      -- reached the end of the array
    finalPalindromes curPal curMaxPals (curPal : curMaxPals)
  | rightmost − curPal == first ∨ a ! rightmost ≢ a ! (rightmost − curPal −1) =
      -- the current palindrome extends to the start
      -- of the array, or it cannot be extended
    moveCenter a rightmost (curPal : curMaxPals) curMaxPals curPal
  | otherwise =
      -- the current palindrome can be extended
    extendPalindrome a (rightmost + 1) (curPal + 2) curMaxPals
  where (first, last) = bounds a
```

In two of the three cases, function *extendPalindrome* finds a maximal palindrome, and goes on to the next center by means of function *finalPalindromes* or *moveCenter*. In the other case it extends the current palindrome, and moves the rightmost position one further to the right.

Function moveCenter. Function *moveCenter* moves the center around which the algorithm determines the maximal palindrome. In this function I make essential use of the PALINPAL property. It takes the array as argument, the current rightmost position in the array, the list of maximal palindromes to be extended, the list of palindromes around centers before the center of the current palindrome, and the number of centers in between the center of the current palindrome and the rightmost position. It uses the PALINPAL property to calculate the longest palindrome around the center after the center of the current palindrome.

If the last center is on the last element, there is no center in between the rightmost position and the center of the current palindrome. I call *extendPalindrome* with rightmost position one more than the previous position, and a current palindrome of length 1.

If the previous element in the list of maximal palindromes reaches exactly to the left end of the current palindrome, I use the PALINPAL property of palindromes to find the next current palindrome using *extendPalindrome*.

In the other case, I have found the longest palindrome around a center, add that to the list of maximal palindromes, and proceed by moving the center one position, and calling *moveCenter* again. I only know that the previous element in the list of maximal palindromes does not reach exactly to the left end of the current palindrome, so it might be either shorter or longer. If it is longer, I need to cut off the new maximal palindrome found, so that it reaches exactly to the current rightmost position.

```
moveCenter a rightmost curMaxPals prevMaxPals nrOfCenters
  | nrOfCenters == 0 =
        -- the last center is on the last element:
        -- try to extend the palindrome of length 1
      extendPalindrome a (rightmost + 1) 1 curMaxPals
  | nrOfCenters − 1 == head prevMaxPals =
        -- the previous maximal palindrome reaches
        -- exactly to the end of the last current
        -- palindrome. Use the palindromes in palindromes
        -- property to extend the current palindrome
      extendPalindrome a rightmost (head prevMaxPals) curMaxPals
  | otherwise =
        -- move the center one step. Add the length of
        -- the longest palindrome to the maximal
        -- palindromes
      moveCenter a
        rightmost
        (min (head prevMaxPals) (nrOfCenters − 1) : curMaxPals)
        (tail prevMaxPals)
        (nrOfCenters − 1)
```

In the first case, function *moveCenter* moves the rightmost position one to the right. Here we use the SINGLE property of *palindrome*. In the second case it calls *extendPalindrome* to find the maximal palindrome around the next center, and in the third case it adds a maximal palindrome to the list of maximal palindromes, and moves the center of the current palindromes one position to the right.

Function finalPalindromes. Function *finalPalindromes* calculates the lengths of the longest palindromes around the centers that come after the center of the current palindrome of the array. These palindromes are again obtained by using the palindromes in palindromes property. Function *finalPalindromes* is called when we have reached the end of the array, so it is impossible to extend a palindrome. We iterate over the list of maximal palindromes, and use the palindromes in palindromes property to find the maximal palindrome at the final centers. As in the function *moveCenter*, if the previous element in the list of maximal palindromes reaches before the left end of the current palindrome, I need to cut off the new maximal palindrome found, so that it reaches exactly to the end of the array.

$$
\begin{aligned}
&finalPalindromes\ nrOfCenters\ prevMaxPals\ curMaxPals \\
&\quad |\ nrOfCenters == 0 = curMaxPals \\
&\quad |\ otherwise \qquad = \\
&\qquad finalPalindromes \\
&\qquad\quad (nrOfCenters - 1) \\
&\qquad\quad (tail\ prevMaxPals) \\
&\qquad\quad (min\ (head\ prevMaxPals)\ (nrOfCenters - 1) : curMaxPals)
\end{aligned}
$$

In each step, function *finalPalindromes* adds a maximal palindrome to the list of maximal palindromes, and moves on to the next center.

I have discussed the number of steps this algorithm takes for each function. At a global level, this algorithm either extends the current palindrome, and moves the rightmost position in the array, or it extends the list of lengths of maximal palindromes, and moves the center around which we determine the maximal palindrome. If the length of the input array is n, the number of steps the algorithm is n for the number of moves of the rightmost position, plus $2n+1$ for the number of center positions. This is a linear-time algorithm.

3.4   Variants

The algorithm for finding palindromes given in the Section 3.2 applies to palindrome predicates satisfying the EXTEND property, and the algorithm in the Section 3.3 additionally requires the PALINPAL property. So the first algorithm can be used to find approximate palindromes, and neither can be used to find word palindromes.

Finding approximate palindromes. Approximate palindromes can be found using the algorithm in Section 3.2. If I only allow substitutions as edit operation, this algorithm is linear in the sum of the lengths of the palindromes found, which might be quadratic in the length of the input string in the worst case, but is linear in almost all real-world applications. This raises two questions:

- How can I also deal with insertions and deletions as edit operations?
- Can I somehow extend the *approximatePalindrome* predicate or the linear-time algorithm for finding palindromes from Section 3.3 to also find approximate palindromes?

The first question is answered by applying standard dynamic programming techniques, as also used to determine the edit-distance between two strings. As for the second question: I have spent many hours on designing algorithms for finding approximate palindromes using the palindromes in palindromes concept, but failed. Anyone?

Finding word palindromes. Since the *wordPalindromes* predicate doesn't satisfy the various palindromic properties, none of the algorithms for finding palindromes can be used to find word palindromes. It is relatively easy to change the *wordPalindrome* property such that it satisfies an adapted EXTEND property. Instead of three, I now split a list into five components and I add a boolean *word*, $((before, (before', s, after'), after), word)$, such that the *string* consisting of $before' + s + after'$ is a text palindrome, and s is the longest word palindrome with the same center contained in *string* if *word* holds. If *word* doesn't hold, then there is no word palindromic substring with the same center.

type $CString' = ((String, (String, String, String), String), Bool)$

$wordPalindrome' :: CString' \to Bool$
$wordPalindrome' \ ((before, (before', s, after'), after), word) =$
   let $string = before' + s + after'$
  in $textPalindrome \ string$
      $\land \ (\neg \ word$
        $\lor \ wordPalindrome \ (before + before', s, after' + after)$
          $\land \ ((null \ before' \land null \ after')$
           $\lor \ (\ and$
              $\circ \ map \ (\neg \circ surroundedByPunctuation)$
              $\circ \ sameCenterSubstrings$
              $\$ \ (before, init \ before' + tail \ after', after)$
           $)$
        $)$
     $)$

$sameCenterSubstrings$ $:: \ CString \to [CString]$
$sameCenterSubstrings \ (before, [\ ] \ , after) = [(before, [\ ] \ , after)]$
$sameCenterSubstrings \ (before, [a], after) = [(before, [a], after)]$
$sameCenterSubstrings \ (before, xs \ , after) =$
    $(before, xs, after)$
   $: sameCenterSubstrings \ (before + [head \ xs], tail \ (init \ xs), last \ xs : after)$

I adapt the EXTEND property by requiring the concatenation of the three strings in the middle to be a text palindrome, and by calculating from the text palindrome the contained word palindrome, if such a word palindrome exists. Using this property, I can now develop a quadratic-time algorithm for finding word palindromes.

4   Conclusions

I have introduced several variants of the palindrome problem, the palindromic properties satisfied by these variants, and two algorithms that can be used to find palindromic substrings, depending on the properties satisfied by the particular palindromic variant sought. The description of the variants and their properties is new to my knowledge; the algorithms for finding palindromes have already been described in the last century by Galil, Manacher, myself, and others [1,4,2].

Acknowledgements. I discussed many aspects of finding palindromes in DNA with Anjana Ramnath of the Indian Institute of Science on Bioinformatics and Computational Biology. Jennifer Hughes of the Whitehead Institute of the MIT Department of Biology helped me finding approximate palindromes with gaps in the male DNA. Bastiaan Heeren commented on a previous version of this paper.

References

1. Galil, Z., Seiferas, J.: A linear-time on-line recognition algorithm for "palstar". Journal of the ACM 25, 102–111 (1978)
2. Jeuring, J.: The derivation of on-line algorithms, with an application to finding palindromes. Algorithmica 11, 146–184 (1994)
3. Jeuring, J.: The history of finding palindromes. In: Liber Amicorum Doaitse Swierstra. Department of Information and Computing Sciences, Utrecht University (2012)
4. Manacher, G.: A new linear-time 'on-line' algorithm for finding the smallest initial palindrome of a string. Journal of the ACM 22, 346–351 (1975)
5. Skaletsky, H., Kuroda-Kawaguchi, T., Minx, P.J., Cordum, H.S., Hillier, L., Brown, L.G., Repping, S., Pyntikova, T., Ali, J., Bieri, T., Chinwalla, A., Delehaunty, A., Delehaunty, K., Du, H., Fewell, G., Fulton, L., Fulton, R., Graves, T., Hou, S.-F., Latrielle, P., Leonard, S., Mardis, E., Maupin, R., McPherson, J., Miner, T., Nash, W., Nguyen, C., Ozersky, P., Pepin, K., Rock, S., Rohlfing, T., Scott, K., Schultz, B., Strong, C., Tin-Wollam, A., Yang, S.-P., Waterston, R.H., Wilson, R.K., Rozen, S., Page, D.C.: The male-specific region of the human y chromosome is a mosaic of discrete sequence classes. Nature 423(6942), 825–837 (2003)

Beautiful Imperative Code
A Functional Ace in the Hole for Imperative Programmers

Marco T. Morazán

Seton Hall University, South Orange, NJ, USA
morazanm@shu.edu

Abstract. The beauty of functional programs stems from clear semantics, referential transparency, and the high-level of abstraction that permits programmers to focus on problem solving. In contrast, this beauty is rarely seen or appreciated in imperative code. In addition to solving a problem, imperative programmers focus on the bug-prone sequencing of assignment statements to obtain efficient code. Imperative programmers that learn functional programming, however, can derive an efficient imperative program from a functional program. This is achieved through a small series of meaning-preserving transformations. This article illustrates the transformations using a small example that yields code that is beautiful and efficient.

1 Introduction

There is no doubt that functional programmers write beautiful code. It would not be a stretch to describe a functional program as poetry in Computer Science. This beauty stems from the fact that functional programming envisions computation as the the evaluation of mathematical functions. Thus, functional languages benefit from referential transparency–that is, $(= (f\ x)\ (f\ x))$ is a tautology. This property allows for the development of code that emphasizes the solution to the problem rather than the machine that evaluates the code. Furthermore, functional languages can largely be described as an implementation of an extended lambda calculus [2] which endows these languages with clear semantics.

In contrast, imperative programmers are rarely associated with beautiful code. Imperative languages envision computation as the sequencing of assignment statements causing changes in state by altering the bindings of mutable variables. If f changes the binding of a variable, then $(= (f\ x)\ (f\ x))$ is not a tautology. Thus, imperative languages do not provide the benefit of referential transparency. This means code development that emphasizes the mutation of variables much like the underlying machine mutates registers. This usually deprives imperative programs of the beauty that stems from easily associating a program with the solution to a problem.

P. Achten and P. Koopman (Eds.): Plasmeijer Festschrift, LNCS 8106, pp. 273–284, 2013.

```
(define (fib n)
   (if (<= n 1)
       1
       (+ (fib (- n 1)) (fib (- n 2)))))
```

Fig. 1. Functional Fibonacci Function

It is common for imperative programmers to dismiss the elegance, the beauty, the clear semantics, the ease of maintenance, and the fewer bugs associated with functional programming in the name of efficiency. After all, they claim, recursion is inefficient and that is what functional programming is mostly about. It is all too common to see such misunderstanding that ignores the level of abstraction that functional languages provide which makes them such a powerful programming tool. This power, in fact, extends to the development of imperative code. Thus, an imperative programmer that has studied functional programming can also develop beautiful code (without sacrificing efficiency). This article presents a small example of how imperative code can be derived from functional code. In essence, it illustrates the equivalence between a functional program and its corresponding imperative counterpart bringing to the foreground that it is erroneous to dismiss functional languages as inefficient and that, instead, imperative programmers can benefit from learning about functional programming. The techniques used to go from a functional program to an imperative program are well-known to functional programmers, but are not well-known by imperative programmers. This article contributes to the bridging of this gap by walking the reader step-by-step through the transformation of a functional program to an imperative program. The transformations used are semantics-preserving and, thus, endow the imperative code with the same beauty of the functional code. That is, it brings forth the meaning of the program and the association with the problem being solved.

2   Functional Fibonacci

In mathematics, the nth Fibonacci number, where $n \geq 1$ is a natural number, is defined as follows[1]:

$$fib(n) = \begin{cases} 1 & if\ n <= 1 \\ fib(n-1) + fib(n-2) & otherwise \end{cases}$$

This recursive definition naturally leads a functional programmer to the function definition in Figure 1 to compute the nth Fibonacci number. This function is recursive and it is easy to see how it is a literal translation from the mathematical definition of the nth Fibonacci number to Racket syntax. Its development is not prone to bugs and is easy to understand. A simple induction of n, its input, suffices to establish partial correctness. Observing that the function is based on

---

[1] An alternative definition has $n \geq 0$ and $fib(0) = 0$.

structural recursion suffices to establish total correctness. In other words, it is easy to see how the program is related to the problem being solved and it is easy to see that the program is correct.

3   Imperative Fibonacci

An imperative programmer would state that the such a function is inefficient, because it is recursive and the control context grows with every recursive call. Correctly observed, for a naive implementation of a programming language, the control context grows due to the delayed + operation that must wait for the evaluation of two recursive calls before it can be applied. In this example, this means that the memory required to evaluate (fib n) is proportional to 2^n. Furthermore, the evaluation engine must *jump* back after the evaluation of each recursive call to complete the delayed + operation.

In response to the functional programmer's solution, an imperative programmer proposes a more efficient solution:

```
(define (fib-imp-bug N)
    (define k (void))
    (define fn2 (void))
    (define fn1 (void))
    (begin
        (set! k N)
        (set! fn2 1)
        (set! fn1 1)
        (while (> k 1)
            (set! k (- k 1))
            (set! fn1 (+ fn2 fn1))
            (set! fn2 fn1))
    fn1))
```

Testing, however, quickly reveals that this functions does not work. For example, (fib 5) evaluates to 16 instead of 8. The imperative programmer, thus, must start a debugging process that involves several rounds of trial and error to determine that the third mutation inside the while loop is incorrect. After the debugging process, the imperative programmer offers the solution in Figure 2.

The function in Figure 2 does, indeed, compute the nth Fibonacci number without growing the control context utilizing three *state* variables (k, fn1, and fn2) that are repeatedly mutated. That is, it is an *iterative* function that can be evaluated with a constant amount of memory. It is not obvious, however, how the imperative programmer developed the code nor how it is related to the mathematical definition of $fib(n)$.

Establishing the correctness of the function requires the development of a loop invariant and the use of Hoare logic [6]. A loop invariant must contain the conjunction of invariant properties for each state variable such that the loop invariant and the negation of the while-loop driver imply the post-condition of

```
(define (fib-imp N)
    (define n (void))
    (define fn2 (void))
    (define fn1 (void))
    (begin
        (set! n N)
        (set! fn2 1)
        (set! fn1 1)
        (while (> n 1)
            (set! n (- n 1))
            (set! fn1 (+ fn2 fn1))
            (set! fn2 (- fn1 fn12)))
        fn1))
```

Fig. 2. Imperative Version of the Fibonacci Function

the function. In this case, the state-variable invariants and $k \leq 1$ must imply that $fn1 = fib(N)$ when the loop terminates. There is little, if anything, to guide the programmer in the development of the loop invariant–a task that is not always straightforward and frequently ignored by imperative programmers.

A functional programmer, nonetheless, inspects the imperative function and concludes that it is beautiful code. In fact, the functional programmer tells the imperative programmer that it is exactly the same recursive function fib from Figure 1. Furthermore, the functional programmer can tell the imperative programmer what the loop invariant is and prove the imperative code correct.

4   From Functional to Imperative Fibonacci

This section traces the thought process of the hypothetical functional programmer above who concludes that fib-imp from Figure 2 is beautiful code. The conclusion is reached by applying several transformations to fib from Figure 1. First, fib is rewritten in continuation-passing style (CPS) to yield a program in which all function calls are tail-calls. Second, the continuations are inlined in the CPS version. Third, the representation of the continuations is changed, from functions to data structures, to yield to an accumulative recursive function for which accumulator invariants are easily developed. Finally, the accumulative recursive function is registerized yielding imperative code, a loop invariant, and a proof of partial correctness.

4.1   CPS Transformation

The major criticism of the fib function in Figure 1 is the growth of the control context. This growth can be eliminated by rewriting fib in continuation-passing style (CPS) [10,13,14]. The control context grows when *the evaluation of an argument* involves a call to a programmer-defined function. In CPS, all such

```
(define (fib N) (fibk N (endk)))

(define (fibk n k)
  (if (<= n 1)
      (apply-k k 1)
      (fibk (- n 1) (fib-cont1 n k))))

(define (fib-cont1 n k)
  (lambda (fn1) (fibk (- n 2) (fib-cont2 fn1 k))))

(define (fib-cont2 fn1 k)
  (lambda (fn2) (apply-k k (+ fn1 fn2))))

(define (endk) (lambda (val) val))

(define (apply-k k val) (k val))
```

Fig. 3. The CPS version of fib

function calls are in the tail position and, therefore, there are no delayed operations that require the growth of the control context to "remember" where to jump back to after the call is evaluated. Instead of delaying an operation, CPS code evaluates operands first and builds continuations that are used to complete the computation. A continuation, therefore, is an accumulator of knowledge required to finish the computation that makes the control context explicit. We can think of the remaining part of the computation, after an argument has been evaluated, as requiring the value of the argument and producing the result. That is, we can think of the rest of the computation as a function that is applied to a value and that returns the value of the program. This observation naturally leads to representing continuations as functions.

Algorithms to transform recursive programs to CPS are extensively described [3,4,9,11,12]. In CPS, functions get an additional parameter–a continuation–that contains the necessary information to complete the computation. If continuations are represented as functions, then a continuation is a function that "knows" how to complete the evaluation of an expression. In order not to change the program's interface, the main function calls an auxiliary function with a continuation to end the computation–a function that returns the program's value it gets as input. A function call to compute an argument that is not in a tail position is eliminated by evaluating the function call with a new continuation to evaluate the remainder of an expression/computation once the value of the argument is known. If the remainder of the evaluation does not require a call to a function that requires the growth of the control context, then the continuation is applied to a result.

The CPS-transformed function fib in Figure 1 is displayed in Figure 3. The function fib calls an auxiliary function, fibk, to compute $fib(N)$ with a continuation to end the computation. The continuation to end the computation is a

```
(define (fib N) (fibk N (lambda (val) val)))

(define (fibk n k)
   (if (<= n 1)
       (k 1)
       (fibk (- n 1)
             (lambda (fn1) (fibk (- n 2)
                                 (lambda (fn2) (k (+ fn2 fn1)))))))))
```

Fig. 4. The inlined version of CPSed fib

function that takes as input a value, $fib(N)$, and that returns it. The auxiliary function, fibk, performs the work of fib from Figure 1 without growing the control context. If n is less than or equal to 1, then the computation is completed by applying the continuation to the value, 1, that is returned in the original program. Otherwise, observe that the else-branch in Figure 1 adds the results of two recursive calls (that require the growth of the control context): one to compute $fib(n-1)$ and one to compute $fib(n-2)$. Both recursive calls need to be evaluated before the addition can take place. Due to referential transparency, we can arbitrarily choose to first compute $fib(n-1)$ in a control context (i.e., with a continuation) that computes $fib(n-2)$ and then performs the addition. This results in a call to fibk with (- n 1) and a continuation that remembers n, to compute $fib(n-2)$, and that remembers the current continuation, k, to complete the computation. The constructor for this new continuation, fib-cont1, returns a function that when applied to the value $fib(n-1)$ computes $fib(n-2)$ in a context that remembers the value of $fib(n-1)$, to perform the remaining addition operation, and the current continuation to finish the computation. The constructor for this third continuation, fib-cont2, returns a function that takes as input the value of $fib(n-2)$ and that completes the computation by applying the saved continuation to the sum of $fib(n-1)$ and $fib(n-2)$. Finally, since continuations are represented as functions, applying a continuation is simply applying a function to a value as done in apply-k.

If we consider the continuation constructors, fib-cont1, fib-cont2, and endk, as primitive operations that do not require the growth of the control context, then all function calls that are not to primitive operations are tail calls. That is, the program in Figure 3 is iterative and does not grow the control context.

4.2   Inlining

An imperative programmer would be quick to point out that a non-tail-call to a continuation constructor in Figure 3, given that it is a function defined in the program, requires growing the control context. Furthermore, the imperative programmer may object, because six functions, instead of one, are required. To eliminate the need to define and call a continuation constructor, the program in Figure 3 is transformed by inlining the continuation constructors. That is, references to the continuation constructors can be substituted by their bodies. Thus, eliminating the need for defining the continuation constructors as functions in the program. Such a transformation is easily done given that the continuation is built to remember existing values and, therefore, a continuation constructor is not called with values that need to be computed.

In addition, references to apply-k can also be inlined. This follows from observing that it is not necessary to call an auxiliary function in order to apply an existing function to a value. Instead, the existing function can be applied directly to the value, thus, eliminating the call to (and the need for) the auxiliary function. The result of inlining is the program in Figure 4.

In addition to reducing the number of functions, the inlined code in Figure 4 makes it explicit that the primary role of the continuations is to remember the value of $fib(n-1)$ and the value of $fib(n-2)$ and to use them to compute the value of $fib(n)$. This means that the continuations are trackers and producers of natural numbers which suggests using natural numbers, instead of functions, to represent the continuations.

4.3   Transformation to Data-Structure Continuations

Changing the representation of continuations from functions to data structures is a common technique used in compilation. The origins of this technique are probably found in the RABBIT compiler [7]. Other Scheme compilers [8] and ML compilers [1] also perform this type of transformation.

To transform a program to use a data-structure representation for continuations each kind of continuation that "remembers" a value is made a parameter–an accumulator–and recursive calls are made with values that need to be remembered. These values are computed without growing the control context. For each accumulator we can define an invariant property that holds every time the function is called. The result is an accumulative recursive function for which we can establish its correctness.

The code in Figure 4 is transformed to an accumulative recursive function that has two accumulators as parameters to fibk. These accumulators are the continuations represented as natural numbers for which we can precisely define the accumulator invariants. If N is the input to fib, then in the transformed program the function fibk has the following accumulator invariants:

$$fn2 = fib(N - n)$$
$$fn1 = fib(N - n + 1).$$

Observe that, with these accumulator invariants, $n = 1 \Rightarrow fn1 = fib(N)$ which is precisely the value the function needs to compute.

The result of the transformation is displayed in Figure 5. Observe that fib and fibk are both tail-recursive functions. That is, the program implements an iterative process as done by a while-loop. Furthermore, the program does not use higher-order functions. These observations suggest that the program in Figure 5

```
(define (fib N) (fibk N 1 1))

(define (fibk n fn2 fn1)
  (if (<= n 1)
      fn1
      (fibk (- n 1) fn1 (+ fn2 fn1))))
```

Fig. 5. Accumulative Recursive Version Using Data Structure Continuations

can serve as the basis for the transformation to an imperative program that can be implemented in any modern imperative programming language. Additionally, the accumulator invariants assist the programmer in developing a while-loop invariant.

4.4 Registerization

An imperative program is obtained by making the parameters of functions state variables (or registers as done by several compilers [1,5,7,8]). The functions in the program communicate values through these state variables, instead of making function calls with arguments, to become 0-argument tail calls. That is, function calls become jumps. The state variables are mutated before every function call (eliminating redundant assignments of a state variable to itself). These assignments are safe to make, because all delayed operations have been eliminated and there is not need to grow the control context and, thus, to remember pre-mutation values for later in the computation. Nonetheless, care must be taken to make sure that the mutations preserve state-variable invariants.

For the program in Figure 5, three state variables are required: n, fn1, and fn2–one for each parameter of fibk. Observe that the iteration continues as along as $n > 1$, which is the loop *driver*. To develop correct code, it remains to identify the loop invariant. The state-variable invariants for fn2 and fn1 are the same as the corresponding accumulator invariants:

$$fn2 = fib(N - n)$$
$$fn1 = fib(N - n + 1),$$

where N is the input to fib. The state-variable invariant for n needs to be identified to complete the loop invariant. For the code in Figure 5, n is not an accumulator. Instead, it is a piece of recursively defined data, specifically a natural number, used to develop a structurally recursive function that uses two accumulators. This suggest that the state-variable invariant for n must be an inequality. Furthermore, Hoare logic states that:

loop invariant $\land \neg driver \Rightarrow postcondition.$

We can plug-in the pieces that we know and solve for the state-variable invariant for n (denoted as "...")：

```
(define n (void))
(define fn2 (void))
(define fn1 (void))

(define (fib N)
  (begin
    (set! n N)
    (set! fn2 1)
    (set! fn1 1)
    (fibk)))

(define (fibk)
  (if (<= n 1)
      fn1
      (begin
        (set! n (- n 1))
        (set! fn1 (+ fn2 fn1))
        (set! fn2 (- fn1 fn2))
        (fibk)))))
```

Fig. 6. First Imperative Version

$$\ldots \wedge fn2 = fib(N-n) \wedge fn1 = fib(N-n+1) \wedge \neg(n>1) \Rightarrow fn1 = fib(N)$$

$$\ldots \wedge fn2 = fib(N-n) \wedge fn1 = fib(N-n+1) \wedge n \leq 1 \Rightarrow fn1 = fib(N)$$

Observe that:

$$fn1 = fib(N-n+1) = fib(N) \Rightarrow n = 1$$

For $n = 1$ to hold when the loop terminates, the state-variable invariant for n is the inequality: $n \geq 1$. Thus, yielding the following loop invariant:

$$n \geq 1 \wedge fn2 = fib(N-n) \wedge fn1 = fib(N-n+1)$$

For the code in Figure 5, fib achieves the invariant by respectively initializing the state-variables, n, fn2, and fn1, to N, 1, and 1. The resulting code for fib is displayed in Figure 6.

After the initial achievement of the invariant, fibk must iterate making sure the invariant is preserved after each iteration. Hoare logic above demonstrates that (as with the accumulative recursion version) when (<= n 1) the correct value to return is stored in the (state) variable fn1. Otherwise, when the driver is true, progress must be made towards termination while always maintaining the loop invariant. Progress towards termination is made by decreasing n by 1 (as in the accumulative recursion version). From this point on imperative code development proceeds by making assertions based on the loop invariant and the mutations executed. To start, we have:

$$n > 1 \wedge fn2 = fib(N - n) \wedge fn1 = fib(N - n + 1)$$

```
(set! n (- n 1))
```

$$n \geq 1 \wedge fn2 = fib(N - n - 1) \wedge fn1 = fib(N - n)$$

Observe that $fib(N - n + 1) = fib(N - n - 1) + fib(N - n)$. This suggests the following mutation:

$$n \geq 1 \wedge fn2 = fib(N - n + 1) \wedge fn1 = fib(N - n + 2)$$

```
(set! fn1 (+ fn2 fn1))
```

$$n \geq 1 \wedge fn2 = fib(N - n + 1) \wedge fn1 = fib(N - n + 1)$$

The only part of the loop invariant that needs to be restored is the value of fn2. This value needs to be the pre-mutation value of fn1 suggesting this final assignment:

$$n \geq 1 \wedge fn2 = fib(N - n + 1) \wedge fn1 = fib(N - n + 1)$$

```
(set! fn2 (- fn1 fn2))
```

$$n > 1 \wedge fn2 = fib(N - n) \wedge fn1 = fib(N - n + 1)$$

The invariant has been restored and, thus, we have the program displayed in Figure 6. This program evaluates using a constant amount of memory just as the program in Figure 2.

An imperative programmer would still complain that our imperative program needs two functions to do the work that can efficiently be done using a single function. In Figure 6, the function fibk repeatedly performs the same mutations until $n \leq 1$. That is, fibk is a while loop. We can, therefore, use a while expression to capture the tail-recursion of fibk in Figure 6[2]. This leads to a new version of fibk:

```
(define (fibk)
  (while (n > 1)
         (set! n (- n 1))
         (set! fn1 (+ fn2 fn1))
         (set! fn2 (- fn1 fn2)))
  fn1))
```

Finally, by inlining fibk and the the state-variable declarations into fib we obtain the code displayed in Figure 7. That is, the imperative version of the function to compute the Nth Fibonacci number in Figure 2 is derived from the functional version in Figure 1. Furthermore, the presented transformations provide an imperative programmer with a guide to develop loop invariants, imperative code, and a proof of partial correctness.

---

[2] The reader wishing to implement this in Racket must extend the language's syntax using a macro to implement a while loop.

```
(define (fib N)
    (define n (void))
    (define fn2 (void))
    (define fn1 (void))
    (begin
        (set! n N)
        (set! fn2 1)
        (set! fn1 1)
        (while (> n 1)
            (set! n (- n 1))
            (set! fn1 (+ fn2 fn1))
            (set! fn2 (- fn1 fn2)))
        fn1))
```

Fig. 7. The Result of Transforming the Functional Fibonacci Function

5 Concluding Remarks

Imperative programmers ought not dismiss the beauty found in functional code as a sign of inefficiency. Instead they ought to view functional programming as a powerful tool for problem solving. When faced with a difficult problem for which it is not clear what the correct sequence of assignment statements is, writing a functional program can be insightful. Once a functional solution to a problem is obtained, this solution can be transformed to a tail-recursive function and then translated to imperative code.

In tandem, the transformations done to functional code yield insights into the correctness of the imperative code. In other words, semantics-preserving transformations of functional code make it easier to establish the correctness of the corresponding imperative code. In addition, these transformations can be done by programs which can have a dramatic impact on development time by reducing debugging time. The resulting programs can be examined after each transformation possibly providing the imperative programmer with insights for improved design choices. The result is beautiful imperative code whose meaning, correctness, and relation to the problem solved are clear. Imperative programmers learn functional programming!

Acknowledgements. To my good friend Rinus Plasmeijer, a continued source of inspiration and constructive debate, Gelukkige Verjaardag!

References

1. Appel, A.W., Jim, T.: Continuation-Passing, Closure-Passing Style. In: Conference Record of the Sixteenth Annual ACM Symposium on Principles of Programming Languages, pp. 293–302. ACM Press (1989)
2. Barendregt, H.P.: The Lambda Calculus Its Syntax and Semantics, revised edition, vol. 103. North-Holland (1984)

3. Danvy, O., Filinski, A.: Representing Control: A Study of the CPS Transformation. Mathematical Structures in Computer Science 2(4), 361–391 (1992)
4. Danvy, O., Nielsen, L.R.: A First-Order One-Pass CPS Transformation. Theor. Comput. Sci. 308(1-3), 239–257 (2003)
5. Friedman, D.P., Wand, M.: Essentials of Programming Languages, 3rd edn. The MIT Press (2008)
6. Hoare, C.A.R.: An Axiomatic Basis for Computer Programming. Commun. ACM 12(10), 576–580 (1969)
7. Steele Jr., G.L.: Rabbit: a Compiler for Scheme: A Study in Compiler Optimization. Technical report. Massachusetts Institute of Technology, Cambridge, MA, USA (1978)
8. Kranz, D.A., Kelsey, R., Rees, J., Hudak, P., Philbin, J., Adams, N.: Orbit: An Optimizing Compiler for Scheme. In: Proceedings of the 1986 SIGPLAN Symposium on Compiler Construction, pp. 219–233 (1986)
9. Plotkin, G.D.: Call-by-Name, Call-by-Value, and the λ-Calculus. Theoretical Computer Science 1, 125–159 (1975)
10. Reynolds, J.C.: The Dicoveries of Continuations. Lisp and Symbolic Computation 6(3/4) (1993)
11. Sabry, A., Felleisen, M.: Reasoning about Programs in Continuation-Passing Style. Lisp and Symbolic Computation 6(3-4), 289–360 (1993)
12. Sabry, A., Wadler, P.: A Reflection on Call-by-Value. ACM Trans. Program. Lang. Syst. 19(6), 916–941 (1997)
13. Strachey, C., Wadsworth, C.P.: Continuations: A Mathematical Semantics for Handling Full Jumps. Higher-Order and Symbolic Computation 13(1/2) (2000)
14. Sussman, G.J., Steele Jr., G.L.: Scheme: An Interpreter for Extended Lambda Calculus. In: MEMO 349, MIT AI LAB (1975)

Author Index